THE RISE AND DECLINE OF U.S. MERCHANT SHIPPING IN THE TWENTIETH CENTURY

TWAYNE'S EVOLUTION OF AMERICAN BUSINESS SERIES

Industries Institutions, and Entrepreneurs

Edwin J. Perkins
SERIES EDITOR
UNIVERSITY OF
SOUTHERN CALIFORNIA

THE RISE AND DECLINE OF U.S. MERCHANT SHIPPING IN THE TWENTIETH CENTURY

René De La Pedraja

TWAYNE PUBLISHERS • NEW YORK
Maxwell Macmillan Canada • Toronto
Maxwell Macmillan International •
New York • Oxford • Singapore • Sydney

The Rise and Decline of U.S. Merchant Shipping in the Twentieth Century
René De La Pedraja

Copyright © 1992 Twayne Publishers

Twayne Publishers
Macmillan Publishing Company
866 Third Avenue
New York, New York 10022

Maxwell Macmillan Canada, Inc.
1200 Eglinton Avenue East
Suite 200
Don Mills, Ontario M3C 3N1

Macmillan Publishing Company is part of the Maxwell Communication Group
of Companies.

Library of Congress Cataloging-in-Publication Data

De La Pedraja Tomán, René.
    The rise and decline of U.S. merchant shipping in the twentieth
century / René De La Pedraja.
        p.   cm.—(Twayne's evolution of American business series ; no. 8)
    Includes bibliographical references and index.
    ISBN 0-8057-9826-9 (hc: alk. paper).—ISBN 0-8057-9827-7 (pb: alk. paper)
    1. Steamboat lines—United States—History—20th century.
    2. Merchant marine—United States—History—20th century.
    3. Shipping—United States—History—20th century.   I. Series.
    HE745.D4   1992
    387.5'0973'0904—dc20   92-17754
                                                                            CIP

The paper used in this publication meets the minimum requirements
of American National Standard for Information Sciences—Permanence
of Paper for Printed Library Materials. ANSI Z3948-1984.

10 9 8 7 6 5 4 3 2 1

Printed in the United States of America

To Beatriz

THE RISE AND DECLINE OF U.S. MERCHANT SHIPPING IN THE TWENTIETH CENTURY

CONTENTS

ACKNOWLEDGMENTS

THE ORIGINS OF THIS BOOK CAN be traced very precisely to the encouragement provided by Robin Higham at Kansas State University in 1986–87. After frequent luncheons with him, during which I explained the nature of my book-length study of the Latin American merchant marine, he suggested that I pause from this vast research project (still unfinished today) in order to write about U.S. steamship companies. Why did American steamship companies appear and then collapse? There was no historical survey available to provide the explanations, and since information on U.S. firms was easier to obtain and certainly nearer than that on the Latin American steamship companies, Robin finally asked, "why don't you write the book on the U.S. first?"

Robin's enthusiasm for the project was soon shared by Edwin Perkins, and the latter decided to include a volume on U.S. steamship companies in Twayne's Evolution of American Business Series. While I remained in Kansas, Robin continued to provide valuable guidance, and until the last stage Perkins raised important issues and made sharp observations; I am sure that if I had followed all their recommendations, the finished product would have been better than it is now.

Gathering information on U.S. steamship companies turned out to be no picnic, and it was only with the courteous and efficient help of library and archive staff members that I was able to obtain the necessary accounts. For attention and service beyond any reasonable demands for official records, I must mention John K. Vandereedt at the U.S. National Archives, and Donald Post and Mary Jane Harvey at the Maritime Administration. William Kooiman in the San Francisco Maritime National Historical Park was very helpful and he also cooperated in other ways.

This book has not received any support, aid, or guidance from private companies, business groups, or organized labor, and it is solely the result of an effort to satisfy my easily aroused intellectual curiosity.

The History Department at Canisius College has provided the time and support that allowed me to complete this project, and my colleagues David Costello, Bruce Dierenfield, Edwin Neville, and David Valaik, also took time to critically comment on many chapters of this book. Paulette Kirsch typed the manuscript, and I also received help from my student assistant Karen Aavik. My friend Paul Taparauskas helped with the proper phrasing of legal and related issues in chapter 9. Copyeditor Carla Thompson skillfully rooted out awkward sentences and made the text more readable. The editors at Twayne sponsored this publication; without their support this book would not have been written or published. Elvira and Terry Butler, and Helen Toman shared their hospitality with me for still another research project. Beatriz, my wife, to whom this book is dedicated, was a permanent source of support and counsel through many challenging stages; my son, Jaroslav, did more this time than classify documents; he actually came up with better versions of several sentences. To all of the persons listed above I am immensely grateful. Any errors or shortcomings in the text remain the responsibility of the author.

INTRODUCTION: THE STRUCTURE AND EVOLUTION OF THE U.S. MERCHANT SHIPPING INDUSTRY

THIS BOOK TRACES THE RISE, decline, and fall of U.S. steamship companies from 1900 to the present. The emphasis is on individual accounts of the principal steamship companies, a generally neglected area of business history. Clear and non-technical narrative moves in chronological order through the twentieth century. The two world wars, which had a huge impact on the companies, divide the book into its three main parts: The Prewar Period, the Shipping Board Era, and the Container Age. New information derived from unpublished sources and hard-to-find facts provides the basis for this survey of the U.S. steamship companies.

This book is the first historical survey to appear about U.S. steamship companies in the twentieth century. Up to now, scholars have preferred to concentrate on topics like government policy, organized labor, and the ships themselves, partly because readily available data and abundant publications guide readers through a familiar story. A few hardy souls have pushed ahead to write histories of some of the steamship companies, but a global view of the firms, rather than just the ships, has been sorely lacking. This book attempts to fill this gap by tracing the management aspects of the principal companies from 1900 to the present, in effect providing a narrative account as well as an explanation of their evolution. The reader eagerly awaiting sea stories should be aware that the view will be from the executive suite, rather than from the captain's bridge.

Trying to provide a synthesis of the life and death of hundreds of highly diverse U.S. steamship companies in a slim volume has been a daunting undertaking. One of the recurrent problems has been the scarcity of information about management. I have devised complex research strategies to overcome the shortage of facts on many fleeting and obscure companies. Ultimately, the type and nature of the information located has been the overriding constraint in shaping the final book. Companies that left little or no trace in publications or open archives have inevitably received brief if any treatment. For other companies, the search has turned up abundant and even overwhelming information, in which cases the goal has become not an exhaustive narrative but rather an insightful synthesis. How to balance an over-abundance of information with gaps in the data has been a constant task in this study, which does not pretend to exhaust the subject or much less be definitive. Many individual companies are waiting for book-length treatment, not to mention the need for maritime studies focusing on chronological periods or geographic areas.

Even a book ten times the size of this one could not hold the histories of all U.S. steamship firms that have existed in the twentieth century. Strict limitations have been absolutely necessary. All companies operating in inland waters, whether rivers, lakes, bays, or sounds have been excluded. The primary focus has been on those companies engaged in foreign trade; nevertheless, the author's original intention to limit the book exclusively to the foreign trade routes proved untenable, and several important exceptions had to be made. Intercoastal shipping (between the East and West coasts of the United States) appeared frequently in the histories of many steamship firms, and consequently has been included. Similarly, coastwise shipping (from Maine to Texas and from Puget Sound to San Diego) proved crucial in the life of many steamship firms engaged in the foreign trade, and so the book takes into account these linkages, without, however, claiming to present a complete picture of the vast field of shipping along the coasts of the United States. Finally, Hawaii and Puerto Rico, two insular parts of the United States, have received careful attention in this book because their coastwise shipping has had extraordinary significance for the U.S. merchant shipping industry.

To avoid expanding the book to unmanageable length, a further selection of firms into three main categories was inevitable. The author apologizes to those whose favorite steamship company did not receive the space it surely deserved, or even more unpardonably, was not even mentioned in the text. In some cases lack of information was the culprit, and the author would be glad to hear from those willing to share oral or written evidence.

The first main category covered in this book, and forming its core, are the following groups or "families" of steamship companies:

□   The International Mercantile Marine (I.M.M.) and United States Lines group of companies with their many affiliates, which from 1901 to 1986 constituted the largest U.S. presence on the foreign trade routes, with their strongest concentration in the North Atlantic.

☐ The American President Lines and its predecessor companies such as Dollar Line and Pacific Mail Steamship, a group of companies that dated back to the nineteenth century and comprised the largest U.S. presence in the trans-Pacific trade.

☐ The group of companies with origins in the Gulf of Mexico, in particular Lykes Brothers, Waterman Steamship, and Sea-Land.

☐ American-Hawaiian and Matson, the companies most closely connected to Hawaii.

☐ The group of companies serving the West Indies trade, including Puerto Rico.

☐ A sample of other steamship companies, such as American Export Lines and the Isbrandtsen firm, both of which merged in 1960.

All of the above firms are called "liner" companies. Liner companies provide regularly scheduled and fast service to any shipper (the client or customer who pays to have the goods carried aboard the vessel to a destination). These liner services are distinct from a second category, the slower but cheaper tramp vessels, which scrounge for cargo in any of the world's ports. When cargo appears in a port the tramps rush there to load like bees to honey, and as soon as they complete the voyage they set off to look for their next cargo. The development of modern communications, in particular the wireless telegraph in the 1910s, gave tramp steamers a permanent place in world shipping, because ship brokers could contact the tramps not only in port, but also on the high seas. The tramps seemingly exemplify a highly efficient market mechanism, as the ships rush to supply any unforeseen or sudden demand for shipping space. In practice, however, they serve primarily shippers who have plenty of time to deliver full cargo loads, usually consisting of low value bulk commodities, but also oil in the case of the tramp tankers. The tramps will attempt to combine cargoes of several shippers, or steam with less than full cargo holds if nothing else is available, but for smaller lots shippers usually find that the tramps are not interested or are vague about delivery dates. A liner company, by contrast, carries small lots quickly and according to a fixed schedule of departures and arrivals, and there is no need to negotiate over rates and conditions. In an approximate but familiar comparison, many individual passengers may book seats on a commercial airline. If they form themselves into a group large enough, it is cheaper to charter the plane. The same basic principle holds for the tramps. While the bulk of this book deals with liner services, two sections describe the efforts to create a fleet of U.S. tramps.

Tramps are fine for occasional voyages, but if a shipper frequently fills entire vessels, he would be wise in most cases to purchase or at least charter his own vessels for a long-term period. It is out of this practice that a third category discussed in this book emerges, the proprietary steamship companies, that is, those shippers owning both the vessels and the bulk of the cargo. One surprising discovery I made in writing this book was the large number of major liner companies with proprietary origins. Thus, Dollar Line and Lykes Brothers began carrying their own cargoes and gradually evolved into liner services. Other proprietary companies such as United Fruit and W.R. Grace developed important liner services, but remained essentially dependent on the cargo generated by the parent firm.

Proprietary steamship companies are usually subsidiaries of parent firms like United Fruit, Alcoa, and United States Steel. Proprietary steamship companies can operate as either tramps or liners, can change from one to the other, or even combine the two. They operate as liners when, besides carrying their own cargo, their ships also serve trade routes on a regular announced schedule, as was most notably the case with United Fruit and W.R. Grace & Co. When the ships steam exclusively to meet the parent company's schedule and cargo space needs, the proprietary steamship company is operating like a tramp, even though at times very regular voyages may be scheduled. Tankers owned or chartered ("rented") by the major oil companies have historically comprised the majority of the vessel tonnage held by proprietary companies, with the fleet of Exxon (formerly Standard Oil of New Jersey) being the largest. Other tankers belong to independent operators who carry petroleum on the open market or charter their vessels to the oil companies on either voyage ("one trip") or long-term (usually in years) charters.

Since the shipper or customer is also the owner of the proprietary steamship company, the shipper-owner enjoys absolute control over the vessels. Parent companies which ship oil, ores or coal, as well as bulky perishables like bananas, have learned the hard lesson that they must themselves own and operate a merchant fleet able to carry a significant portion of their cargo. This lesson is sometimes forgotten, and when new management trained in modern cost cutting but not in shipping takes over, it often makes the mistake of slashing or abolishing a company's fleet because the tramps' rates are irresistibly lower. Once the principle is painfully relearned, management must determine what changing percentage of cargo should move on the company's own ships, a never-ending and difficult exercise for proprietary steamship companies.

Some readers may be disappointed by the relatively little attention this book gives to the flags of the ships, and in particular to the highly publicized issue of "flags of convenience" (Panama and Liberia, among others). In effect, this book considers most U.S.-owned vessels flying flags of convenience as one more type within the long historical tradition of U.S. ships flying foreign flags. As an introductory book surveying a vast field, this study is not intended to propose new conceptual approaches, but the clarity inherent in a new simplifying idea was too much to resist. In this book, ships and companies are considered U.S. operations when they meet two conditions. First, the ships and companies must be owned by U.S. citizens and second, the company must be run directly by U.S. management. All other issues, such as where the ship was built, the flag or registry of the ship, the nationality and language of the crews and officers, are secondary. If this approach sounds radically new, it should not, because it is already implicit in a number of company histories, and is now only stated directly and publicly. The chief drawback of this approach is that a case by case analysis of each company and its subsidiaries is required to separate those ships under direct U.S. management from those merely owned by U.S. interests. Companies have not been eager to share this information about the very heart of their shipping operations, but for the cases discussed here, enough evidence is available to allow this book to identify U.S. companies irrespective of which flags their ships flew.

A chronological overview will describe the main steps in the rise and decline of U.S. steamship companies and the structure of the book.

The first stage is 1900 to 1914 (chapters 1 and 2), the pre-World War I period when steamship companies used mostly foreign-flag ships, usually British. Vessels of other registries, even one Cuban, also existed. Crews were mainly Chinese, British, and natives of other parts of the British empire. In liner services in the foreign trade, International Mercantile Marine and Pacific Mail towered above the rest. The remainder of U.S. steamship companies tended to fall into the proprietary category, that is, they owned most if not all of the cargo carried aboard their vessels. Some true liner services did exist that were owned and run by major shippers. Matson and Dollar Line, originally just proprietary steamship companies, were actively seeking new business from other shippers, thus evolving gradually into liner services.

The outbreak of World War I in 1914 abruptly and permanently ended the pre-war shipping world. The British flag suddenly became a liability, because England could and often did requisition many ships for wartime service. Some shipowners began to ponder how to create a registry that would keep their vessels safe from interference from the British and other governments, but they could not take the first steps until after the war was over. In direct response to World War I, the U.S. government in 1916 established a specialized and powerful agency, the Shipping Board (chapter 3). The establishment of government shipyards to construct a large merchant fleet, the training of tens of thousands of civilians to become seamen and officers, the operation of ships, and the control of all vessels in ocean transportation were the Shipping Board's extraordinary achievements, which proved to be of the utmost significance for the war effort. The long-term consequences for the merchant shipping industry came only after the war had ended, when the Shipping Board took two fundamental decisions.

First, the Board elected to finish building the huge number of ships planned for a war that had been expected to last into 1919; indeed, the Board launched more ships after the war was over than during hostilities. Second, with this huge wartime surplus fleet, the Shipping Board embarked on a campaign to create and subsidize a distinct U.S.-flag merchant marine able to challenge England's, which was still the largest in the world. Some ships were operated directly by the government. The Shipping Board's preferred, policy, however, was to pay private operators to run the government-owned ships until the new companies could afford to buy them on easy payment plans at bargain basement prices. This giveaway program to create a private U.S.-flag merchant fleet on such a large scale has remained a unique phenomenon in world shipping; at one moment in the early 1920s, two hundred private operators were paid to operate government vessels. Important new companies were born at this time, most notably Waterman and American Export, while small companies from pre-World War I days such as Dollar Line and Lykes Brothers received an enormous boost thanks to the government's generosity. A weeding-out process got underway even before the government till began to run out, until the two hundred firms shrank to fewer than twenty, which largely continued to depend on some form of government subsidy.

During the Shipping Board era, a crucial event took place that more than cancelled the huge government investment in private shipping. In a burst of Anglophobia, International Mercantile Marine agreed in 1926 to divest itself of the bulk of its British-flag ships in exchange for promises of generous subsidies for its U.S.-flag ships. The largest U.S. steamship company was permanently undermined, and became another burden on the federal budget. With the approval of very generous mail subsidies in 1928, U.S. steamship companies entered their most lucrative years ever, but soon revelations of scandals, misappropriation of funds, as well as outright corruption and fraud, generated public pressure to overhaul the subsidy system. The New Deal addressed but could not permanently solve the problem of how to maintain a strong U.S.-flag merchant marine. In landmark legislation of 1936 (chapter 7), Congress replaced the discredited Shipping Board with a new U.S. Maritime Commission, drastically slashed subsidies, which were henceforth stipulated in rigid terms, and outlawed foreign flags to any company receiving shipping subsidies. By the late 1930s management found that to survive on the strictly limited subsidies without foreign flags or foreign crews required a careful balancing act that only a few firms operating in choice routes and possessing extraordinary entrepreneurial talent could accomplish. The second largest U.S. steamship company, the Dollar Line, was soon near bankruptcy; to save this crucial service to the Far East, the U.S. Maritime Commission purchased the line in 1939, and embarked on the task of paying off the creditors and reconstructing the company under the name of American President Lines.

In the late 1930s most firms decided to run the aging World War I vessels to the limit of their service lives, but not to replace them; the dwindling of their fleets foreshadowed the eventual disappearance of the U.S. merchant marine in foreign trade routes. The vessel replacement problem was effectively bypassed when the U.S. Maritime Commission launched a crash World War II shipbuilding program. A parallel program trained a new generation of seamen and officers, until the U.S. government by the end of World War II had created and was operating the largest merchant fleet in the world, outstripping even England's (chapter 8). For the first time the United States had become the leading maritime power, and with most of the world in ruins, the United States appeared guaranteed commercial supremacy on the sea-lanes for at least fifteen to twenty years, the normal service life of the ships built during World War II.

After 1945 Europeans expected the U.S. government to spawn another large group of new U.S. steamship companies, just as it had after World War I, but these fears proved groundless. Although several dozen proposals were entertained, no more than six new liner companies actually operated, and only two, Pacific Far East Line and Central Gulf Lines, lasted over a decade. On the other hand, at least fifty U.S.-flag tramp outfits did emerge. In general, the goal of the government was to return as soon as possible to the status quo ante, namely the shipping situation existing in the late 1930s. The government rapidly dismantled the wartime institutions and offered for sale at bargain prices the merchant fleet of surplus ships to U.S. citizens as well as foreigners. Soon Europeans acquired the vessels necessary to rebuild their shattered merchant fleets, and in the case of the South Americans, to create a new merchant marine.

From 1945 to the present, the steady decline of U.S. steamship companies has only been briefly halted when military emergencies like the Korean, Vietnam, and Gulf Wars provided powerful but temporary stimuli. The introduction of containers, rather than giving U.S. companies a technological edge, actually backfired. Containers hit U.S. companies just as the World War II generation of ships was reaching the end of its useful life, and vessel replacement with more costly containerships proved a burden too crushing for most companies to bear. The collapse of one company after another has become almost a routine occurrence, and no longer evokes any surprise. As the end of the twentieth century approaches, almost nothing is left of U.S. liner and tramp services; only the proprietary companies that sought refuge in foreign flags have survived. The contrast was all the more striking because the United States at the start of the twentieth century could boast of a powerful merchant fleet, whose emergence forms the subject of the first chapter.

Part I.
The Prewar Period

1

The American Challenge

As THE TWENTIETH century began, there were few indications that the United States would attempt to claim a preeminent position in world shipping. Britain owned and operated the largest merchant fleet in the world, and the only foreseeable rival was a rapidly industrializing Germany, whose two main lines, Hamburg-America and North German Lloyd, were already challenging British shipping in many sealanes. In contrast to Germany's feverish expansion of her merchant fleet, the United States, since the end of the Civil War, had followed a policy of maritime neglect, so that U.S.-flag vessels virtually disappeared from the foreign trade routes except in the Pacific Ocean.

The greater U.S. presence in the Pacific Ocean rather than in the Atlantic was the result of two factors. U.S.-flag lines enjoyed the intercoastal privilege that excluded foreign-flag ships from the trade between the East and West coasts of the United States, a tremendous advantage totally lacking in the routes to Europe. Second, U.S. lines in the Pacific Ocean used highly efficient and low-cost Chinese crews for their ships. Pacific Mail Steamship Company, discussed in the third section, stood out as the premier U.S.-flag line in the transpacific trade, a position the company held until World War I. The fourth section reveals the existence of other U.S. companies of growing importance in the Pacific Ocean.

U.S. success in the Pacific Ocean should not be overstated, however: The North Atlantic was the center of world trade and shipping, and by comparison the Pacific Ocean was largely deserted in 1900. Not until 1982 did transpacific shipping finally overtake the Atlantic in cargo volume. The North Atlantic was the center of world shipping at the beginning of the twentieth century, and there the British lines of Cunard, White Star, and Leyland carried the bulk of the cargo and passengers, with the German lines Hamburg-America and North German Lloyd in second place. The prevailing situation was abruptly altered when in 1901–1902 the Wall Street financial magnate J. P. Morgan created in the North Atlantic the largest single merchant fleet then existing in the world, the International Mercantile Marine. The first two sections of this chapter explain how this dramatic development took place, and how I. M. M. operated until World War I.

☐ The Creation of the International Mercantile Marine

The United States burst into North Atlantic shipping with a suddenness that surprised many Europeans accustomed to dismiss American steamship efforts as ridiculous. America's invasion may have seemed to be just one more manifestation of the young republic's flexing of its industrial and financial muscles, but in reality it answered the structural need to consolidate shipping services in the North Atlantic. The Leyland Line, the White Star Line, and Cunard were the three main British firms on the North Atlantic, although there were some smaller companies as well. On the American side, the Atlantic Transport Company of Bernard N. Baker and the International Navigation Company of Clement A. Griscom constituted the modest American presence in the North Atlantic; both companies pried a variety of subsidies out of Congress to keep their U.S.-flag ships running, but the bulk of their ships were operated under the lower-cost British flag. Holland-America was a Dutch line also prominent in the North Atlantic services, but none could match the swift rise and massive presence of two new German lines, the Hamburg-America under the aggressive Albert Ballin, and the North German Lloyd. From the 1890s Germany had been determined to build up a merchant fleet eventually rivaling England's, and the immediate result had been overtonnaging the routes. The massive German intrusion in turn provoked a response from the French Compagnie Générale Maritime, a state-owned line charged with keeping at least a share of cargoes out of German hands and in French vessels.[1]

By 1900 the situation in the North Atlantic was critical, and with all the lines planning to build bigger and faster liners to carry freight and the teeming immigrant traffic, rapidly rising investment costs and sharp competition guaranteed a reduction in the number of firms. If the smaller lines did not act quickly, they would be the first to be eliminated, a fact first appreciated by Bernard Baker of Atlantic Transport, who traveled to England to approach the Leyland Line with a proposed merger in March 1900. By combining freight and passenger business, the merger of the two companies justified and financed the construction of fewer but bigger and faster liners. Ownership of Leyland Line had fallen to John R. Ellerman, who was not a steamship man but rather a financial manipulator. Ellerman was willing to sell, but only if he could make a killing on the sale. Perhaps if left alone Ellerman would have lowered his price down to Baker's level, but soon other individuals with rumors of more promising offers were buzzing in Ellerman's ears. The Germans, in particular Ballin, did not want to see this merger go through, or for that matter any deal in which they did not have a substantial interest. On the American side, Griscom strongly pressured Baker to drop the Leyland merger, on the grounds that as American steamship executives, they had mutual interests.[2]

Baker now took a back seat in the subsequent developments, while Griscom himself temporarily took the lead with a bold proposal. Griscom since 1899 had been trying to secure a loan from a J. P. Morgan subsidiary to build six new vessels to be placed under the U.S. flag after the passage of a subsidy bill in Congress. In the middle of 1900 Griscom now entered into contract with J. P. Morgan with the proposal to merge not only the two U.S. steamship companies but one or more British lines as well. The consolidation would provide considerable savings and make for a more regular and profitable operation. J. P. Morgan had long considered the competition between the individual firms to be ridiculous: their ships all rushed out of New York on the same day to try to be the first to reach Europe, when if they just distributed their voyages to have one sailing each day of the week, the passengers and the shippers of cargo would enjoy a more dependable service with enough profits for all the steamship lines. If the Congress passed the subsidy, the ships would be built and registered in the United States; if the subsidy bill failed, the cheaper and well-tried route of British shipyards and registry would be followed.

The risks seemed small, and J. P. Morgan agreed to provide the financial backing for the proposed combination. The first step was relatively easy, and by December 1900 the negotiations for the merger of Griscom's International Navigation and Baker's Atlantic Transport were

completed; both remained as directors and stockholders in the gradually
emerging combine, but from then on J. P. Morgan was the driving and
controlling force. The next step was to acquire a British line, and J. P.
Morgan's London associates began negotiations to acquire the Leyland
Line. The majority stockholder Ellerman drove a hard bargain: he demanded not only one-third more than the Americans' generous offer
but also that the high price be extended to the remaining stockholders
who had not been a party to the negotiations. Ellerman's prices were
outrageous, and here Morgan faced his first decision on whether to drop
the deal or proceed with the formation of the shipping combine.[3] Morgan pushed ahead and in April 1901 the sale of Leyland Line was announced, causing a tremendous public sensation in England. Newspaper
accounts of the deal reported that "Liverpool had learned with very
considerable astonishment" about the sale; "it was never imagined that
a large interest in a Liverpool shipping company with such a history as
this would be transferred to American capitalists."[4]

And this was not the last shock awaiting the British public. The
largest and most prestigious British line on the North Atlantic was the
White Star Line, which had recently launched the *Celtic*, then the
world's largest passenger liner. In 1899 the founder of the White Star
Line had died, and a rift had developed between his son and heir, J.
Bruce Ismay, and the second-largest stockholder in the company, the
shipbuilder William J. Pirrie. The internal squabbles provided the opportunity for Morgan to acquire the White Star Line, and soon Pirrie
was safely in the Americans' camp; he himself conducted the negotiations with the rest of the stockholders and finally with Ismay to convince them to sell. Once again Pirrie secured a price one-third higher
than that offered by the Americans, but this time only one-fourth of
the price was given in cash, the rest being in the form of preferred stock
in the new combine; in effect the sellers were being asked to finance
the sale on the prospects of favorable profits in the future. The sale
took place in July 1901, but it was not announced until April 1902, although rumors of important happenings were circulating long before
the disclosure.[5]

With the two U.S. companies and the two British firms already
under his control, Morgan needed only to add the Cunard Line to turn
his North Atlantic combine into a near monopoly in the North Atlantic.
Stock ownership of Cunard was more widely diffused than had been the
case for either Leyland or White Star, while the directors of Cunard
with small but significant blocks of shares were confused over whether
to accept the many offers proffered by Morgan's associates. Morgan
should have been more insistent and more generous with the Cunard

stockholders; the Cunard directors could easily see that the terms received by the White Star Line stockholders had meant surrendering profits and control over their company in exchange for promises of future profits. Morgan hesitated and did not push the Cunard takeover while there was still time, especially before news of the White Star Line sale had been formally announced. Instead, Morgan had to deal with the sudden maneuvers by Albert Ballin of Hamburg-America.

For the German lines, the proposed consolidation of U.S. with British lines was a real threat. The Germans had been able to rise rapidly thanks to the competition among these rival lines, but against a single combine the goal of German supremacy in North Atlantic shipping could never be attained. Through the commercial intelligence network, Ballin and the German government were soon aware of the Morgan combine, and they were determined to take all steps necessary to neutralize this movement. Morgan's takeover of Leyland and White Star had been so swift as to prevent countermoves, but the Germans thought that perhaps they could do something to avoid the danger from the new combine. Ballin of Hamburg-America and the officials of North German Lloyd began a series of trips to England and New York, even talking with Morgan himself. Quite naturally the German lines refused to enter the combine, but, using a "community of interest" argument, they asked for an informal association. German nationalistic pressure was very strong, and when Ballin agreed to Morgan's purchase of a minority share in Hamburg-America stock, violent anti-American protests in the German press forced the cancellation of this arrangement. Instead, in February 1902 a mutual exchange of shares was agreed to by the German lines and Morgan's combine, as part of a traffic agreement dividing freight and passengers in the North Atlantic for 10 years.[6]

The agreement was attractive to the Morgan combine, which, having neutralized its formidable German rivals, could now try to recover in assured future earnings the high price paid for the Leyland stock. The German-American agreement was soon known in shipping and official circles, and it provided the Cunard directors the answer to their previous indecision. The alliance with the Germans had increased the bargaining power of Morgan, who now could threaten to shut out Cunard from the North Atlantic unless it agreed to sell out to the new combine, but this ploy backfired. Up to the time of the German alliance, much as Cunard tried, they could never picture J. P. Morgan—son of an English financial family, raised in England to be thoroughly Victorian and having many British associates—as posing a mortal threat to British economic or strategic interests. But with the German alliance,

England's political enemy and most likely military enemy in any future war suddenly entered the equation to shake a somnolent British government out of its free-market dreams and into action. The only way Cunard could escape the grip of the Morgan combine and the German lines was by a subsidy from the British government to build two of the largest liners in the North Atlantic; with the new faster ships, later named the *Lusitania* and the *Mauretania*, Cunard could not only hold but also increase her market share. After complex negotiations the British government and the company reached an agreement, which they signed in September 1902.[7]

Long before then Morgan knew the stage of acquisitions was over, and as he watched Cunard slip from his grasp, he contented himself with organizing his new shipping combine, which had operated informally since April 1902 but was not formally incorporated as the International Mercantile Marine or I.M.M. until October of that year. In 1909 the International Mercantile Marine was the fourth-largest industrial corporation by assets in the United States surpassed only by U.S. Steel, Standard Oil, and American Tobacco Co. To emphasize as much as possible the purely business aspect of the venture, the name International had been chosen to avoid any identification with a particular country, and the legal title was for a company whose fleet was 85 percent British flag, 12 percent U.S. flag, and 3 percent Belgian flag.

As part of the negotiations with the Germans and to neutralize any Dutch surge in the North Atlantic, the Morgan combine had forced Holland-America to sell 25 percent of its shares to International Mercantile Marine and 25 percent to the two German lines, the latter being fierce rivals of the Dutch. The Dutch resented this agreement, and finally during World War I they were able to repurchase the shares held by I.M.M. and the German lines. I.M.M.'s fleet was the single largest in the world, and while it incorporated only a modest fraction of the total British flag tonnage scattered all over the world's oceans, there was no doubt that by buying established English lines the Americans had managed to propel themselves into a commanding position in North Atlantic shipping. Only the tests of experience would tell whether the venture would be a financial success and how long it would last.[8]

□ I.M.M. on the North Atlantic

From 1902 until 1914, control of I.M.M. rested in a five-man voting trust, consisting of J. P. Morgan himself or his son, two of the Morgan associates, and two English representatives. Initially they were J. Bruce

Ismay, also president of the subsidiary White Star Line, and William J. Pirrie, the shipbuilder who had exchanged 75 percent of his White Star stock for I.M.M. shares and the agreement that during 10 years all ships of the new combine would be built in his shipyard. President of I.M.M. was Clement A. Griscom, ably aided by a young and enthusiastic vice president, the American Philip A. Franklin. Ismay chafed at being subordinate to Griscom whose International Navigation Co. had been much smaller than the White Star Line. I.M.M.'s financial performance in 1902 and 1903 was very poor and the combine as a whole failed to declare any dividends, but the White Star Line continued to declare dividends that were actually handed over to I.M.M. to cover the losses in the other subsidiaries. The British stockholders felt duped, and they decided to make Griscom the scapegoat for I.M.M.'s misfortunes. In early 1904 the $100 stock of I.M.M. was down to $4 for the common and $19 for the preferred. Ismay was full of new ideas to turn around I.M.M., while Griscom was at the end of a long and distinguished business career. J. P. Morgan submitted to the mounting pressure and agreed to kick Griscom upstairs to the chairmanship of the largely decorative board of directors of I.M.M. Ismay in 1904 became president of I.M.M. with headquarters in New York, while retaining his presidency of the subsidiary White Star Line.[9]

Ismay was eager to make his mark in the shipping world, but he soon discovered that the poor performance of I.M.M. in the North Atlantic was due to factors beyond the control even of a company with more than 130 steamers, the largest merchant fleet in the world. The year 1900 had been exceptionally good for shipping, but a slump began in 1901 and continued through 1903, which was the real reason behind I.M.M.'s initial poor profit earnings. Bad years usually give way to good ones, but at this time underlying structural changes in trade required difficult adjustments by the steamship companies. Whereas prior to 1900 the regular trade patterns on the North Atlantic had been the export from the United States of foodstuffs and raw materials and the import from Europe of manufactures and immigrants, the rapid industrialization and high tariffs in the United States dried up the flow of European manufactured goods after 1900. Fortunately for the steamship companies, the total number of immigrants continued to rise; if the Europeans were considered as goods, then the trade imbalance disappeared. Clearly a new type of versatile vessel was needed, one able to cram at least a thousand immigrants on board and then return from the United States loaded with raw materials and foodstuffs (if necessary, grains and other low-value bulk commodities). A percentage of disappointed immigrants always returned to Europe, and some of the successful residents liked to travel to visit relatives back home, but there were never enough passengers to make up for the shortage of goods; to fill the holds of the larger liners, steamship lines had to compete against tramp steamers for the low-value bulk cargoes.

The steamship lines of the North Atlantic had become excessively dependent on the immigrant traffic (the steerage passengers or class) for their profits and survival. First-class passenger facilities did not enter into the financial equation, because the upper-class travelers, although willing to pay high prices, were in a position to demand matching service. The value of the first-class service was in public relations, as a way of generating massive publicity that would draw second-class passengers and, most importantly, the steerage-class immigrants.[10]

To make the situation worse on the North Atlantic, Cunard had withdrawn in March 1903 from the Atlantic Conference, which set rates on passengers and freight, and the ensuing rate war had contributed to I.M.M.'s poor financial showing. The rate war was really between Cunard and the German lines whose government-sponsored control over the immigrant traffic passing through Germany from Eastern Europe had given them a commanding position over British lines. The new I.M.M. president Ismay was not about to dwell on these details, and as soon as he took office in the middle of 1904, he began a series of sharp rate cuts to cripple both the German and the English lines. Cunard met the price cuts, and more significantly it signed an agreement in 1904 with the Hungarian government providing for the carriage of immigrants to the United States via the Mediterranean ports of Fiume and Trieste. By this clever flanking movement Cunard diverted part of the immigrant flow into its ships and away from the German ships in Hamburg and Bremen. Nevertheless, no great advantages resulted from this action: the German lines brought pressure on the Hungarian government to cancel the agreement; rates remained low; I.M.M., the German lines, and Cunard piled up losses; and attempts to end the rate war foundered. Finally in 1908 the German emperor intervened and "said he was going to tell Mr. Ballin that he must settle things with the Cunard; that it was absurd this fighting and cutting of rates and throwing away money."[11] Shortly afterward an agreement was reached in April 1908 restoring the rates to their level before the rate war.

The end of the 1903–1908 rate war shifted the focus of competition from prices to the quality of the service. Cunard had taken the lead with the delivery of the *Lusitania* and the *Mauretania* in 1907, the two ships the British government had earlier agreed to subsidize in response to the I.M.M. challenge. The *Lusitania* and the *Mauretania* were the largest and fastest liners in the world; the elegant ships were popular with first-class travelers, and the lower decks were easily filled with immigrants and could also hold many commodities for the return voyages. The German lines were working on bigger and better ships to match Cunard, but they were beaten by I.M.M., which prepared a trio of vessels to gain supremacy in the North Atlantic.

Ismay's strategy was to design ships better and more luxurious than the *Lusitania* and the *Mauretania*. As the price tag on the proposed ships mounted, something had to be sacrificed; I.M.M. chose to forsake speed, so that at 22 knots the ships were slower than the Cunard liners, which were able to travel at 25 knots. The first of the three ships, the *Olympic*, was delivered in 1911, and since its luxury features were a big success with the wealthy traveling public, I.M.M. decided to increase its emphasis on the luxury aspects in the second sister ship, the *Titanic*, delivered in 1912. The name of the third scheduled ship, the *Gigantic*, was later changed to the more modest *Britannic*.

Ismay had gotten himself into a corner, because to match the service of the two faster Cunard liners, he needed three of his slower ships. By the time the *Titanic* was launched, the failure to build more speed into the ship was evident, but Ismay counted on a huge publicity campaign to attract enough travelers in spite of the lower speed. Unlike the Cunard ships, the *Titanic* class vessels lacked double hulls and instead had watertight compartments, which led a shipbuilding journal to label the ship "practically unsinkable." Public relations experts dropped the distracting "practically" and the press soon talked about the "unsinkable *Titanic*," convincing many persons to book passage on the safest of liners afloat. For the maiden voyage in April 1912, Ismay himself traveled aboard with a fabulous collection of millionaires and personalities, in order to make a media splash both upon departure from England and upon arrival in New York. It was imperative that the *Titanic* be no less a success than the *Olympic*, for otherwise the White Star Line, the real money earner of I.M.M., would not be able to pull the parent holding company out of its unbroken record of yearly losses. Under pressure to reach New York as fast as possible, the *Titanic*'s engines were driven to the maximum, and when the reports of icebergs ahead began to pour in with alarming frequency, the captain, at the insistence of Ismay, declined to shift course south for the longer route out of range of the icebergs or to slow down to allow the giant ship more time to avoid obstacles. On 12 April 1912 the *Titanic* struck an iceberg and sank less than three hours later; of the 2,206 aboard, only 703 were rescued after two hours at sea in open boats when the old Cunard liner *Carpathia* arrived at maximum speed in response to the distress call.[12]

For world shipping, 1912 was a boom year, with steamship companies earning record profits and declaring dividends on the average of 7 percent, but for I.M.M. the loss of the *Titanic* in that year turned a large surplus into a certain loss. While the captain of the *Titanic* had bravely gone down with his ship, J. Bruce Ismay had escaped among the survivors; after a few months of disgrace and humiliation, he was removed from all positions at I.M.M. and the White Star Line. With him went the bulk of the remaining British stockholders, who always had been uncomfortable with their minority status since 1902 and who now proceeded slowly to dispose of their I.M.M. shares. By 1916 more than 90 percent of the stockholders were U.S. citizens. A caretaker president took over at I.M.M. to try to pick up the pieces, but the company was in deep trouble. No dividends had ever been paid, and the debt incurred to pay the extravagant prices for the purchase of the subsidiaries in 1901–1902 crushed I.M.M. The subsidiaries had continued to operate largely on their own, so that the expected savings from consolidation of services did not occur. The 1902 expectation of future profits had turned out to be groundless for the first 10 years, and in 1912 the loss of the *Titanic* weakened the White Star Line, usually the most profitable of the British-flag operations, while the U.S.-flag subsidiaries continued with their traditional losses.[13]

Steamship shares thus gained a bad reputation on the stock market, which was henceforth reluctant to invest in or even speculate on ships. I.M.M. managed to meet its debt payments on time, but the outbreak of another rate war in January 1914 again plunged I.M.M. into a precarious situation. The largest merchant fleet in the world was now Hamburg-America, followed by North German Lloyd, and these two German lines started a rate war that raged until the outbreak of World War I. This shipping rivalry provides an example of how excessive commercial competition can easily contribute to violent confrontation. World War I caused a tremendous temporary disruption in shipping, increasing the pressure on an already weakened I.M.M., and in October 1914 the company failed to meet its interest payments.[14]

Technically the company was in bankruptcy, but the vice president, Philip A. Franklin, detected a unique opportunity for the company and for himself. Franklin convinced the creditors to appoint him the receiver of I.M.M., on the promise of turning the company around. He gambled on the temporary shipping dislocations giving way to an acute and highly profitable shipping shortage, and his strategy worked. With the large wartime profits, the company quickly paid all overdue interest payments, and in 1915 it paid dividends for the first time on the preferred stock (dividends were never paid on the common stock). Franklin was now confirmed as president of I.M.M., beginning more than 50 years of his family's grip on the company's management. The Morgan associates agreed to dissolve the five-man voting trust, but Franklin knew the importance of having the Morgan firm backing the steamship company, and for nearly 20 more years he managed to persuade three of the Morgan associates to continue serving on the board of directors long after all official financial links had disappeared. As long as the Morgan associates were on the board (and even for decades after their departure), their presence sufficed to scare away prospective speculators wishing to take over I.M.M. Nevertheless, after paying off the company's debts and stabilizing its management, Franklin still had to find a way to keep I.M.M. modestly profitable once the extraordinary shipping profits of World War I came to an end.[15] I.M.M., by its reliance on foreign-flag ships, had remained the premier U.S. line in the North Atlantic. In the Pacific Ocean U.S. lines had combined intercoastal privileges with Chinese crews to attain a strong position in transpacific shipping since the late nineteenth century, but would the success last into the twentieth century?

☐   Pacific Mail Steamship Company

In 1900 few doubted that the Pacific Mail Steamship Company, operating a transpacific service since 1867, would continue to be the main U.S. line in the Pacific Ocean. Created in 1848 to provide regular service between the East and West coasts of the United States, the route along the Pacific coast had remained important and had grown to include calls in Mexico and the hauling of profitable coffee cargoes from Central America. For the transpacific service, the company ordered two new combination cargo-passenger vessels in 1902, the *Korea* and the *Siberia*, and two more in 1904, the *Manchuria* and the *Mongolia;* the company then had the fastest and largest steamers in the Pacific Ocean. The company also purchased and chartered additional ships to meet the continuing expansion in freight. Since 1893 Pacific Mail Steamship had been owned by the Southern Pacific Railroad, which, in one of its wisest decisions, had appointed Rennie P. Schwerin as vice president and general manager of the shipping line, a position he held until 1916. Schwerin, a graduate of the U.S. Naval Academy, was the rare navy officer who combined a knowledge of merchant ships with uncanny business ability and foresight. The changing executives of Southern Pacific Railroad who knew little about ocean shipping were more than glad to leave the steamship line safely in Schwerin's hands.[16]

The new general manager immediately managed to turn around the steamship line, which resumed paying dividends in 1897–99 for the first time since 1885. Nevertheless, after 1899 the company never again paid dividends because of the rapidly growing Japanese competition. Japan, as part of its drive to capture export markets, had decided to create a large merchant marine, and the Japanese government poured subsidies into lines such as Nippon Yusen Kaisha, which also profited by being able to pay low wages to Oriental crews. The Japanese lines were not about to risk a premature rate war, so they concentrated instead on undermining the cargo foundations of non-Japanese firms like Pacific Mail. The strategy was deviously simple: Nippon Yusen Kaisha offered a very low rate to a non-Japanese merchant in Japan who decided to use the cheaper steamship service. The Japanese line then passed on the names and addresses of all the clients of the non-Japanese exporter to Japanese merchants who promptly contacted them and underquoted the foreigner's prices. The non-Japanese exporter was driven out of business, and the grateful Japanese shippers were only too eager to send the freight aboard the Japanese lines. Gradually the foreign exports of Japan, at this time mainly silk, started to fall under the control of the Japanese exporters; a monolithic block of Japanese merchants, lines, and later industrialists and bankers slowly began to take shape after 1900.

Although Pacific Mail did not receive government subsidies for its U.S.-flag vessels like the Japanese lines had received before World War I, the U.S. company was still in a position to fight back. The ships traditionally had been run by very efficient Chinese crews, so as far as costs were concerned, Pacific Mail could match any price cut of the Japanese lines. Deferred rate rebates (a refund of part of the payment six months or a year after the shipment was completed) did not become illegal in the United States until 1916; thus, by tying the non-Japanese shippers to Pacific Mail, the company retained considerable cargo bookings. The remaining non-Japanese merchants in Japan, seeing what had happened to their former colleagues, became more cautious about accepting the bait of tempting freight rate offers from the Japanese lines. The Japanese threat could be countered, but only by means of vigorous, long-term company action supported by the U.S. government.[17]

Pacific Mail did not ask for subsidies but rather wanted constant legal and moral support for its activities in the ruthless trade competition of the Far East. While the Japanese shippers and steamship executives were subsidized and otherwise rewarded and encouraged to devise new and more ingenious ways to capture all foreign trade and cargoes, Pacific Mail, because it was owned by Southern Pacific Railroad, immediately was suspected—if not openly deemed guilty—of monopoly charges in the minds of many Americans. Schwerin himself was repeatedly brought before Congress—not to receive a well-earned recognition for his untiring efforts against Japanese competition, but to be treated with hostility. One of his replies there plainly reveals his exasperation:

> Why, you do not know what water competition is. I am here before this committee, and my crime is that I am trying to keep the American flag on the ocean. The questions that are asked me here before this committee are along the line that I am doing something wrong, and that I ought to be fined for doing something wrong. I tell you, gentlemen, it is a pretty hard proposition that we are up against. . . . Leave us alone; let us go and do what the other fellows are doing, and let the government help us to do these illegal things that the other fellow is doing.[18]

Schwerin decided to take advantage of the opportunity provided by the expected opening of the Panama Canal in 1914 to strike a crushing blow against the Japanese. He obtained the financing to build four gigantic cargo-passenger ships of 37,000 deadweight tons—the total weight of each ship's cargo, fuel, stores, crew, and passengers—to serve the route between New York and the Philippines. The ships would also carry cargo in the protected intercoastal trade and serve the Far Eastern ports from New York as well as from San Francisco. Even if the Japanese built ships as big, they still would be excluded from the intercoastal trade, and with its loyal and tireless Chinese crews Pacific Mail could still meet any rate cut by the Japanese lines, who for the first time would experience a decisive setback. Nevertheless, this seemingly foolproof strategy failed. In a bizarre move, Congress came to the rescue of the Japanese, and in 1912 passed the Panama Canal Act, which prohibited steamship lines owned by railroads from using the Panama Canal. In the costliest peacetime construction project of the first half of the twentieth century, the U.S. government had built a canal that admitted without discrimination the ships of all other nations of the world but excluded some of its own U.S.-flag ships! Selling Pacific Mail to non-railroad owners was not a real option, especially after the poor financial results of I.M.M. Everyone in the steamship business knew about the Japanese menace, and although possible investors were impressed with how well Pacific Mail had held up against the grueling Japanese competition, they were not about to risk their capital.

Schwerin felt betrayed by his own government and people:

> If you had struggled for 20 years as I have, taken a line that was a million and a quarter in debt, and practically in the hands of a receiver, doubled that line up by slow, hard process, until you had gotten into *Korea* and *Siberia,* which you were told would be your graveyard, and then you got *Mongolia* and *Manchuria,* and were told that would settle it; and then, against all the better judgment of your associates and friends, you raised $12,000,000 to build four 37,000-ton ships to put in the trade from New York to the Philippine Islands, and a million and a half to change these four ships to the latest modern types, and you were defeated by Congress—prohibited by Congress from building those ships—I think you would be a little discouraged. I want to say that I am done with the American flag forever. I would not raise my hand to raise a dollar for the American flag. My interest in this business before this committee to-day, gentlemen, is absolutely because I am practically subpoenaed here. I have no interest in the shipping business. I am about to retire. I have given 20 years of my life, morning, noon, and night—slept and breathed with it—to see that flag on the ocean, and I am just as certain as I sit here that if those four ships had been built I would have had four more for the coast of South America, and four more equal to the *Imperator* that is going to run to Europe, all under the American flag.[19]

Schwerin had gone sour on U.S.-flag shipping, yet the existing vessels of Pacific Mail operated by highly efficient Chinese crews still guaranteed years if not decades of lively competition against the Japanese. Congress could not leave well enough alone, and under intense pressure from white labor unions passed the La Follette Seamen's Act of 1915, which mandated that at least 75 percent of the crews must be fluent in English, a measure aimed in particular against the Chinese crews of Pacific Mail. The cheapest English-speaking crews were from the British Empire, but they would not be cheap enough to compete with Japanese crews; Pacific Mail's labor costs would increase enough to turn its marginal profits into permanent losses. Also, the Chinese crews provided superb attention to the passengers and were excellent seamen as well, and Pacific Mail did not want to risk its reputation for quality service at the hands of new and untried crews of other nationalities.[20]

Pacific Mail had repeatedly stated that if the seamen's bill became law, the company would either leave the U.S. flag or sell off the business. Prior to 1914 Pacific Mail could have avoided any manning requirements by shifting to the British flag, but once World War I began, the British flag exposed the company's vessels to requisition by the English government. Rather than seeing the war as a handicap, Southern Pacific Railroad and Schwerin saw it as a blessing in disguise. The tremendous shortage of tonnage in the North Atlantic caused by World War I provided the perfect opportunity to recover the investment in the thankless steamship business. In 1915 the five main steamers of the transpacific trade, including the *Korea, Siberia, Manchuria,* and *Mongolia,* were sold to the International Mercantile Marine for operation under the U.S. flag at the exorbitant rates prevailing in the North Atlantic. The gap left in the transpacific services gave the Japanese the green light to take over many steamship routes in the Far East. W. R. Grace and Company purchased Pacific Mail itself as well as its remaining ships in the U.S. West Coast, Mexico, Central America, and Panama routes. Pacific Mail's services nicely complemented Grace's own routes between the west coast of South America and the United States. As a Grace subsidiary, Pacific Mail continued a rather hectic career until its surviving ships were incorporated into other Grace operations in 1925.[21]

□ U.S. Lines in the Transpacific Trade

Until World War I Pacific Mail Steamship was the leading U.S.-flag company in transpacific trade. Three other firms tried to challenge the supremacy of Pacific Mail Steamship, and out of their strivings finally emerged the post–World War I successor. The first challenger was Oceanic Steamship Company, incorporated in 1881 by Claus Spreckels, a German immigrant who had settled in Hawaii. Spreckels had built a fortune in the United States, and from 1876 on he added extensive sugar plantations in Hawaii to his holdings. To carry the Hawaiian sugar to his refinery in California, Spreckels created the Oceanic Steamship Company in 1881, initially running sailing vessels. He then chartered British-flag steamers, and in 1883 the first steamers he had ordered, the *Alameda* and *Mariposa,* entered into service. Spreckels soon learned that there was not enough Hawaii cargo to keep the steamers busy, so he turned his eyes on the route to Sydney and Auckland served by Pacific Mail with a subsidy from Congress. After adroit lobbying in Congress, Spreckels secured the transfer of the subsidy from Pacific Mail to Oceanic Steamship in 1885, which was a major coup and also a nice complement for his Hawaiian service.[22]

In 1890 Oceanic Steamship received an additional subsidy for the route from the New Zealand government, on the condition that the

Union Steamship Company of New Zealand participate in the joint venture with a third ship. The annexation of Hawaii to the United States in 1898 raised the fear that soon the coastwise laws would extend to those islands. The next year Congress mandated only U.S.-flag vessels for the trade between Hawaii and California. This extension of the U.S. coastwise laws ended the arrangement between Oceanic Steamship and the Union Steamship Company of New Zealand, because henceforth foreign-flag ships were excluded from the California-Hawaii route. In 1900 Oceanic Steamship received the *Sierra, Sonoma,* and *Ventura,* three new vessels, that met the speed and size specifications Congress had required to qualify for mail subsidies. Congress refused to increase the subsidies in 1907, and Ocean Steamship Company simply laid up the three new ships; only the older *Alameda* and *Mariposa* remained serving the Hawaii-California routes. Congress finally increased the mail subsidy in 1912, and the Oceanic Steamship Company put back into the South Pacific route the remodeled *Sierra, Sonoma,* and *Ventura,* which, among other changes, had been converted to oil burners. Meanwhile the economic and political position of the Spreckels family had declined considerably, and the family split into opposing factions. From 1910 on Oceanic Steamship barely limped along until only its purchase by a powerful financial group could make it a successor to Pacific Mail.[23]

A second challenge to Pacific Mail's supremacy had come early in the twentieth century. In 1893 James J. Hill had completed the Great Northern Railway, the last of the transcontinental railroads, with its final terminal in Seattle, Washington. For the Great Northern to be a success, a transpacific steamship extension was necessary to generate cargo, but steamship companies that were well established in California were reluctant to extend any but coastwise service to Seattle. Hill quickly discovered Nippon Yusen Kaisha, a Japanese line struggling to secure a minimal position in the transpacific trade. Soon an agreement was signed providing for an exchange of cargo between the railroad and the steamship firm on the condition that Nippon Yusen Kaisha provide at least a monthly service between Seattle and the Far East. In 1896 the Japanese steamers began to call on Seattle, and the agreement with Nippon Yusen Kaisha remained in force until World War I.

Hill was glad to have the Japanese call on Seattle, but this was just the beginning. He believed that the millions of Chinese and Japanese were markets just waiting to be tapped. According to Hill, if the Chinese would switch from rice flour to wheat for their noodles, the individual consumption multiplied by millions of persons would mean a tremendous cargo volume for the Great Northern Railroad passing through the wheat-growing areas of the U.S. northern plains. Since Nippon Yusen Kaisha's ships were not enough, Hill needed his own fleet, and for that purpose he incorporated the Great Northern Steamship Company on 3 August 1900.

Hill was not about to charter ships or buy second-hand vessels. He wanted not only the best but also the biggest ships possible. To carry the huge cargoes expected in Far East trade, Hill wanted four ships of 22,250 deadweight tons, larger than any then afloat, with accommodations for 200 first-class passengers and 1,200 in steerage. The contract for the ships was signed on 28 February 1900 with the Eastern Shipbuilding Company, a shipyard so new it did not yet have a business address. Hill's shipping venture had proceeded uneventfully until he contracted with this untried and inexperienced shipyard. Knowing that construction of such large ships would take longer than usual, he had counted on about two years, but the *Minnesota* was not delivered by the shipyard until August 1904, and the second ship, the *Dakota*, was not delivered until 1905. By then Hill had become thoroughly disillusioned with the shipyard, and he did not enter into contracts for the last two planned ships. He explained his decision thus: "I had an experience in the building of two very large ships, and I am quite sure I do not want any more . . . I would rather undertake to build a thousand miles of railway than to build two ships."[24]

Delivery of the ships only meant new problems for Hill, because his shipping subsidiary, the Great Northern Steamship Company, could not find enough cargo to fill the huge deep holds of the vessels. The shipyard had installed obsolete and ill-suited equipment, while Hill himself had cluttered the design with radical innovations that turned out to be costly failures. Breakdowns, malfunctions, bunker fires, and a whole host of other mishaps marred the early careers of these ships. The two ships were also very slow, making definite schedules difficult. To create some semblance of a more regular service, the steamship company chartered five ships for combined operations from Seattle to the Far East. With seven ships in service in 1906, including the two largest in the Pacific Ocean, the Great Northern Steamship Company appeared to emerge as a serious and growing menace to Pacific Mail.

As it turned out, Rennie Schwerin of Pacific Mail had no reason to worry. Because of a gross mistake on the part of the captain, on 10 March 1907—a clear, calm day—the *Dakota* struck a reef off the coast of Japan at full speed. The ship was a total loss and the captain spent the rest of his life as a night watchman. The Japanese, whom Hill had first introduced to Seattle, now had become formidable competitors, and the lower rates of the subsidized Japanese lines soon made the operations of the chartered vessels unprofitable. One by one Hill withdrew his vessels, until in 1908 only the *Minnesota* was left. Because the ship was so big, economies of scale were possible, and the use of Chinese seamen for its very large crew matched the lower labor costs of the subsidized Japanese lines. The *Minnesota* settled into a trade pattern of four seasonal voyages each year: spring, summer, fall, and winter. Extended stays in each Far East port of call gave the company's agents more time to fill the vessel's apparently bottomless holds prior to the return voyage to Seattle. In spite of all these efforts, the Great Northern Steamship Company still suffered small losses, but since the cargo brought to Seattle earned high profits for the parent railroad, the operation was allowed to continue until World War I. At that time the *Minnesota* became another casualty of the La Follette Seamen's Act of 1915, because without the Chinese, the cost of its crew of at least 175 men made the losses of the unsubsidized company unbearable even for the Great Northern Railroad. The vessel was sold in 1917 to the International Mercantile Marine for profitable operation on the North Atlantic, where steamship companies were enjoying record freight rates. The possible transpacific threat from the Great Northern Steamship Company had disappeared.[25]

The third challenge to Pacific Mail's pre–World War I supremacy was the Dollar Steamship Company, which was organized in 1900 and entered the transpacific trade in 1902. The company belonged to Robert Dollar, a naturalized American citizen born in Scotland and a longtime resident of California. Shipping had been a natural outgrowth of Dollar's lumbering activities in the Pacific Northwest. To reach the isolated camps from the coastal cities, he had depended on wooden steamships called "lumber schooners" to bring supplies in and take the logs out, but unreliable service had convinced him that he needed to buy his own lumber schooners, starting with the first one in 1892. In two years the ship had earned its full purchase value, and this accidental discovery of shipping profits did not go unnoticed. Dollar bought additional ships and finally bigger steel steamers, until the capacity exceeded the cargo needs of his lumber camps. He still had sufficient logs and lumber for the outbound voyages, but he had run into one of the eternal problems of merchant shipping, the need to find return cargoes. The most natural solution was to enter the coastwise trade along the Pacific coast by shipping loads of lumber as far as southern California and returning with cargoes for any of the intermediate cities on the voyage back to the northwest.[26]

Up to 1902 Dollar's operations had been with U.S.-flag vessels on the coastwise trade or with British registry for the Canadian northwest trade. Profitable as these routes were, Dollar sensed that with the annexation of the Philippines great prospects were opening in the Far East trade that should not remain the exclusive preserve of Pacific Mail Steamship. For operation in the routes to the Far East, the Dollar Steamship Company purchased several steel steamships beginning with the *Arab* in 1902. There was a strong demand in the Far East for his lumber, so the outgoing cargoes were guaranteed, but return cargoes were largely monopolized by Pacific Mail. Dollar decided he would have to drum up his own business to fill the cargo holds of his ships on their return voyages, and he went ahead of the *Arab* on the first of many combined pleasure and business tours to the Far East. The first step was to acquire an agency network. This supposedly easy task took more time than expected, because the English agencies in the Far East, accustomed to handling the accounts of long-established and venerable firms, were reluctant to deal with an unknown upstart. Finally an agency network was established, but Dollar realized these agents would not be particularly aggressive about securing cargoes, a task he himself had to solve. The first thing he did was to land a cargo of sulfur for the *Arab*, which otherwise would have returned home with only the small load the agents had managed to scrounge.

When the *Arab* made its return call in Japan, Dollar set out to confirm reports of large oak forests in northern Japan. His keen business eye immediately detected a great opportunity and that prime oak timber remained a very profitable cargo for the Dollar Steamship Company up to World War I. The ships loaded with lumber sailed from the United States and landed part of the lumber cargo in Japan, where the holds were replenished with Japanese oak ties for shipment with the rest of the American lumber to China. On the return voyage, the ships loaded Japanese oak ties for shipment to the Southern Pacific Railroad. As if shipping Japanese oak had not been enough, Dollar made another coup when he signed a contract with Southern Pacific to supply Japanese oak ties for its railroad construction in Mexico, bypassing Southern Pacific's own subsidiary, Pacific Mail Steamship Company.[27]

With lumber cargoes in both directions complemented by general cargo, the Dollar Line's Far East service was profitable, and the company continued to acquire new oil-burning vessels. Dollar, always the merchant, had begun to buy pig iron in China during his tours for shipment aboard the vessels, since the ships were still returning home not fully loaded. He then proceeded to buy enough stock in the Western Steel Company, a small outfit, until he became one of its directors. He convinced the board that it was cheaper to buy low-price iron from China than from the East Coast of the United States. With his market guaranteed, he returned to China to negotiate a contract with Han Yeh Ping, the state-backed firm that produced the iron. From 1910 on Dollar Steamship carried the Chinese iron, and at last its vessels had full return cargoes.

With the initial three-year contract for the iron, the Dollar Steamship Company began to operate on more regular schedules, although up to World War I it resembled a hybrid between a proprietary line (owning the cargo on board) and a tramp outfit (chasing after cargoes in any port). There were limited first-class accommodations aboard the steamers, but there was room for many Oriental immigrants in the highly profitable steerage class. The crews were almost all Orientals, a staffing policy the Dollar Line retained even into the early 1930s, while until World War I all ships engaged in the foreign trade were under British registry.[28]

Dollar had rejected all suggestions of abandoning his lumbering business, which had continued to expand with the growth of his shipping business until they had become two mutually complementary activities. The Dollar family had begun to invest in real estate and shore facilities throughout the world and was also entering other fields, thus creating a rather diversified company. Enriched further by the high World War I shipping profits, the Dollar Steamship Company was in a very strong position to challenge and eventually replace Pacific Mail Steamship. Starting in the late 1910s, however, old age gradually removed Robert Dollar from active management of the powerful business he had built so carefully. Unfortunately, his son Stanley had not inherited his father's business talent, but he had another kind of useful talent: he was a master at manipulating the federal government. This ability held tremendous promise for shipping from the 1920s onward.[29]

2

A Merchant Fleet for an Empire

IN 1898 THE ANNEXATION of the Philippines, Puerto Rico, and Hawaii, as well as the acquisition of informal control over most of the West Indies and Central America, gave the United States its first "empire." The extension of the coastwise laws to Puerto Rico and Hawaii made urgent the establishment of U.S. shipping services to these two annexed islands as well as to the Cuban protectorate. In the West Indies, as in Hawaii, economic penetration had preceded political annexation, so that the fleets of United Fruit Company and W. R. Grace and Company acted as important instruments of imperial expansion.

☐ American-Hawaiian Steamship Company

American annexation of the Hawaiian Islands on 7 July 1898 created a great and unique opportunity to develop a new steamship service. The extension of the coastwise laws to Hawaii in 1899 made the trade between mainland United States and the islands a U.S. preserve. In spite of foreign and Hawaiian protests, the coastwise exclusion remained permanently in force in the Hawaiian Islands (unlike the Philippines, where all attempts to extend the coastwise laws failed). Since 1882 George S. Dearborn had wanted to send steamships rather than clipper ships around Cape Horn, but investors were skeptical about another service just between New York and California. The annexation of Hawaii opened a new dimension to his proposal, and he found enough backers to incorporate the American-Hawaiian Steamship Company on 7 March 1899.

To provide their share of the capital, investors like Dearborn and Wallace Flint sold their clipper ships that had served the intercoastal route around Cape Horn. Another major subscriber was Lewis Henry Lapham, owner of a major leather company, who in 1901 became the largest single stockholder in American-Hawaiian. The additional capital needed to order new steamships was raised by two bond issues in 1900 and 1901. The two main officers running the company were George S. Dearborn, president until his death in 1920, and Captain William D. Burham, manager until his retirement in the fall of 1914. The engineering side was under the direction of a brilliant Danish immigrant, Valdemar Frederick Lassoe, already famous because of his collaboration with John Ericsson, the inventor of the *Monitor*, the warship that revolutionized the art of naval warfare.[1]

The key to success for American-Hawaiian lay in securing a major share of Hawaii's cargoes. In his first visit in 1899 Dearborn convinced Sugar Factors, the main exporter of Hawaii, to purchase a large chunk of stock in the new steamship company; Sugar Factors was also ready to sign a contract for the hauling of sugar cargoes. In a subsequent visit by Capt. Burham, Sugar Factors signed a six-month contract with American-Hawaiian on 17 August 1900. The contract was renewed for another six months and then for a two-year period. On 1 December 1906 the contract's duration was extended for four years; only with the approach of World War I did American-Hawaiian and Sugar Factors return to annual periods. These multi-year contracts which were quite common between large shippers and steamship firms in the pre–World War I period, provided a remarkable stability for American-Hawaiian. At the same time the abundant sugar exports solved the constant, major problem of the pre-1898 intercoastal trade around Cape Horn—namely, lack of eastbound cargoes. With ample cargoes in both directions and protection from foreign competition provided by the coastwise laws, American-Hawaiian discovered a fountain of wealth that seemed guaranteed to last at least until the end of the twentieth century.[2]

Nevertheless, American-Hawaiian was not content to sit back and reap the profits; instead, it became a pioneer in three noteworthy shipping innovations. Capt. Burham had spent a lifetime aboard wooden sailing vessels and Dearborn had dispatched them for decades, yet both had no hesitation about abandoning sailing vessels for steamers. At the end of the twentieth century, now that the superiority of steam over sail is so manifest, it sometimes is hard to realize that at the end of the nineteenth century the controversy in the United States surrounding the question of steam versus sail had still not been settled. American-Hawaiian ordered four new steel steamers at first and more subsequently; although in the beginning, during shipping shortages, the company still chartered wooden sailing vessels, eventually even the charters were only for steel steamships. The Pacific Ocean was rapidly becoming the last ocean refuge for wooden sailing vessels, yet there too companies like American-Hawaiian were rapidly introducing the new era of steel and steam.[3]

American-Hawaiian had planned to inaugurate the intercoastal service between New York and Hawaii in 1900, but the Boxer Rebellion in China intervened, so that the *Californian*, just delivered by the shipyard, was requisitioned by the military to transport and supply American forces. With the end of the Boxer Rebellion, American-Hawaiian began service from New York to Hawaii, with stops on the West Coast, in January 1901. On the first trip the company made a second significant innovation. For sailing vessels the Straits of Magellan had generally been a deathtrap, and they had preferred the much longer and stormier route out on the open sea beyond Cape Horn. Capt. Burham calculated that his modern steamers could safely cross the Straits of Magellan, thus saving the shipper time as well as coal. The insurance companies, looking at the historical record of wrecks by sailing vessels in the Straits of Magellan, did not share Burham's optimism and demanded twice the usual insurance rate of 3 percent on the hull. Capt. Burham decided that those extra costs were the inevitable start-up expenses of a pioneer and went on to send his steamers through the Straits of Magellan. No catastrophes occurred, and afterward, with a proven track record, Captain Burham negotiated the insurance rate of American-Hawaiian down to 3½ percent by 1903; henceforth neither nature nor the insurance underwriters blocked the passage through the Straits of Magellan.[4]

Despite saving time and fuel on the new route, American-Hawaiian still had some logistical problems, one of them being the fuel supply itself. Except in Colombia, high-quality coal deposits are rather scarce in South America, unlike in North America. The American-Hawaiian steamers soon discovered how unsatisfactory coal supplies were along the route, because after bunkering in the British West Indies, they generally had to steam all the way to Coronel, Chile, to refuel with low-quality coal. Marine engineer Lassoe was hard at work on a solution and, in conjunction with Luther D. Loveking, invented the Lassoe-Loveking oil burner. American-Hawaiian shared Lassoe's eagerness to test the invention and had the oil burners installed in the *Nevadan* and *Nebraskan*. A trial run on the Hawaii-California route was a complete success, and American-Hawaiian prepared the *Nebraskan* for the real test through the Straits of Magellan. The American shipping world, which with its excessive traditionalism still had not fully accepted coal steamers, was shocked again in April 1904: "The sensation of the time is the recent extraordinary successful oil-fuel burning voyage of the American-Hawaiian steamship *Nebraskan* from the Pacific coast to New York."[5]

The savings in space, time, and efficiency were too great to be ignored: American-Hawaiian promptly converted its entire fleet of nine ships from coal to oil, and made all its new shipyard orders for oil-burning ships. The U.S. Navy, inspired by the *Nebraskan*'s success, decided to convert its warships to oil. As the shipping operations had been highly profitable, the company was able rapidly to repay its original two bond issues, while plowing remaining profits into new steamers and the purchase of a large portion of Texaco stock. All seemed well for American-Hawaiian when in 1903 Sir Weetman Pearson (later Lord Cowdray) walked into the company's offices to deliver an ultimatum. The Mexican dictator Porfirio Díaz had granted Pearson a concession and more than $60 million to build a railroad across the Tehuantepec Isthmus. If American-Hawaiian sent its cargo through the new port terminals of Salina Cruz in the Pacific and Puerto Mexico in the Gulf, transit time would be at least 20 days less than by the Straits of Magellan. The savings in time and cost would assuredly attract larger volumes of cargo. So as not to be confused with a salesman, Sir Pearson finished his presentation by saying that if American-Hawaiian did not care to participate, he would create his own fleet of steamships.

The management of American-Hawaiian was deeply divided on this issue. Capt. Burham, convinced that his steamers could meet any competitors in this new intercoastal service, wanted to fight, but Dearborn's view of seeking an accommodation with Sir Pearson prevailed. By an agreement signed on 9 May 1905, Sir Pearson became a stockholder in American-Hawaiian, which would receive two-thirds of the revenue from the cargo, while one-third would go to the railroad. By a price-support clause, the Tehuantepec railroad guaranteed that the earnings per deadweight ton of American-Hawaiian's fleet would fall no lower than those of 1904. Since 1904 had been a very prosperous year, the steamship company received payments from the railroad in addition to the company's actual earnings every year except in 1912.[6]

Service through the Tehuantepec railroad began in January 1907, and American-Hawaiian then divided its ships into two fleets, one bringing cargo from New York to Puerto Mexico, the other to Salina Cruz in the Pacific. The Pacific fleet originally sailed only a triangle route between Hawaii, Salina Cruz, and the U.S. West Coast, but eventually a second run operated just on the West Coast between Puget Sound and Salina Cruz. Pearson's claims about saving 20 days proved false during the initial years, because moving the cargoes from ship to railroad and back to ship proved immensely time-consuming. For the untrained stevedores—initially forced Indian laborers from the region—the modern machinery introduced by Sir Pearson was beyond comprehension. Unloading the first ship in Puerto Mexico took 17 days, and the first ship in Salina Cruz a full 30 days. The learning process was slow and arduous, but the Mexican foremen eventually mastered their task, and on the Pacific side Chinese coolies assisted the local stevedores. The savings in time gradually increased until at least 15 days were saved by this route, and shippers sent more cargo once they saw that American-Hawaiian advertised faster delivery dates.[7]

A problem never permanently solved was that of pilfering and large-scale theft. In the first two years over 20 percent of the cargo was damaged because of poor or improper handling. By 1910, when damages were finally brought under control, many boxes had been smashed, leaving exposed valuable contents that inspired organized looting efforts. In spite of increased police protection, the petty pilfering gave way to gangs who broke into railroad cars and wagons to steal merchandise. Attempts to wreck the trains became more frequent, and at least once freight cars were derailed and the valuable merchandise carefully replaced with stones. Two big shippers refused to ship by the Tehuantepec route, but others like the Sugar Factors whose cargoes were unattractive to looters were more than satisfied with the increased savings in time.[8]

The agreement with the Tehuantepec railroad allowed for its cancellation on six months' notice when the Panama Canal opened. President Dearborn regarded the Panama Canal as the big opportunity to capture a large percentage of the low-value transcontinental bulk traffic handled in the United States by the railroads. The all-water route via the Panama Canal would be cheaper and faster than Tehuantepec, but American-Hawaiian would need to expand its fleet of 14 steamers to as many as 43 eventually. By the end of 1913, 12 more steamers had been added to bring the total up to 26, creating the largest U.S.-flag fleet; and more were in order and under study. The crucial decision hinged not upon the expansion itself, which was a very sound business proposition, but upon the financing. Dearborn had begun favorable negotiations with an investment firm to float a third bond issue. Investor bankers were asking questions and scrutinizing the company's operations and prospects before signing bond issues, which was a purely routine matter for a well-run company like American-Hawaiian. But to avoid these prying glances, Dearborn preferred to borrow short-term commercial loans at a higher interest rate from eager lenders who asked no questions. Thus Dearborn made his first mistake.

The commercial credits were renewed from year to year until they reached their maximum amount in July 1914, putting the company in an extremely vulnerable position as it groaned to meet repayments. Dearborn had counted on the Panama Canal entering into service when the locks were completed at the end of 1913, but new landslides postponed the opening until 1914. Meanwhile in Mexico the dictator Díaz had been overthrown, revolutionary turmoil disrupted the Tehuantepec route early in April 1914, and on 21 April 1914 the United States occupied Veracruz in what appeared to be the beginning of a large war. The U.S. Navy requisitioned four vessels of American-Hawaiian for the military operation in Mexico, but this was not enough to save the company. On 24 April, American-Hawaiian decided to abandon the Tehuantepec route and to return to the Straits of Magellan, because the company, buried under the short-term commercial debt, could not afford to lose any income. When the Panama Canal at last opened on 15 August 1914, American-Hawaiian was waiting in line with three vessels that were the first commercial ships to use the new waterway. With the opening of the canal and the outbreak of World War I in the same month, the company was not just saved—it was launched on a course of solid prosperity.[9]

Unfortunately, the short-term problems blocked a realization of the real long-term opportunities. The company had just started to profit from the use of the Panama Canal when new slides closed the waterway on 13 September 1915 and the ships were rerouted one last time through the Straits of Magellan. By the time the Panama Canal reopened permanently on 15 April 1916, all the company's ships were already under war charter. Since 1915 the company had been considering abandoning the intercoastal trade because wartime dislocations had reduced considerably the cargo moving between the East and West coasts. Dearborn also wanted to be rid of the short-term commercial debt as quickly as possible, and dangling right in front of him were the tremendous opportunities to charter his entire fleet at record-breaking prices on the North Atlantic runs. Hawaiian trade was a priceless jewel of permanent value, but the cost of keeping it seemed too high. Dramatic strategies—oil burners, Tehuantepec, and the Panama Canal—had distracted Dearborn and finally misled him as to where his company's long-term interests really lay. Sugar Factors was shocked by American-Hawaiian's January decision to abandon the islands; as the only concession, on 7 September 1916 the steamship company signed a final contract that left two ships behind to ferry the sugar harvest from Hawaii to San Francisco. That same day American-Hawaiian announced the suspension of its intercoastal service from Hawaii and the West Coast. The Honolulu Chamber of Commerce and newspapers in Hawaii were outraged and felt betrayed at the company's sudden withdrawal for the sake of lucrative but temporary wartime charters.[10]

Dearborn, now nearing the end of his life, was determined to leave behind a company free of debt, but despite large profits he was not fully satisfied with operations since 1916, as he confessed to Lord Cowdray (Pearson): "Most of our ships have been on time charter, others have been freighting them, so it is making big money with very little effort. Though I must say I enjoyed our trade, which belonged to us and in which I took pride, much more than under the present method of doing business."[11] When the United States entered World War I, the government requisitioned the last two company ships on the route between the islands and San Francisco. American-Hawaiian never returned to the islands, but it retained the name in remembrance of its most profitable and exciting years as the largest U.S.-flag merchant fleet. Hawaii, unjustly spurned, now eagerly sought another company willing to make a long-term commitment to the islands' prosperity.

□ Matson Navigation Company

Captain William Matson, a Swedish immigrant, had gradually built up—through purchase, partnerships, and charters—a small fleet of sailing vessels in Hawaii by the end of the nineteenth century. Further expansion was impossible, because since 1890 a joint venture between Oceanic Steamship and the Union Steamship Line of New Zealand had amply served the California-Hawaii trade as part of their route to Australia and New Zealand. The annexation of Hawaii by the United States on 7 July 1898 and the subsequent extension of the coastwise laws to the islands excluded the ships of the Union Steamship Line from the Hawaii-California routes, an exclusion sorely resented by some New Zealanders even as late as the 1930s. Oceanic Steamship hesitated and failed to fill the gap quickly with American-flag vessels. Instead, Capt. Matson seized the unique opportunity, promptly borrowing sums from San Francisco banker William H. Crocker to buy three more sailing vessels and three old steamers for service in the California-Hawaii route. The Matson Navigation Company was incorporated on 9 February 1901, with Capt. Matson as president, a position he held until his death in October 1917.[12]

Oceanic Steamship did not see how its route to Australia and New Zealand could be threatened by Matson, and so it was content to let the latter carry the excess cargo on the Hawaii-California route. Matson did not enjoy his comfortable niche for long: When the modern steamers of American-Hawaiian reached Honolulu in early 1901, he knew he was finished—unless Matson Navigation took drastic action. Shippers in California and Hawaii would rush to send their goods via the modern fast steamers of American-Hawaiian rather than the three rust buckets Matson had bought at great sacrifice. Competition against the new rival was out of the question: American-Hawaiian was too big, and as a heavily capitalized firm it had well-established agencies and connections on both the East and West coasts of the United States.

A brainstorm occurred to Matson to save his struggling steamship company: "Why not use oil for fuel on Hawaiian plantations and in the sugar mills?"[13] The islands were still importing coal from faraway Australia, even though oil fields had been discovered in California. There was one problem, though: if he began to import oil, American-Hawaiian would undercut his rates. Matson decided to buy oil fields in California, making some important oil and natural gas discoveries in the process. He even had a 106-mile pipeline built to carry the oil to the docks for loading aboard his vessels. Matson converted his three steamers to oil burners, but he was in no rush to buy new ships, because for carrying his oil to guaranteed buyers in the islands or for stockpiling it, his remaining sailing vessels were more than satisfactory. Owning most of the cargo he carried, Matson operated like a proprietary carrier, which was the only way he could escape the otherwise crushing competition of American-Hawaiian.

Already a millionaire by 1907 and the head of highly profitable oil and shipping companies, Matson could have retired or sat back to watch the natural growth of his enterprises; however, Matson could never stay still, and he continued eagerly to seek the way to enter shipping in a big way, and not just through his proprietary cargoes. His talents and operations had not gone unnoticed, and Edward Tenney, president of Castle and Cooke, a prestigious Hawaiian exporting firm, approached Matson in early 1907 and dictated terms for an association, but "Captain Matson is reported to have bellowed right back, emphasizing where he stood in the shipping business and where he intended to go, 'and by God it isn't to Hell, either, Mr. Tenney.'"[14] A thoroughly rattled Tenney, accustomed to submissive behavior from supposed underlings in the islands, walked off, but the chairman of the board immediately changed Tenney's mind and sent him back that same day to agree to all the captain's conditions. Thus began a half-century of close association between the two firms. Castle and Cooke bought large chunks of stock issued by Matson, enabling the steamship firm to purchase new steamers. Matson could have built the ships with his own money, but what was really valuable was Castle and Cooke's commitment as Matson's agent to supply outbound cargoes, thereby breaking American-Hawaiian's grip on the export of sugar. Castle and Cooke—just like Alexander and Baldwin, C. Brewer and Company, American Factors, and Theo. H. Davies and Company, the rest of the "Big Five," the major conglomerates in Hawaii—hoped that American-Hawaiian would always continue to provide regular steamship service, but just in case it didn't, they needed Matson Navigation as a backup.

With the powerful backing of Castle and Cooke, Matson ordered steamers from the shipyards to expand operations and also began his campaign to eliminate competitors. His first target was the Planters Line, a fleet of 10 sailing vessels owned mainly by the Big Five; they were hesitant to make a long overdue investment in steel steamers. Matson, who already controlled Castle and Cooke's shares in the Planters Line, was able to convince the other stockholders after some extended negotiations to sell the Planters Line to him. Agreement was finally reached in January 1908; Matson had not only eliminated a potential rival but had gained sailing vessels that nicely complemented his existing operations for the rest of their useful lives.[15]

With his growing fleet and sugar cargoes from Castle and Cooke, Matson could not be kept from challenging American-Hawaiian, his second target. Matson's smaller ships could enter many ports in Hawaii and on the West Coast of the United States that were inaccessible to American-Hawaiian's large steamers, but ships are power: American-Hawaiian was the only line with ample tonnage to move Hawaii's entire sugar crop. In 1910 the Big Five, interested in stability and regular service, blocked Matson's proposed rate war and promised American-Hawaiian that they would not increase Matson's share of the sugar cargoes. In return American-Hawaiian agreed to charter the *Honolulan*, a passenger liner under construction, to Matson for the Hawaii-California run. Nevertheless, before finalizing this deal, the Big Five authorized Matson in January 1911 to make a purchase offer for American-Hawaiian. The company refused to sell and thereby passed the Big Five's last test of its determination to stay serving the islands. The Big

Five trusted that all these maneuverings had made amply clear to American-Hawaiian that if it left the islands, it would never be allowed to return. [16]

Matson, now reaching the end of his life, realized that he could do no more to expand his fleet, and he reluctantly resigned himself to a secondary if important position in Hawaii's shipping. Then, with the outbreak of World War I, the shipping world totally changed, and Matson watched his powerful rivals miraculously disappear one by one. First to go was Oceanic Steamship. World War I had created a tremendous shipping shortage in the South Pacific as England had shifted her ships to the North Atlantic. The field was left wide open for Oceanic Steamship, which was making huge profits supplying Australia and New Zealand from the mainland United States, but the company's ships, steaming full, could neither load nor unload cargo in Hawaii. Next to go was Pacific Mail, whose ships on the Far East service had called on Hawaii since the nineteenth century. All U.S. lines in the Pacific had traditionally used Oriental crews, but Pacific Mail had developed a particularly close relationship with its Chinese crews. Not only did they work for low wages, Pacific Mail considered the Chinese the finest seamen in the world. Although Pacific Mail was a highly successful American steamship firm, it was unfortunately hounded out of business by union leaders and the government. When Congress passed the La Follette Seaman's Act in February 1915 limiting the Chinese to only 25 percent of each U.S. crew, this was the last straw for the company. [17]

Matson was extremely glad to see these two formidable rivals leave Hawaii, and the struggle was once again between Matson and American-Hawaiian, but it was no contest. Matson had grown, but American-Hawaiian was then the largest U.S.-flag merchant fleet, able to carry not only all of Hawaii's sugar but also large volumes of intercoastal trade through the recently opened Panama Canal. As confrontation with American-Hawaiian was out of the question, Matson had to limit itself to the oil cargoes and to a secondary position under Castle and Cooke's protection; the dream of operating the largest fleet in Hawaii was forgotten.

Unexpectedly, in January 1916, American-Hawaiian contacted the Big Five to announce the withdrawal of all its vessels from the Hawaii service except for two that would ferry the 1916 sugar crop to California for shipment to the transcontinental railroads. American-Hawaiian's decision was a colossal blunder, ranking among the worst mistakes in twentieth-century American shipping. The outcry in Hawaii ensured that the company would never be allowed to return there. Nevertheless, the shipping disaster that befell Hawaii ironically meant the fulfillment of Matson's wildest dreams, offering him what his company on its own could never have attained.[18]

Swamped with cargo and passengers, Matson Navigation rushed to buy and order new ships to meet the unexpected surge, while old steamers as well as sailing vessels were kept running past their service lives. It would take several years to fill the huge gap left by American-Hawaiian, but Matson Navigation—through its own efforts as well as the backing of the Big Five—had become the chosen shipping company of Hawaii. When the government requisitioned all steamers over 2500 deadweight tons in October 1917, Matson did not give up but instead made heroic efforts to keep some semblance of services by running relics, rust-bucket steamers rescued from scrap yards, and sailing vessels. Not until the government returned the requisitioned vessels after World War I did service resume normal levels, but in the meantime Matson had done everything within its power to ease the shipping crisis. Matson's loyalty to serving the islands was well received by the Hawaiian people and the Big Five, who had now found in Matson the steamship line for the twentieth century.[19]

□ The West Indies Trade

In the 1880s a group of U.S. firms decided to complement the wooden sailing vessels plying their trade between New York and the West Indies with regular steamship service. The earliest incentive and the greatest demand for cargo space came from the island of Cuba. Not counting many tramps and smaller outfits providing sporadic services, the route to sugar-rich Cuba was served from the 1880s on by three main companies: the Ward Line, the Clyde Line, and Munson Steamship. The competition soon became too tough for the Clyde Line, which switched its service to the Dominican Republic and stayed in that comfortable niche for the next 70 years. For Puerto Rico its turn came in 1885 when Archibald H. Bull created the New York and Puerto Rico Steamship Company, which also called occasionally in Haiti and more frequently in the Dominican Republic. These steamship lines formed part of the advance wave of American economic penetration into the West Indies during the last quarter of the twentieth century.[20]

As American investment and citizens flowed into those islands, the demands for faster links with the United States increased, and in turn the better transportation attracted further waves of Americans and investment. As the frontier in the west came to an end, the United States appeared to have found another open space to the south in the largely untapped islands of the West Indies. Economic penetration was soon followed by a desire for political control, which was finally achieved by the Spanish-American War in 1898. Spain, the only European power with a direct interest in the West Indies, had become a hindrance to the outpouring of American energies in this new potential southern frontier. Spain, however, failed to prepare adequately to defend its lingering imperial pretensions, and in a war barely five months long it was unceremoniously expelled from the West Indies as well as from the Philippines. The United States received outright possession of Puerto Rico; Cuba underwent two military occupations (1898–1902 and 1906–1909) and remained a protectorate until 1934. Caught between U.S. control in Cuba and Puerto Rico, Haiti and the Dominican Republic were subjected to constant U.S. interventions punctuated by lengthy military occupations during the first 40 years of the twentieth century. American economic penetration in the last quarter of the nineteenth century had undermined Spain's political control, but once the war was over this drive for economic dominance slowed. After a decade of U.S. protection and fostering, American companies in the West Indies became fat and bloated, with their competitive edge dulled.

Cuba, the largest and most fertile island, always remained the heart of the West Indies trade. Sensing the opportunities brought by the Spanish-American War, Walter D. Munson replaced earlier partnerships with the formal incorporation of the Munson Steamship Company in 1899. The north coast of Cuba was the special preserve of the Munson Line which called on the sugar ports of Matanzas, Cárdenas, Sagua, Caibarién, Nuevitas, Puerto Padre, Gibara, and Nipe Bay. The main route was from New York, but another originated in Mobile, Alabama, thereby beginning what would be a somewhat turbulent relationship with the Gulf States region. From Mobile the Munson Line also steamed with lumber cargoes to Argentina, but that part of the business really did not get going until 1910. By 1913 Munson was chartering more than one hundred British-flag ships to provide its main service to Cuba and its secondary service to Argentina. The sugar operations were closely tied to the harvest season, since during the rest of the year cargo movements slackened considerably. By chartering British ships the Munson Line hoped to keep its fixed costs down by avoiding having idle ships during the long months after the sugar harvest. Certainly purchasing all the ships needed for the sugar trade would have been a gross error, but by failing to buy even a modest percentage, the Munson Line passed up the opportunity to accumulate any assets in ships, which were the ideal collateral for loans and placing new vessel orders in the shipyards. Contracts with the sugar plantations, usually of at least three years' duration and easily renewed, guaranteed large northbound sugar cargoes and provided stability for the company. But as a charterer anybody else could appear to undercut with chartered vessels, as companies like Isbrandtsen-Moller began to do starting in the 1920s. Munson's long race to balance charter prices with cargo rates and volumes began easily enough in the stable prewar years, but it became an increasingly harsh struggle once the World War I shipping boom had collapsed.[21]

Havana, the largest and most prosperous city in Cuba and in the West Indies, was not served by Munson. In an informal understanding, Cuba was distributed in geographic market shares between Munson and the Ward Line. Havana was the standard port of call for the Ward Line, which provided frequent scheduled service from New York City on its own ships, soon replaced by new liners with a larger cargo-passenger capacity; the liners flew the U.S. flag thanks to a mail subsidy. The second city in Cuba was Santiago, located in the eastern part of the island that was then undergoing a tremendous sugar expansion and offering mounting volumes of cargo. The Ward Line established two new routes to meet this demand. In one route, Ward vessels called at Guantánamo, Santiago, Manzanillo, and Cienfuegos before returning home; another loaded at Santiago and then "topped off" the cargoes at the Mexican ports of Progreso, Veracruz, and Tampico before steaming back to New York. Without any subsidy for these last two routes, the Ward Line had no choice but to order cheaper British vessels for operation under the Cuban flag (curiously enough). Seasonal sugar was obviously the most important northbound cargo, but by concentrating service on the two main cities of Cuba, the Ward Line was able to generate sufficient general cargo and passenger volumes to keep the regular services operating at a profit during most of the year, while the Mexican calls added another nice margin of profit.[22]

As U.S. railroads reached farther south down the Florida Peninsula, first to Tampa and Miami and finally to Key West in 1912, the obvious advantages of a direct link with Cuba only 90 miles to the south were too much to be overlooked. A consortium of railroads incorporated the Peninsular and Occidental Steamship Company (not to be confused with the famous British steamship firm Peninsular and Oriental) on 21 June 1900 to provide regular cargo and passenger service to Cuba from Tampa, Miami, and Key West. Quietly but efficiently, the Peninsular and Occidental plied the Florida Strait for the next six decades.[23]

The annexation of Puerto Rico to the United States in 1898 and the subsequent extension of the American coastwise laws henceforth protected the New York and Puerto Rico Steamship Company from any foreign competition. The company, which had operated British-built and British-flag steamers between New York and Puerto Rico since 1885, now had to replace them with the more expensive U.S.-built and U.S.-flag steamers. This complication scared one of the two partners who demanded to sell his shares, the beginning of many misfortunes that befell American steamship companies serving Puerto Rico. Bull, the other stockholder, was then forced to sell his shares, because he had already borrowed to the limit, and the new buyer insisted on full ownership of the company. The sale agreement was finally closed when Bull posted a bond pledging not to operate rival steamers for 10 years. The clever Bull was quick to use the sale proceeds to buy wooden sailing vessels, which he put on the Puerto Rico run under the Bull Steamship Company, incorporated on 19 June 1902. Most of his former shippers preferred the faster steamers of the New York and Puerto Rico Steamship Company, but enough could afford to wait for the slower sailing vessels—in order to receive the 20 percent lower rates—to leave him a minimum of West Indies business, nicely complemented by coastwise trade from Florida to New York as well as calls in Haiti and the Dominican Republic.[24]

In 1911, after the expiration of the 10-year prohibition, Bull Steamship reentered the trade with steamers. The steamship trade was now monopolized by the New York and Puerto Rico Steamship Company and the new smaller Insular Line. A ferocious rate war promptly broke out, with the established companies doing everything possible to block the return of Bull Steamship. The crews and staff of the companies fully participated in the competitive spirit, and numerous brawls and clashes occurred between the crewmen. As the open violence subdued, the crews turned to ambushing the messengers of the rival companies either to steal or tear up the bills of lading. Bull Steamship had entered the trade with its own steamers, but when one of them sank in January 1912, the New York and Puerto Rico Steamship Company quietly exerted its influence to freeze Bull out of the charter market. Blacklisted on the charter market, Bull Steamship was repeatedly rebuffed when it tried to buy used vessels, and it was able to escape the deadly grip of its major rival only by ordering new vessels from the shipyards—an alternative that a financially weaker company could not have considered. The rivalry came to an end in 1915 when the Insular Line sold out to Bull, leaving the latter and the New York and Puerto Rico Steamship Company as the two U.S. lines providing service from New York to Puerto Rico.[25]

The reason that the New York and Puerto Rico Steamship Company could wield so much influence in many sectors was because it was part since 1908 of the large combine (the twenty-seventh–largest industrial corporation by assets in the United States in 1909) called Atlantic, Gulf, and West Indies Steamship Lines, whose main subsidiaries were the Ward, Clyde, and Mallory lines, as well as the New York and Puerto Rico Steamship Company. Mainly a holding company, Atlantic, Gulf, and West Indies Steamship had left considerable freedom to the individual lines, but it was ready to support a subsidiary engaged in a bitter struggle against a new rival like Bull. As the title of the holding company indicated, coastwise services from the Gulf to the Atlantic and along the East Coast of the United States formed the bulk of its activities; for ships steaming between New York and the Gulf and passing in front of Havana, the West Indies service was a natural extension.

The idea of consolidating the rival services in the West Indies was powerfully aided by the example of the International Mercantile Marine in the North Atlantic. The promoter was Charles W. Morse, who had made his initial fortune in the ice trade. Wanting to build his wealth on something more solid than ice that melts, Morse plunged into speculating on Wall Street mergers. He acquired control of banks, insurance companies, public utilities, and sundry other corporations, and his rise appeared to have no bounds. In early 1907 he cast his acquisitive eye on the steamship companies in the coastwise and West Indies trade, and price offers considerably higher than their assets brought them under his control by March 1907. His steamship combine lasted but a few months, and in October 1907 his whole financial empire toppled like a deck of cards, triggering the Panic of 1907 in the United States.[26]

The former owners and bondholders of companies Morse had bought out created the Atlantic, Gulf, and West Indies Steamship Lines on 25 November 1908 to take over the steamship firms then in bankruptcy proceedings because of the collapse of Morse's short-lived empire. The first president, Henry R. Mallory, turned the company around, and after erasing as unpayable a large part of the debt contracted by Morse, the constituent lines began to earn moderate profits. Atlantic, Gulf, and West Indies remained active in the West Indies until 1955 but after World War I it lost its supremacy because of increasing competition from a firm whose existence was barely noticed in the pre-1914 period: Lykes Brothers Steamship Company. As a small tramping outfit shipping cattle and lumber to Cuba on chartered British-flag vessels from 1898, Lykes Brothers was indistinguishable from other tramping operations that came and left without leaving a lasting trace. Unlike the other steamship companies serving the West Indies, Lykes Brothers initially carried products from its other land properties in the South as well as in Cuba.[27] Thus in the early years before World War I, Lykes Brothers shared important similarities with the proprietary steamship companies discussed in the following section.

□ Proprietary Steamship Companies: United Fruit and W. R. Grace

A proprietary steamship company is one that owns the bulk of the cargo carried in its ships; the investment in ocean transportation is at least equaled and usually exceeded by the company's assets in other activities. The purest proprietary steamship companies have been the tanker fleets that carried the oil of parent companies like Exxon and Texaco. Alcoa Steamship belonging to the Aluminum Company of America and the Isthmian Line belonging to United States Steel were two proprietary companies, sometimes called industrial carriers, that found it profitable to carry other cargoes as well, in particular for the return voyage. Two companies dating back to the nineteenth century were good examples of the rise of proprietary steamship companies: United Fruit, which in spite of numerous efforts remained closely tied to its own cargoes; and W. R. Grace, which built a successful steamship business around its own substantial cargoes.

□ **United Fruit Company.**   Bananas had been imported sporadically into New England as exotic curiosities since the early nineteenth century. From 1871 on, after the annual fishing season was over, Captain Lorenzo D. Baker employed his wooden sailing vessel to carry bananas from Jamaica during the remainder of each year. In 1884 Capt. Baker abandoned fishing to concentrate on bringing bananas to Boston from Jamaica; soon he settled in the island to expand the banana plantations. An associate, Andrew W. Preston, began the long marketing struggle—which was finally won in the early 1920s—to make the American public like and purchase this previously unknown fruit. No matter how much marketing and production was done, however, the enterprise would fail if the fruit arrived rotten in Boston. Wooden sailing vessels depended on the winds, and thus their arrival was easily delayed. The circulation of air through the holds was discovered to retard the fruit's spoilage, but there was little chance of fresh air for a sailing vessel stalled in a windless sea. The promoters decided as a first solution to have their banana plantations located in the West Indies, the producing area closest to the United States. From Jamaica plantations spread to the Dominican Republic, but attempts to tap Cuba—the largest, most fertile, and nearest location of all—were postponed because of a long bloody and destructive insurrection there in 1895–1898. A second solution was to switch exclusively to steamers, thereby guaranteeing delivery times and preventing any spoilage of bananas. Some of the early steamers kept their sails as an emergency backup in the increasingly unlikely case that the steam engines failed, but otherwise the company eagerly accepted steam over sail.[28]

With Preston as the first president, the United Fruit Company was incorporated on 30 March 1899 after the merger of several banana companies, most notably the holdings in Central America and Colombia of Minor C. Keith, a later United Fruit president. Cuba, now at peace under U.S. occupation, provided the perfect opportunity to acquire large stretches of land for banana cultivation. Too late United Fruit discovered that because of the semitropical climate in the West Indies, the banana yields were lower than in the hotter areas of Central America and Colombia. Gradually over the coming decades the company disposed of its earlier banana plantations in Jamaica and the Dominican Republic. In Cuba, however, the company had stumbled upon a rich discovery: the lands acquired in the eastern part of the island were unusually fertile and ideally suited for sugar cultivation. These lands, which until 1960 remained the largest single holdings among the company's vast plantations in Latin America, grew the sugarcane that was processed in two local sugar mills and converted to white sugar in the company's Boston refinery. The sugar operations remained the company's main money earner and chief hedge against any temporary difficulties in the banana trade. An example of complete vertical integration (that is, owning all the steps in the production process from the land itself to the final refinery processing), the sugar was naturally transported on the company's rapidly growing "Great White Fleet," so named because the ships were all painted white to retard heat absorption.[29]

Only the adoption of modern rapid steamers made possible the shift away from the West Indies (except for the Cuban sugar plantations) and to Central America and Colombia much farther south. The longer distances also made the company more vulnerable to any breakdown in ocean transportation, so that to feel truly secure, United Fruit changed its nineteenth-century policy of chartering most vessels to owning the bulk of its tonnage after 1900. By 1913 the company's sugar and bananas were carried aboard the company's own ships, numbering more than 60 while for peak demand or unexpected cargo movements the company chartered tramps (usually Norwegian) until it was operating in total as many as 100 steamers. The company's own ships were under British registry until World War I, not only because of lower costs but also to prevent any requisitions by the U.S. government like those that occurred during the Spanish-American War, the Boxer Rebellion, and other international incidents. While nonproprietary steamship companies like American-Hawaiian were amply compensated for lost cargoes by generous government charters, for United Fruit the lack of ships meant the paralysis of all operations and the swift bankruptcy of the firm.[30]

When United Fruit purchased four surplus U.S. Navy steamers, the ships came with facilities that easily accommodated 60 passengers. From 1900 on United Fruit began an intensive public relations campaign to promote cruise travel by wealthy tourists. First-class passengers did not generate big profits, but since the travelers made the round trip, at least the ships were earning some income on legs of the route otherwise short of cargo. During the first three decades of the twentieth century the company also felt that cruise travel aboard the Great White Fleet was important for public relations, particularly to supplement the company's marketing campaign to secure acceptance for the banana in the United States. After 1903, the introduction of refrigerated ships provided travelers an attraction unrivaled for many years:

> Ducts lead from these huge cooling chambers to all of the staterooms. If the passenger finds it too warm at any hour of the day or night, he pulls the slide overhead and lets in a sufficient amount of fresh cool air to lower the temperature to the degree required. What millionaire in New York, London, or Paris can boast of this inestimable luxury? What terror is there to tropical heat or humidity when a touch of the hand can "turn on the cold" as easily as a child can turn the valve of a steam radiator? That is what I call a real luxury.[31]

For the fast steamers arriving on schedule, forced-draft ventilation had sufficed to keep the bananas from spoiling, but refrigeration brought additional advantages. With refrigerated ships, the bananas arrived greener and thus could withstand a longer inland transportation to the very center of the United States. Furthermore, Europe was now within reach, and starting in 1903, the same year of the introduction of the refrigerated steamers, United Fruit pioneered banana imports to Europe, becoming the largest supplier to this large new market. Refrigeration lessened the concern for speed in the ships, the company's formula for safe deliveries up to 1903. Speed remained an issue only for the "candy boats," the freighters that hauled the sugar cargoes from

Cuba. Once the sugar harvest season was over, the candy boats were redeployed to carry bananas from Central America and Colombia; fast speed and forced-draft ventilation delivered the bananas without any spoilage.[32]

By the first decade of the twentieth century United Fruit had taken the form it would retain until the 1960s. No new developments occurred to change the company's operations, which increasingly fell into a routine if not a rut. Proprietary cargo had risen from 16 percent in 1900 to 32 percent in 1912, but soon this percentage slipped and the fleet survived thanks to the company cargoes. Only by stops in Havana was any substantial southbound freight obtained; the rest of the countries remained too poor to afford any substantial imports, beyond importing the company's own equipment and supplies. By the 1930s the passenger service had diminished, and after World War II it was avoided: "Every Banana a guest, every passenger a pest"[33] became the rule. Otherwise the first decade of the twentieth century was hardly distinguishable from subsequent ones in the structure and shape of United Fruit's operations, a company where time seemed to have stopped.

☐ **W. R. Grace**   Peru in the second half of the nineteenth century was rather isolated from trade with the United States. Wooden sailing vessels traveled around Cape Horn loaded with cargoes from the East Coast of the United States to California, leaving no room for freight to Peru; furthermore, the sailing distance between Peru and the United States was roughly the same as to Europe. Pacific Steam Navigation Company, a British firm, provided ample service to Europe, and not unexpectedly Peruvian foreign trade largely bypassed the United States. Nevertheless, the Peruvian guano boom created more opportunities for profit than even the established British trading houses could handle. In 1851 an Irish immigrant, William R. Grace, came to Peru, where he made his initial fortune as a merchant and left an organization behind after he decided to shift the seat of his trading house to New York in 1866. While in Peru he already had invested in ships and formed partnerships to charter sailing vessels to transport goods from the United States. In 1882 he took the step of establishing the first line of sailing vessels regularly serving trade between Peru and New York. As his trading house drummed up more business between the two countries, the need to complement the sailing vessels with scheduled steamers became more acute. In 1893 Grace finally established a regular and dependable service between New York and Peru. By 1902 the line owned six steamers and chartered additional vessels, and it planned to acquire still more ships, all under the British flag. The company planned further expansion in its own fleet to take advantage of the expected increase in trade volume and to avoid the drawbacks of too much chartering. In 1903, just prior to his death the following year, Grace established a separate British-flag line to steam along the Pacific coast from Canada in the north to Chile in the south.[34]

The company continued to grow after 1904 under William's descendants. The advantages of oil over coal as a fuel were evident to the new management; the conversion from coal to oil began with the first two steamers in 1906, and was gradually completed in subsequent years. In South America, the center of W. R. Grace & Company's activities, remained Peru, where the company branched out from purely trading transactions into running business enterprises. In 1882 the Grace company purchased its first sugar plantation, the first of many land purchases in Peru over the next fifty years. Beginning in 1902, Grace also invested in the textile industry, until by 1918 its mills produced 45 percent of Peruvian textiles.[35]

As the investments in land multiplied, the significance of the steamship services increased: "It is no doubt disappointing, as you say, that this line should not be an El Dorado, but it is not, all the same. It is of great use and assistance to our business generally, and might almost be considered the mainstay of our export and import business today, and must be fostered and cared for in every possible way."[36]

Shipping services had brought Grace to trade and then to invest in Chile. The steamer service from 1893 on reinforced the strong trade links of the 1880s, and the ships inevitably made calls along the Chilean coastline prior to reaching Peru. In 1901 the company began to purchase nitrate fields in Chile, and nitrates became a profitable export which also conveniently lengthened the life of the company's remaining sailing ships. Until World War I, the sailing ships carried lumber from the Pacific Northwest and returned with nitrate cargoes, a slower but cheaper service that paralleled the company's line of steamers.[37]

The company's stake in Chile was second only to that in Peru, and the lucrative trade with Chile had to be protected at all costs. The only serious challenge came in 1901 when the Chilean government asked the Brazilian and U.S. governments to join in subsidizing a fast steamship service from New York to Chile. Brazil and the U.S. declined to participate in the scheme, but the Chilean government, under political pressure to provide faster steamship service, decided to open bids for a subsidized Chilean-flag line. Grace saw the real danger not from the existing private Chilean line, Compañía Sud Americana de Vapores, but from Beeche, Duval and Company, the main British competitor on the New York-Peru route. To keep the very generous subsidy out of the hands of its rival, Grace decided after painstaking examination, to shift its ships from the British to the Chilean flag, but only if no other alternative was left. Adroit lobbying in Chile dragged out the issue through 1902, until the Chilean government abandoned the proposal altogether. The outcome could not have pleased Grace more: "In regard to the subsidy, we are in a very happy frame of mind. We will take the subsidy if we get it on our terms, and will be perfectly satisfied if no subsidy is given to us provided none is given to our competitors."[38] The timely ordering of faster steamers consolidated Grace's prosperous trading and business position in Chile for many decades to come.

Would the Chilean success be repeated in neighboring Argentina? Grace officials definitely thought so, and during the first two decades of the twentieth century they attempted to expand into Argentina. The ships on the way to Chile and Peru steamed near long stretches of Argentina's coast. On the inducement of U.S. Steel Company, which needed to send cargoes to southern Argentina, Grace began to make occasional calls in Bahía Blanca starting in 1908, and was considering making regular stops at this and other ports along the Patagonian coast. The company's Chile office, however, could not book enough cargo from Argentina, and by 1909 relations with U.S. Steel had soured. To make things worse, a crucial local agent in Argentina had secretly become a competitor. Unlike in Peru and Chile, Grace had failed to establish a trading house or branch office in the capital city to make investments and promote the flow of cargoes to its ships. By the time the company corrected the mistake in 1918 and opened an investment firm in Buenos Aires, it was too late. Other competitors had already parceled out the really lucrative aspects of Argentina's trade among themselves. Furthermore, the opening of the Panama Canal radically changed the shipping routes: the company's ships no longer steamed along Argentina's coast on the way to the Straits of Magellan, but now used the shorter and more direct route by the Panama Canal to both Peru and Chile. Grace thus missed the opportunity to establish itself in Argentina, and left the door open for Moore-McCormack and Delta to enter this shipping route in the years between the two world wars. Not until sixty years later would Grace make one last attempt to break into Argentine ocean transportation.[39]

The setback in Argentina did not detract in the least from the extraordinary success the company had attained along the Pacific coast of South America. The volume of cargo continued to grow until by 1912 W. R. Grace was making 22 scheduled voyages from New York to Peru each year. On the one hand, the opening of the Panama Canal ended the option of easily calling on Argentina's ports; but on the other, and more importantly, consolidated the company's position in Peru and Chile. The steaming time to Peru from the United States was halved, and at last reflected the shorter distance between Peru and the United States as opposed to Europe. The abandonment of the Straits of Magellan route clearly marked the decline of British commercial influence in Peru and Chile. Henceforth the Pacific coast countries of South America would increasingly turn to the United States rather than to Europe.[40] W. R. Grace and Company, benefiting from the U.S. business offensive of the pre-World War I period, could confidently look forward to decades of high returns from its investments in South America and in ocean transportation.

Part II.
The Shipping Board Era

3

World War I

THE END OF AN ERA in shipping was one of the many consequences of World War I. For U.S. shipping, World War I made its influence felt in three main ways. The first section explains how the U.S. handled the initial disruption caused by the outbreak of the war in August 1914. The shipping crisis continued to grow to the point that the United States recognized the need for a specific government agency, the Shipping Board, whose creation in 1916 is explained in the second section. How the Shipping Board struggled to meet the extraordinary demands created by U.S. entry into World War I in April 1917 is the topic of the last section.

☐ The Initial Shipping Crisis

When World War I began on 4 August 1914, the Woodrow Wilson administration proclaimed neutrality, but much more than this declaration was required to overcome the ensuing shipping crisis. Prior to the war, 58 percent of American foreign trade was carried by British ships and 15 percent by German and Austrian ships. The outbreak of hostilities drove from the seas the German and Austrian ships, many of which sought refuge in the neutral United States. The gap left in shipping services could not be filled by the remaining European countries or by the U.S.-flag ships that had comprised barely 8 percent of the net tonnage in American foreign commerce.

Charter rates for vessels increased, and freight rates rose even more because they included the war-risk insurance, which was climbing rapidly. The effect finally reached the ships themselves, whose value steadily mounted. The shipping shortage came just as one of the largest bumper crops in recent history was reaching the market, and the produce, without transport abroad, piled up on the seaboard. Cotton was hit hardest: without transport to foreign markets the commodities lost value, and the cotton prices fell to half of their 1913 level. Panic swept the financial community in the United States; the New York Stock Exchange closed its doors in August 1914, not to reopen until December 1914. Only the most vigorous action by the Woodrow Wilson administration, in particular by Secretary of the Treasury William G. McAdoo, prevented an economic disaster in the United States. To many accustomed to look to Europe for guidance, the outbreak of the war seemed the end of the world, and indeed there was no denying that one era was coming to a close, especially in the case of shipping.[1]

Secretary of the Treasury McAdoo, working in close consultation with President Wilson, prepared the government's initial response to the world shipping crisis in August 1914. The enthusiastic and effective McAdoo—rather than the secretary of commerce or the secretary of state, who actually had more direct jurisdiction over shipping—convinced Congress to approve two important bills by the end of August. The first was the ship registry law, which allowed the transfer to the U.S. flag of foreign-built vessels, a step that heretofore had been illegal. The second was the war-risk insurance law, which allowed the government to shoulder part of the increasingly exorbitant war insurance rates. With those two laws, the government counted on the transfer to the U.S. flag of many vessels, which henceforth would be available to carry U.S. seaborne commerce.

McAdoo knew that even more vessels were needed, and so in August he presented to Congress a ship purchase bill allowing the government to buy and operate a merchant fleet. McAdoo had been the first high-ranking government official in the United States to grasp the simplicity and logic behind partial government ownership of an essential service. He had been impressed by the government's construction of the Panama Canal, which was opening in August 1914, and by the efficiency of U.S. Army operation of the Panama Line for the Canal Zone government. Initially the only ships available for purchase were the interned German and Austrian vessels. The British themselves had toyed with the idea of buying the ships, which included the second-largest passenger liner in the world, the *Vaterland*, later known as the *Leviathan*. McAdoo first left the field wide open for private business to acquire the German ships, but when International Mercantile Marine demanded a federal guarantee of the bonds as a condition of the purchase, McAdoo decided it was time to present the ship purchase bill to Congress so that the government could acquire and operate the ships for itself.[2]

Wilson and McAdoo naively believed that all the support they had extended to private business to weather the financial panic allowed them to count at least on its neutrality, if not on its support. So many advantages flowed from government ownership of a merchant fleet that using government funds for this purpose seemed very natural to them: "It seems to me that if this enterprise must depend upon the credit of the government to succeed, or to raise the necessary means, the government might as well do the thing directly."[3] The House Committee on Merchant Marine and Fisheries under Joshua Alexander fully agreed with the merits of the bill and reported very favorably on it to Congress—but unfortunately the proponents of a government-owned fleet had failed to learn a key political principle: Although subsidizing private profits with public funds was a way of life for many U.S. businesses, these same businesses would bitterly oppose the use of government funds for a public service. A double standard was at work in the twentieth century: while private firms could go broke or bankrupt without evoking any comments on the weaknesses of private enterprise, any successful government operation quickly evoked protests against unfair competition by the government in the private sector.

The conservative ideology opposed to any form of government ownership of the merchant fleet has been the bane of U.S. maritime policy, starting with the defeat of the ship purchase bill. By September 1914, the bill had died in Congress and a false lull in the shipping shortage convinced most in the business sector that ship registry and war-risk insurance were the only government measures needed. McAdoo did not take this defeat lightly, and he bitterly contrasted how eagerly private banks had welcomed support from the U.S. Treasury with how strongly they then opposed a shipping service that would benefit all Americans; rightly he believed that he had been deceived and, further, that valuable time was slipping by that could have been used to build up a larger merchant fleet as insurance against the war's intensifying. The belief in a war of short duration died hard, however, and 1915 found the United States trying to assess what other measures should be taken.[4]

Charter and freight rates continued to climb in early 1915, constituting a clear warning signal about the need to take action, yet business leaders conveniently interpreted the higher prices as proof that the private steamship companies were prospering. Their theory went like this: As freight rates increased, the higher profitability of the business would naturally attract more investment capital, and government could simply sit back and watch as the efficient market mechanism effortlessly supplied the tonnage needed to catch up with the demand for cargo space. This position, strongly espoused by the Republican party, while plausible for temporary dislocations in tranquil periods, did not answer the need for long-term shipping services or the specific acute emergency caused by World War I. Every shipyard in the United States was swamped with foreign orders and U.S. Navy construction, while no ships were for sale abroad. The high freight rates, rather than stimulating adequate capital investment, were serving mainly as a rationing device to allocate the scarce shipping space only to those able to pay the extravagant rates. The market mechanism had become clogged, and the government needed the tools—in this case, its own merchant fleet—to restore the normal functioning of market mechanisms in foreign trade.

By the middle of 1915 the policy of doing nothing, of waiting out the shipping crisis, was quite obviously not working. The registry of foreign-built vessels had brought under the U.S. flag few new vessels; most of the recently registered vessels had previously plied the same routes for U.S. companies usually under the British flag. The main addition to the foreign trade fleet of the United States had come from those vessels previously engaged in the domestic shipping services, partly in response to a slight decrease in the coastwise trade because of the wartime disruptions in trade routes. Since most of the coastwise vessels were small, they could easily increase the number of U.S.-flag ships in the foreign trade, but not the total volume; by the middle of 1915 the percentage share of foreign trade carried on U.S.-flag vessels had risen to only 12 percent, a modest increase from the 8 percent of the year before.[5]

Perhaps one of the few real additions of the U.S.-flag fleet as the result of the ship registry had been the transfer from the German flag of 17 tankers owned by a German subsidiary of Standard Oil (later called Exxon). England and France looked critically at flag transfers from German ships, but after considerable misgivings finally accepted these because ownership of the ships had always remained with a U.S. corporation irrespective of the actual flag of registry. Another 9 German flag tankers had been caught in German ports, but they remained profitably employed, hence Standard Oil had not attempted their transfer to U.S. registry. To avoid the confiscation of the 9 tankers by the German government in April 1917, when the U.S. declared war on Germany, Standard Oil arranged for a fictitious transfer of the tankers to purely German interests; once the war was over, Standard Oil confidently expected to reclaim the 9 tankers, which in the meantime would have been earning profits.[6]

Whatever the final fate of the Standard Oil tankers, by 1916 it was becoming amply clear that the U.S. government could no longer afford to stand by and hope the shipping crisis would peak and then recede; at the very least the government needed to endow itself with a specialized agency to deal with the complex issues of shipping, which were foreign to many Americans still living in a rural environment or viewing the world from an isolationist perspective.

□ The Shipping Board

The only legislation passed in 1915 affecting shipping was the Seamen's Act. Signed into law in April, the measure aggravated the shipping situation, because owners refused to comply with the crew regulations that stipulated no more than 25 percent of seafarers on a given vessel could be Orientals, and because some were opposed to improving the living and working conditions aboard the vessels as well as the seamen's wages. The Robert Dollar Company shifted all its ships to Canadian registry, while for Pacific Mail Steamship, the Seamen's Act was the last straw, and it decided to get out of the shipping business altogether. In August the company sold its five transpacific steamers to the International Mercantile Marine for service in the newly lucrative North Atlantic route, and it sold the rest of the fleet to W. R. Grace and Company for use in the Latin American routes. As for the Seamen's Act, although attempts at repeal by legislation and executive action foundered, the main provisions of the act were quietly allowed to become dead letter because of diplomatic pressure and were not rigorously enforced until the 1930s.[7]

The sinking of the *Lusitania* on 7 May 1915 brought home to many Americans their extreme vulnerability to disruptions in overseas shipping. British ships carried the bulk of U.S. overseas trade, but what happened when these ships were sunk by submarines? Clearly the United States needed its own merchant ships—not only for commercial purposes but also as part of military preparedness. Secretary of the Treasury McAdoo quickly realized that no matter how overwhelming the commercial arguments for a strong merchant marine, the American people were more easily swayed by military considerations. Sitting around in Washington, D.C.—like the passive Secretary of Commerce William C. Redfield—was accomplishing nothing, so again McAdoo took the lead, embarking this time on a month-long western tour in October 1915. Although ostensibly he wanted to reach the Pacific Coast region, his real goal was to convince the farmers to support a government-owned merchant marine. Speaking stops in Nebraska, North Dakota, and Montana widely reported in the local press spread the message among farmers. In the Pacific Coast area, McAdoo managed to bring over some important business groups to accept the idea of government ownership; a major coup was gaining the support of Robert Dollar, the archconservative, who now agreed to tolerate a very limited government ownership during periods of emergency.

The legislative struggle would not be easy, but McAdoo had other measures in hand to build upon the momentum of the duly publicized western speaking tour. He had laid the groundwork with the Pan-American Financial Conference of May 1915 held in Washington, D.C., which had convened a subsequent meeting of the International High Commission in Buenos Aires for April 1916. McAdoo headed the American delegation to Buenos Aires, and he used the tour as another publicity device to convince Americans of the need for shipping services between the United States and Latin America. One delegate, John Fahey, a former president of the Chamber of Commerce of the United States, "returned a transformed man on shipping matters" and confessed that after the trip he was "convinced that it will be long years before private interests will ever undertake the establishment especially of the fast lines which are needed in South American countries."[8]

McAdoo returned from the trip even more enthusiastic: "The great cry throughout South America is for merchant ships to carry on trade between the United States and these countries."[9] Both the Pan-American Financial Conference and the International High Commission had concluded that any further talk about increasing trade between the United States and Latin America was meaningless until regular steamship services were established. In case the Latin American delegates failed to realize what was required, McAdoo kindly provided them with briefs so that they could adopt and publicize the appropriate resolutions. The Latin American delegates duly complied, but an undercurrent of dissent remained in South America, with many people believing that their countries should have their own ships and not rely on U.S. services. But that was an issue for future decades; in 1915–16 the choice was between no ships or U.S.-flag ships, and the Latin Americans enthusiastically supported the latter.

A similar choice befell the American businessmen who preferred private steamship lines but had to choose between no ships or government-owned ships in 1916; regretfully they began to support the latter alternative. The legislative struggle had begun in January 1916 with the introduction of bills in both houses. Upon the return of McAdoo with the favorable publicity from his South American tour, the bill was reported on favorably by Alexander's House Committee on Merchant Marine and Fisheries and passed the House in May. Senate passage appeared more difficult if not impossible without crippling amendments, but just in time the British provided much-needed ammunition when they held the Paris Economic Conference in June 1916. Americans quickly interpreted the conference not as an attempt to restrain the economic ravages of World War I, but rather as a discriminatory attempt to create an exclusive economic union by the Allies against the United States. First target would be the rich Latin American trades, an easy prey for the Europeans after the war unless the United States established its own steamship services. Forced to choose between swallowing their antigovernment principles or forsaking profits, the U.S. businessmen reluctantly chose the former. The Senate passed the bill, but with some amendments, and after ratification by the House, President Wilson signed the revised bill into law on 7 September 1916.[10]

The long and arduous legislative struggle had begun in August 1914, and even in the early bills the proponents had dared not include one important feature. The law patterned the Shipping Board after the only other available example, the British Board of Trade, about which Americans knew very little. Because the Federal Trade Commission and the Department of Commerce already existed, only a titanic legislative struggle could have created an umbrella organization with broad powers over foreign trade and not just shipping. Unfortunately, the artificial separation of shipping from other foreign trade issues remained a constant in government policy, a gap aggravated by the failure to create one board or department with overriding authority over foreign trade.

The Shipping Board was composed of five members appointed for fixed terms by the president with the consent of the Senate; no cabinet members could belong to the board, so the result was an agency independent but also isolated from the executive branch. Shippers and farmers had been promised an independent and impartial agency to perform regulatory functions concerning rates, agreements, and services much in the manner that the Interstate Commerce Commission did for the railroads. The Shipping Board had full regulatory powers over the steamship lines offering regularly scheduled service, but the law said nothing about the tramp vessels that wandered from port to port seeking cargo wherever available.[11]

Congress granted the Shipping Board a large initial sum to buy, charter, and construct vessels for U.S.-flag steamship services. The

Shipping Board was also authorized to establish a subsidiary corporation to build ships on its own, as well as to operate the government vessels, provided that direct government operation of the vessels ended five years after the emergency was over. This last provision had been inserted in one of the Senate amendments, destroying McAdoo's goal of a government-owned fleet to solve the country's shipping needs permanently; quite rightly, he thought that the original bill had been "tremendously emasculated."[12] The limitations of the Shipping Board became clearly visible as the years went by, but at least and at last the United States had a single authoritative agency endowed with funds to face the shipping crisis of World War I.

□ The Shipping Board in World War I

The law creating the Shipping Board had been approved on 7 September 1916, yet four months passed without any action. Finally, in January 1917, the five members of the Shipping Board took office, with William Denman, an admiralty lawyer, as chairman. Four precious and irreplaceable months had been lost, and not even Germany's declaration of unrestricted submarine warfare on 31 January could galvanize the Shipping Board into action; its last commissioner, because of an unexpected resignation, was not appointed until March. When Congress declared war against Germany and the Central Powers on 6 April 1917, the Shipping Board was not at all prepared to address, much less solve, the tremendous wartime shipping crisis.

Ten days after the declaration of war, the Shipping Board used the authority in the 1916 legislation to create a subsidiary, the Emergency Fleet Corporation. Originally designed to study and award contracts for shipbuilding, the Emergency Fleet Corporation and its parent soon realized that the government would have to embark on a massive construction program of its own. All available shipyards were booked solid for years with foreign orders for merchant ships and navy contracts. The role of the Emergency Fleet Corporation changed from being a bureaucratic office to being the largest industrial enterprise of the war. By now serious doubts existed over the capacity of lawyer Denman to conduct the gigantic shipbuilding program, and in April Major General George Goethals was brought in as general manager of the Emergency Fleet Corporation, with full authority over shipbuilding but subordinate to Denman, who was its president.

Gen. Goethals's credentials were impressive: in addition to having had a distinguished military career, he had overseen the construction of the Panama Canal. Goethals was also accustomed to running a one-man show without interference from anyone, making a clash with his weak superior Denman inevitable. The rivalry between the two compounded the earlier four months' delay in getting the Shipping Board organized. If the Wilson administration had wished to use Goethals's extraordinary organizational talents and driving force, he should have been put in charge either of the Shipping Board or of an entirely separate agency devoted exclusively to shipbuilding. Instead, his subordinate position of general manager was guaranteed to generate the maximum strife; soon the Shipping Board was divided into Goethals and Denman factions, and the controversy surfaced in the press starting on 26 May. Last-minute efforts to patch up the differences merely prolonged the crisis, and finally President Wilson intervened to accept the resignation of both Goethals and Denman on 24 July.[13]

The vast amounts of money, resources, and personnel the government had poured into the Shipping Board and the Emergency Fleet Corporation had helped them grow into strong organizations, but the fact remained that the Denman-Goethals controversy had resulted in the misuse, if not outright loss, of six more months. President Wilson at last found the right man for the job, appointing Edward N. Hurley as the new chairman of the Shipping Board and president of the Emergency Fleet Corporation. Hurley took office on 27 July 1917 and promptly established clear lines of authority for the subordinate managers. A successful businessman with prior government experience, Hurley was a driving, energetic individual who was happy to surround himself with highly competent people. Once Hurley was in charge, the United States rapidly began to catch up on all the lost ground and wasted time.

The shipping difficulties were tremendously compounded by the U.S. entry into World War I on 6 April 1917. Hurley inherited the large and apparently insoluble problem of carrying and supplying U.S. troops. To transport General John J. Pershing and the vanguard of the American Expeditionary Force to France, the Shipping Board had to strip the coastwise and intercoastal steamship companies like Luckenbach, American-Hawaiian, and the Ward Line of their passenger liners and add three of the navy's four troop transports, one of the U.S.-flag passenger liners of the International Mercantile Marine, and two passenger-cargo ships of the United Fruit Company. The motley flotilla sailed under U.S. Navy escort on 14 June but it was unable to carry the whole force. As only one of the ships had been designed for transatlantic travel, they were simply too small. Reluctantly the Shipping Board had to turn to British-flag ships, including those of the International

Mercantile Marine, to transport the overwhelming majority of the American Expeditionary Force, with Navy escorts along part of the voyage being the only U.S.-flag participation.[14]

The Shipping Board had no time or resources to build passenger liners, because each boatload of American soldiers delivered by the British ships to France increased the pressure to supply larger amounts of supplies and equipment. Quite naturally, the Shipping Board focused almost exclusively on freighters for its shipbuilding program. The shortage of freighters, rather than abating with the delivery of new ships, became more critical as the war continued, because Gen. Pershing gradually shifted his target goal from a 60-division, to an 80-division, and finally to a 100-division army. The fear always remained that whenever the war ended, Britain would use its near-monopoly over passenger liners to blackmail the United States by refusing to return home the million American soldiers in France; if the Shipping Board refitted freighters at immense cost into troopships, then the gap left in commercial trade routes would promptly be filled by the British steamship companies eager to regain control over the world's commercial sea lanes.[15]

Distrust of British imperial and commercial designs never left the Shipping Board or the Wilson administration, but it could not shake the determination to field and support the large army that was needed to defeat Germany in France. All vessels already existing or under construction were mobilized by the Shipping Board in a three-step process.

The first measure was to commandeer the German and Austrian vessels interned in American ports since the outbreak of World War I in 1914. Customs officials seized the 97 vessels on 6 April 1917, the day of the declaration of war, but some of the German crews still managed to damage the ships. All the enemy ships were welcome, and in tonnage they vastly exceeded the prewar U.S.-flag foreign trade fleet; particularly valuable were the passenger liners, including the *Vaterland*, renamed the *Leviathan*, the second-largest ship then afloat in the world. By midsummer 1917, the German ships were repaired and put back in service under the U.S. flag, a task complicated by the location of many of these ships in overseas possessions ranging from Puerto Rico to the distant Philippines and Samoa.[16]

The second step was the requisition on 3 August 1917 of all vessels under construction in U.S. shipyards, except for U.S. Navy orders. Allied countries and many neutral nations had placed considerable orders for ships, to the point that the shipyards were booked for years to come. Hurley realized upon assuming office that this backlog would not allow the Emergency Fleet Corporation to carry out an efficient shipbuilding program, and hence he requisitioned the 431 hulls under construction. In effect, the government took control of the private shipyards, which, although technically still under private ownership, now could be coordinated into the larger shipbuilding program. Only navy orders were spared, and the navy's own yards continued to work feverishly on military construction.

The third measure came on 12 October 1917 when the Shipping Board requisitioned all U.S.-flag ships over 2,500 deadweight tons. Prior to that date, the Shipping Board had requisitioned individual vessels from the steamship companies for specific voyages or indefinite periods, but by that last measure the Shipping Board in effect took full control of the entire oceangoing fleet of the United States, both in domestic and foreign trades. The owners of the ships became operators for the Emergency Fleet Corporation and were very generously compensated for the use of the ships by special expense-sharing arrangements, but full authority to allocate the vessels rested with the government.[17]

The Shipping Board now had to coordinate the movements of the seized German ships, the 431 hulls requisitioned and soon to be completed, and the vessels from its own rapidly growing shipbuilding program. Primary responsibility for allocating and controlling the vessels assigned to the private operators fell initially to the special Division of Operations created within the Shipping Board in September 1917. This division essentially took care of the government-owned or requisitioned fleet; to deal with the skyrocketing freight rates in neutral vessels, the Shipping Board created a separate Chartering Committee shortly thereafter. No chartered vessel could clear a U.S. port unless its charter had first been approved by the Chartering Committee; this power was used to force neutral vessels at reasonable rates into those routes that had been neglected but that were considered essential for the war effort and for the supply of raw materials into the United States.[18]

Coordination between the Chartering Committee and the Division of Operations was a time-consuming task for the Shipping Board, which was enmeshed in countless technical and commercial issues. Chairman Hurley decided the time had come for some wise delegation, and on 11 February 1918 he created the Shipping Control Committee and placed it under the most prestigious American steamship executive of the day, P. A. S. Franklin, who stepped down as president of the International Mercantile Marine for the duration of the war. Hurley made the appointment on his own because he feared that some past squabble might lead President Wilson to block the appointment, but soon the president became a strong believer in Franklin's abilities. Franklin introduced a very simple principle: All merchant ships belonged to a single pool and were utilized as soon as the need to move cargo materialized. All departments and agencies of the government forwarded to Franklin their shipping needs, and he made sure the ships appeared and the cargoes were delivered. In Hurley's term, Franklin was a "shipping dictator" who with the full backing of the Shipping Board strove for the most efficient allocation of all merchant vessels. As a seasoned steamship executive, Franklin performed the delicate chess game of moving the right ships around the world to pick up and deliver the cargoes without wasting time or equally valuable space.[19]

The Shipping Control Committee's outstanding success could not hide the fact that the United States was critically short of ships and that repeatedly during the war it had to turn to British and other Allied tonnage to move not just the American Expeditionary Force but also cargoes vitally needed both in Europe and the United States. The submarine campaign made the shortage more critical, but even without submarines the shipping shortage was real enough. The ultimate solution lay in building more ships and in training more Americans to become seamen and officers in the merchant fleet. A crash recruiting and training program produced large numbers of competent seamen, but foreign crews continued to remain vital throughout the war; it was simply impossible to create such large numbers of experienced seafarers on such short notice, no matter how much money and personnel the government suddenly deployed to meet the crisis situation.[20] Even an intensive shipbuilding program could not compensate for many years of maritime neglect. Hurley launched the Emergency Fleet Corporation into a full-speed-ahead building program that eventually was highly productive, but nothing could hide the fact that the United States rode the waves to victory in World War I on British ships. With the existing shipyards clogged with orders, the Shipping Board had to assume the immense start-up expenses of creating its own yards from scratch. Government yards were established throughout the country, but the greatest concentration of them, including the largest (Hog Island), lay within 50 miles of Philadelphia. If the shipbuilding program had begun promptly upon the creation of the Shipping Board in September 1916, a larger number of ships would have been delivered sooner, but instead the program was barely getting off the ground by late 1917. When the war unexpectedly ended on 11 November 1918, the Emergency Fleet Corporation had laid a little over 1,400 keels but delivered only about a third that number of completed ships. Yet the shipbuilding program was in full swing at last, and Hurley had to decide what the Shipping Board should do about the huge projected output for 1919.[21]

4

The Rebirth of the U.S.-Flag Merchant Fleet

THE WORLD WAR I shipbuilding program endowed the United States with a vast merchant fleet. England's tonnage was still greater, but for the first time since the Civil War, the United States had a merchant fleet able to carry a substantial share of the country's oceanborne trade. Building the ships was only the first—and perhaps easiest—step toward establishing regular steamship services under the U.S. flag. The Shipping Board groped to formulate a coherent policy for the disposition of the ships, as the first section explains. The most logical alternative—namely, favoring the previously existing firms, such as the International Mercantile Marine discussed in the second section—was unfortunately rejected. As the last two sections of this chapter and the next two chapters will detail, the Shipping Board embarked instead on the often chaotic policy of creating new U.S.-flag steamship companies, not always with favorable results.

☐ The Shipping Board and Demobilization

The unexpected end of World War I on 11 November 1918 found the United States in the middle of the vast shipbuilding program. By Armistice Day the shipyards had delivered only 470 ships but had laid 1,429 keels. Except for the additional 276 ships launched but not yet delivered, should the rest of the building program be canceled and the partly built hulls scraped? Edward N. Hurley, the chairman of the Shipping Board, asked Sir Arthur Salter, the British shipping representative in Washington, D.C., for his best advice. Sir Salter said that "he anticipated for a year or two shipping of all kinds would have plenty to do with the aftermath of the war; but thereafter surplus vessels would be a drug on the market, and the British were planning to curtail their building."[1] Unfortunately for Hurley, he had not yet learned what he later realized, that while British officials often did not tell the whole truth, they rarely stated falsehoods. Consequently the chairman "hurried back to his Shipping Board colleagues to urge them to go ahead and build because the British were scared to death of American competition." The construction program was carried out, with 757 vessels completed in 1919, 406 in 1920, 68 in 1921, and the last 3 in 1922. The emergency shipbuilding program formally ended in May 1922, nearly four years after the war was over.

While the Shipping Board had the responsibility of deciding how many vessels to build, it had much less control over their disposition once they were finished. Supplying U.S. forces still in Europe and carrying soldiers home initially called for more ships; but, once the troops had come back—by the end of 1919—the military cargoes to Europe drastically declined. The tremendous dislocations in food and coal supplies for devastated Europe kept cargo space at a premium during all of 1919 and at least into early 1920, but the board knew more normal conditions were bound to return. To dispose of its rapidly growing fleet, the Shipping Board offered many of the new ships for sale, but it did not pursue a very aggressive selling campaign. Since not enough buyers materialized (even at bargain prices), from the middle of 1919 on the Shipping Board began to assign ships to "managing operators," an arrangement whereby the profits were retained by private individuals while the losses were transferred to the government.

Another idea behind the managing operators was to stimulate the creation of new U.S.-flag steamship companies in order to break the grip that a few predominantly foreign-flag combines—such as the International Mercantile Marine and the Atlantic, Gulf, and West Indies Lines—had on U.S. shipping. Soon there were 200 managing operators, who were distributed between lines and who plied regular routes on schedule, and tramps who wandered about whenever cargo appeared, although initially there was considerable overlapping and confusion between both groups. The flood of surplus vessels was so great that many of them were allocated to the older lines for operation alongside their foreign-flag ships. The coastwise trades were eventually overtonnaged, and by 1919 the Shipping Board was able to revoke the temporary permission granted foreign vessels to serve the coastwise trade during the wartime emergency. Throughout the world's seas, the U.S. flag appeared in many ports that had not been visited by American ships sometimes in generations; it seemed to many that a lasting maritime revival had taken place.[2]

The allocation of ships to the managing operators (the most important decision of the Shipping Board with regard to U.S. steamship companies) had taken place in a disruptive, haphazard, and overlapping manner. The lack of a clear plan or any type of long-range program resulted in deficits for the government, while many get-rich-quick operators reaped a bonanza of private profit at government expense. The Shipping Board claimed to maintain a "confidential" file on all operators to prove their reliability, but examination of these files quickly revealed that the government had little or no idea about who was receiving the ships, much less whether they were likely to make a long-term commitment. But with freight and passenger rates sky-high after the Armistice, the managing operators were extremely eager to run the government ships in order to reap the windfall profits.[3]

Clearly the Shipping Board should have paid close and constant attention to the managing operators, at the very least by allocating ships to no more than 20, rather than 200 as actually happened. Other issues of greater immediate urgency but of fleeting importance to U.S. steamship companies dominated the Shipping Board, which increasingly was disrupted by a rapid turnover of top leadership. Chairman Hurley, though well-suited to carry out the merchant marine policy, resigned because of illness in late May 1919; even before then his excessive involvement in European relief and his membership in the U.S. delegation to the Paris Peace Conference had left little time for any coherent shipping policy. His successor as chairman, John Barton Payne, was in office only seven months and concentrated his attention on the single issue of bargaining the German passenger liner *Imperator* for nine tankers claimed by Standard Oil. President Wilson's incapacity after a stroke gave Payne unusual freedom to bring extraordinary pressure to bear against the Allies on behalf of the oil company, to the point that the assistant secretary of state wrote that "if the government is going to have me represent the Standard Oil, I think they should at least allow me to charge the usual legal rate of corporation lawyers."[4]

Standard Oil kept control of the tankers for a number of years until they ceased to have a crucial role, and Payne himself was promoted to secretary of the interior, leaving the chairmanship again vacant. President Wilson appointed Admiral William S. Benson, who recently had retired from the U.S. Navy as chief of naval operations. He took office as chairman of the Shipping Board in March 1920, but inexplicably his Senate confirmation was not pressed by the Wilson Administration even when no opposition was apparent. Benson tackled his job with gusto and became the most outspoken and courageous defender of the U.S. merchant marine. His aggressive shipping policy called for even more U.S. lines to reach different parts of the world that he believed were not adequately covered by the existing 200 managing operators. Benson went so far as to demand vessels from the War Department because they were needed to establish new steamship services before the foreign competitors captured the remaining routes.

Working with Senator Wesley Jones of the Commerce Committee, Benson rushed through Congress the Jones or Merchant Marine Act of 1920, virtually without congressional debate and with no recorded vote. A not fully recovered President Wilson signed the bill on 5 June 1920 after the most cursory discussion in the cabinet. Controversy quickly erupted over three of the main aspects of the new law: the extension of the coastwise laws to the Philippines; the granting of preferential rail rates to shippers using U.S. vessels; and the authorization given the president to abrogate treaties that prohibited discrimination in favor of U.S. shipping. The Jones Act was the United States' first and only declaration of war against foreign shipping; as Sen. Jones explained, "They say it will drive foreign shipping from our ports. Granted; I want it to do it."[5] Unfortunately for the merchant marine, the backlash was strong from U.S. shippers who did not relish a general rate war against the whole world as much as Benson and Jones did. A stunned Benson could only watch with dismay as each of the three key provisions in the law was allowed to lapse; soon he was saying that it had been easier to run the navy as chief of naval operations. He was not the first naval officer—nor would he be the last—to learn that it was harder to run a merchant fleet than a navy. Benson's interim appointment ended in March 1921 when the incoming Republican administration of Warren G. Harding withdrew his nomination and appointed its own officials, who unfortunately continued the high turnover.

The rest of the Jones Act remained in force—in particular, those sections recognizing the right of the Shipping Board to hand over and eventually sell (at rock-bottom prices) ships to private operators in a graduated transition designed to create strong U.S. steamship companies. Benson had built the whole merchant marine plan on the shifting sands of the new managing operators, most of whom were in the business only as long as they could make quick and easy profits. Only a handful of operators had planned for the future in what was inherently a business of many years' duration, so that when the shipping market collapsed in the summer of 1920, just after the passage of the Jones Act, few were able to survive. Those who had bought vessels at higher prices and on borrowed money in 1919 now went into bankruptcy. Many of the ships steamed with half their full loads or even less, transferring the mounting losses to the Shipping Board. Likewise, the demand for chartering government ships dried up, and the Shipping Board was left with a growing number of idle ships.

The most urgent step was to stop the outflow of government funds with a first drastic slash of 80 managing operators by June 1920. By June 1921 the number had dropped to 97 operating 744 government vessels, and in June 1922 the Shipping Board had reached the more reasonable figure of 39 with 394 vessels. The tramp services had been eliminated, but there were still too many overlapping routes among the existing lines, so in a resolution of 30 November 1923, the Shipping Board proceeded to consolidate the 39 operators into 25 steamship companies. This was the maximum number that the Shipping Board should have allowed in 1919, and for 1923 was still too large.[6]

The cost of subsidizing these 25 operators, although more tolerable, was still burdensome because losses continued to be transferred to the government. Increasingly the Shipping Board began to assign the trade routes to those managing operators who had bought part or all of the government vessels in their respective routes, a step many were reluctant to take until a generous mail subsidy program was created in 1928. The turnover in Shipping Board officials and the frequent bureaucratic quarrels continued throughout the 1920s. The Shipping Board became a captive of shifting coalitions of private steamship companies, so unscrupulous executives had ample opportunity to reap considerable personal gains by favorable allocations of ships, routes, and funds from the government. For too many private executives, the battle in Washington, D.C., became more important than the competition against foreign rivals. A selection of cases in the rest of this chapter and the next two describes the relations the Shipping Board maintained with individual steamship firms. In the first case, the International Mercantile Marine, the Shipping Board failed to realize what were the real issues at stake in the struggle for survival of the largest U.S. steamship company.

□ I.M.M. at the Crossroads

World War I had not modified the fundamental characteristics of International Mercantile Marine—namely, a U.S. corporation owning foreign-flag ships, overwhelmingly of British registry. The solid financial position of the company was meaningless to many Americans obsessed with the charge that I.M.M. was merely a front for British interests. After the wartime alliance with England was over, the fears of British domination returned with perhaps even greater force. P. A. S. Franklin, the head of I.M.M., had worked hard to correct the impression, but all his public relations efforts were in vain. I.M.M. regretfully concluded that the sale of its British-flag subsidiary, the White Star Line, was the only action that would satisfy nationalistic clamor in the United States. By November 1917 I.M.M. had reached a tentative agreement to sell the White Star Line to a "British syndicate." After the Shipping Board and President Wilson both stated on 19 January 1918 that there were no objections to the proposed sale, I.M.M. received a firm offer from the undisclosed syndicate, which was obviously a dummy corporation created to hide the true buyer.

The financial transaction was of such magnitude that further negotiations with the U.S. Treasury were necessary to avoid upsetting the financial markets in New York and London by the sudden transfer of such large sums from England. By the time the monetary arrangements were finally cleared, the U.S. government had reconsidered its earlier approval of the White Star Line sale, because "this is the greatest fleet and the largest ships in the world, and no company except the Cunard has such ships."[7] The mystery over the buyer only heightened the anxiety: "They are to be sold to what Mr. Franklin calls a private shipping syndicate, but he believes it is backed by the British Admiralty." A worried secretary of the navy explained on 18 November 1918 to President Wilson: "I suppose you know all of these facts, but this is such an epoch-making transaction I felt it my duty to bring it to your attention. No American shipping ought to be sold, even if it is to be used by Great Britain." That same day President Wilson sent a note asking I.M.M. to suspend the sale, and the results were expressed in a subsequent letter:

> My Dear Mr. Franklin:
> Allow me to acknowledge receipt of your letter of November 21st and to express my appreciation of the action of the Board of Directors of the International Mercantile Marine Company in resolving to take no further action in the matter that has been under discussion until the views of the government are fully presented and considered.
> I hope and believe that I can give you the views of the government in a very short time, because I realize that it is not fair to keep the Board of Directors in uncertainty.
> With appreciation,
> Sincerely yours,
> Woodrow Wilson[8]

Franklin knew very well that the immediate acceptance of the president's request did not suffice to dispel the popular belief that I.M.M. was a dummy front for British control, so he received with interest the proposal (alive in U.S. official circles at least since 23 November 1918) that the U.S. government purchase the shares of I.M.M., thereby removing the private stockholders out of the line of fire of U.S. ultranationalists. British government opposition to the sale could be taken for granted: "An important shipping agent" went so far as to say that "he believed England would declare war rather than see this fleet pass under the American flag."[9] President Wilson believed that he could convince the British government, but he still was not clear on the right course of action: "I have given a great deal of thought to the question of the purchase of the Mercantile Marine but still find myself in doubt as to what is the right and just conclusion."[10] The Shipping Board worried over where to find such huge sums at a moment's notice and without time to risk a potentially messy request in Congress. The Shipping Board finally informed I.M.M. on 1 April 1919 that the company was free to deal in any way with the White Star Line.

I.M.M. now received a second offer from the mysterious British syndicate whose identity was then unknown to the U.S. government but, thanks to private British business archives, may now be revealed: the Royal Mail Steam Packet Company. Franklin and the rest of the directors unanimously endorsed the sale and urged stockholders, in the strongest terms possible, to approve the contract of May 1919 so that I.M.M. would be free at last of the foreign-flag taint so repulsive to U.S. nationalists. A small group of stockholders had different ideas, however, and a confusing intrigue followed. If the sale was rejected, Chairman Hurley of the Shipping Board promised to hand over a large number of ships to I.M.M., which not only would consolidate its position as the largest single fleet in the world but also would extend its influence to new areas like Australia, South America, and later even Africa. The Royal Mail Packet Company sensed the opposition and raised its offer $5 million above the previous $125 million of 1918, but to the dismay of the British company and the directors of I.M.M., the stockholders voted down the sale.[11]

The outcome left I.M.M. exposed as a supposedly British monopoly, an ideal target for U.S. propagandists. Franklin knew well that the Shipping Board was bypassing I.M.M. in the allocation of the war-surplus vessels, in spite of the earlier vague assurances of Chairman Hurley. In the case of the Philadelphia/Baltimore run to Hamburg, "we under the circumstance are eminently well equipped and established to handle this business, and we really cannot understand why we should not be given an opportunity of doing so."[12] Franklin was forced to state that "it is quite evident to us that there is a direct discrimination against us for some reason which we regret."[13] The Shipping Board, determined to create small new U.S.-flag lines to foster competition, refused to assign vessels to I.M.M. for the Hamburg route, but the only real beneficiary of this policy was the German line Hamburg-America, which quickly recovered its prewar position. The pattern of U.S. shipping policy was set: In order to foster competition between U.S. lines, the road was left open for large foreign combines to pick off one by one the small U.S.-flag companies.

When the Shipping Board assigned the route for New York–Manchester, I.M.M. (with previous service to that port and a very strong base in Liverpool) was the only logical choice, but the Shipping Board preferred to create a series of small U.S.-flag firms to handle the government vessels in the Manchester service; all of these small firms eventually were driven under by the powerful British firms. The bitter anti-British sentiment in the United States prevented the Shipping Board from making mutually beneficial arrangements with I.M.M. The final break came when on 17 January 1920 I.M.M. made a bid to purchase 30 German steamers, including the *Leviathan*; I.M.M. was the only firm large enough to operate these vessels under the U.S. flag, and combining their services with those of the British-flag subsidiary, the White Star Line, guaranteed great savings and substantial profits, thereby further ensuring a commanding position for U.S. shipping in the North Atlantic.[14] No matter how hard I.M.M. and the Shipping Board tried to convince the public otherwise, the whole plan was dismissed as a British conspiracy to gain control over U.S. shipping. The Hearst newspapers launched a ferocious publicity campaign and filed a lawsuit to prevent the Shipping Board from selling the vessels to I.M.M. Sentiments reached a fever pitch: "When in England has anyone heard of an Englishman lauding the I.M.M. as such, or the American Line? Are Messrs. Lord Pirrie, Grenfell, and Harold Sanderson taking orders from P. A. S. Franklin? Perhaps the *dominating presence* of the latter is the chief reason why he was selected to act as the *figurehead* behind which these designing scoundrels are enabled to pull the strings of our very government. Don't give up the ships to the British BASTARDS."[15]

The sale of the German steamers was blocked, although I.M.M. remained operating the vessels but not for long: "Considerable friction exists between the Shipping Board and the I.M.M., Admiral Benson being particularly unpleasant to Mr. P. A. S. Franklin, and it is anticipated by the I.M.M. that the Shipping Board will withdraw from that organization the boats allotted to it, which number about sixteen. Formerly the I.M.M. operated about seventy or eighty of the Shipping Board boats but only sixteen are left."[16]

The last ships were duly withdrawn, and in 1921 the Shipping Board placed passenger liners such as the *Leviathan*, which were too big for any other U.S. firm to handle, under the control of a newly created government-owned and operated firm, United States Lines. All these blows had been too much for Franklin, who tried to save face when talking to the British ambassador but finally broke down when negotiating with Cunard about rates: "I know how pessimistic he is about the future; in fact I thought when I saw him before he left this side that he was verging on a panic."[17]

Franklin certainly had ample reasons for his worries: the nature and economics of North Atlantic passenger travel had radically changed since the imposition of immigration quotas by the United States in 1920. The real profits had always been gained by cramming wretched immigrants into the lower decks; the deluxe passengers on top were mainly a means of advertising the lines, as the newspapers filled the gossip and other columns with reports of how the beautiful people traveled in the first-class accommodations. With the drying up of the immigrant traffic, the first-class passengers, who never had been very profitable, lost their crucial role: "New York society women who travel with maids and poodles and countless wardrobe trunks are no longer besieged by agents for steamship lines as they used to be in days when there were plenty of steerage passengers."[18] Instead the passenger liners sought to replace the destitute immigrants with boatloads of tourists. The goal was to convince tens of thousands of Americans to travel to Europe, which was not so hard to do after World War I because many of the U.S. soldiers who had served in Europe wished to return with their friends and families. The economics of the change in passengers reduced the profits of the liners, which now required ever-larger investments with better facilities for all passengers, not just the first-class ones; above all, a large labor force was required to cater to the tourists, and the U.S.-flag ships with higher labor costs were put at an additional disadvantage. The ownership of the British-flag White Star Line insulated I.M.M. from the higher labor costs, but the tremendous political pressure of the widespread Anglophobia in the United States made continued ownership a dangerous liability.

Franklin realized it was time to dispose of the problem, and in April 1926 he negotiated the sale of the White Star Line to Sir Frederick W. Lewis, of Furness, Withy, and Company, "one of the few men left in the shipping business with a full share of optimism and who has always craved a big position in the North Atlantic puddle."[19] In spite of Lewis's optimism, by July the negotiations had collapsed. An undeterred Franklin pushed on to sign a contract on 27 November 1926 with the Royal Mail Steam Packet Company, the old suitor of 1918 and 1919 with whom contacts had been sporadically maintained. Control of the White Star Line passed on 1 January 1927 to the Royal Mail Steam Packet Company, which then emerged as the largest single shipping combine in the world, the proud achievement of its dynamic director, Lord Kylsant. The sale and final transfer of the White Star Line to a British company evoked concern in the U.S. press, but it was too late to stop this momentous transaction. British concern now shifted to the future employment of the rich shipping experience accumulated in I.M.M.:

> With regard to Franklin, Lord Kylsant seems to think that Franklin may, after all, be content to confine his shipping activities in the future to what is left of the I.M.M. He told me that Franklin has more than once expressed a wish to divest himself of the anxiety that has always haunted him since the *Titanic* of a similar catastrophe to one of the other ships; but while this may be a genuine expression of thought on the part of Franklin, I doubt whether he has yet arrived at a state of mind when he would be content to devote his time to golf and gardening.[20]

I.M.M. still retained ships under British and Belgian registry in very profitable trades, but its principal source of revenue after the sale of the White Star Line became the intercoastal service between the East and West coasts of the United States. The latter service was a protected trade, so that I.M.M. could just sit back and count the profits, but the excitement of foreign competition and the romance of oceangoing ships was too much for Franklin. Rather than allow the foreign-flag ships to finance their own vessel replacements, Franklin wanted the proceeds from those ships gradually to be diverted to U.S.-flag foreign operations, a suicidal move unless I.M.M. could obtain government subsidies to compensate the lower construction and operating cost of his foreign rivals. Forgetting past resentments against the government, on 1 October 1927 Franklin made his first public appearance with Shipping Board officials since 1919. He hoped that the U.S. public had finally buried the Anglophobia against I.M.M.[21]

Improving relations with the Shipping Board guaranteed I.M.M. eventual approval of government subsidies, but Franklin knew he needed vessels if he was going to return to the major league of world shipping. The British firms would never let go of their ships again, so that the only other large fleet left in the North Atlantic was the government-owned and operated United States Lines, whose flagship was the *Leviathan*. To pry loose United States Lines from the Shipping Board, Franklin needed more than to dispose of his remaining foreign-flag services—he also needed powerful allies with direct access to the Republican administration in Washington, D.C. Also, a new generation was starting to take charge, in particular his son John Franklin. The latter, with Vincent Astor, James A. Farrell, Jr., and Kermit Roosevelt, son of former president Theodore Roosevelt—all from "the finest and most representative American families"—managed the Roosevelt Steamship Company, although the major stockholder was the new financier Basil Harris.[22] In June 1930 this new generation heavily subscribed for a stock issue of I.M.M., in effect taking over the company, although P. A. S. Franklin remained the leader and chief executive of this group, with the understanding that upon his retirement his son John would be his successor. The Shipping Board approved the consolidation, and the Roosevelt Steamship Company became another I.M.M. subsidiary. With so much political and financial capital at its disposal, I.M.M. was ready to participate in the struggle to gain control of United States Lines.

□ The Struggle for United States Lines

As explained in the first section, the Shipping Board planned to dispose of its huge World War I fleet by assigning government-owned ships to private operators. The rule also was to give preference to newcomers over previously established firms and, above all, not to increase the share of the largest firms. When the time came to assign the North Atlantic liners, including the former German vessel the *Leviathan*, the Shipping Board faced a dilemma. No new private operator had the minimum resources needed to operate passenger liners with their supporting freighters across the North Atlantic, yet it was political suicide to assign the vessels to the International Mercantile Marine, the only one of the established firms enjoying the necessary capital and organization to run the ships. After a brief ill-fated experiment, the only alternative left was direct government operation, no matter how ideologically repugnant to some; in 1921 in order to run the passenger liners itself, the Shipping Board created the United States Lines.

Government operation began under most inauspicious circumstances: "The two best ships are thirteen years old, the other twenty-one years old and should be off the owner's books long before this, so it is no time for a new owner to come into the field and expect to make any money."[23] The consensus was "that as an owner's operation, the

Line won't pay." Expensive and frequent repairs tied up the liners, especially the *Leviathan*—which, among other mishaps, ran ashore in
New York harbor on 21 December 1923 and was refloated only with
considerable difficulty. In spite of these mishaps, government-operated
United States Lines at least broke even, and it did it without the rampant profiteering and looting already becoming typical of the private
managing operators (as discussed in later chapters). Trapped by a probusiness ideology in the 1920s, the Shipping Board failed to be impressed with the achievements of direct government operation. When
Congress reduced appropriations, the Shipping Board sought to reduce
expenses not by clamping down on the wasteful and reckless practices
of the majority of the private operators, but rather by selling off United
States Lines and the supporting freighter service of the American Merchant Lines in the belief "that experienced American shipping men can
take these lines, consolidate them and operate them at substantially less
cost than under government operation."[24]

In July 1926 the Shipping Board called for bids because "we do
desire to find out just what the market is and whether these ships can
be sold on satisfactory terms, and the only way to do so is to offer both
the steamers and the services for sale."[25] An important consideration in
the Shipping Board's decision was the recent sale of the White Star Line
by the I.M.M., leaving the latter with "a considerable amount of American capital for use at home. It has been felt for some time in Shipping
Board circles that, provided he divest himself in his foreign ship interests, P. A. S. Franklin, President of the International Mercantile Marine, would be the proper purchaser of the United States Lines."

When the bids were opened on 8 November 1926, I.M.M. did
make an offer, but only for the *Leviathan*, while another firm wanted
to buy either the *President Roosevelt* or the *President Harding*. Since
the goal of the Shipping Board was to dispose of the entire line, the bids
were rejected, and United States Lines continued under government
operation. The hard fact remained that without foreign-flag ships to
generate profits, direct government operation and ownership was the
only economical alternative left. A scheme surfaced in 1928, however,
which appeared to make more attractive the economics of the venture.
The French government, tired of piling up losses on the subsidized passenger services, was prepared to sell the French line Compagnie Générale Maritime, but no buyers could be found. If the sale of the French
line was combined with that of United States Lines, they could unite
their routes and sailings to provide a competitive cargo and passenger
service. The Shipping Board was easily convinced to put on sale United
States Lines and the supporting freighter service of the American Mer-

chant Lines; opening bids were set for November 1928. Upon receipt of unconfirmed reports that Germany had radically changed the designs of the superliners under construction, the *Bremen* and *Europa,* President Calvin Coolidge agreed to postpone the sale until January 1929 so that the reports could be verified. Special missions to Germany confirmed that the *Bremen* and *Europa* when finished would undercut and outclass any U.S. passenger liners; news of the German move also stiffened the resolve of the French who, for patriotic and prestige reasons, had to retain their line against the German danger.[26]

When the bids were opened in January 1929, the only serious bidder was I.M.M., which, because of the economics of competing against the British lines and the forthcoming German liners, felt only a low bid was justified; the high bidder was a new player, Paul W. Chapman, who in a contract of 20 March 1929 was confirmed as the new owner of United States Lines. Chapman was elated and claimed that the purchase of the United States Lines and the American Merchant Lines from the government "has received the enthusiastic endorsement of industrial leaders throughout the country who regard it as the beginning of a new era in American shipping."[27] To allow others to participate in the enthusiasm, he offered in June a prospectus giving Americans the opportunity to buy shares in the venture; in the prospectus Chapman claimed the assets of United States Lines were $32.5 million, when he had just promised to pay the government $16 million for those same assets! These and other discrepancies soon led to mounting criticism of the rush to sell this government operation:

> In the past, the bidders on these various lines have been steamship people and only remotely speculators, but when Mr. Chapman and his associates entered the field, the question became one which is almost entirely a speculative proposition. This is proven in Chapman's actions with United States Lines. I do not question the price he paid for the ships, because, it is possible they are worth what he paid for them, but no sooner had he secured the line, than he made a public announcement that he was going to sell it to the people of the United States. His plan, which seems to be widely known and authenticated by public announcement, means that he is placing the entire burden of the purchase of this line on the public, but will retain controlling interest by issuance to himself of one million shares of no par value common stock.
>
> This is the old promoter's game, by which the public buys something and presents it to the promoter without any material cost to him.[28]

Chapman was riding high, and he continued to push his stock with "a partial payment plan for purchasing this stock which requires a down payment of only 20 percent."[29] The sluggishness of the stock subscription did not deter him from bidding on two other lines owned by the Shipping Board but managed by private operators, the American Diamond and the America-France Line. By combining these cargo services with those of United States Lines, Chapman believed he could face foreign competition successfully. To ensure his position on the North Atlantic, on 24 May 1930 he signed a contract with the New York Shipbuilding Co. to build two new passenger liners, later named the *Manhattan* and the *Washington,* with money borrowed from the Shipping Board. Chapman's actions were all the more surprising, since from the middle of 1929 on he was in deep financial trouble. His highly optimistic prospectus to the stockholders torpedoed his application for a mail subsidy: "The Interdepartmental Committee found it hard to reconcile this rosy financial statement with a request for a government subsidy. Mr. Chapman is then stated to have hurried to Washington to explain to Mr. Brown that his Corporation's optimistic prediction was based on the presumption that they would secure the mail contracts for which they had applied. It was with this expectation that he had bought United States Lines for some $16,000,000; his application had been pending almost from the time the sale took place."[30]

For Chapman, the whole United States Lines acquisition was a giant speculation not justified by any possible returns from the operation of the ships. He should have never bought the line, and the Shipping Board should have looked at his credentials more carefully: Of the original $16 million purchase price, he had managed to pay only $5 million by the middle of 1931. He was in arrears with numerous payments, the *Leviathan* was losing money on its voyages, and as a Shipping Board official explained: "They were all through. I don't know whether they were technically in bankruptcy, but they had let a contract for the *Manhattan* and *Washington,* and were unable to make their payments, and the New York Shipbuilding Co. was stopping operations, and it looked as though the whole enterprise was gone."[31]

When Chapman rejected a last-minute offer by I.M.M. to purchase United States Lines in July 1931, the Shipping Board was left with no choice but to resume control of the line, if only for the sake of promptly making a call for new bids in August 1931. The Shipping Board in conference with Franklin stipulated the terms and conditions for the purchase of United States Lines, which were all met in the bid presented on 13 August 1931, the last deadline. Five days later, on 17 August, Chapman, in partnership with Stanley Dollar and Kenneth D.

Dawson, submitted a better bid (which the Shipping Board decided to consider despite the deadline), whereupon I.M.M. placed a second bid as well, topping its original offer. After hectic and confusing negotiations, the Shipping Board told I.M.M. and the Chapman-Dollar-Dawson group to combine their efforts into a single proposal.[32]

The sudden entry of the Dollar family had been a most unexpected move, and John Franklin (son of P.A.S. Franklin) and Kermit Roosevelt went as representatives of I.M.M. to San Francisco to negotiate with the Dollar family and Dawson. They quickly reached an agreement over United States Lines by establishing a Nevada holding company in which each group held a 50 percent share. The other agreements and discussions revealed the Dollar family's real interest in the United States Lines acquisition: The family demanded recognition of its supremacy over Pacific Coast shipping, in exchange for granting recognition of supremacy over the Atlantic to I.M.M. No detail was too small to be overlooked; for example, the Dollar Line secured the monopoly over the use of the name "President" for its ships. The bulk of the agreement centered on the mutual allocation of routes and services, which essentially was a division of the U.S. steamship business into spheres of influence. The understandings reached in early October 1931 reflected the need to trim and rationalize services if these lines were to survive both the Great Depression as well as the sharper foreign competition.[33]

A contract with the Shipping Board on 30 October 1931 ratified those aspects affecting United States Lines, which then fell under the joint control of I.M.M. and the Dollar-Dawson group. Chapman was gradually eased out; in 1934 he filed lawsuits against I.M.M. over supposed grievances. Stanley Dollar became president of United States Lines for a brief time, but his residence in San Francisco as well as a managing contract left effective control to I.M.M. The 30 October 1931 contract with the Shipping Board had granted I.M.M. full operational control over United States Lines as well as half-ownership; by 1934 ruin had engulfed the Dollar family, and I.M.M. was able to gain full ownership. The struggle for United States Lines was finally over.[34]

□　American Export Lines

Another of the firms organized in early 1919 to operate Shipping Board vessels was the Export Steamship Corporation, soon better known by the name of its main service, American Export Lines. In 1920 the firm was acquired by Henry Herbermann, who ran it with characteristic boldness during the next 15 years. Herbermann was a product of the

New Jersey waterfront; he started out as a longshoreman, and through hard work and borrowed money he rose to control firms engaged in warehousing, trucking, and lighterage (barge service for loading and unloading ships). The boom years of World War I allowed him to amass enough profits and expand his credit until in 1920 he achieved his real goal of acquiring a steamship line. His rapid rise did not stop there: during the 1920s he was determined to turn American Export Lines into one of the largest steamship companies in the United States, and while this goal remained his main driving force, American Export Lines prospered.

The 1920s were a period of expansion, thanks to the Shipping Board assuming all losses on the operation of government vessels. American Export Lines, along with A. H. Bull Company and C. D. Mallory and Company, served overlapping routes to the Mediterranean and the Black Sea from New York. The overlapping of the routes was supposed to keep any one firm from acquiring a monopoly, which actually was a groundless worry given the intense European competition. Nevertheless, the Shipping Board would not underwrite forever the losses of the three firms, and the one with the strongest grip on cargo would be the sole survivor whenever the inevitable consolidation took place.[35]

The key long-term commodity in the Mediterranean was Egyptian cotton, normally all imported into the United States on British ships. To break the English stranglehold, two obstacles had to be overcome. First, Egyptian cotton was traditionally loaded on board as it came from the fields, and this warehouse service required that the vessels stay in port at least a week and usually two until the ships were full; then the process repeated itself with the next ship. British lines were very accommodating in providing this warehouse service, but in turn they bound the cotton shippers with deferred rebates, "fidelity commissions," and other conference arrangements legal everywhere in the world except in the United States. The Shipping Board and the U.S. consul at Alexandria decided only force could break this British grip, and in June 1921 they threatened to close U.S. ports to British ships carrying Egyptian cotton. A round of conciliatory negotiations took place in London, and in October an agreement was reached to divide the cotton cargoes in half between U.S. and British ships. This was a major boon to American Export Lines, which could build its Mediterranean service upon the long-term and solid foundation of the 1921 cargo-sharing agreement (it remained in force until the 1930s).[36]

In spite of its Egyptian cotton cargoes, American Export Lines was still showing a larger loss than Bull Steamship Company, so that when the Shipping Board began the process of consolidation in early 1923 to reduce the hemorrhage of government funds, a tough fight seemed inevitable. The president of the Emergency Fleet Corporation strongly urged the Shipping Board to award the Mediterranean service to Bull Steamship, but this action would have meant favoring an older firm (established in 1902) over one of the Shipping Board's own young offspring, when an important statutory goal had been to introduce new firms into the formerly closed ranks of the older shipowners. Yet if the service went to American Export, Bull Steamship—with all its influential connections—would be unjustly punished. C. D. Mallory and Company provided a ready solution to this dilemma. Through lack of executive oversight, C. D. Mallory and Company had foolishly allowed its government ships to deteriorate:

> In the four years that I have been in this position I have never seen any case showing an unwillingness to cooperate and a disregard of the desires of this office any more plain than this one . . . The Mallory staff . . . in the past has been extremely inefficient and unsatisfactory . . . in view of the inability of the Mallory Line to properly direct and control the efforts of its port staff insofar as the work of maintenance and repair is concerned, it is the strong recommendation of the office that the ships be withdrawn from the Mallory Line and that they be not allowed to handle government vessels.[37]

C. D. Mallory's repeated failure to heed the constant warnings from government officials, as well as its undistinguished earnings record, had placed it in a very vulnerable position. Since C. D. Mallory also ran services to Africa, overlapping those of the Bull Steamship Company, the outcome was obvious. On 27 August 1924 the Shipping Board terminated the Mediterranean and African services of C. D. Mallory and handed them over to American Export Lines and Bull Steamship Company, respectively. The owner, C. D. Mallory, a fourth-generation shipping man, did obtain a hearing at the Shipping Board to ask for a reconsideration of the decision. Mallory believed the odds were stacked against him at the hearing and he failed to obtain any satisfaction; clearly any redress would have had to come through the judicial system, but on closer analysis Mallory decided not to file suit.[38]

Henry Herbermann was now the undisputed master of the U.S.-flag services between the East Coast and the Mediterranean, with the exception of the Dollar Line's westbound round-the-world service. When the Shipping Board put the 18 vessels in the Mediterranean service up for sale, his very low offer of $1 million, payable to the government on easy terms, was the only bid. As the proud owner of one of the largest U.S.-flag fleets, Herbermann was the product of another rags-to-riches success story. He had no intention of selling out, as he needed the prestige from his high-ranking position to compensate for years of deprived status. Unfortunately, he wanted not only to gain the prestige but also to make a splash with the money, and from the early 1930s he began to exhibit many of the obnoxious traits often associated with the newly rich. He expanded his staff to a number he considered commensurate with his rank. He extended his routes and increased sailings more out of a desire to show the house flag than any real cargo possibilities. Finally, he lavished on himself a splendid salary and a bulging expense account, yet to maintain his overblown style of living he also took large sums from the company's funds as personal loans. Technically speaking, there were no laws against what he was doing, but since the survival of U.S.-flag operations ultimately depended on the taxpayer, such wasteful practices and conspicuous consumption exposed the company to serious criticisms.[39]

A flood of mail subsidies from 1928 on enriched Herbermann and kept afloat American Export Lines, which still managed to pull off some commercial coups. The Black Sea run had given the line a way into the Soviet Union, and the occasional Soviet cargoes increased until in 1929 the Soviet government signed an exclusive one-year contract for service to the Black Sea ports. In 1930 the Soviet government signed a second contract, this one for three years. For the Black Sea service, American Export Lines provided a vessel every 10 days, and more if requested by the Soviet government. The reason for this unusual contract was the largest bulk movement of freight from a single country since World War I. The Soviet Union had placed huge orders for equipment in the United States—the farm machinery alone was worth $40 million, while 20 percent of the cargo was oil-drilling equipment—and all these imports had to be shipped to Soviet ports. Return cargoes, in effect the payment for these imports, consisted of coal, lumber, chrome, and manganese. All the latter loads were bulk cargoes traditionally carried aboard tramps, and American Export Lines had pulled off a major commercial coup by beating the Norwegian tramps to this profitable cargo, which was particularly attractive because of its long, legally specified duration.[40]

When almost by accident the company began to carry passengers aboard the freighters in 1927, American Export Lines believed it had discovered a sure profit earner, and soon each ship was fitted with accommodations for 12 passengers. The ships overflowed with passengers in the summer months, and the idea of owning prestigious passenger liners was very appealing to status-conscious Herbermann. The company took the momentous decision to order four combination freighters with accommodations for 100 passengers each. The first of these "Four Aces," as they were dubbed, was delivered in 1930, the last three in 1931. With a speed of more than 16 knots, they were very fast for freighters but too slow to be competitive as liners, and the consequences of entering passenger service soon became evident. The demand for passenger travel was greatest to Italy, whose lines owned very fast superliners; only those wishing a slower service at a higher price bothered to sign up on the Four Aces, which carried less than 5 percent of the traffic to the United States. Also, by turning to passengers, American Export neglected the backbone of its Mediterranean business, the Egyptian cotton. This trade had been hit hard by a high American tariff in 1930, and now American Export, for fear of losing its passengers, could not afford to have the liners waiting around for weeks until the cotton was loaded. Thus the company itself undermined the highly profitable 50 percent agreement of October 1921; the British gladly picked up the slack, but not without reminding shippers that the U.S. lines were notoriously unreliable over the long run.[41]

With freight revenues declining, American Export Lines was not able to meet the government loans taken out for the construction of the Four Aces; furthermore, earlier government loans for the purchase of the original 18 freighters were still outstanding. The Shipping Board showed a patience that no private financial institution could afford to show, but in spite of repeated extensions and postponements, American Export remained about $800,000 behind on the payment of the low-interest government loans. By 1934 the company had received over $8 million in mail subsidies, and to make appearances worse, the $800,000 deficit coincided with the amount Herbermann had received in salaries and expense accounts—but excluded the dividends received or the sums he had borrowed from the company. These and other revelations were made in the public hearings of a special Senate investigative committee headed by Senator Hugo Black; coming at a time when tens of millions of unemployed Americans were suffering the effects of the Great Depression, they necessarily forced the Shipping Board to take action.

When word leaked that the government as a first mortgage holder was about to foreclose on the company, the second mortgage holders panicked and promptly pressured Herbermann to relinquish his control of American Export to New York Shipbuilding Company in April 1934. The latter company's sole interest was to protect its outstanding loans; it had no overriding wish to enter the steamship business. New York

Shipbuilding Company demoted Herbermann to vice president at a modest salary, and hired William H. Coverdale, a naturalized U.S. citizen of Canadian origin with tremendous shipping experience, to turn the company around. Because the Shipping Board had stipulated that shipbuilding and steamship operations should not remain in the hands of the same company, Coverdale's first task was to find a new owner. The Wall Street firm of Lehman Brothers put together an investment group including Lehman people, Coverdale himself, and Charles Ulrich Bay; with the proceeds from a loan, the group acquired American Export Lines for a very low price in May 1935.[42]

Lehman Brothers wisely retained Coverdale in spite of the inevitable Anglophobic accusations, and in his more than 10 years as president, he effected a total reorganization of the company. Herbermann's death in October 1935 proved an unexpected boon, since his $600,000 of life insurance went to the company. The most important priority was to reduce administrative expenses, which Coverdale did by firing many of the staff, slashing salaries, and sharply cutting the excessive expense accounts. The new management focused attention on rationalizing the routes, for without profitable voyages the company could not survive. Herbermann had spread his growing fleet thinly over many ports, and he had developed the bad habit of sending ships out of the routes to pick up small cargoes. With ships wandering about, American Export needed to have a costly reserve fleet ready to fill the gaps in the established schedules, or else forfeit the mail subsidies. Coverdale, working closely with J. E. Slater, his executive vice president, limited the ships' voyages to only the scheduled ports, and from then on these received reliable and predictable service. Fewer ships were now needed, and the sale of 6 ships reduced the fleet to its former number of 18. The company then paid off the government loans and other mortgages, and just prior to the outbreak of World War II it was in a very sound position.[43]

Even with the reduced subsidies instituted after the passage of the Merchant Marine Act of 1936 (discussed in chapter 7), American Export was running well. The steamship company felt strong enough to experiment with aviation, and it set up a subsidiary to try to compete against the world monopoly of Juan Trippe's Pan American Airlines. Once this experiment had run its course, American Export returned to the steamship business, earning record profits during World War II and reaping tremendous gains during the postwar shipping shortage. The rescue package arranged by Lehman Brothers and Coverdale had set the company back on track, and American Export Lines once again became one of the United States' leading steamship companies.[44]

5

The Rise of Gulf Shipping

UNTIL THE 1920S U.S. steamship companies had been concentrated primarily on the Atlantic coast and secondarily on the Pacific. The initial expansion of the U.S. merchant marine had largely bypassed the states bordering on the Gulf of Mexico, and although companies based on the Atlantic provided some service to the Gulf, the region generally felt it had been neglected. The Shipping Board's determination to create many new steamship firms thus answered long-felt needs of the Gulf.[1] To provide service to foreign ports from the Gulf, three companies rose to prominence, of which only one, Lykes Brothers, had existed prior to World War I. For all three companies—Lykes, Waterman Steamship Corporation, and Delta Line— their real expansion and consolidation took place under the Shipping Board, which later could point with pride to these success stories in the Gulf.

☐ Lykes Brothers Steamship Company

When in October 1918 the Shipping Board assigned Lykes Brothers the first contract to operate government vessels, the real growth and consolidation of the company began. The only one of the Gulf steamship firms predating World War I, Lykes Brothers had been limited to voyage and short-term charters of foreign-flag ships. Lykes Brothers had sailed mainly to Cuba and other ports in the Caribbean, and since its operations were not well known outside the Gulf, the company escaped the "taint" of association with foreign-flag vessels. Lykes Brothers was perhaps the first of the pre–World War I firms to realize that the Shipping Board was offering a priceless and unique opportunity to transform a small steamship outfit into one of the top three merchant fleets of the United States. With strong backing from Lykes family members (who owned cattle, meat-packing, and other interests throughout the American South and Cuba) the steamship company firmly pursued since October 1918 not only profits but also the more important goal of becoming the largest merchant fleet in the South.[2]

To enter the ranks of the Dollar Steamship Company and the International Mercantile Marine, Lykes Brothers first had to gain a commanding position—if not a monopoly—in the Gulf of Mexico. Its strategy called for excluding steamship firms not native to the South while quietly gobbling up the local outfits. United Steamship Company operated government vessels between Galveston and the West Indies, but when its owner, H. Mosley, died on 31 January 1921, Lykes Brothers promptly intervened to obtain the ships from the Shipping Board. Just a month afterward, what was left of United Steamship Company fell under the control of the New York–based firm of Munson Steamship Company, and the latter applied in April 1921 for a reallocation of the Shipping Board's ships now under Lykes. In the ensuing ferocious struggle, Lykes Brothers, with its extensive network in Texas and ports in the South, effectively mobilized local sentiment against New York control, until Munson's request was rejected by the Shipping Board.[3]

Munson was out of Lykes's way (but not yet out of the Gulf); however, another outsider, W. R. Grace and Company, was not so easily eliminated. In 1919 the Grace Line had inaugurated a service from the Gulf to the Pacific coast of South America with Shipping Board vessels. Lykes did not like this entry at all, and to make things worse its strong local connections with the Gulf community were canceled by Grace's powerful influence in New York and Washington, as well as the latter company's control over considerable amounts of northbound cargo from Peru. Erratic skirmishing broke out between the Grace Line and Lykes Brothers, but the latter knew this was a battle it could not win. Grace Line, however, did not want to win at the price of a messy fight with adverse publicity, including the revelation of its own heavy-handed tactics. In 1931–32 both sides agreed to create a subsidiary, Gulf and South American Steamship Co., in which each parent company owned a 50 percent interest, to handle the trade with the Pacific coast of South America. The agreement proved lasting, and Lykes not only had neutralized a larger and more powerful outside rival but also had effortlessly gained a share in the profits of the trade with the Pacific coast of South America.[4]

Lykes's rapidly expanding control was not further challenged by outside lines. Indeed, the neglect of the Gulf services by American lines that concentrated more on Atlantic and Pacific services had been primarily responsible for the rise of locally controlled steamship firms such as Lykes. Lykes could now turn to the second part of its strategy— namely, to eliminate the other local firms. Slated as first to go was Daniel Ripley and Company, which provided service between Texas and France/Belgium; since Lykes served Germany and Holland from both New Orleans and Texas, the advantages of this merger (approved by the Shipping Board in December 1924) were obvious. Besides eliminating a potential rival, the creation of the new combined firm, Lykes Brothers– Ripley Steamship Company, served the additional valuable purpose of disguising Lykes's operation of foreign-flag vessels prior to World War I. As this new company apparently resulted from the merger of two previous Shipping Board operators, nobody would be likely to dig up Lykes's past; and this lack of scrutiny would give the Lykes family, with 70 percent of the holdings, time to digest Ripley's 30 percent share in the new company. In another move in 1925, Lykes-Ripley bought Tampa Interocean Steamship Company, then operating Shipping Board vessels to the Mediterranean and the Far East. With these acquisitions, Lykes-Ripley emerged with 68 Shipping Board vessels under its operation, the largest fleet in the Gulf.[5]

Lykes Brothers now decided in 1929 to capture all remaining rivals in one big swoop. Lykes, with powerful influence in the Shipping Board, planned to create another parent company in which Delta Line, Waterman Steamship Corporation, and Dixie Line would pool their ships and receive in exchange a corresponding amount of stock. As the operator of the largest number of Shipping Board vessels in the Gulf, Lykes Brothers (the Ripley interests by the early 1930s were gradually reduced) would have majority control. Lykes, however, met stiff resistance from the targeted victims; and by the time the trap closed, the elusive prey had escaped. Lykes had not emerged empty-handed because Delta Line, in a struggle to the death with Munson Steamship, had to give up the France/Belgium service, which nicely complemented Lykes's existing runs in Europe.[6]

Lykes reassessed its tactics and concluded that the consolidation attempt had failed because Delta and Waterman had become formidable Gulf rivals; in contrast, Dixie Line was tottering on the verge of collapse and was open to capture by an all-out attack by Lykes, a move that would keep the other Gulf lines from merging with Dixie. The opportunity was provided by the government's decision to sell off as many as possible of the vessels whose operating expenses were covered by the Shipping Board. U.S.-flag shipowners knew that competition against foreign steamship companies was impossible without this financial support. In exchange for buying the vessels, the Shipping Board promised the operators they would qualify for very generous mail subsidies. Lykes made more attempts to purchase directly the ships of Waterman and Delta, but to no avail. More successful was the bid for the Dixie Steamship Line; its Shipping Board vessels were assigned to Lykes on 13 April 1932. On 18 April, Lykes submitted a purchase offer for its own and Dixie's ships (a total of 52) and the next day the Shipping Board approved the sale.[7]

The breakneck speed of these transactions was not an example of government efficiency but rather reflected the desire to rush the proposal through while a probusiness Republican administration was still in office. The sale had not been advertised, and no bids had been solicited or received. The files later revealed that an offer by Isthmian in 1930 to purchase the ships in the Gulf–Far East service had been ignored, and many other irregularities appeared. Lykes purchased the 52 ships at rock-bottom prices, at an average of $50,000 each. As the special Senate investigative committee of Hugo Black poured over these and other transactions, the new Democratic administration of Franklin D. Roosevelt was forced to face some harsh facts about Lykes: "This brings us to the question of possible fraud, which incidentally is peculiar to the Lykes case and has not been suggested in the case of the other lines. . . . There is no question but that the picture there presented has some ugly aspects. That it falls short, however, of constituting a provable cause of fraud as such is the considered opinion of our Special Counsel in charge of litigation."[8]

The Shipping Board Bureau (the temporary successor of the Shipping Board) decided to retain 9 of the 52 ships sold to Lykes Brothers, on the grounds that well-established statutory procedures had not been followed in the sale. Lykes Brothers was free to file claim in court against government abuse, but that action would also allow the government to elicit evidence and develop the case for fraud charges. The Shipping Board Bureau still felt it was on somewhat shaky ground in its decision and asked for an opinion from the attorney general. After three years, neither the attorney general nor Lykes Brothers had taken any action, and the matter of the missing 9 ships (subsequently chartered to the company) was quietly buried by the tacit consent of both sides.[9]

Owning 43 ships and using others in time charter (one or more years), and enjoying as well very generous mail subsidies until 1937, Lykes Brothers reaped a financial windfall. Its position as the largest U.S. steamship firm in the Gulf was amply confirmed. From 1935 on the cover of Ripley was slowly dropped, and the Shipping Board learned to its surprise that the funnel marks or company emblems of Lykes-Ripley were gradually giving way to those of just Lykes Brothers Steamship. The closely held family company was in an extremely solid position, with assets exceeding liabilities by a factor of six. At many times in its career during the 1920s and 1930s, Lykes Brothers could have made a tremendous gain by selling out of the steamship business, but a get-rich-quick attitude had never dominated the family management. Profits were essential to achieving the primary company goal of becoming the largest line in the Gulf.[10] As the 1930s came to a close, Lykes discovered that in spite of all the plotting and countermeasures since 1919, the Waterman Steamship Corporation had managed to emerge as a formidable rival in a Gulf of Mexico that was no longer big enough for both.

□ Waterman Steamship Corporation

Of the new steamship operators, John B. Waterman was not among the poorest, although a shortage of funds had kept him from entering the tightly closed steamship circles in his early life. Born in New Orleans of an old established family, he had learned the shipping trade and then moved to Mobile in the hope of expanding his horizons. No competitors blocked Waterman's advance in Mobile, but the city's small capital resources precluded any permanent entry into ocean transportation. The Shipping Board's decision to share vessels offered a tailor-made solution to the capital shortage problem, and Waterman was among the first interests lobbying to obtain the ships on the most favorable terms. The Shipping Board was impressed with Waterman's steamship credentials, while his two Mobile associates—C. W. Hempstead, owner of a local lumber company, and Thomas M. Stevens, head of a prestigious law firm and modestly wealthy—provided added guarantees of the soundness of the venture.[11]

The first stage of operations began with the sailing of the *Eastern Sun* from Mobile to Liverpool in November 1919. One year later the company was managing 6 vessels, totaling 47,788 deadweight tons, for the Shipping Board. Waterman vessels carried coal and grain to Italy,

Spain, and the rest of the Mediterranean. At other times the ships took grain to Rio de Janeiro in Brazil and then steamed south to the River Plate to pick up grain for a return trip via Europe. A tendency to serve the East Gulf–United Kingdom trade route was gradually emerging, but Waterman and too many of the other managing operators continued to function more like tramps. The high freight rates prevalent since the end of World War I as well as the lavish Shipping Board compensation sustained this haphazard and irregular pattern of operation. The collapse of freight rates in 1920 and the heavy drain on its funds finally forced the Shipping Board to assign the routes to fewer companies. The Waterman Steamship Corporation escaped this major thinning of the ranks and in 1923 received as its allocation the trade from the East Gulf to the United Kingdom and the north European continent—the zone of its greatest strength.[12]

Thus in 1923 a second stage in the company's shipping operations began, but Waterman knew that to ensure the success of the trade route to the United Kingdom and the north European continent, much more than the Shipping Board's decision was needed. According to President Waterman, the "naturally tributary territory" running 300 miles inland from the coastline and extending from Maine to Texas belonged quite properly to key ports served by their own steamship services.[13] The cargo originating in this tributary territory guaranteed successful steamship lines for major ports like New York, Baltimore, and New Orleans, but this was not the case for Mobile, which had to look farther for enough cargo to sustain the Waterman company. The railroad was simply crucial, and fortunately the Central Freight Association Territory (extending east of the Mississippi and north of the Ohio River) provided cheaper rail rates to Mobile than to its rival port of New Orleans. With regard to inland water transportation, although the Mississippi Barge Line quoted more favorable rates to New Orleans, the Warrior Barge Line quoted better rates for Mobile.

The Waterman Steamship Corporation thrived, but John B. Waterman did not let his guard down and instead imposed the management practices that prepared the company to seize new opportunities as well as to face sudden setbacks. The three associates—Waterman, Stevens, and Hempstead—doubled as the company's executives, receiving modest salaries and keeping overhead to a minimum. The profits were generally plowed back into the ships, whether to refurbish them or to purchase for the first time (and not just operate) vessels from the U.S. Shipping Board. The growing cargo volume generated by the Florida boom, a wave of investment fueled by frenzied real estate speculation, convinced the corporation to create in 1925 a new subsidiary, Mobile,

Miami, and Gulf Steamship Company, to manage the *Lake Capens*, *Lake Fairport*, and *Lake Benton*, three vessels purchased from the U.S. Shipping Board.[14]

The prospects for renewed expansion and more profits were abruptly interrupted when a series of setbacks during 1926–27 plunged the company into its first crisis. The Florida boom collapsed, paralyzing the three vessels of the Mobile, Miami, and Gulf Steamship Company, which could not even earn the income to meet the easy payment terms on the Shipping Board mortgages. Waterman secured a payment extension from the Shipping Board, but before he could gather enough funds from his other operations, a second blow hit the company. To counter the railroad rates that favored Mobile, rival steamship companies began to absorb the rail differentials of the Central Freight Association Territory in their ocean rates. To make things worse, New Orleans had at this time secured from the barge lines more favorable rates that made significant inroads into Mobile's "naturally tributary territory." The crisis had to be solved quickly, or Waterman Steamship Corporation would soon join the growing number of Shipping Board operators who had folded. Nearer to home, the preference of the barge lines for New Orleans could not go unchallenged, and the corporation proceeded to absorb the barge differentials into the ocean rates, for, as President Waterman explained, "it is perfectly sound to make up our minds to fight the devil with fire."[15]

Something big was still necessary to save the company from ruin. The mortgage payments on the three new vessels (although postponed) would soon fall due, and only a bold, risky move could secure permanent employment for those ships. The highly competitive European route, as well as other foreign routes, could absorb no more vessels; but why not sidestep foreign competition by reaching beyond Florida into Puerto Rico, which enjoyed the exclusive privileges of U.S. coastwise laws? Puerto Rico, an island possession of the United States in the Caribbean, was chronically short of regular steamship services, yet taking the readily available cargoes was a big gamble because little return cargo came from Puerto Rico. If the homebound ships deviated slightly from course, the company could quote lower rates to entice sugar cargoes from Santo Domingo, Haiti, and above all Cuba. Exploiting this discovery to the maximum made the Waterman Steamship Corporation a permanent carrier for Puerto Rico throughout the pre–World War II period, and the route also provided the opportunity to outflank New Orleans by opening service to Puerto Rico from Houston and other West Gulf ports, in addition to the regular sailings from Mobile.[16]

The 1926–27 crisis marked the beginning of the third stage in which the Puerto Rican/Caribbean trade rivaled the United Kingdom/ north European continent route. By this time, a new management team had formed under President Waterman, who was eventually promoted to chairman of the board. The new executives, characterized by fine competence and tremendous motivation, also took advantage of the invitation to become shareholders in the company. The first ones to come aboard were Edward A. Roberts as vice president and H. C. Slaton, who served more than 10 years as secretary-treasurer. Another very dynamic individual was Captain Norman G. Nicolson, who soon was second only to Roberts in the corporation.[17]

A major challenge soon tried the new management team. The threat of consolidating all the Gulf coast steamship lines into a single company had been only partially averted in 1923, and ever since then the Shipping Board had been toying with the possibility of a more complete consolidation of Gulf services. The Shipping Board decided in early 1929 to sell off its remaining lines, but the bitter struggle that raged over the disposition of the North Atlantic routes postponed until 1930 any action on the vessels in the Mobile-Europe trade. It was clear, however, that unless the Waterman Corporation moved quickly to purchase the vessels on its European run, another rival could buy them from the Emergency Fleet Corporation and leave the company with tonnage barely sufficient for the Puerto Rican/Caribbean trade.[18]

To fortify its position as the steamship line of the East Gulf, the company added Tampa, Florida, to the regular services. "The weak spot in our defense armor," Waterman declared, was return cargo from Europe, and to justify its claim to the European route, the company opened a general agency to solicit cargo on the Continent.[19] More funds were needed to make a valid bid to the Shipping Board for the purchase of the vessels the company had operated, but doubts first had to be overcome: "I am sorry to say that I have not gotten rich, as you seem to assume. It has been a hard struggle to develop a service in the East Gulf, because so few people outside of myself had any real faith in the success of the venture and could not, or would not grasp the idea that the East Gulf was an economic unit, in itself, and capable of competition with other sections of the Gulf."[20]

Lykes Brothers made several attempts to neutralize the Waterman Steamship Corporation. As early as the stock reorganization of 1927, Lykes Brothers had sounded out stockholders about selling their shares, but rumors of this move reached President Waterman in time to abort any takeover. Lykes then pressured the Shipping Board to accept one single consolidated company in the Gulf; according to the proposal the number of vessels controlled by each of the previously independent firms determined their voting rights, and Lykes (as the largest) was assured of full control.

Only a most vigorous counterattack saved the Waterman Steamship Corporation from absorption by Lykes. The lobbyist H. B. Arledge mobilized the support of elected officials from Alabama, Mississippi, and western Florida in Washington, D.C., while President Waterman did the same in the East Gulf among chambers of commerce and other business groups of shippers. Yet to secure Shipping Board approval for the purchase he had to abandon the Texas and Louisiana routes, which had long been a problem for Lykes. This concession temporarily pacified Lykes, and at last in 1931 the Shipping Board approved the purchase of the vessels previously operated by Waterman Steamship in the East Gulf to northern Europe trade.[21]

As owner of its own vessels, Waterman Steamship entered into another successful phase of operations starting in 1931. The corporation remained as deeply dependent on government subsidies as before, but there were other reasons as well for the company's success. Foremost among them was the untiring dedication of its founder, John B. Waterman, who had conceived the project of creating a major company and pushed it through to completion despite the risks involved and skeptical advisers. He claimed that "the development of this company has been the climax of my life's efforts," and indeed he had laid a solid foundation for the company between 1919 and 1937.[22] But Waterman Steamship did not end with the founder, and from 1929 on, when Waterman was frequently incapacitated by illness, the new management team of Roberts, Nicolson, and others showed the ability to successfully pursue the steamship business. The fact that the company executives were the majority stockholders of the Waterman Steamship Corporation was also a strong advantage.

The corporation continued the policy of reinvesting profits. While the mail contracts for foreign trades were the essential source of profits, fierce competition discouraged further expansion into overseas routes. The possibility of purchasing other American steamship firms met no success, and Waterman instead decided upon the expansion of its coastwise services. A new subsidiary, Pan-Atlantic Steamship Corporation, began weekly sailings from Gulf ports to Philadelphia, New York, and Boston in 1933. The coastwise laws excluded foreign competition from this trade route, which though less profitable, guaranteed regular sailings and did not depend upon mail or other subsidies.[23]

Besides entering the coastwise trade, the Waterman Steamship Corporation also channeled profits into other areas, like the Ryan Stevedoring Company, a subsidiary since the early 1920s. The corporation also increased its qualified shore personnel until in 1933 it could offer full maintenance services for ocean vessels. The investment in repair facilities took a major step forward when in 1937 the firm purchased shipyards henceforth run by another subsidiary, the Gulf Shipbuilding Corporation. By 1937 Waterman Steamship was well represented in the main parts of the shipping business, including foreign, insular, and coastwise services, as well as stevedoring and shipbuilding. Furthermore, the company had the flexibility to shift resources among the different activities within the maritime field. Waterman Steamship had emerged as the most successful of the Shipping Board's offspring.[24]

□ Delta Line

The Mississippi Shipping Company (soon to be known by its trade name of Delta Line) was organized in New Orleans on 24 March 1919 to take advantage of the opportunities offered by the Shipping Board. As one of the latter's few successful offspring, Delta Line was similar to Waterman Steamship Corporation, although differences were obvious from the start. While the personal goal of creating a successful and long-lasting steamship firm was the overriding consideration for John B. Waterman, Delta Line's primary motivation was more mundane: To provide coffee merchants in New Orleans with regular direct shipments from Brazil, thereby preventing New York from monopolizing the coffee import market. Regular steamship service to Brazil would also provide additional export markets for goods produced in the Mississippi Valley; this second objective resembled Waterman's other goal of promoting Mobile's foreign trade.

Quite naturally, 40 percent of Delta Line's original capital was subscribed by coffee interests, and two of the original seven directors were from the coffee trade. The investors, including the members of the board of directors, were swamped by other business activities, and so they were looking for someone to whom they could entrust the new company. The election of the president and other officers from the ranks of the seven members of the board of directors was largely pro forma, since none could devote enough time to run the day-to-day operations. By unanimous consensus the board created the position of general manager for Norman O. Pedrick, a recognized steamship expert. Thomas F. Cunningham remained the president from 1919 until his death in 1937, but since he devoted most of his time to his warehouse business, it was Pedrick who in fact ran the company. Not surprisingly, numerous links and a strong friendship developed between

Waterman and Pedrick, and the latter was finally promoted to president of Delta Line in 1937, a position he held until his death in 1942.[25]

Delta Line began operations on 7 August 1919 when the *Bound Brook* sailed from New Orleans to Brazil, the first of eight sailings in that year. Northbound coffee cargoes were plentiful, but the ships were sailing south with too many empty holds. After a year the company realized that unless enough southbound exports materialized, the service might not be feasible. Fortunately a solution was ready at hand. Argentina was importing large amounts of agricultural implements and other American machinery, so that with the approval of the Shipping Board, Delta Line obtained authorization to sail south as far as Uruguay, Paraguay, and Argentina. On 15 September 1920 the *Lorraine Cross* sailed for Argentina, returning via Brazil with coffee. Before, in June 1920, the Shipping Board had assigned Delta Line the routes to Glasgow, the Baltic, and Scandinavia. Subsequently, in April 1921, the Shipping Board shifted Delta's European service to only Le Havre, Antwerp, and Ghent.

With enough time, the European route could become as important for Delta as it had been for Moore-McCormack, another firm serving the east coast of South America but only from the East Coast of the United States. Delta was well established in its trade patterns in South America. For the ships sailing south, lumber for Argentina had become the main cargo, followed by packaged petroleum products (mainly lubricating oils and grease from the Port Arthur refinery on the Gulf coast). Iron and steel products had fallen to third place because of revived European competition after 1920. The return of coffee cargoes from Brazil provided stability and the bulk of the revenue for the company. In some years Argentina's imports declined, to be matched by higher imports from Brazil, so that Delta, by rerouting voyages between the two countries, was able to maintain a stable operation.[26]

Just as for Waterman Steamship Corporation, domestic competition for cargo was crucial, but while Waterman concentrated mainly on Mobile's position against the port of New Orleans, for Delta the real competitor was New York City. In the vast area of the United States north of the Ohio River and between Buffalo and St. Louis known as the Central Freight Association Territory, Delta had difficulty filling the trains that frequently reached New Orleans with less than full carloads because the railroad rates favored New York City. As far as proceedings before the Shipping Board went, in 1924 the steamship lines from New York agreed to settle the case out of court, but separate proceedings before the Interstate Commerce Commission about the railroad rates dragged on into the 1930s. Delta, just like the rest of the Gulf steamship

lines, had to lobby hard to make sure that New York City, by discriminatory rail rates, did not siphon off an undue share of the export commerce of the Central Freight Association Territory.[27]

A different type of competition turned into a life-and-death struggle for Delta starting in 1926. Munson Steamship, an older firm dating
back to the pre–World War I years, was desperately trying to survive
in a vastly changed shipping environment. Being accustomed to running foreign-flag ships and not having adequate financial backing,
Munson needed to pry enough routes in Latin America out of the Shipping Board just to survive. Munson was already running a passenger
service to South America, and, taking advantage of the Shipping Board's
policy of consolidating routes, the company also proposed to run the
freighters operated by Delta. Quick lobbying countered this thrust, and
on 24 November 1926 the Shipping Board did consolidate the services,
by placing Delta as the sole operator of the government-owned ships in
the two previously separate routes.

Under normal circumstances that decision would have meant the
end of Munson, but as an older and prouder firm still operating some
profitable routes to Cuba, it deeply resented being squeezed out of the
Gulf. When early in 1929 the Shipping Board opened bids for the purchase of Delta's steamers, Munson prepared to strike a crushing blow.
When the bids were opened on 11 March 1929, Moore-McCormack had
offered $10.50 per deadweight ton, Delta $12, and Munson a whopping
$28, more than twice Delta's bid. A major crisis ensued, and Pedrick
rushed to provide damage control. Delta's board of directors authorized
Delta to meet the bid of Munson. In a delaying action by the Gulf
coast's chief lobbyist, Hardin B. Arledge, called attention to the weaknesses of Munson's financial position, as well as the "taint" of having
some operations under foreign flags. New Orleans interests swung into
action with powerful political support, and Waterman Steamship Corporation put its own resources into the struggle. The Shipping Board
met and decided to reject all the bids, but it agreed to negotiate with
Delta for the sale of the vessels at a price equal to Munson's bid. Delta
promptly filed the new offer on 27 March 1929 and it was accepted that
same day by the Shipping Board. This coup took considerable effort, as
Arledge explained: "I can assure you that this result was only accomplished after one of the most strenuous fights we ever had."[28]

The 12 government vessels, the entire fleet in this service, were
sold to Delta, on the condition that their speed be increased to 13 knots
and that accommodations for 25 passengers be installed in each ship.
The price was the highest ever paid for vessels sold by the Shipping
Board. The fact that Delta had been able to match the Munson offer

was due in great part to management's prudent practices. From the start Delta Line had instituted the practice of distributing profits in the form of stock dividends, and during the first 16 years of its existence it had stipulated that existing stockholders had the right of first refusal if anyone decided to sell the shares. With careful management under Pedrick and a policy of plowing profits back into the company, the sound financial position of Delta—achieved by methods similar to those of Waterman Steamship Corporation—allowed the company to face the continuing challenge from Munson.

The profits of all Shipping Board routes were based on the assumption of government subsidies. While the Shipping Board operated vessels, the principle was simple. Essentially, the losses were transferred to the government; however, this assumption of loss was a huge burden, considering that even efficient operators like Delta lost an average of $5,000 per voyage. Once the government sold the vessels to private individuals, operation could be sustained only by a government subsidy, which would come in the form of a contract for carrying mail; the tacit understanding was that the buyers of the ships would have first claim on the mail subsidies. When the Post Office Department opened the bids in May 1929, Munson offered to carry the mails at a lower rate, again beating Delta to the punch. Munson's lower bid created an embarrassing situation, and only after much counterlobbying did the Post Office reject all bids.

Munson had been able to survive by operating a number of vessels under foreign flags, but for firms like Delta operating only under the U.S. flag, "failure to obtain the contract would have resulted in financial destruction of Delta line."[29] The time had come to teach a lesson to Munson Steamship, especially after its president, Frank C. Munson, threatened to submit another low bid for the mail subsidy unless he was allowed 50 percent control of Delta. Munson's threat was no bluff, and when refused, Munson submitted a third bid even lower than the first two for the mail contract. Obviously there was not enough room in the Gulf for both Munson and Delta; one would have to go, but the Shipping Board was at a loss as to how to handle an older firm like Munson. Waterman Steamship concluded its best interests were served by a close alliance with Delta, partly because the latter would contract for Waterman's shore facilities and stevedoring services in Mobile. A whole campaign was mobilized to bring pressure upon the government, but the Shipping Board decided that higher guidance was required. The steamship companies brought into the struggle senators who soon passed a Senate joint resolution calling on the postmaster general to award the contract to Delta. Presidential interference could still have been fatal, but after careful briefings by senators, President Herbert Hoover endorsed the U.S. Post Office's decision to grant the mail contract to Delta on 1 July 1930.

Delta was now permanently confirmed in its route to the east coast of South America, and Munson Steamship Company never recovered from this blow. Munson went into a sharp decline, and in 1934 it began lengthy bankruptcy proceedings. Delta's victory had been far from complete, however: the exhausting struggle had so monopolized the company's attention that an equally serious danger had been overlooked. While Munson and Delta had been tearing each other to pieces, in the background Lykes Brothers Steamship had been pulling the strings for a swift move against Delta's European service. Too late, Delta tried to form a partnership with Waterman Steamship to run the service to Le Havre, Ghent, and Antwerp, but the only concession that the Shipping Board granted was minority stockholder status for Delta in a larger and reconstituted Lykes Brothers Steamship Corporation, which took over the European run in August 1930. Lykes could not expand further because both Pedrick and Waterman were too smart to engage in a senseless struggle; instead they gravitated more toward each other in a loose alliance during the 1930s against the menacing size of Lykes.[30]

While all these domestic battles were raging, Delta also faced constant and sometimes ruthless competition from foreign lines. From 1919 to World War II the permanent competitor was the state-owned Brazilian line, Lloyd Brasileiro. Hamburg-America provided a triangular service between Germany, Brazil/Argentina, and the Gulf, while Osaka Shosen Kaisha (O.S.K.) operated a westbound round-the-world service for Japan that routinely stopped in Brazil to bring coffee to the Gulf. To carry shiploads of bulk commodities, foreign tramps routinely appeared. During the 1930s a series of rate wars and underpricing campaigns caused by the Great Depression seriously disturbed the trade between the Gulf and the east coast of South America.

In 1940 the outbreak of World War II left Lloyd Brasileiro and Delta as the only two regularly scheduled liner services between the east coast of South America and the Gulf. As always, coffee remained the basis of the trade, on the average providing 75 percent of the return cargoes, and in some years as high as 90 percent. Lumber was the main export item (accounting for more than 40 percent of the cargo weight) followed by petroleum products whose volume was in gradual decline during the 1930s, because of competition from tankers as well as local refineries in South America. The downward trend in petroleum exports did not worry Delta, which counted on lumber to provide the bulk of the general southbound cargo. After World War II the unexpected happened: lumber virtually disappeared as a cargo item, while petroleum products made a surprising revival. In any case, the overall prospects looked bright enough, and in 1938 Delta entered into a subsidized ship-building program to replace nine of the old World War I vessels with six new and faster cargo-passenger ships, drawing on the designs of the newly created U.S. Maritime Commission. Clearly Delta was one of the handful of Shipping Board–inspired firms that prospered and survived after World War II.[31]

6

Asia and the South Pacific

By THE ESTABLISHMENT of U.S.-flag lines in the states bordering on the Gulf of Mexico, the Shipping Board had successfully met the long-felt desires of that region. Another important priority for the Board was to create permanent U.S.-flag services in the trade routes to Asia and the South Pacific, but here it was harder to repeat the success stories of Gulf shipping. The heart of the trade was transpacific shipping to the Far East, which is discussed in the first section. In spite of all the Shipping Board's efforts, U.S.-flag lines were gradually squeezed out by the powerful Japanese lines, a process that began before World War I. The Shipping Board felt that the new route to India from New York offered a more propitious field for U.S.-flag lines, but as section 2 reveals, the Board's efforts ended in costly disillusionment. The last section describes how imaginative management by the Matson Navigation Company converted the Shipping Board's backing for the U.S.–Australia / New Zealand route into a surprising success story.

☐ Turmoil in the Far East

World War I was the catalyst for major changes in Far East shipping. The three principal Japanese steamship companies, in spite of massive government subsidies, were burdened by debt and had been running large deficits prior to 1914. Thanks to the war, Nippon Yusen Kaisha, Osaka Shosen Kaisha, and Toyo Kisen Kaisha cleared the debt and, besides paying large dividends, accumulated large reserves to finance a permanent expansion as well as to weather any adversities after the wartime boom. World War I also marked the beginning of the rapid growth of transpacific shipping; as the French consul in Hong Kong explained: "Formerly few ships sailed on the Pacific, but now it has become one of the most frequented oceans in the world.[1]

The virtual absence of hostilities in the Pacific Ocean, in particular the lack of German submarines, meant that vessels could safely cross the ocean without encountering the dangers present in the North Atlantic combat zones. The surviving sailing vessels, easy prey for German attacks in the Atlantic, flocked to the Pacific Ocean where during the war they made their last stand against the more formidable steel steamers. The closing of the Suez Canal and the opening of the Panama Canal in 1914 rerouted more vessels across the Pacific. World War I sparked a burst of economic growth that propelled Far East trade into a position of importance not imagined before: for example, the tonnage in the transpacific trade in 1920 was five times higher than it was in 1914.[2]

Unlike China, which had no merchant marine, Japan with its steamship companies was ready to take maximum advantage of the wartime opportunities. The withdrawal of most British vessels to the Atlantic and the disappearance of German steamers left the Japanese in command of Far East trade. The Japanese were not content just to enjoy the good winds blowing in their favor—they wanted to exploit the opportunities to the maximum, and they were determined to drive out those American steamship companies like the Dollar Line that still maintained services to the Far East:

> Notwithstanding the dislike of the average shipper for the Japanese lines, we are nevertheless feeling the Japanese competition more and more and their tactics are most difficult to combat.
>
> Their game is to use their European steamers as a means for obtaining transpacific trade. They play one against the other and they can do this to good advantage as space to Europe is in great demand.
>
> We have lost business from quite a few shippers who are friendly towards us, and when we pinned them down for reasons for not giving us business we have on each occasion been told it is because of the Japs' hold on them. In other words, if they did not give the Japs their transpacific freight, they could get no European space and many shippers regard their European business worth as much to them as their American business, so when the

Japs frankly tell them 50 tons of transpacific freight will secure them 10 tons of European space, they have no alternative but to meet the Japs' demands.[3]

The end of World War I meant the return of British shipping to the Pacific, as well as the entry of large numbers of surplus Shipping Board vessels under the U.S. flag. The shipping market collapsed worldwide in 1920, and in the Pacific uncontrolled competition erupted between all the lines: "Rates were utterly unstable and fluctuated violently in an unduly depressed range. On many occasions, rates on the same sailing changed several times during the same day."[4] To try to stop this senseless competition, which was harmful to the steamship firms but even more so to the shippers who could not count on stable rates for regular services, the Shipping Board organized the Far East Conference among its managing operators in 1920. Soon the Shipping Board realized that unless the foreign lines were also brought into the conference, any attempt to stabilize rates could not be successful. On 1 September 1922 all the foreign lines, including the British and Japanese, joined the Far East Conference, which set rates for trade between the East Coast of the United States and the Far East. The next year the Pacific Westbound Conference was similarly established for the trade between the West Coast of the United States and the Far East.

The creation of the conference system guaranteed the survival of regular liner services in the Far East, but the conference alone did not determine what share of the trade would be carried aboard each nation's vessels. The resourcefulness and vision with which each company managed its assets ultimately decided its market share. The task of defending U.S.-flag shipping fell to many small American firms easily picked off one by one by the large foreign enterprises. One prewar firm, the Dollar Line, emerged as the main instrument to retain a share of transpacific trade for the United States. As explained in chapter 1, Robert Dollar had created the steamship line as a consequence of his need to ship his lumber. By the 1920s the family-owned firm had branched out into many ventures, and although lumbering remained crucial, shipping occupied most of management's attention and resources. Also by the early 1920s control had passed to the sons—in particular, Melville and Stanley Dollar—who, however, continued to consult with their father, Robert, until the latter's death in 1932.[5]

The Dollar Line purchased surplus ships at very low prices from the Shipping Board, and soon they had extended services running from the West Coast of the United States to the Far East. The Dollars knew that as a purely transpacific outfit they would never be able to challenge successfully the British and Japanese lines. The Dollars wanted to buy more vessels to establish a permanent round-the-world service under the U.S. flag. They had sent freighters in trial runs along the route, and although the voyages lost money, the potential of the service had been more than confirmed. At this point a profound and permanent division occurred within the family. The oldest brother, Melville, a "freighter" man, strongly agreed with the round-the-world cargo service, but he was totally opposed to entering the risky passenger business. He maintained that for running freighters there was always the company's lumber cargo to fall back on in hard times, but once the firm entered the passenger business, the demands for capital for newer and better ships would escalate out of control.

Melville had spoken prophetically, but the glamor of the passenger liners was too much for his father, Robert, and his brother Stanley to resist. Melville was overruled, and in 1923 he withdrew to manage the lumber side of the family business. However, Melville's advice had been partially heeded, and the seven vessels purchased from the Shipping Board in 1923 for the round-the-world service were the 502s, freighters modestly fitted to carry 87 first-class passengers each. The cabins were a complement to the cargo, so that the initiation of round-the-world service on 5 January 1924 need not have been a risky move at all. Nevertheless, the allure of bigger liners proved irresistible, so that the 1923 decision to enter the passenger business with the 502s appears from the perspective of later events as the move that ultimately doomed the Dollar Line.[6]

The Dollar Line insisted on buying the Shipping Board vessels as soon as possible, unlike most managing operators. By the purchase the Dollar Line insured its trade routes against rival competitors who could no longer bid or intrigue for the ships, but it also forsook the highly profitable agreements whereby the company operated the ships for the government at the Shipping Board's expense. Stanley Dollar had no reluctance about making a huge profit from deals with the government, but like his father, he resented any government oversight, no matter how lucrative. Other poorer managing operators had no choice but to swallow their pride along with the government funds, but Stanley could afford an alternative. In spite of the Seaman's Act, his ships continued to be manned heavily with Oriental crews, dramatically slashing his labor costs. Conditions for the seafarers on board, whether American or Oriental, were among the worst of U.S.-flag ships. The steerage trade, that is carrying Chinese coolies supplemented by Filipinos to Hawaii and to the West Coast of the United States, lingered on for years, and it never disappeared between Far East ports. The Chinese coolies, the Pacific equivalent of the wretched immigrants on the Atlantic side, were the most valued cargo, and stuffed in holds and decks in ramshackle arrangements, provided profits too large to resist. The sailing schedules of the ships in the Dollar fleet were so arranged to take care of most of their repairs and maintenance in the lower-cost Far Eastern ports. Ownership of stevedoring and dock facilities provided more gains, while the many other ventures of the diversified Dollar Company provided additional profits for the family.[7]

Stanley Dollar had a booming and lucrative business, but he still could not forget his dream of running large modern passenger liners. The 1928 Merchant Marine Act offered juicy mail subsidies to those operators who would build and run new vessels on the essential trade routes. The bait was too tempting for Stanley who signed up for the mail contract; with this subsidy he could have ordered new vessels, but instead he preferred to borrow 75 percent of the price from a separate loan fund of the Shipping Board and the rest from private banks. The large modern passenger liner the *President Hoover* was launched in 1930, followed by the *President Coolidge* in 1931; also with the Shipping Board loans, four of the 502s were thoroughly reconditioned and their passenger accommodations increased to 175.

Stanley Dollar had overestimated the demand for passenger traffic to the Far East, and he had counted on the boom times of the 1920s to supply a growing number of wealthy passengers for his ships. The Great Depression dashed all these expectations, and just as his brother Melville had predicted, the Dollar Line found itself with large excess passenger capacity built with borrowed money whose repayment had become pressing. There were additional problems with the Dollar Line, as the next chapter explains. Hopes of trying to make up for the lost passenger business with increased earnings from freight were likewise dashed by the general decline of the cargo volumes in the Pacific caused by the Great Depression.[8] Equally deadly was the entry (into the already-depressed freight business) of an outsider, Isbrandtsen-Moller Steamship Company, beginning in 1928.

Hans Isbrandtsen, who was of Danish origin and became a naturalized U.S. citizen in 1936, operated a partnership in New York with his Denmark-based cousin Arnold Moller. The ships of the latter operated as the Maersk Line, which still thrives today. Moller had hoped, by putting his older and slower ships into the partnership of Isbrandtsen-Moller, to stimulate his younger cousin to more aggressive cargo solicitation for the newer Maersk vessels sailing from New York to Europe and the Far East, but he succeeded beyond his wildest expectations. Isbrandtsen quickly discovered that if he quoted rates 10 percent under those of the Far East Conference, a few shippers who otherwise could not sell their products were willing to book with Isbrandtsen. Since his cousin Moller scrupulously adhered to conference agreements, Isbrandtsen sought application to the Far East Conference in 1928, on the condition that he be allowed to quote rates 10 percent lower because of his older and slower ships. The Conference Secretary replied, "Why can't you fellows build fast boats like the rest of us? If you can't afford faster boats, you don't belong in the business." An infuriated Isbrandtsen replied with a declaration of war: "All right, we'll operate outside the conference," and so he did, with crusading fervor, during his entire life.[9]

Isbrandtsen-Moller began service from New York to the Far East in 1928, so that when the Great Depression struck the next year, a rate war was assured. The Pacific Westbound Conference suffered a rate war, but the deadliest and longest—from 1931 to 1934—was in the Far East Conference, which bore the brunt of Isbrandtsen's rate-cutting practices. He capitalized on the discovery that by quoting rates 10 percent under the conferences, he could lure shippers away, and soon he began to expand: "He started off his service with comparatively slow and small boats and is now making ships for the trade. The first boat sailed from New York on Saturday, one of the new boats called Isbrandtsen-Moller, the modern type 14-knot ship, and the first of a fleet coming on of that speed. Competition will become more and more intensive unless something radical is done."[10] Isbrandtsen became the prototype of the "outsider" who would come to skim the cream off the trade, ready to retreat into low-bulk commodities as a glorified tramp operator if necessary. Isbrandtsen did not build up a trade but rather entered it whenever he could undercut the conference rate, at least for a few voyages.

Isbrandtsen's survival was due not so much to his particular tactics as to his decision to operate in those trades under the umbrella of U.S. antitrust law. In purely foreign-line conferences, Isbrandtsen was promptly frozen out of the trade by practices such as the deferred rebate (a discount refunded by the company usually six months or a year after the date of shipment), which was illegal only in the United States. Instead in conferences within the jurisdiction of U.S. antitrust law, not only were these conferences weakened but so were the U.S. steamship companies, whose resolve to stay in the business was further undermined by the tactics of outsiders like Isbrandtsen both before and after World War II. Thus Isbrandtsen was both a cause and a result of the decline of the U.S. merchant marine.

The real beneficiaries of Isbrandtsen's outsider activities were the

Japanese lines, which rebounded from the Great Depression into a period of expansion. In 1936 the Dollar Line could only report helplessly their ever-widening influence: "The Japanese lines are apparently making strong efforts to gain a foothold in all trade routes throughout the world."[11] Because of wasteful management, the Dollar Line was not able to prepare even a belated response until after 1938. The British, seeing their vaunted shipping supremacy rapidly eroding, were more concerned: "The speed at which Japanese competition grows is phenomenal . . . It is now quite apparent that the shipping industry is to be fostered by the government through the employment of every means at Tokyo's command. The purpose is twofold. First, this subsidized shipping is part of a deliberate political policy of advancement; second, it is hoped through increased shipping receipts to offset the adverse balance of trade."[12]

The British, with all their maritime experience, could not bring themselves to take the strong measures required to counter the growing Japanese shipping presence in the Far East:

> The fundamental cause of the recent Japanese success is the superior Japanese methods of organization and in particular the system whereby Japanese banking firms, exporting houses, and shipping companies work in close cooperation. [. . .] It follows from this that the real remedy for the decline in British shipping would be for the British shipowners to rationalize their organization and to take a leaf out of the Japanese book and work in closer contact with the banking and exporting interests concerned. To be effective such reorganization would have to be drastic, and unfortunately there is little prospect that the British shipping firms will be moved, by stress of circumstances, to abandon their present helpless attitude and to adopt such a policy. Whereas the peculiar history of Japanese industry has brought about the concentration of many enterprises of various characters into the hands of a few big families, involving forms of industrial and commercial organization of the horizontal cartel type, the English individualist tradition has led to a certain inelasticity and to a reluctance to cooperate with outside interests.[13]

If even the British steamship companies, which still had the largest tonnage in the world, were confronted with such problems, then the less formidable U.S.-flag lines operating in the Far East on the eve of World War II did not offer much hope for meeting the Japanese challenge. Thus, as the Pacific Ocean rose in importance among the world's trade routes, the foundation needed to maintain a strong U.S. presence in those sea lanes began to weaken.

□ Indian Ocean Adventure

Americans had long felt a certain curiosity about exotic and mysterious India; U.S. concern for India was further awakened by its common misfortune of English colonial rule which in the case of the subcontinent lasted until 1947. Trade followed sentiment, and by the late nineteenth century the United States discovered in British India a market for U.S. manufacturers and a source of raw materials. A lively trade developed that for years was channeled through London, whose merchants reaped hefty middleman profits. When British lines realized they could obtain larger cargo volumes by steaming directly from New York to Calcutta, they inaugurated the service in 1897. The German line Hansa entered the trade in 1900 and pushed out the British firms, until by 1914 the Germans controlled half of the cargo. World War I interrupted the sailings, and Germany, stripped of her merchant marine by the Armistice, was unable to return to the trade. The gap was quickly filled because "at the end of the war many British lines thought they were poaching on no one's preserves if they collected something the Hansa Line had had."[14] The Ellerman Line emerged with the lion's share of the New York–Calcutta trade, followed by the Cunard subsidiary Anchor-Brocklebank, which had entered the trade route in 1923.

Prior to World War I, the United States had been content to have the trade with India handled by foreign lines, but after the war, the Shipping Board promptly took action. In 1920 one of the managing operators, the Kerr Steamship Company, received Shipping Board steamers to provide the first direct U.S.-flag liner service to India. The outward leg of the journey was unsatisfactory, because India's market potential had been overestimated. To keep the ships from sailing empty to India, Kerr Steamship loaded cargo for the Mediterranean, thereby undercutting the other managing operators who provided the regular service between the United States and the Mediterranean. Burlap and jute provided abundant return cargoes from Calcutta, but Kerr adopted the wrong strategy: "In place of going all out to secure cargo from the major port to a major port, the vessels were filled at various ports en route with the result that the shippers in Calcutta and the consignees in the U.S. became considerably dissatisfied with their cargo being delayed when routed by Shipping Board vessels."[15] Quite rightly Cunard was able to claim that "the Shipping Board from time to time [has] operated a rather half-hearted service, which left the merchants cold."[16]

Kerr was also running very heavy losses for the Shipping Board, which on 22 October 1924 decided to transfer the steamers to the Roosevelt Steamship Company because the latter promised successful voyages without drawing cargo away from the Mediterranean. The Roosevelt Steamship Company, another offspring of the Shipping Board, had been created in 1920 by a group of associates including Kermit Roosevelt, the son of former president Theodore Roosevelt. Kermit was no figurehead, and he put tremendous force into the shipping business. He did keep his promise not to load Mediterranean cargo, but the losses remained the same as under the Kerr Steamship Company. An increasingly budget-conscious Shipping Board wanted to start taking his steamers away, but he convinced the government that a profitable service could not be created overnight.

The Shipping Board proceeded with a separate plan in early 1926 to consolidate the Australian and Indian routes into a new around-the-world service. Australia imported vast amounts of American products but exported little to the United States except during the wool season; India exported large volumes of burlap and jute but imported little from the United States. If the Shipping Board vessels could steam to Australia to deliver American products, then dashed to India to pick up the Calcutta cargoes for the return trip via the Suez Canal, the profitability of the service would be assured. Some steamers still made occasional trips from New York to serve Bombay and the outer Indian ports, while others still carried the seasonal wool cargoes from Australia back to the United States. Roosevelt had made two trips to India, where his status as a president's son was a natural calling card; he built up tremendous goodwill among Indian merchants, who were impressed by his efficiency in meeting their needs and in securing the direct Calcutta–New York service. Roosevelt had considerable influence in the Republican party, and quite naturally the new consolidated service to Australia and India (the American Pioneer Line) was allocated to the Roosevelt Steamship Company.[17]

The British lines had enjoyed making fun of Kerr Steamship Company, but they easily recognized a new formidable foe: "Sir John R. Ellerman began by impressing on us the danger and seriousness of the Roosevelt Line opposition in Calcutta–New York trade. He stressed the fact that sentiment would drive American consignees to support the American flag, and said that they regard a period of cut rates as inevitable unless we got together in an agreement between the three lines."[18] Roosevelt could not have agreed more on the need for cooperation, and to reach an agreement, he went on a mission to England in June 1927. His first task was to convince the skeptical British that this was not another passing fancy for the Americans:

> Mr. F. A. Bates asked whether the Shipping Board would really continue to show interest in what was after all a comparatively

small trade from their point of view, dealing with cargo ships, and with small prospects of profits. It was pointed out that their main interests and that of the American public centered in their arrangements for Atlantic service on a *Leviathan* scale. Mr. Kermit Roosevelt replied that we had got quite a wrong impression. The Shipping Board had given up their ideas of the importance to America of *Leviathans*. They regarded that type of ship as an advertisement figure, and not of real importance. Their main idea now was to concentrate on building up a series of long distance American cargo ship services, which would secure a supply of certain essential products, such as wool and jute, to America in the event of another war.[19]

Roosevelt's mission benefited from the highly unusual circumstance of disunity among British lines: "I had previously known of the bitter feeling between Sir John Ellerman and the Cunard Group, but had not been prepared to find it quite so virulent. He continually referred to them as having 'knifed him in the back' and said that he believed it totally impossible to come to any agreement with them. He said he had been negotiating with them but had been unable to get anywhere."[20] For once Americans were able to enjoy the infighting between the two British lines, so that the day before Roosevelt returned home he received a very favorable offer from Ellerman for a 25 percent share of the sailings, to which Cunard agreed. The situation was too good to last for long, and Roosevelt returned home to find that the Isthmian Line had obtained an injunction against the just-concluded agreement. The Isthmian Line was a subsidiary of U.S. Steel and had made about four sailings annually to India since the end of World War I. The Isthmian Line loaded the parent company's steel cargoes for India, so any jute and burlap for the return voyage was pure profit. Furthermore, Isthmian was closely associated with the Ellerman Line, which secured the return cargoes from India in exchange for part of the steel freight.[21]

With slowly rising cargo volumes, Isthmian wanted to increase its sailings beyond four per year, while the Roosevelt Line claimed that because of the former's close ties to the British, this simply meant reducing the American share below 25 percent. Cunard and Ellerman refused to reduce their sailings to accommodate Isthmian's request, and they began to freeze the Roosevelt Line out of cargo. To keep shippers loyal, Roosevelt Steamship slashed rates in half in December 1927, and the long-feared rate war at last erupted in full force. Isthmian's insistence on increasing its share precluded a prompt settlement, but by the middle of 1928, all lines were suffering heavy losses, and they finally agreed to end the rate war in early August 1928. By the agreement, the

United States retained its 25 percent share of the total sailings, now increased to 72, thereby allowing Isthmian 2 extra sailings without having to reduce the sailings of the Roosevelt Line. The British were worried by "the new arrangement which really represents a victory for the aggressive methods of the Shipping Board and will encourage them to employ similar tactics in relation to other trades of which they covet a share."[22]

The Roosevelt Line feared that Isthmian would not live up to the agreement and would seek even more sailings; to try to commit the lines to stability, a New York–India Conference was finally established on 1 January 1929. Prior to that date, no conference had existed, and the fluctuations in rates had aggravated the competition over the number of sailings. Before the New York–India Conference could stabilize this trade route, however, the Great Depression disrupted world shipping. The conference itself was the first casualty, and it was dissolved in December 1930 because of the cutthroat competition that had erupted. The Kerr Line, now under British flag and control, shifted some of its empty ships into the New York–India route and began to quote rates one-third lower. In February 1932 Kerr Line could not stand the pressure any longer and withdrew from the trade; Cunard had meanwhile done the same, leaving only the Ellerman and Roosevelt lines in the New York–India route, except for the less frequent sailings by Isthmian, which was also hard hit by the Great Depression.[23]

The Roosevelt Line had merged with the International Mercantile Marine in 1930, and the combined influence of both Kermit Roosevelt and I.M.M. was needed to keep the Shipping Board from eliminating the Indian service as a long-overdue budget cut. The losses on the route were so great that the Shipping Board planned to eliminate the whole service. Roosevelt still retained sufficient influence in the final months of the Herbert Hoover administration to block the move, while John M. Franklin vigorously defended the need for the service:

> We cannot help but feel that the elimination of the Indian service would be a very serious mistake; it would destroy the effort and the investment expended in developing this service, and surrender control of this important service to foreign steamship interest; this would lead to increases in rates to the detriment of our trade and to the advantage of our European competitors; it would mean to tie up the Diesel ships now in service, for which there is no other suitable employment; it would place in jeopardy the further successful operation of the remaining branches of the American Pioneer Line and thereby practically destroy the potential sales value of the line.[24]

In desperation, the Shipping Board now secretly proposed to consolidate the Indian service with Isthmian's sailings, but when news of this proposal leaked to I.M.M., relations with the government agency became particularly intense.[25] To make things worse, from 1935 on the Diesel ships operated on this service began to suffer breakdowns, mishaps, and other difficulties that caused delays and cancellations of announced sailings. The volume of trade with India had not recovered as rapidly from the Great Depression as other routes, and increasingly I.M.M. tired of the whole Indian service. In an attempt to preserve sailings on schedule, the Shipping Board recommended reductions in the revolutions of the Diesel engines: "From a traffic standpoint it cannot be pointed out too strongly that if breakdown of vessels, which have occurred so frequently of late, continue, the American Pioneer Line services will suffer serious damage in their competitive position with foreign lines."[26] The company adopted the suggestion at the cost of lowering speed by a half-knot.

Nobody talked about vessel replacement, and gradually the Roosevelt subsidiary, I.M.M., and the government all became disenchanted with the Indian service. The ships managed to hang on until 1939 when the outbreak of World War II disrupted the trade patterns. After the war, other U.S.-flag ships returned to call on Indian ports as part of around-the-world services or as occasional extensions of established routes, but with diminishing frequency after the 1960s. The direct New York–Calcutta service, begun with so much enthusiasm in 1919 and lavishly bankrolled by the Shipping Board during 20 years, was never revived again.

□   Tempest in the South Pacific

Until 1926, Matson Navigation Company had concentrated on the protected coastwise trade between Hawaii and the Pacific Coast. That trade always remained the backbone of the company's shipping, and it was strengthened in 1930 by the takeover of a potential rival, the Los Angeles Steamship Company. During the first three decades of the twentieth century, Matson had also invested in a variety of businesses in Hawaii and on the mainland, such as sugar, hotels, and oil, so that by the late 1930s the ships were only 27 percent of its assets. Since 1917 the solid growth of the company had been largely the work of William P. Roth, a hard-driving executive who had acquired his position by marriage to Lurline Matson, the only daughter of Captain William Matson, the principal stockholder and founder of the firm. The lure of foreign trade proved too strong for Roth, who prepared to extend the service to Australia and New Zealand; he had carefully calculated that by combining an aggressive campaign with government subsidies, Matson could earn important profits in the South Pacific.[27]

As a first step, Roth bought for Matson the Oceanic Steamship Company whose owners had fallen on hard times and were willing to sell the line for a low price; the three ships were 26 years old, but the line itself remained profitable thanks to the mail subsidy. In 1928, in a joint venture with American-Hawaiian, he bought the Oceanic and Oriental Navigation Company from the Shipping Board; Matson kept the 11 10-knot freighters operating on the route to Australia and New Zealand, while American-Hawaiian kept the other ships on the China trade. Another mail subsidy kept the 11 freighters profitable, but Roth was not simply a mail bounty hunter—he had bigger plans. The *Malolo,* the first luxury passenger liner in the Hawaii-California service, had been a success since 1927, and Roth believed that by synchronizing cargo with luxury passenger liners, he could repeat the same success in the service to Australia and New Zealand.

The Shipping Board eagerly backed this idea, and loaned more than two-thirds of the construction costs to Matson Navigation, which also qualified for a higher mail subsidy than before. In 1930 the company ordered two ships from the shipyards, the *Mariposa* and the *Monterey,* both of which entered service in the South Pacific run in 1932; a third sister ship, the *Lurline,* was later ordered, but it served only the Hawaii-California route. The vessels carried 700 first-class and cabin-class passengers, but no third-class ones; these ships would not cram Orientals into the decks as the Dollar Line still did. With a 22-knot speed, the vessels were faster than anything ever seen before in the South Pacific, and their cargo holds were designed for high-paying items such as fruits, automobiles, rugs, and pianos; Coast Guard safety laws prohibited carrying gasoline aboard, but it did allow packaged petroleum products such as lubricating oil. Shippers wishing the speed and safety of the combination liners were more than glad to pay the higher cargo rates on the *Mariposa* and the *Monterey*; for the carriage of the bulky low-grade commodities like lumber, copra, and asphalt, Matson's recently acquired fleet of old freighters provided slow but cheap transportation.[28]

The success of the two liners depended on developing tourist traffic. A well-established tourist agency network in the United States easily drummed up curious Americans eager to see the exotic places of Hawaii, Samoa, and Fiji plus the more distant New Zealand and Australia. The trick was to convince large numbers of New Zealanders and

Australians to pick Matson over the British lines and Union Steamship Company of New Zealand, a line affiliated with the British firm of Peninsular and Oriental. Matson placed advertisements in Australian and New Zealand newspapers praising the amenities of its plush liners, and by means of this aggressive publicity campaign (with even the novelty of a direct-mail campaign to every prospective passenger), many New Zealanders and Australians were finally convinced that the British way to travel to England in tramplike ships was not the best and certainly not the only way to enjoy sea travel. In spite of slightly higher passenger rates, they began to flock to the Matson ships, using them even for the short haul from Australia to New Zealand across the Tasman Sea. Matson had improved the standards of travel with movies, dancing, games, swimming pools, and many other luxurious attractions. The venture was profitable, but its success ultimately depended on the continuation of the mail subsidies from the U.S. government.[29]

The Union Steamship Company felt mortally threatened by the entry of the subsidized Matson liners into the New Zealand–Australia trade. From 1931 stevedores sided with the New Zealand company and refused to handle cargo carried between Sydney and Auckland, so that the *Monterey* and *Mariposa* could take only passengers between Australia and New Zealand. As a stopgap measure, this response was understandable, but it could not hide the real weakness of the Union Steamship Company: "If Mr. Shaw had placed two reasonably suitable ships in the trade during the ten-year period when he had plenty of opportunity to do so, the present situation would not have developed, and it seems to me that the whole debate hinges on just that."[30] In merchant fleets as in navies, the only answer to a superior ship has been to build an equal or better vessel; to do nothing is highly dangerous. Union Steamship could have ordered a ship when the construction plans for the *Mariposa* and *Monterey* were announced in 1930, or, to be on the safe side, it could have waited until 1932 to study the rival ships and measure their success.

Instead, Union Steamship, together with the governments of New Zealand and Australia, engaged in a long struggle to close the trade between Australia and New Zealand to non-British shipping. The arguments drew on remote historic events: for example, Union Steamship, which had pioneered the trade between Hawaii and California in the nineteenth century, resented its exclusion in the twentieth century by the U.S. coastwise laws. The company's ships could sail from California but could not discharge passengers and cargo at Hawaii on the route to New Zealand; Matson's ships could do so, as well as share in the trade between New Zealand and Australia on the route across the

Tasman Sea. On the grounds that the latter route was within the British Empire, Union Steamship wanted to exclude Matson from the Tasman Sea trade unless the New Zealand line received access to the California-Hawaii route as in the nineteenth century. Britain had almost made a colony of Hawaii, but unfortunately for Union Steamship, the United States annexed Hawaii in 1898, and it was political suicide to try to repeal the coastwise laws excluding foreign-flag vessels.

New Zealand and Australia proposed to close unilaterally the Tasman Sea trade to non-British vessels, and enabling legislation was passed in 1936 and 1937, with the Australian government stating "that it would go to the limit in protesting" the entry of the Matson vessels.[31] Nevertheless, the United States held the trump card: any closing of the Tasman Sea to U.S.-flag shipping was easily countered by invoking the authority (reaffirmed in the Merchant Marine Act of 1920) to extend the coastwise laws to the Philippines. Through an unusual set of circumstances, British shipping was carrying over 20 percent of the trade between the United States and the Philippines; British steamship companies were most hesitant to risk losing their profitable trade over two ships in the Tasman Sea. Indeed, the Philippines privilege was a powerful weapon of reprisal that, always dangling over British and other foreign competitors, gave the companies created by the Shipping Board additional protection.[32]

The superior service of the *Monterey* and *Mariposa* had created a loyal following: "If the Matson line ships cease to call at New Zealand, about one-third of the population would complain."[33] When the Union Steamship Company asked Matson in 1935 to suspend the Tasman service, "Mr. Roth replied in the negative, stating that in view of the labor troubles last year in San Francisco (which had cost the line a large sum of money), the increased costs of operation, and the uncertainty as to the American government's policy regarding shipping subsidies, the Matson line could not contemplate giving up any of the business it now held."[34] President Alexander Shaw of Union Steamship had no choice but to withdraw his company's vessels from the San Francisco–Australia run in November 1936 to reduce losses because of Matson's competition, although the latter carried only 11 percent of the passengers on the Tasman Sea run. The Canadian-Australian Line, a Canadian company, was also threatening to withdraw, and it seemed as if Matson was on the verge of acquiring a near-monopoly on passenger traffic between North America and Australia/New Zealand. The Australian government presented a tough bill directed at Matson, but British intercession removed its most aggressive discriminatory clauses.

The controversy over Matson's service was now in diplomatic channels, but the State Department did not want to get involved in correspondence, because if requested by the Congress for publication, still another wave of anti-British feeling would probably ensue. In off-the-record conversations U.S. and British diplomats sought to create an understanding between the shipping companies. By 1937 the governments of both the United States and New Zealand were anxious to reach a settlement. New Zealand's position softened with the realization that if the U.S. lines were excluded, the Japanese were more than ready to enter South Pacific shipping. As World War II neared, the United States did not want to have friction in the South Pacific. The governments of Australia, New Zealand, Canada, the United Kingdom, and even the colony of Fiji agreed to subsidize the construction of passenger liners comparable to Matson's, a measure that, if taken years before, would have avoided the whole controversy. As a sign of goodwill, Matson promised not to bring the sister ship *Lurline* into the South Pacific trade, and gradually all parties reached an accommodation. There was no denying that by aggressive marketing Matson had developed a passenger trade well-integrated with cargo services and that the company had attained a degree of success beyond the amount of mail subsidies received.[35]

7

The Passing of an Era

BY THE LATE 1930S one stage in the history of steamship companies had come to a close, even before the outbreak of World War II. The most obvious sign was the abolishment of the old Shipping Board, never again to be revived in any similar form. At another level, one generation of steamship executives gave way to a younger breed. Previous chapters witnessed the departure of John B. Waterman, Henry Herbermann, and Robert Dollar; to this list will now be added P. A. S. Franklin. Lastly, and perhaps the most significantly, the strategy of combining foreign-flag with U.S.-flag operations was largely abandoned, an extremely risky move given the nearly simultaneous decline in the coastwise and intercoastal trade.

☐ The New Deal for Shipping

By the late 1920s, the Shipping Board had poured vast sums into private steamship companies without in any way halting the decline of the U.S. merchant marine. To rescue the previous investment, the government decided to subsidize the private steamship companies permanently. Since the word "subsidy" was heresy to most Democrats, a long and bitter congressional battle was only to be expected. The clever parliamentary tactic of dropping the tainted word "subsidy" for "mail contract" eased many ruffled feelings, and England's timely decision to shift the Cunard passenger liners during the winter into the New York–Havana route (formerly an American preserve) provided the right amount of urgency to secure approval of the 1928 Merchant Marine Act. The Post Office was authorized to award contracts to steamship companies for the carriage of mails. Since the legislation contained few fixed rules, the Post Office and the Shipping Board used the appropriations as a slush fund to award almost all lines the maximum rates; later disclosures revealed all too frequent instances of ships sailing thousands of miles just to carry a few pounds of mail at immense profit to the steamship owners. The previous arrangements with operating agreements with the Shipping Board had not been replaced completely, so in many cases the result was "subsidy piled upon subsidy."[1]

Other forms of assistance also contributed to the flood of money pouring into the pockets of steamship executives, "individuals who publicly posing as patriots, prostituted those laws for their private profit."[2] The generosity of the federal government, rather than building up a merchant marine to serve the public good, had instead enriched a small privileged group. The mismanagement and favoritism of the Post Office and Shipping Board had grown to alarming proportions, but not until the onset of the Great Depression in 1929 did criticism of the subsidy giveaway program begin to mount. As many Americans sank into unemployment, homelessness, and poverty, the spectacle of a few shipping companies wallowing in government funds became harder to accept. A number of government studies pointed out the most flagrant cases of waste, and finally in April 1932 President Herbert Hoover proposed to transfer the Shipping Board to the Department of Commerce, so that the executive branch could exercise direct control to halt the spreading abuses. Hoover had waited too long to propose this measure, and Congress decided to wait until the new Democratic president took office in April 1933 before taking any final action.

The Franklin D. Roosevelt administration immediately launched a flurry of legislation known as "the Hundred Days"; three of these measures had a direct impact on steamship companies. The Independent Offices Appropriation, as an economy measure, authorized the president to abolish, consolidate, or transfer many existing government agencies. The Democratic administration abolished the Shipping Board and the Merchant Fleet Corporation as independent agencies and transferred their functions to a newly created Shipping Board Bureau within the Department of Commerce, effective on 9 August 1933. All understood the arrangement was temporary, awaiting in particular the results of a Senate special committee established to investigate the air mail and ocean mail contracts. Senator Hugo Black plunged the special committee into the most exhaustive examination of the U.S. merchant marine since the Alexander Committee of 1913–14; whatever findings the Black Committee might make, it appeared they would come too late because a separate process was already at work to implement government policy toward the steamship companies.[3]

In June 1933, also during the Hundred Days, Congress created the National Recovery Administration to ensure a government partnership with private business in the task of ending the Great Depression. Under its jurisdiction, each sector of the economy was authorized to draw up a code of self-regulation to create maximum employment and to set prices, wages, and levels of competition; the codes allowed pooling and other arrangements, all exempt from antitrust prosecution if approved by the National Recovery Administration. After four months the National Recovery Administration had approved more than seven hundred codes drafted by private business; unfortunately no agreement could be reached about the steamship code. After immense difficulties, the competing interests of the rival U.S. lines were papered over, but an even larger problem loomed with the question of foreign steamship lines. A shipping code without the foreign lines was meaningless, while including them meant taking jurisdiction away from foreign governments. The National Recovery Administration wrestled with the hot potato of the shipping code during the rest of 1933 and 1934 and, following the experience of the Shipping Board, was reluctant to regulate the world's shipping lanes unless clear cases of blatant discrimination against U.S. lines could be proved. On their part the foreign lines did not want a confrontation with the U.S. government, and they proposed instead a separate National Recovery Administration code just for the foreign lines. From here on lengthy drafts and counterdrafts for shipping codes flew endlessly back and forth until the nightmarish experiment was mercifully put to death by the Supreme Court's 1935 decision declaring the National Recovery Administration unconstitutional.[4]

The delay had not worried the steamship companies, as they had continued to receive their juicy mail payments. The end of the good times appeared on the horizon when the Black Committee delivered its scathing report in June 1935. Through a careful listing by name, date, place, and amount, the committee exposed a "saturnalia of waste, inefficiency, unearned exorbitant salaries, and bonuses" and also explained the mechanisms utilized by unscrupulous operators:

> Holding companies, subsidiaries, associates, affiliates, and whatnots have been used by shipping companies for the uniform purpose of siphoning the income of subsidized operating com-

panies into the pockets of individuals. When discovered, it was always found that these corporate devices concealed salaries, bonuses, secret expenses, and purloined revenues, which in equity and good conscience should have remained in the treasury of the subsidized company. . . . inexcusably heavy profits have been made by some ocean-mail contractors and excessive salaries, fees, commissions, and expense accounts have been paid to officers, agents, and high-powered "fixers" plying their art in Washington. . . .

While the clamor has always been made that our marine subsidy would provide funds for the payments to American seamen of wages set at a proper level, and substantially in excess of foreign wages, in many instances the proper wage scale has been cut, and money transmitted to mail contractors in constructive trust for American seamen has been diverted by contractors to their own private profits for exorbitant salaries and unearned bonuses. This practice and result is wholly indefensible.[5]

To this depressing tale of misappropriation of public funds, the government operation of steamship companies formed a salutary contrast: from 1921 to 1929 the Shipping Board had run without private intermediaries the United States Lines, while the Department of the Army ran the Panama Line; when the government directly operated the lines, not a single case of mismanagement occurred thanks to the well-tried and proven methods of government accounting and supervision. The problem was with the interface between the government and the private sector; in particular, when private business received public funds during long periods. The conclusion of the Black Committee was inescapable and has remained valid to this day for the maintenance of any substantial merchant marine: "This committee, therefore, recommends that whenever the taxpayers' money is invested in ships or shipping enterprises, the government shall retain full and complete ownership and control."[6] The Black Committee was not so politically naive as to ignore that such a proposal, although the only logical conclusion from the mass of evidence gathered, was on purely ideological grounds unacceptable to many Americans. As a secondary alternative the Black Committee paraded a long list of requirements and "thou shall nots" that any policy of subsidizing private ownership and operation would have to include. The complexity of the safeguards, to prevent more looting of the public treasury for private benefit, contrasted with the simplicity of government ownership and operation; furthermore, the ingrained opposition to subsidies within the Democratic party was another potent factor that just might swing the legislative outcome.

Unfortunately, the reform of shipping policy had become just one more pawn in the larger political struggle. By 1935 business had turned against the New Deal—even though large segments, such as banking, had been saved by the New Deal. With the mounting and increasingly hostile opposition from business and conservative groups, the Black Committee's recommendation for a government-owned shipping enterprise was precisely the kind of high-visibility item that would generate fears of a socialist takeover by a power-mad Roosevelt administration. In March 1935, even before the final recommendations of the Black Committee were in, President Roosevelt had announced his support for government subsidies to private steamship firms; the Department of Commerce had reached similar conclusions as early as May 1934, and both worked toward passage of the Merchant Marine Act of 1936. The sound proposal of a government enterprise never had a chance, although lingering traces survived in the final law.

Quite expectedly, Congress found that the administration's proposals left too many loopholes for a repetition of private profiteering, and it proceeded to tack on an impressive list of controls, requirements, and safeguards, in a classic case of locking the barn door after the horse has fled. In this respect, the Merchant Marine Act of 1936 was an unqualified success, for under its detailed, complex, and rigid provisions, no cases of misappropriation or diversion of government funds for private profit ever took place.[7]

The goal of the Merchant Marine Act passed in June 1936 was not honest public finances but rather the development of a merchant marine capable of carrying "a substantial portion" of the country's foreign trade on U.S.-flag ships. To qualify for subsidies, U.S. steamship companies could not own or operate foreign-flag ships. The heart of the law was the criteria to assign "differentials" between the higher U.S. costs and lower foreign costs. These differentials were the basis for a "scientific subsidy policy" whereby the government, after a careful determining of the exact prices, covered the higher costs private operators faced when running U.S.-flag ships. Subsidies were distributed for shipbuilding "construction differential subsidies" and for running the ships "operating differential subsidy." To administer the program Congress established an independent agency, the U.S. Maritime Commission, which also performed the regulatory functions for the entire shipping industry. The five members of the commission were appointed by the president with the consent of the Senate for six-year terms.[8]

The first duty of the new U.S. Maritime Commission was to replace the old mail contracts with the new operating subsidies. This task was accomplished by the new energetic chairman, Joseph P. Kennedy, appointed with the other permanent members in April 1937. Kennedy conducted a vigorous program of activity, but left after barely ten months in office. No matter how vigorous the application of the Merchant Marine Act of 1936, the decline of the American steamship industry continued unchecked through 1937, 1938, and 1939. The policy of differential subsidies was simply not adequate to maintain a U.S. merchant marine in private hands, a harsh fact temporarily obscured by the dramatic expansion during World War II.[9]

What needs to be explained is not the failure of the New Deal maritime policy (a result grasped even from the moment the bill became law) but rather its remarkable survival into the 1990s. Government agencies changed, but for the rest of the twentieth century the maritime subsidy policies established in the Merchant Marine Act of 1936 have remained in force and basically unaltered. Essentially, factors outside the law itself have been responsible for its continued functioning. Certainly the most important factor has been the appearance of military conflicts, most notably World War II with its postwar shipping shortage, but also the Korean, Vietnam, and Persian Gulf conflicts. The differential subsidy could not preserve by itself the U.S. merchant marine, but when combined with ships built during World War II and sometimes also with military or government cargoes, substantial profits were possible.

The long stretches between the wars proved rough sailing for many steamship companies, and their perseverance cannot be accounted for solely by the differential subsidies. First of all, a number of steamship executives showed a marked preference to remain in the steamship business even when other more profitable alternatives were available. Some finally caved in to the temptation and withdrew from shipping, but the fact that they were willing to remain for long periods in a business not among the most profitable reveals underlying motives of prestige, status, and often simply a particular liking for the type of work. Much as the Black Committee rightfully castigated the get-rich-quick practices of most operators, the hard fact remained that individuals such as those in the Lykes family or John B. Waterman preferred to stay in this business and planned for long-term survival.

An influential group that was almost entirely absent from the New Deal shipping policy debates was organized labor. After World War II the organized labor movement, run by a tight leadership in an almost dictatorial fashion, emerged as the primary backer for the subsidy provisions of the 1936 Merchant Marine Act. For most private operators, the amount of money they would receive under the stringent clauses did not justify the incredible paperwork, complex applications, delays, rigid rules, and restrictions, not to mention the congressional struggles to include adequate appropriations in the national budget. From the late 1940s, organized labor took the lead and assumed the task of securing government approval for the subsidies. This allowed steamship companies to meet the union's demands for bloated salaries—they would be covered by the government subsidies. Unlike anything foreseen under the 1936 act, the companies became intermediaries transferring official funds into labor's salaries. Subsidy policy changed from its original goal of maintaining a merchant marine to the different goal of perpetuating the power of big-labor leadership.[10] As later chapters show, the point was reached when the moderate subsidies could cover only the high wage costs but not the rest of the expenses necessary to face foreign competition. Under the Merchant Marine Act of 1936 the virtual disappearance of U.S. steamship companies was inevitable but not immediate, and without any fixed timetable the end could be repeatedly postponed.

□ The Rescue of Dollar Line: American President Lines

Dollar Line's inability to counter the Japanese challenge discussed in the previous chapter was largely due to the policies pursued by its owner, Stanley Dollar. He was an expert at making juicy deals with the federal government, but his performance as a steamship executive was notoriously poor. When Dollar tried to acquire American-Hawaiian (which no longer sailed to Hawaii) in order to increase the Dollar Line's share of the trade between Hawaii and California, he met bitter stockholder opposition, and to prevent the takeover, Matson Navigation Company counterattacked by threatening to enter the Far East routes of the Dollar Line. Rather than face this frontal challenge, Dollar turned and ran to sign a shameful surrender on 23 April 1930. By that agreement the Dollar Line not only abandoned any attempt to increase its share of the Hawaii trade but also handed over 50 percent of its annual gross passenger and freight revenues on that trade to Matson. Euphemistically called a "division of territory" agreement, which is something quite different, the accord with its large annual payments was of doubtful legality. No similar agreement has yet been uncovered for other steamship companies.[11]

Dollar Line was drowning in debt by the early 1930s; to replace its fleet of older liners, it had borrowed heavily from private banks and the Shipping Board. Only a most rigorous control of expenses and careful husbanding of resources could have repaid these growing debts, yet management's goal was exactly the opposite: "Every conceivable device was adopted to drain the earnings and the working capital from the company as rapidly as possible."[12] By numerous subterfuges, government subsidy funds were diverted from the Dollar Line to the many subsidiaries of the Robert Dollar Company. As a minimum figure, Stanley Dollar admitted to receiving in compensation $2.5 million between 1923 and 1934, while his brother J. Harold Dollar received slightly more than a million, which were fabulous sums for those preinflation years.

The draining of the company to enrich the Dollar family reached such extremes that the Shipping Board finally felt compelled to act on 11 April 1933. Loan repayments were overdue, and to prevent the company from going into bankruptcy the Shipping Board set up a joint account on 11 April 1933 to handle future disbursements of government subsidies. Dollar Line could make no disbursement from the mail subsidy without the Shipping Board's signature, but without access to the company's books, this control by itself could not remedy the situation. Seven times Stanley Dollar refused to provide the information, and, not surprisingly, the company drifted closer to bankruptcy. By 1937 the situation had become critical: "The maintenance of the vessels had been so long neglected that they were in an unsatisfactory condition from the point of view of safety. The Dollar Line was notorious for its almost callous neglect of the conditions and accommodations of its crews' quarters. The past history of the Dollar operations made it obviously clear that the management was shockingly incompetent."[13]

From April 1937 on the new U.S. Maritime Commission, under the leadership of Joseph P. Kennedy, confronted this highly unsatisfactory situation and decided in June to suspend all further subsidy payments to the Dollar Line until the latter provided all necessary information. When at last Stanley Dollar consented to open the books, the company was already in crisis. The U.S. Maritime Commission plunged into a first round of negotiations to try to reorganize the Dollar Line and prevent it from collapsing into bankruptcy. The main protagonist in the June–December 1937 negotiations was the Anglo-California Bank, which was afraid that, as the holder of many outstanding Dollar Line loans, it would be dragged into bankruptcy with the steamship firm. Dollar's heart was not really in the negotiations, and in spite of having siphoned off the subsidies into the family pockets, his firm attitude always remained that the government had the obligation to bail him out. Kennedy himself had tired of the whole shipping business and rumors were already rife that he was eager to resign and accept a more prestigious government position. Nevertheless, all parties agreed by 9 December 1937 on a reorganization plan, but before it could be signed, the *President Hoover* (one of the company's two modern passenger liners) ran aground off Formosa on 11 December 1937 and was judged a total loss.[14]

The first reorganization plan, whose budget had counted on the revenues from the sunk passenger liner, was now unworkable. The insurance money and a temporary subsidy gained time for the U.S. Maritime Commission to embark on a second round of negotiations with the Anglo-California Bank, Stanley Dollar, and a mounting number of creditors in February–August 1938. The task now fell squarely on the new chairman of the U.S. Maritime Commission, Admiral Emory S. Land, who replaced Kennedy in February 1938. By the end of that month, "the problem of putting the ships into proper condition and getting them back into service had proved much more difficult than had been anticipated."[15] Public opinion opposed spending more federal funds for the enrichment of private steamship operators, and by 1938 the U.S. Maritime Commission had simply run out of funds to pour into the bottomless pit of the Dollar Line. Any request for a congressional appropriation would turn into a grueling replay of the Senate hearings under Hugo Black, and the ensuing public outcry necessarily would have destroyed any rescue attempt for the now-bankrupt Dollar Line.

The only way the U.S. Maritime Commission could tap additional funds was by approaching another federal agency, the Reconstruction Finance Corporation, to obtain a bailout for the Dollar Line. The Reconstruction Finance Corporation had been lavishly funded by Congress to rescue individual private enterprises from the ruin of the Great Depression. However, the corporation was not a slush fund, and it demanded stringent conditions before approving the loan for the Dollar Line. Most significantly, collateral was required, and since the company was already clogged with overdue payments to the Anglo-California Bank, the U.S. Maritime Commission, and many private creditors, there were no assets left to pledge except the company itself (the ships were already overmortgaged). Stanley Dollar tried to avoid the inevitable, but finally on 15 August 1938 an agreement was signed whereby, for about 90 percent of the Dollar Line's stock, the U.S. Maritime Commission assumed liability for all debts. As Stanley Dollar himself wrote a year later, "the government owns 90 percent of the stock."[16]

Why did the U.S. Maritime Commission conclude that it had to bail out the Dollar Line by means of a takeover? The consensus was "there is only one possible alternative if this plan is not accepted and that of course is bankruptcy or receivership."[17] The experience of the

Dollar Line case and the subsequent history of the U.S. steamship companies clearly shows that this was a major mistake on the part of the commission, which should have allowed the company to collapse into bankruptcy proceedings. Powerful reasons mainly concerned with the Japanese threat, such as the need to bring Americans stranded in Asia back home and to move vital cargo to the Philippines, argued on behalf of the government's decision, but the real protagonist was the Anglo-California Bank, which saw in the government takeover a bailout of itself and not just the Dollar Line. The rest of the desperate creditors eagerly supported the government intervention as the quickest and safest way to recover their money. Thus, in the takeover of the Dollar Line, just as during the previous years of mail subsidy, the government was trying to provide a public service, only to have its intentions both times converted into private profit. The contract and related instruments carefully drawn up by the lawyers clearly stated that a sale had taken place, but these documents (more than sufficient in a purely private transaction) would turn out to be woefully inadequate when one of the parties was the government. Throughout all the negotiations in the 1930s, never once did the Dollar family members admit the slightest regret over having drained government funds for their own private profit; this unrepentant and unreformed attitude was the only warning sign available to the government, which should have heeded the warning and allowed the company to fold. In bankruptcy court the government's bid for the Dollar Line's vessels would have won because no other U.S. steamship company was in a position to make a serious offer.

To try to make a clean break with the cloudy past, the U.S. Maritime Commission promptly changed the name of the company to American President Lines. In a historical vindication, the first chairman of the government-owned and operated company was none other than William McAdoo, who, as Secretary of the Treasury in the Woodrow Wilson administration, had been the first high-ranking official to realize and propose the merits of government ownership in merchant shipping. The appointment was a personal triumph for McAdoo, who in the last years of his very active life threw himself with great enthusiasm into the task of rebuilding a looted and demoralized company.

With the outlays from the U.S. Maritime Commission and the Reconstruction Finance Corporation, American President Lines began to repair the damages of the previous Dollar management. The debts were gradually repaid, the company's fleet was refurbished, new C-class ships were ordered, and gradually the company's position in the Far East was restored. The strict government operation from 1938 on marked a period of efficiency, reliability, and profitability. During World War II the company reaped large profits, but it scrupulously avoided the many profiteering scandals that rocked most of the private steamship companies. Government ownership and operation had turned American President Lines into one of the largest U.S. steamship firms (soon rivaling United States Lines), but it remained to be seen for how long private business would allow such a successful venture to survive.[18]

□ Crisis in Coastwise and Intercoastal Shipping

The coastwise trade along the Pacific Coast and from Maine to Texas and the intercoastal trade between the East and West Coasts played an important role in the rise and survival of U.S. shipping in the foreign trade. The three main components of coastwise and intercoastal shipping had been the tankers, the tramps, and the liner services.

□ **Tankers**   In 1937, 70 percent of the cargo moving in the coastwise trade was petroleum carried aboard 293 tankers, and the growing oil volume appeared to dispel any signs of crisis. During the 1930s, 85 percent of the tankers were owned by oil companies, the largest fleet belonging to Standard of New Jersey (today Exxon) and the rest to other U.S. oil companies such as Texaco, Gulf, and Mobil. The 85 percent share of the tankers owned by the oil companies seemed proof of the high degree of vertical integration in the industry, but in reality it marked a shift from the prewar position, when the oil companies had carried nearly 100 percent of the domestic oil shipping in their own ships. The gap between 100 and 85 percent was filled by the appearance of independent tanker operators, or "independents," who were another legacy of the Shipping Board.

The massive wartime construction program had included tankers, but the market for tankers was sluggish after the war, with only 17 sold to the oil companies; even after transferring 12 to the Navy Department, the Shipping Board was still left with 88. In 1922, a temporary decline in output from Mexico increased the demand for oil from the California fields, and with longer sailing distances the shortage of U.S.-flag tankers became critical, as the oil companies could not transfer their foreign-flag tankers of the Mexican run into the domestic trade. The Shipping Board was only too glad to dispose of its remaining tankers now that prices were strong, so it sold most of them in 1923–24.[19]

The oil companies did not believe that the 1922–24 shortage was likely to repeat itself, but other unpredictable disturbances in the tanker market could never be ruled out. Should the oil companies buy up all the remaining Shipping Board tankers, or should they allow small independent tanker firms to emerge? The Shipping Board preference for favoring new operators was no threat to the oil companies as they had ample experience in setting up dummy corporations. Most oil companies, including Exxon, decided to "undertonnage" themselves either by not having enough U.S.-flag tankers to carry 100 percent of their needs, or by not leaving any reserve capacity to meet unexpected cargo volumes. For their additional tanker needs, the oil companies chartered, usually for extended periods, the vessels of the independent operators. The independents also met the specialized needs of foreign oil companies such as Shell, which entered the refinery and marketing business in the United States but was prohibited by the 1916 Shipping Act from owning U.S.-flag tankers.

If demand for tankers slumped, as happened during the Great Depression, the oil companies operated their fleets at near-capacity and transferred the losses to the independents whose vessels were idled; this was the case with the largest independent, C. D. Mallory and Company, whose 19 vessels were laid up from 1930 to 1934. The severity of the Great Depression was such an extreme case that even after canceling all its charters, Exxon was forced to lay up 26 of its U.S.-flag tankers. Hard times ended with the 1935 boom, which marked the beginning of years of prosperity for tanker operations. The oil companies went so far as to have 52 U.S.-flag tankers operating frequently in the foreign trade, though mostly as a reserve to the domestic tankers: U.S.-flag tankers in the foreign trade could be quickly redeployed to meet any sudden demand in coastwise and intercoastal shipping, but the more profitable and numerous foreign-flag tankers of the oil companies were excluded by the coastwise law from the domestic trades.[20]

The U.S. Maritime Commission confidently counted the tankers as the one sector of the U.S. merchant marine able to replace its vessels and ensure proper service, but warning signs were already visible. The independent tanker operators worried most about Exxon's decision in the late 1930s to meet 110 percent of its average domestic needs with its own U.S.-flag tankers. Ultimately, the coastwise and intercoastal trade in petroleum depended on three things: large demand for oil in the East Coast, large oil production within the United States, and lack of alternate transportation for the oil. If any of these three elements failed, the coastwise and intercoastal trade in petroleum was doomed, irrespective of the laws excluding foreign vessels. Only the demand for oil in the East Coast could be taken for granted: not only was consumption there growing but it was starting to displace coal. As for the other two, only time could show whether there were any grounds for worry.[21]

□ **Tramps**   During the days of wood and sail, U.S.-flag tramps had traveled far throughout the world's seas, chasing after cargo and having no schedules and no regular service. In the last 30 years of the nineteenth century, the British pioneered the development of the steel steamer until they controlled the world's tramp shipping, followed closely by the Norwegians. By 1910, U.S.-flag tramps had virtually vanished from foreign trade, and only a small number survived in the protected domestic trade. The evolution of the more successful lumber tramps into regular liner services further depleted the ranks of the coastwise tramps.

The wartime construction program left among the surplus ships a large number of vessels of slow speed and large capacity, ideal for tramps. The Shipping Board made an effort to revive foreign-trade service by U.S. tramps between 1919 and 1922. The results were disastrous, with the Shipping Board losing as much as $25,000 on each round-trip voyage, but those same ships when chartered to foreign companies earned a nice profit for the government. In 1922, the Shipping Board went sour on U.S. tramps and refused to support them anymore, whether in foreign or domestic routes.[22] Many factors accounted for the failure of U.S.-flag tramps in the foreign trade:

> It has not been the custom of American seamen to sign on for the indefinite articles that are normally required by tramp ships, i.e., American crews normally sign up for voyages between specific points and return. Tramp ships, due to the nature of their service, may not return to American ports or home ports for long periods of time. Tramp ships also are often maintained by the ships' crews, which is not an American practice. Further, tramps operate at and for the convenience of shippers, often operating at a very definite loss in order to build up future business or to take a ship from one port to another in order to obtain cargoes.[23]

There was no prohibition against running tramps in the protected coastwise trade, and the Shipping Board, faced with sluggish ship sales, was only too glad to unload the surplus vessels at the usual low prices to any U.S. operators. The vast size of the United States, endowed with many natural resources, meant that there was always a considerable movement of low-value, heavy, bulk commodities, the backbone of the tramps' cargo. Phosphates, soda ash, sulfur, and other inputs or by-products of the chemical industry, as well as sand and gravel, were among the most reliable cargoes for U.S. tramps in the coastwise trade. Occasionally U.S.-flag tramps, in spite of strong foreign competition, could pick up sugar cargoes as they sailed by the north coast of Cuba. Coal was always a good cargo for tramps, but the rise of liner services of colliers to supply the normal demand eliminated coal cargoes except in peak periods. The same was the case for logs and lumber, cargoes almost entirely taken over by U.S.-flag liner services.

The indifference, if not hostility, of the Shipping Board (and after 1936 of the U.S. Maritime Commission) was an additional hindrance to the remaining U.S.-flag tramps. Some, like Clifford D. Mallory, continued to operate tramps right up to World War II, but most had gradually transferred their ships to foreign-flag operation in other countries, leaving only a small number in the domestic trade. The U.S. Maritime Commission claimed in 1937 that there were "very few tramps in the coastwise trade," and it predicted the eventual demise of tramps not only in the United States but in world shipping as well; therefore, any attempt to develop U.S.-flag tramps was considered "a backwards policy" since the tramps had supposedly become obsolete in the world trade.[24] Nevertheless, in a subsequent 1939 report, the U.S. Maritime Commission discreetly admitted that "tramp carriers are important, particularly in the Atlantic-Gulf coastwise trade."[25] Predictions about the demise or disappearance of tramps in world shipping were wrong, but the survival of any U.S.-flag tramps in what was regarded as a "cutthroat business" was certainly far from certain.

□ **Liner Services**   Unlike tramps (who wander about without any fixed schedule), liner services follow previously announced regular sailings, much like the itineraries of cruise ships in the late twentieth century. Liner services in turn were divided into those primarily engaged in either the domestic or the foreign trade, with considerable overlap between both. Traditionally, since the nineteenth century, tonnage in domestic trade had far exceeded the U.S.-flag ships in the foreign trade; only with the inclusion of foreign-flag ships of U.S. companies (in particular the International Mercantile Marine after 1902) did the foreign-trade sector acquire a more respectable size. After World War I, operators bought surplus Shipping Board vessels for the domestic trades, which were soon overtonnaged. Rivalries between the lines in domestic service led to rate wars, and by the late 1930s the coastwise and intercoastal operators had been reduced to 10 principal companies and a fluctuating number of smaller outfits. Firms like Luckenbach, Pope and Talbot, and American-Hawaiian provided the liner services; the Admiral Line (predominant in the Pacific coastwise trade) had not survived the bankruptcy in 1938 of the Dollar family, its main stockholder.[26]

The decline of the coastwise and intercoastal lines was caused primarily by competition from the railroads who, in order to grab the cargo, obtained the approval of the Interstate Commerce Commission to undercut the water carriers. The 1912 law prohibiting the railroads from operating ships via the Panama Canal had essentially given the railroads a green light to try to destroy the intercoastal lines. As the railroads laid more track, they also reached cities and communities whose only previous link with the outside world had been coastal steamers. Passenger traffic was also sharply curtailed by the spread of the railroad and highway network between the two world wars. By the end of the 1930s, many domestic steamship lines were bankrupt, and those who had survived lacked funds to replace their vessels, which were on the average at least 20 years old. There were few new vessels and quite a few relics in the domestic coastwise and intercoastal service, and although in some cases unsound management was responsible for the bankruptcy of individual firms, in general the prospects were bleak for domestic services.[27]

The gradual collapse of coastwise and intercoastal service meant that American consumers would soon have to pay the higher prices associated with other forms of cargo transportation. For the lines in U.S. foreign trade, the crisis in coastwise and intercoastal service eliminated an important if not vital safety net. In cases like Waterman and Lykes Brothers, coastwise operations had been a complement to their foreign services, providing a dependable base of revenue. The intercoastal trade had the added advantage of being easily worked into the Far East runs of U.S. lines. Whether the coastal service had been considered as a complement, a safety net, or just a final retreat, the crisis in coastwise and intercoastal shipping necessarily adversely affected the lines engaged in foreign trade, whose survival strategies were thus dangerously undermined.

□   The End of the International Mercantile Marine

The successful acquisition of United States Lines in October 1931 had not improved I.M.M.'s financial position. The mail subsidies did not bail out I.M.M. for long either, and the company's annual losses increased from 1932. The executives of I.M.M. had believed that the takeover of United State Lines would cancel the effects of the crucial 1926 decision to sell the British-flag White Star Line, but they had greatly miscalculated. To make things worse, the buyer of the White

Star Line, the Royal Mail Steam Packet Company, had gone bankrupt, leaving large payments to I.M.M. outstanding. For the latter, it was imperative to receive the large sums still pending on the sale, but as late as 1934, I.M.M. had obtained no satisfaction and was finally forced to bring a lawsuit in English courts to defend its contract rights. Royal Mail Steam Packet Company had originally toyed with the possibility of selling the White Star Line back to I.M.M., the most logical solution to the problems of both companies, but unfortunately anti-British sentiment (at a fever pitch in the United States) precluded this option for I.M.M.

In January 1934 the White Star Line was finally acquired by Cunard, I.M.M.'s most formidable competitor on the North Atlantic. The British government lavished subsidies on Cunard to finish building two new superliners, the "Queens," which would immediately make obsolete and ridiculously small the *Manhattan* and the *Washington* (the two recently launched U.S.-flag passenger liners of the I.M.M.). Germany was competing no less vigorously for traffic on the North Atlantic with the new liners the *Bremen* and the *Europa*. As I.M.M. explained, "there never was a time when the United States Lines and our other properties were more desperately in need of the full support and backing of the United States government."[28] Unfortunately for I.M.M., the fierce foreign challenge coincided with tremendous hostility in the United States because of the Senate mail investigation under Hugo Black. The revelations of the Black Committee created strong public sentiment against the U.S. steamship companies but failed to trigger a government takeover of the private firms.

I.M.M. had no choice but to begin cutting losses, starting with the largest steamer then afloat, the *Leviathan*, which was finally laid up in September 1934. The *Leviathan* had already exceeded its 20-year service life, and it had been showing losses on its voyages for some time because it was slow compared to the new rival superliners. The fact that the *Leviathan* was laid up just three years after its acquisition by I.M.M., after the Shipping Board had operated it successfully for years, seemed suspicious to many Americans.[29] A bitter anti-British campaign flourished in the media and in the Hearst press, which cited the laying up of the *Leviathan* as incontestable proof of a wicked British plot to destroy the U.S. merchant marine. The headlines blared titles like "British Deals Duped America in Ship Rivalry," "*Leviathan* Rotting in Plot to Wreck Merchant Marine," "More U.S. Ships Face Scuttling in Secret Pact; American Financiers Aided in Conspiracy."[30] The text of the articles explained the nature of the charges: "High-powered finance, the British government and the Shipping Board have wrecked the American merchant marine. This conspiracy began thirty-two years ago and is not yet finished. Its perpetrators have a juicy bit of business yet to consummate. . . . Congress should put an immediate end to the whole brazen scheme whereby a part of American mail money is findings its way, or will find its way, into the cash register of a company under contract with the British government to serve the interests of British trade and the British merchant marine."[31]

These and other sensational accusations drove I.M.M. into a corner; its president P. A. S. Franklin, described the journalistic articles as "absolutely inaccurate, unfair, unsound, most unkind—they are terrible," but to no avail.[32] I.M.M. and all other foreign-flag operators had already been condemned by American public opinion. Without any chance to explain or present their side, all U.S. steamship companies owning foreign-flag ships were considered unpatriotic; no logical argument was possible against highly nationalistic anti-British feelings, and the codification of the prohibition against ownership of foreign-flag ships by subsidized U.S. lines was a foregone conclusion in the 1936 Merchant Marine Act. The inflamed charges against I.M.M. were most unjust because the company, sensing the rising nationalistic wave of anti-British sentiment in the United States, had been slashing its foreign-flag fleet since 1926. Those ships still not disposed of in the early 1930s were mainly still there because of the Great Depression: the company saw no need to take a heavy loss on selling them at depressed prices when buyers were not available and when the ships continued to earn profits in their regular runs.

By 1935, I.M.M. had disposed of almost all its foreign-flag ships, a major sacrifice that the company understood would be compensated by the award of generous government subsidies indispensable to maintain the costlier U.S.-flag services. Initially the government kept its side of the bargain and assigned the mail contracts to some of I.M.M.'s routes. However, the 1936 Merchant Marine Act substituted the operating-differential subsidy, which supposedly covered the difference between the higher U.S. and lower foreign cost of operating a ship; in fact, the new subsidies were considerably less generous than the mail contracts and also subject to stringent regulations. I.M.M. should not have accepted the change from mail to operating subsidies, and in retrospect it also should have considered abandoning the shipping business as Pacific Mail had done in 1915. Franklin's emotional attachment to ocean shipping and his son John's desire to equal his father's prestige convinced them to persevere at a time when many other firms were "coming ashore" to more stable businesses on land. I.M.M. agreed in 1937 to the terms of the operating subsidy, but at the same time it realized that the practices of previous decades had to be drastically overhauled if the firm was to survive under the more modest government support and without the safety net of foreign flags.

A penetrating inquiry of I.M.M. in 1937 revealed areas in need of change. Before anything else, management had to pinpoint exactly the nature of the losses since 1932, but fortunately there was no reason for immediate alarm: "These deficits would constitute a serious drain on the company were it not for the fact that the losses reported above are the result in large part of substantial depreciation charges which, in our opinion, are excessive."[33] Thus management could simply juggle the figures to make most losses disappear; lowering depreciation charges made vessel replacement harder in the future, but this problem was left for another generation to solve. A second reason for the losses was discovered to be more political: "There is likewise ample reason to believe that it is to the advantage of the management that this group not show a profit. So long as deficits be reported it is possible to lay claims for the maintenance and perhaps increase of ship subsidies. Successful operation would obviously raise the question as to whether American shipping needed such subsidies."[34]

Government observers had always been baffled by the high operating costs of I.M.M.; for example, the same ships run by the Shipping Board when handed over to I.M.M. had costs from 20 to 25 percent higher—one more powerful argument for lower-cost government operation. The explanation tied in with management's need in the 1920s and 1930s to avoid declaring profits:

> Payments for a great number of services for which I.M.M. makes charges to subsidiaries are in turn made over to small service companies privately owned by various officers and directors of I.M.M. The imposition of these charges to that extent accounts in part for the high cost of operations. . . . Total salaries, including commissions, bonuses, etc., paid the officers and executives of I.M.M. and affiliated companies receiving over $7,500 per year have averaged during the depression years about $600,000 per year. We do not believe that this point needs further elaboration or additional evidence need be presented that the I.M.M. is largely run by the management for their own particular benefit.[35]

These comfortable arrangements were possible so long as I.M.M. was running foreign-flag ships and receiving abundant government subsidies, but with none of the former and a sharp reduction in the latter, management proceeded to prune its organization. A lot of fat had appeared in managerial ranks, and the branch offices scattered in all the major cities of the United States and many in Europe had overgrown their cargo volumes. On 1 July 1937, I.M.M. ceased to provide the agency services for its main subsidiary, United States Lines. I.M.M. retreated to its original conception of simply being a holding company with few operating functions. Instead, United States Lines proceeded to create its own smaller network of offices throughout the country and Europe; it tapped the best brains and personnel of I.M.M., but those not called were out of jobs. Supposedly a leaner and smaller managerial team would allow United States Lines to survive future circumstances less propitious than any I.M.M. had ever faced before.

No less urgent for United States Lines was the need to maintain its position in the North Atlantic trade routes against sharp foreign competition. The *Leviathan* was sold for scrap in December 1937, thereby ending the drain of expenses for this obsolete ship. As far as a replacement, no "monster ships" like the *Queens* were possible for United States Lines without a lavish government subsidy. The construction-differential subsidy of the 1936 Merchant Marine Act was supposed to cover the difference between the higher U.S. cost and the lower foreign cost of building a vessel, in fact only allowed placing an order for the *America,* a modest-size passenger vessel, which was finally completed in 1940. The *America,* in combination with the older *Manhattan* and *Washington,* provided a fairly adequate U.S.-flag passenger service on the North Atlantic.[36].

Other I.M.M. operations had to be restructured to ensure the company's survival. The steamers *California, Pennsylvania,* and *Virginia* had been constructed for the intercoastal trade in 1928 and 1929, but from 1931 on they had consistently produced substantial losses, even with ample mail subsidies. The end of the mail subsidies made intolerable the continued operation of these combination cargo-passenger ships, which instead were ideally suited for the New York–east coast of South America service. The Shipping Board had assigned the route to the Munson Line in the midst of complex bankruptcy and bailout arrangements since 1934; to solve both companies' problems, in December 1937 I.M.M. proposed to buy the remaining assets of the Munson Line, thereby acquiring the routes on which to operate profitably the *California, Pennsylvania,* and *Virginia.* I.M.M. had never before served the South American route, and its negative public image as a monopoly trust easily convinced the U.S. Maritime Commission to block the takeover. Nevertheless, the U.S. Maritime Commission purchased the three vessels and agreed either to operate them itself or to assign them to another private operator to keep running the New York–east coast of South America service. The U.S. Maritime Commission spent a large sum modernizing the three vessels, but rather than operate them itself, in 1938 the government accepted the purchase offer of Moore-McCormack for the three ships, now renamed the *Argentina, Brazil,* and *Uruguay* and known collectively as the "Good Neighbor Fleet."[37]

The sale of the three intercoastal vessels turned a tidy profit for I.M.M., which still had to solve a problem with another of its smaller subsidiaries, the Baltimore Mail Steamship Company, created in 1930. Baltimore Mail had failed to qualify for an operating subsidy, and without government funds the company could no longer maintain its service of five vessels between Baltimore and northern European ports. The sale of the *California, Pennsylvania,* and *Virginia* had left a gap in the intercoastal services, and now I.M.M. conveniently filled the need by turning the task over to the Baltimore Mail Steamship Company in August 1938. The older and smaller freighters were better suited for the intercoastal trade, and they performed with satisfactory results in this protected trade.[38]

The outbreak of World War II on 1 September 1939 completely disrupted the sailing schedules of United States Lines as well as the other subsidiaries of I.M.M., and many freighters were laid up. The loss of its foreign-flag ships in 1935 and the failure to receive ample subsidies had put the company in a precarious position. To bail out the company, which was facing cash-flow problems, United States Lines received a government loan from the Reconstruction Finance Corporation on 17 December 1941. Those emergency funds helped support United States Lines until the profits from chartering all its ships to the government started to materialize.

In spite of all the pro-British sentiment during World War II, United States Lines fully understood that American nationalism had not decreased at all and that the older conception of international arrangements to conduct shipping operations was politically unfeasible in the United States. As a U.S.-flag concern since 1935, the company had to do everything in its power to sell itself to the skeptical American public as a loyal and patriotic organization, not subservient in the remotest way to foreign interests. The old I.M.M. name had become not only an anachronism but a liability as well. Without fanfare, the name of that creation of J. P. Morgan, the International Mercantile Marine, was dropped on 21 May 1943, whereupon United States Lines assumed any remaining holding functions. An era in U.S. shipping had come to an end.[39]

Part III.
The Container Age

8

World War II

WORLD WAR II HAD a decisive and lasting impact on U.S. steamship companies, as this and later chapters show. Merchant shipping was also decisive for the outcome of World War II, a conclusion apparently not fully shared by the U.S. government, which so far has declined to write an official history of U.S. shipping during the war. The following three sections sketch selected events and decisions that most influenced the postwar course of U.S. steamship companies.

☐ Neutrality and Flags of Convenience

When Germany invaded Poland on 1 September 1939, most Americans were determined to stay out of World War II. Isolationist sentiment was so strong in the United States that in spite of tough neutrality laws on the books, mounting political pressure called for additional legislation. The sinking of U.S. merchant vessels had triggered the United States' entry into World War I, and isolationists were determined to prevent a recurrence of a similar chain of events. Senator Key Pittman, chairman of the Senate Foreign Relations Committee, introduced a bill that placed sweeping restrictions on shipping to any belligerent country. The State Department with presidential support from Franklin D. Roosevelt was able to limit the bill's coverage to the European area. The

Neutrality Act signed by the President on 4 November 1939 did allow England and France to purchase war goods, but U.S.-flag ships could not go to their ports, nor to those of Germany, Ireland, Sweden, Denmark, Netherlands, Belgium, the Baltic, and Norway south of Bergen. The law, usually called the "cash-and-carry" law, also excluded U.S. ships from areas in the Far East proclaimed by the president to be in a state of war. Roosevelt declined to issue the proclamation because excluding U.S.-flag ships would only help Japan, the aggressor who had a large navy and merchant marine, while punishing China, the victim, who had neither of those resources.[1]

The subterfuge of failing to declare that a state of war existed would not be tolerated for Europe by the isolationists, so another way had to be found around the cash-and-carry provisions in order to help England and France. Two days after the passage of the law, United States Lines applied for permission to transfer 9 vessels to the Panamanian flag. No other steamship company depended as much as United States Lines on the North Atlantic routes for the bulk of its trade, and hence the urgency of the application. The request backfired and turned into a public relations disaster, with claims that "the deal smacked of trickery."[2] Under mounting criticism, the Roosevelt administration worked out an alternate formula, essentially that United States Lines would sell the ships to a foreign dummy corporation, whereupon the U.S. Maritime Commission would approve the transfer of registry. The company first picked Norway for the transfer, but that country, feeling pressure from Germany in January 1940, refused to accept the transfer, whereupon the company placed 9 freighters under the Belgian flag. By December 1940 6 of the 9 had been sunk (only one would survive the war), and as replacements, the company bought from the U.S. Maritime Commission 5 vessels that were quietly registered under the Panamanian flag to bypass the neutrality prohibition. Other steamship companies with less visibility than United States Lines used the Panamanian registry from the outbreak of the war. Between September 1939 and June 1941 the U.S. Maritime Commission approved the transfer of 63 U.S.-flag vessels to Panamanian registry, which provided a convenient way around the Neutrality Act. If the ships were sunk, neither the government nor U.S. citizens were involved, and hence a repetition of the chain of events leading to World War I was impossible.

The Panamanian registry had a lasting impact on the U.S. merchant marine, but in 1939–41 it was only one of four alternatives to the shipping restrictions in the cash-and-carry law of November 1939. Actually, the most important option was the sale and transfer of ships to Britain for operation under the British flag and with no U.S. crews.

From September 1939 to June 1941 the 126 vessels transferred to England were double the tonnage shifted to the Panamanian flag. Selling vessels to neutrals, most notably to Brazil, was a third option of lesser importance, although it eased the demand for British crews, since crews of other nationalities were used. A final alternative carried out without fanfare was the redeployment of U.S. and British vessels. Great Britain gradually relinquished parts or all of certain ocean routes to U.S. vessels, thereby releasing British vessels to carry cargoes on the North Atlantic. In the case of multinationals like Exxon, the shifts took place within the company: Canadian- and British-flag vessels (joined by Panamanian) were redeployed to replace the few U.S.-flag tankers pulled out of the Atlantic by the Neutrality Act.[3]

The growing realization that a victory by Nazi Germany was not in the best interests of the United States gradually paved the acceptance for all of those alternatives as ways to help England. Isolationists were decisively routed on 11 March 1941 when Congress passed the Lend-Lease Act, which provided an effective means to help England and other Allies that were running out of monetary reserves. Lend-Lease repealed the "cash" but not the "carry" part of the November 1939 Neutrality Act, and hence Panamanian registry and the other alternatives remained just as vital to bypass the shipping restrictions, since Americans were still not ready to accept the sinking of the U.S.-manned and U.S.-flag ships on the North Atlantic. The Coast Guard took under protective custody the interned ships of the German, Italian, and Danish merchant fleets on 30 March 1941, and after the passage of the enabling legislation on 6 June, those not transferred to the U.S. flag were placed under Panamanian registry and also armed; the crews of the Danish ships were also trained in the use of the weapons.

The United States was moving inexorably toward the side of England, and on 15 September 1941 a presidential proclamation reduced the British part of the exclusion zone to only the United Kingdom, thereby releasing U.S. ships to steam to the rest of the overseas possessions and territories of the British Empire. From September 1941 on the sinking of U.S. merchant vessels and repeated German attacks on U.S. merchant ships, as well as on a destroyer, provided the needed support for the repeal of the "carry" provisions of the Neutrality Act. Finally on 17 November 1941 Congress authorized the sailing of armed U.S. merchant ships to England.[4]

With the repeal of the Neutrality Act's prohibition against sailing to England, Panamanian registry appeared to have become superfluous, but instead of being phased out it remained as one of the shipping legacies of World War II. Panamanian registry had existed prior to 1939, but it was not widely known, and it had been used mainly by the fleets of the fruit and oil companies. For private companies, the Panamanian flag meant not only profits but also the avoidance of constant government hassles and red tape. For the U.S. government, the Panamanian flag became an effective tool to use when subterfuges were needed either during or after World War II. U.S. official approval and backing was essential to keep the registry system on track: President Arnulfo Arias decided on 6 October 1941 to cancel the Panamanian registry of vessels armed by the U.S., yet three days later, after assurance of U.S. support to plotters, he was overthrown. The new local government rushed to ratify the arming of Panamanian vessels, although the State Department insisted in public there was no coincidence between the two events.[5]

U.S. entry into World War II after 7 December 1941 did not diminish the need for Panamanian registry. Complex legal and labor problems made Admiral Emory Land reluctant to bring the Panamanian vessels under U.S. registry, and actually the number of vessels flying the Panamanian flag continued to increase during the war. One estimate puts the number of Panamanian-flag vessels sunk or captured during World War II at 158, with the loss of over 1,500 seamen.

Panamanian registry also provided steamship companies with a valuable substitute for the traditional alternative of registry under the British flag. As the dissolution of the British Empire accelerated at the end of World War II, many advantages of British registry, such as using Oriental crews, dwindled away. Panamanian registry, in spite of bothersome fees and some quasigraft payments, was quite acceptable, but it did raise the danger that outside pressures on that one weak and volatile country might endanger the registry system. As an additional safeguard, oil companies created another registry at Liberia in December 1948, thereby giving shipowners a choice between Panama and Liberia. The flag of convenience system, called "runaway flags" by opponents, was now fully institutionalized, and it would become one more factor in the troubles of the U.S. merchant marine after World War II.[6]

□ The Road to War

The outbreak of World War II on 1 September 1939 immediately affected U.S. shipping. Rates rose and continued to increase, allowing many companies to recover the losses of previous years. The value of ships skyrocketed; even old hulks and relics on the way to scrapping now found eager buyers, particularly in England. The Allied blockade kept U.S. shipping out of Baltic and German ports, but thanks to the preponderance of the combined English and French navies, the initial disruption of the sea lanes was not very great. Steamship companies expected a repeat of the high profits of World War I, but the illusion of easy profits was shattered on 4 November 1939 when Congress passed the Neutrality Act, which excluded U.S. ships from the majority of European ports, including England.

The loss of the European routes could have been a crippling blow to U.S. steamship companies in peacetime, but the unusual wartime situation and exorbitant rates provided many alternatives. The previous section discussed the transfer of many U.S. ships to foreign flags, but there were other solutions as well. Moore-McCormack rerouted its Baltic service to the north to Bergen in Norway, a port that remained outside the zone excluded by the Neutrality Act until May 1940. Black Diamond Lines chartered its U.S.-flag ships for operation in safe routes, but it maintained its service to Holland by chartering foreign-flag ships. United States Lines, the hardest hit, laid up all its freighters except for nine transferred to the Belgian flag. The company placed its two older passenger liners, the *Washington* and the *Manhattan*, in the Italy to New York run, because the Mediterranean initially remained outside the prohibitions of the Neutrality Act. For several companies like Lykes Brothers Steamship and American-Hawaiian, the best policy was to sell their older ships at inflated prices, thereby reaping a huge windfall profit; with only a small fraction of the proceeds from the sale, these and other companies qualified to place orders for the new state-of-the-art C-type ships the U.S. Maritime Commission had designed and was offering at low subsidized prices.

It is easy to overlook the fact that World War II solved the vessel replacement problem for U.S. steamship companies. Most of the ships in operation were the result of the crash building program of World War I. In 1940 U.S.-flag ships faced block obsolescence, that is, almost all ships had become average and were no longer suited for their trade; obsolescence is generally measured at 20 years, although in Third World countries with lower repair and maintenance costs, ships may be operated for 30 or even 40 years. In the United States, such a strategy has not been feasible, and to avoid mounting repair and insurance charges, the ships must be replaced. The provisions of the Merchant Marine Act of 1936 convinced most shipowners to allow their fleets to shrink if not disappear, foreshadowing what later happened again in the 1960s. Thus, when late in 1938 the U.S. Maritime Commission announced its long-range program of building 50 of the new C-type ships during the next 10 years, that prospective assistance was an essential

but minor consideration for shipowners; unless the expected rates
would cover the rest of their expenses and still allow adequate profits,
they would not purchase additional ships. Steamship executives have
always known that war, when at last the true value of ships is appreciated, means high profits. From 1938 on shipowners and the U.S. Maritime Commission were both in a sense responding to the expectation
of another major war: the latter by beginning the shipbuilding program, and the former by placing the orders and more importantly making the commitment to operate the ships and indeed stay in the
steamship business.[7]

The German offensives in May 1940, the Fall of France in June,
and Italy's entry into the war brought new complications to U.S. shipping. All of Europe, including the Mediterranean, had become a war
zone, and U.S.-flag ships could now sail under the provisions of the
Neutrality Act only to Lisbon, served solely by the American Export
Lines. The "Four Aces" of American Export as well as its freighters
were swamped with passengers fleeing war-torn Europe, and they were
booked solid for months in advance; nonetheless, the U.S. Maritime
Commission refused to allow the United States Lines to shift the liners
Manhattan and *Washington* to the Lisbon routes, not daring to risk big
passenger ships that would soon be in tremendous demand during the
war. To make things worse for the company, in July 1940 the shipyard
delivered the *America,* the largest and most modern U.S.-flag passenger liner. United States Lines placed the *America,* along with the older
Washington and *Manhattan,* on the intercoastal service. After the de-
stroyers-for-bases agreement with England on 2 September 1940, the
liners ferried U.S. troops to the leased Caribbean bases, yet they continued to incur heavy losses until they were finally chartered to the
military in May 1941.

The U.S. Maritime Commission realized that a shipping crunch
was imminent, and on 27 August 1940 it decided to speed up its long-
term program so that 200 C-type ships would be contracted by July
1941. By October 1940 47 ships had been delivered and 130 more were
under contract, considerably ahead of the accelerated schedule. The response of the steamship companies remained decisive, because their expectations of profits had in the first place contributed to fuel the
demands for a larger shipbuilding program. An additional attractiveness
was the quality of the commission's cargo ships. The designs for the C-
1, C-2, and C-3 combined the optimal characteristics for both military
and commercial purposes. The steam turbine ships had the same fuel
consumption as the older 11-knot ships, but they reached greater speeds
(15.5 knots for the C-2, 16.5 for the C-3); in some ships the installation
of different machinery produced even higher speeds. Certainly the

combination of speed and fuel economy was irresistible to both the military and commercial operators. The C-types were sleek, modern ships designed by the Technical Division of the U.S. Maritime Commission, which rightly took pride in its accomplishment.[8]

Britain had begun to feel a shipping crunch after the Fall of France in June 1940. From the start of the war Britain had made the potentially fatal mistake of underestimating the cargo-carrying capacity needed to supply the island. This blunder was incomprehensible, especially because the situation for the island so closely paralleled that of World War I; as a lame excuse, part of the blame was placed on the writers of books about the World War I shipping experience for not being sufficiently clear, and the rest on the "ignorance of the audience" that made no effort to understand these books.[9] Not having adequately digested the World War I lessons, Britain found after June 1940 new obstacles, not the least of which were the conversion of French ports into U-boat bases and the closing of the Mediterranean to British shipping. This last development was particularly significant, because ships coming from Asia could no longer use the Suez Canal route but instead had to sail around the Cape of Good Hope in Africa, adding thousands of miles to their voyages. So while the shortage of ships was real enough, the shortage of cargo-carrying capacity quickly became critical. As the fastest solution, in October 1940 the British established a Merchant Shipping Mission in the United States that placed orders in shipyards for 60 ships of identical design to speed up delivery.

The U.S. Maritime Commission, including its chairman, Admiral Emory Land, wanted to stay as far away as possible from the British ship order. The British wanted a cheap, easy-to-build, blunt-bow 10-knot tramp; they drew a sort of composite of pre–World War II British tramps, but with too many throwbacks to the pre–World War I ships, long since obsolete. For the high-speed battle raging in the North Atlantic, when Royal Navy escort vessels were few and dangerously far between, the British decision to place this big order for tramps rather than faster and better-equipped vessels was certainly a serious mistake. Land waged a campaign against any idea of U.S. participation in the British tramp construction program: "The last thing I want to do is to repeat the mistakes of the last war and have a lot of obsolete vessels on our hands unless the emergency is so great as to make this an absolute necessity."[10] Land's repeated entreaties were unavailing, and President Roosevelt announced on 3 January 1941 that the United States would build an additional 200 ships of similar design to the British 60.

The U.S. Maritime Commission had been overruled by the president, on the argument that speed in delivery was more important than speed in steaming. The British shipping community soon woke up to

the blunder and, after the initial 60-ship order, shifted to faster freighters, but in the United States an unstoppable bureaucratic process had
begun. By existing U.S. statutory regulations, the British design was
substandard, so that the crew's facilities and quarters had to be drastically improved. The most significant difference was using oil rather
than coal as the fuel; also, the installation of a single midship house
made the vessels look different from the British prototype. Called the
"ugly ducklings," they soon were more properly baptized as "Liberty"
ships. The first Liberties went into service in January 1942, and as the
mass-production assembly techniques were perfected, delivery time was
shortened until the vast outpouring of Liberties became the majority of
the merchant shipbuilding program in the United States between 1942
and 1944.[11]

In 1941 the Liberties were still in the future, and so the United
States had to take additional steps to meet the urgent shipping requirements. After the passage of Lend-Lease in March 1941, the U.S. Maritime Commission decided to assume authority over all U.S.-owned
ships, whether U.S.-flag or foreign, and thereby it was able to bring
pressure upon United Fruit Company to shift four of its foreign-flag
vessels of the Great White Fleet to serve the new bases in the British
Caribbean; likewise, the foreign-flag ships of Alcoa became available
for rerouting to critical areas. Yet shipping shortages continued to appear, particularly in Latin America, whose supplies of raw materials and
other commodities were considered vital. As ocean rates continued to
climb sky-high in mid-1941, the pressure for drastic action mounted.

Pressuring the individual companies to serve this or that route was
no longer considered adequate, and in May 1941 the U.S. Maritime
Commission created a shipping pool of about 2 million deadweight tons
to be placed and operated under its central control. Where did the ships
come from? The easiest to use were the Axis ships interned in U.S.
ports and under government custody; they provided about half a million tons. The last of the laid-up vessels from World War I were reactivated and refitted to provide additional tonnage. The new C-type
vessels as they were delivered by the shipyards entered the pool, and
the commission also commandeered 50 U.S.-owned but foreign-flag
tankers to guarantee the supply of oil to Britain from Venezuela. Those
provisions still did not meet the pressing needs, so roughly half of the
intercoastal fleet (the ships most readily available for wartime emergency) was seized to provide another three-quarters of a million tons;
the cargo previously carried aboard the intercoastal ships was now
dumped on the railroads.[12]

Outside of the shipping pool remained almost all the vessels of the
U.S. steamship companies engaged in the foreign trade. The firms con-

tinued to operate traditional routes to Latin America, Asia, and Africa, and increasingly they replaced British vessels pulled out from those regions and sent for service to the North Atlantic. For example, in June 1941 the U.S. Maritime Commission announced that U.S. steamship companies had assumed the Canada-Australia route, thereby releasing British-flag ships. But the most famous or infamous steamship operation took place in the Middle East and was known as the "Red Sea charters." With rates shooting higher all the time, the companies decided to make big profits, when the purpose of this operation was to supply the British under German attack in Egypt. Land, sometimes considered probusiness, correctly summed up the issue: "Rightly or wrongly, the Red Sea operators made excessive profits and the fact that they might have made even more money in some other operation has nothing whatsoever to do with the case. The fact still remains that excessive profits were made and more excess in something would be no justification for less excess in the Red Sea operations. Rightly or wrongly, the Red Sea operators have placed in jeopardy any legislation favorable to the American Merchant Marine which may come before the Congress."[13]

Land's words were prophetic. After the war, the revelations of the Red Sea charters as well as other cases of profiteering were played up in the media. U.S. steamship companies, which never had recovered from the public relations disaster of the Hugo Black Committee in 1933, faced a renewed barrage of public hostility and distrust. In 1941 enough information about such activities did filter out to make the public demands for stricter government safeguards irresistible. The repeal on 17 November 1941 of the Neutrality Act prohibition on U.S. shipping to Europe made government control inevitable. Britain was a high-risk zone for insuring ships, and steamship companies could go only if they charged rates high enough to cover the risks. The U.S. Maritime Commission refused to approve such rates, and consequently to have U.S. ships sail to England from November 1941 to the end of the war the government had to assume the risks. Time was needed to work out the new arrangements, but before they could be put in place, the Japanese attack against Pearl Harbor on 7 December 1941 brought the United States directly into World War II.[14]

□ The War Shipping Administration

The attack on Pearl Harbor found as many as two hundred U.S. vessels exposed to Japanese attack on the wide expanses of the Pacific Ocean. U.S. shipping in the Western Hemisphere was not immediately affected by either the Japanese or German onslaughts, while sailings in the North Atlantic were already under heavy naval escort. But in the Pacific Ocean, the surprise factor so ably exploited by the Japanese did cause serious ship losses, whether the attacks came from planes, submarines, or armed merchant raiders. Against the unified Japanese offensive, U.S. merchant shipping presented a disorganized front. American President Lines had suspended its regular sailing schedules since midsummer 1941, but partial government requisitions had left some vessels in commercial service. In the case of lines like Matson and Lykes Brothers, most of their ships were still plying commercial routes in the Pacific.

Almost all service to Japanese-controlled areas had ended prior to Pearl Harbor, but costly mistakes still occurred, the most noteworthy being the tardy evacuation of U.S. forces from China. The military ordered the American President Lines' *President Harrison* and *President Wilson* to evacuate a U.S. Marine battalion from Shanghai to the Philippines, a mission these two passenger liners accomplished by 4 December 1941. The *President Harrison* then received orders to return to evacuate the legation guard in Beijing, so that on Pearl Harbor day, the liner was steaming near the coast of Japanese-controlled China and was quickly spotted; in an attempt to avoid capture, the captain ran the ship aground. The Japanese soon had the ship back in service, and the United States saw the shortage of passenger space made even more acute by the loss of this liner.[15]

To avoid more costly mistakes, full centralized control of U.S. shipping had become a necessity, and the U.S. Maritime Commission proceeded to take over the rest of the ships of the steamship companies. In January 1942 the government also requisitioned those ships still remaining in the intercoastal service. The shipbuilding program was proceeding rapidly, with all ships previously ordered by private companies requisitioned for official service, while the rest of the vast shipbuilding output was feeding directly into the huge government fleet. Would the five-member U.S. Maritime Commission be able to provide the decisive leadership needed for merchant shipping during the war? Independent regulatory commissions still enjoyed great prestige (which was not seriously eroded until the 1970s), but President Roosevelt did not want to take chances, and already he had packed the U.S. Maritime Commission with three navy men, including the chairman, Admiral Land.

Formal meetings were still held, and the civilian members continued to ponder with all deliberate care the weighty issues of wartime shipping, but Land soon tired of the arrangements: "You know, I don't believe in the commission form of government; I think you ought to have a one-man show and shoot him at sunrise if he doesn't run it right."[16] The British, at the same time, had been pressing the United

States to create a single unified authority to control shipping, both for civilian and military use. The president was convinced and, using the authority of the War Powers Act, he created the War Shipping Administration on 7 February 1942. Land became the head of the new agency but retained the chairmanship of the U.S. Maritime Commission. The other two navy commissioners also received positions within the War Shipping Administration, as did many other executive officials who held joint appointment in both agencies; a number of divisions and bureaus, such as personnel, provided the same services for both agencies. The considerable overlap and dual membership did not hide a clear division of labor: the U.S. Maritime Commission concentrated on shipbuilding, while the War Shipping Administration operated and directed the vessels. Yet this division was never considered final because it was understood that if the two civilian members of the U.S. Maritime Commission needlessly blocked or harassed vessel construction, then under the War Powers Act, the president could at any moment promptly transfer the entire shipbuilding program to the War Shipping Administration, an eventuality that never occurred.[17]

The War Shipping Administration has remained the forgotten agency of the U.S. war effort, and although its operations are largely beyond the scope of this book, which is focused on the business side, some minimal comments are needed to understand postwar events.[18] Two essential characteristics must be stressed. First, the War Shipping Administration was an umbrella organization or, better yet, a holding company; the agency owned or had on long-term charter all U.S.-owned ships irrespective of their flag. For the actual operation of the ships, the agency relied on the individual steamship companies for use of their regular crews. As larger numbers of ships came from the yards, the number of ships assigned to each company was increased accordingly. This way the War Shipping Administration avoided the need to create a new shipping organization for management and operation and instead could concentrate on the heart of the shipping business—namely, space allocation. The key to success was to operate "all merchant ships out of a fluid pool from which the constantly changing requirements for merchant tonnage can be adapted to the available tonnage . . . efficiency is only possible where tonnage is centrally controlled by an agency which can constantly shift vessels from one use to another in order to take advantage of ships in the geographic areas of conflict, in the requirements of the armed forces and in the needs of other claimants for vessel space."[19]

The principle of efficient space allocation was well recognized by the War Shipping Administration from its inception and stoutly defended throughout the war, in spite of later British claims that the English had to restrain themselves from delivering a "lecture" to the Americans on the subject. The obstacle was simply the U.S. military: the Joint Chiefs of Staff had no quarrel with a single government agency running civilian shipping requirements, but when the War Shipping Administration wanted to extend its control to military shipping, the U.S. Army and Navy not only refused but continued to build up their own merchant fleets, a mistake the British had wisely avoided. Put in commercial terms, the army and navy were acting like the proprietary steamship lines, such as United Fruit and Alcoa, while the War Shipping Administration represented the common carriers, which provided scheduled service for all shippers needing to move cargo. Who was right? U.S. military doctrine had grown out of the experience of quick and usually limited conflicts, World War I being too brief to change this line of thinking radically; clearly for such conflicts control by the military of their own shipping was recommended. But for total conflicts like World War II, which required the mobilization of the entire economy for victory, civilian needs assumed a greater importance. The most efficient allocation of cargo space between civilian and military needs (not always incompatible) became mandatory. In a major illustration, the vessels of the War Shipping Administration steamed to the South Pacific to deliver military cargoes and returned loaded with raw materials for the war effort. Ships under army and navy control usually returned empty, and thus the only way out of the conflicting civilian and military demands was to build even more ships, thereby incurring even higher expenses in both shipbuilding and ship operation for the already prohibitively expensive war. The United States was forced to build more ships than were really needed for the war, because the U.S. military refused to allow a universal space allocation system under the War Shipping Administration like the one that existed in World War I under P. A. S. Franklin's Shipping Control Committee.[20]

The War Shipping Administration struggled continuously to convince the U.S. military of the need for universal space allocation. Another issue, labor, was no less trying for the government agency, but at least that problem was solved by the end of 1942. With the U.S. entry into World War II, the demand for seamen dramatically surged and continued to be high, particularly in the early months of 1942 when U-boats took a deadly toll in lives of U.S. seamen. The steamship lines combed their personnel files to track down former seamen, while the War Shipping Administration launched a massive publicity campaign to attract former as well as prospective seafarers. The use of former seamen gave the government enough time to establish massive training programs. The existing state maritime schools were vastly enlarged, and the federal government established the Merchant Marine Academy at King's Point, Long Island, in 1943. Most of the new personnel, however, were prepared in special training camps operating for the duration of the war.[21]

A political struggle erupted over the seafarers: would they remain civilians or become part of the military? The navy wanted to bring the merchant service under its control, much in the same way as had happened with the Coast Guard, the latter of course retaining its own institutions and chain of command: only operational control of the vessels had been shifted to the navy. Starting in the late 1930s, a strong labor movement had emerged among the seamen, and particularly aggressive union leaders saw in militarization a threat to their hard-won leadership positions. Rivalry between navy and merchant marine had been widespread before World War II, and it was not hard to whip up antinavy sentiment among the seafarers. Rumors spread quickly: first, that this move was simply a union-busting plot to reduce U.S. seamen to the atrocious standards of the pre–World War I era; and, second, that the navy would impose all the military trappings so hated by the seafarers—namely, uniforms, protocol, salutes, and excessive paperwork. Seamen's unions had been on strike in the months immediately before Pearl Harbor, and they carried a lot of votes and influence, so President Roosevelt naturally did not want to antagonize them unduly.

The resulting formula, mainly the product of short-sighted union leaders more interested in their own bureaucratic positions than in the welfare of the rank-and-file or in the long-term prospects of the merchant marine, had to be unsatisfactory. Rather than establishing the merchant service as another branch of military service comparable to the navy, army, and Coast Guard, each with their own traditional customs, rules, and practices, the seamen instead were kept in civilian status. The War Shipping Administration could not draw on the draft, so higher wages were necessary to lure civilians into this high-risk occupation; in fact, the merchant service suffered a higher percentage of casualties than any of the other armed services. Many unnecessary complications arose because of the violent opposition of labor leaders to military status. In this study, the postwar consequences are of even greater concern: since civilian seamen could not have access to the GI Bill for education or for veterans' benefits after the war, the slightly higher pay received by seamen during the conflict could not compare with postwar compensation. Union leaders later knew that they had blundered, and to try to make up the loss, they proceeded after the war to push wage demands to the highest levels in the world. In the period 1946–60 when lower union wages would have given some steamship companies a margin to work out a survival strategy, the companies found themselves faced with exorbitant wage demands, which could only be met by government subsidies. Not surprisingly, after the war labor largely replaced the steamship companies as the main proponents of government shipping subsidies.[22]

The legacy of labor was matched by the wartime legacy of ill-suited ships. Once the decision had been taken to build the obsolete Liberties, the blunder simply could not be stopped. The belief in a short war was one of the assumptions underlying the Liberty shipbuilding program, but by 1943 to continue to defend the Liberty as the only merchant ship design went against all shipping logic and experience. The U.S. Maritime Commission under Admiral Land had decided by 1942 to stop the construction of Liberties and instead shift to a faster vessel, the Victory, a simplified C-type design. While it was claimed that 25 percent more of the simple Liberties could be built, the faster C-type ships and the Victory ships had twice as large a cargo-carrying capacity. The War Shipping Administration struggled endlessly to explain to the War Production Board and other agencies the meaning of *cargo-carrying capacity*, as well as other shipping mysteries, but the uninitiated refused to listen. Land finally decided to get a clear military decision as to what ship was best suited for the war effort; after lengthy expositions by shipping adviser John M. Franklin, the Joint Chiefs of Staff finally decided the issue on 9 August 1943:

> Since the beginning of the shipbuilding program, the fast C ships, particularly the C-2 and C-3, have best met the strategic needs and have been seized to meet Army and Navy needs, often as combat ships. They are even now being rapidly converted as combat loaders and as combination passenger and cargo to fill vital military needs. The C-4 is building in direct response to Army requirements. The increased speed of these faster ships reduces the danger of loss of troops and cargo from submarine attack, shortens the time of turn around, decreases the requirements for escorts and saves crew manpower; advantages which it is held have justified their construction in the past and now with greater force will do so in the future.[23]

The decision of the Joint Chiefs of Staff cleared the road for the Victory ship construction, but precious time had already been lost in the bureaucratic wrangling. No Victories were delivered in 1943, and the first was ready only in February 1944, followed by only 14 more before May, so that in 1944 the shipbuilding program still remained weighted toward Liberties. Only in 1945 did the Victories at last displace the Liberties, whose ongoing construction momentum simply could not be stopped. Land had agreed with the British that the building program for the second semester of 1945 should include all Victories and no Liberties, yet it was impossible to turn the tap off, and at the end of the war, in August, Liberties were still being delivered and others remained in various stages of construction. Even before the war was over, the main problem had become lack of cargo for too many ships, the recurrent problem of commercial shipping operations. Clearly the United States wasted money building too many merchant ships for World War II, and the great majority were obsolete Liberties ill-suited to compete against the new and faster designs in the postwar commercial rivalries.[24]

There was no denying, however, that the War Shipping Administration had performed successfully the tremendous task of carrying not only the seaborne trade of the United States but also, for the first and last time in history, a majority of the world's ocean trade. At the end of World War I England's fleet had still been bigger than that of the United States, but at the end of World War II the United States emerged with the world's largest merchant fleet and a majority of the world's tonnage. This remarkable achievement could not disguise a number of serious but not irreparable mistakes. All the United States needed was careful attention to long-term concerns and, above all, the determination to retain at least a significant share of seaborne commerce for the country's merchant fleet, which had finally gained dominance in the high seas.

9

Retreat from Supremacy

THE UNITED STATES emerged from World War II as the leading maritime power, outranking even England, which for generations had owned the largest merchant fleet. Only by the most deliberate mobilization of resources under government control did the United States rise to preeminence by the end of World War II. If the United States was to retain an important presence in the world's sea lanes, a very careful policy, no less challenging than the wartime buildup, was required. Some crucial questions remained: How long would the United States remain a major shipping nation? More importantly, for how long did it *want* to ply the sea lanes?

☐ The Surplus Ship Sales

The question of what to do with the huge merchant fleet built by the government had repeatedly been raised both in public and in private, even before World War II had ended. As early as 1943, a number of Allied countries had requested title to some of the U.S.-built tonnage, yet prewar legislation made any permanent transfer of registry and ownership difficult. The Lend-Lease Act and other emergency legislation did allow the transfer of vessels for the duration of the war. Furthermore, President Franklin D. Roosevelt had promised British Prime Minister Winston S. Churchill that the United States would seek to replace the very heavy shipping losses suffered by England, and soon the United States extended similar assurances to Norway. Other Allied countries in Europe, as well as Brazil, now rushed to file their requests for special consideration in any distribution of the postwar U.S. merchant fleet.

The gathering international momentum to share in American ships was temporarily arrested in Congress when Schuyler Otis Bland, the chairman of the House Committee on Merchant Marine and Fisheries, introduced a bill that essentially prevented the sale of vessels to foreign countries or noncitizens. This was the shipowner's preferred policy: U.S. lines would have first choice of the surplus ships at bargain prices to replace their tonnage lost during the war, and the rest of the 61 million deadweight ton fleet, more than 60 percent of the world's tonnage, would be laid up and held in reserve. Government ownership of this vast reserve fleet endowed the United States with a powerful if unspoken deterrent. Control over vast numbers of ships conferred power, and although the United States did not aspire to retain the position of number one maritime power after the war, the more modest goal of carrying 50 percent of U.S. oceanborne commerce on U.S.-flag ships could easily be attained. In effect, the reserve fleet became a threat hanging over foreign lines, which would not dare risk the reprisal of the sudden entry of large numbers of U.S. ships into world routes.[1]

The deterrent policy was soon abandoned in late 1944 when the shipyards gained the upper hand in determining the disposition of the surplus vessels. The mounting international pressure to award ships to wartime allies served as the perfect argument to shape a policy benefiting the interests of the U.S. shipyards and their labor unions. While U.S. steamship firms still remained mildly optimistic about carrying a share of U.S. oceanborne trade, domestic shipyards knew they were finished unless something drastic could be done. At the very least, foreign shipyards had to be kept from reviving. If large numbers of U.S. ships were sold to foreign countries, shipyards abroad would receive few if any orders, giving the remaining domestic shipyards a rest from foreign shipbuilding competition. Furthermore, shipyard executives held the illusion that once foreign steamship companies operated U.S. vessels with their superior technology and many comfortable conveniences, foreign countries would demand more of these ships and consequently place future orders in U.S. shipyards, in spite of the latter's higher cost. Secrecy was vital for the shipyard rescue plan to work, and when a government official in a confidential report stated the strategy, in a private note he was quickly told to remove all references: "Don't give away our strategy in selling foreigners our ships."[2]

No amount of secrecy could fool the Europeans who, with centuries of maritime experience, were not going to allow their shipyards to be ruined by massive dumping on the part of the United States. European countries were very eager to buy surplus ships, but at the same time they revived their shipyards; access to surplus ships favored European shipyards in the long run since, not needing a crash expansion program after the war, they could concentrate on rebuilding their capacity to handle a permanent workload in both repair and vessel replacement by the 1950s. The real worry of the European steamship lines was that the U.S. government would continue to operate a substantial part of the wartime merchant fleet; the U.S. government already owned American President Lines, and since prewar policies to foster a private merchant marine had generally failed, "it must, therefore, be assumed that there would be considerable extension of state ownership in American shipping as compared with prewar."[3]

The rush to demobilize and strong ideological pressures in the United States soon dispelled the European steamship lines' lingering fear of having to compete against a government-owned and run fleet. In September 1945 Admiral Emory S. Land, head of the War Shipping Administration and of the U.S. Maritime Commission, was pressuring President Truman to obtain passage of the Ship Sales Bill: "this legislation should be in what is generically known as the 'must' column."[4] Every day that the government operated the vast wartime fleet benefited private operators and added to the profit of the U.S. Treasury, so that final passage of the bill came only in March 1946. As a concession to U.S. steamship companies, provisions in the law attempted to place foreign buyers last in the line to acquire ships, but the legislation contained enough administrative leeway to more than cancel these advantages.

Congress had really not faced the problem of the surplus ships, and the law essentially transferred the problem to the U.S. Maritime Commission, now more preoccupied with recovering its bureaucratic powers temporarily usurped by the War Shipping Administration. When the latter was dissolved on 1 September 1946 and its remaining functions were transferred to the U.S. Maritime Commission, a smooth transition was imperative to prevent the creation of an unwieldy and ineffective agency at a crucial moment in the country's shipping history; instead, the Commission, in an emotional outburst, decided to limit itself largely to "changing the hats" of the War Shipping Administration for Maritime Commission "hats." The Commissioners feared a revival of the era of Emory Land and took the position that they wanted to be in complete charge as a body and in direct contact with all operations subordinate to the Commission. The issue of the Chairman versus the other Commissioners crowded out all other issues of sound organization. The Commission emerged with an organization consisting of a vast and unmanageable number of divisions reporting directly to the Commission. They boasted of the fact that virtually all division heads remained unchanged in status and were directly accountable to the Commission.

As presently organized, the Commission is so burdened with thousands of day-to-day operating decisions that it cannot function to formulate and assure the execution of basic policies and programs although this is the urgent need.[5]

Transactions with other government agencies like the Navy and Commerce departments were slowed down but ultimately accomplished; the real danger came in the contact with private business. In effect, the U.S. Maritime Commission, determined not to be left stuck with unsalable ships as had happened to the Shipping Board after World War I, became a vulnerable target for scams and other schemes to spirit money and ships out of the government agency. The period of maritime scandals had begun, with operators like Daniel K. Ludwig being among the first to profit, although for many this was merely the continuation of the lucrative deals during World War II. Since the U.S. Maritime Commission was under relentless pressure to end government operation of ships, the opportunities for turning many a profitable transaction became even greater; rather than working to create a long-term shipping policy, the Truman administration was more concerned with showing "a determined effort on the part of the Commission to get out of the shipping business."[6]

The inherent American ideological bias against government ownership and operation was further reinforced by the "global do-gooders" who all along had wanted the Truman administration to sell the surplus ships first to the foreign countries and later to the U.S. operators. The argument was that the reconstruction of the European economy was of vital interest to the United States. By 1946 the global do-gooders were joined by the Cold War warriors who felt that the fastest possible economic recovery of Europe was necessary to stop Soviet Communist expansion. Out of these demands, the State Department formulated the policy "that sales of ships to citizens and noncitizens should be on the same terms."[7]

By 1946 most European countries had their shipyards in operation, and they used this newly recovered capacity to bargain with the Americans, in effect offering to cut back their shipbuilding program if the United States sold them more surplus ships. Furthermore, starting in 1945 the Europeans had come to inspect all the available surplus ships in order to have first choice on the most modern and fastest vessels, usually the C-2s and C-3s completed in 1944 and 1945. These ships, some of which were completed only after the war was over, were the most suitable for commercial operations; other ship designs—such as the slow Liberties, which were barely suitable for tramping—were generally left for the Americans. In effect the Europeans, joined by some Latin Americans, had skimmed the cream off the wartime merchant fleet.

Overall, U.S. steamship companies also failed to seek out ships aggressively from the surplus fleet; instead they generally limited themselves to restoring their tonnage to its prewar size. In a final move, the U.S. Maritime Commission refused to grant blanket approval to the purchase requests by U.S. steamship companies, and some of the ships it refused to sell to American buyers subsequently were sold to foreigners. The maritime policy was as usual caught in between two opposing and undesirable alternatives: If all the ships requested by U.S. firms were granted, then when the subsidy program resumed functioning, as it did by the late 1940s, the government would have to pay staggering sums to the private owners to keep the lines profitable. If the ships were sold to the foreign lines, then even larger subsidies would be needed to keep the U.S. steamship companies competitive.[8]

By 30 June 1947 the government had sold 3.3 million deadweight tons (306 ships) to Americans and 8 million deadweight tons (799 ships) to foreigners. Since the original authority expired on 31 December 1947, Congress subsequently passed extensions so that sales continued to foreigners until 1 March 1948 and to Americans until 15 January 1951. U.S. investors at last began to avail themselves of the surplus ships, so that their total acquisitions before the Ship Sales Act of 1946 expired climbed to 9.5 million deadweight tons (847 ships), but the foreign share had also climbed to 12 million deadweight tons (1,113 ships). What the figures did not reveal was that many of the ships were sold to U.S. citizens who were fronts or dummy corporations just waiting for the right opportunity to transfer the ships to foreign owners, increasingly for operation under the Panamanian and Liberian flags of convenience. These evasions took place both before the expiration on 1

March 1948 of the authority to sell to foreigners and after that date as part of complex stratagems to pry ships out of the U.S. government at bargain prices.[9]

As the influence of U.S. shipyards waned, the U.S. Maritime Commission tried to take a harder line against foreign ship sales, but to no avail. As more and more ships passed into foreign hands, the share of the country's oceanborne trade carried by U.S.-flag vessels declined from the wartime high of 68 percent in 1945 to 39 percent in 1950, falling below the stated goal of retaining a 50 percent share of ocean-borne commerce for U.S. ships.[10] The downward turn continued irreversibly during the subsequent decades. Other factors were also at work in the U.S. retreat from supremacy, as the following sections reveal.

□ The End of Coastwise and Intercoastal Shipping

The decline of intercoastal shipping—between the East and West coasts of the United States—and coastwise shipping—in the Pacific Coast region and from Texas to Maine—had already begun in the late 1930s. For many seaside communities, steamers had been their only links with the outside world for generations, but the gradual spread of railroads, trucks, buses, and airplanes made deep inroads into the steamship business. Nevertheless, prior to the outbreak of World War II, coastwise and intercoastal shipping still comprised over half of the deep-sea tonnage while domestic shipping, which included the Great Lakes fleet, comprised more than two-thirds of the U.S. merchant marine. Domestic shipping, in particular the coastwise and intercoastal services, provided a large pool of talent, seamen, routes, and cargoes to bolster the position of those steamship companies engaged in the foreign trade. Coastwise and intercoastal shipping, in spite of vigorous competition from other carriers, remained remarkably resilient because water carriage was still the lowest-cost transportation, with savings passed on to the shippers in the form of lower rates.[11]

By the end of the 1930s, the railroads, which had long reigned supreme in the interior of the United States, began to fear the coming competition from trucks and automobile transport on roads and highways. Rather than tackling this formidable challenge directly, the railroads targeted for elimination intercoastal and coastwise shipping, their most serious rival from the perspective of costs. With the cargoes taken away from the ships, the railroads would then be able to face the truckers who, as the most expensive land carriers, did not appear to be as serious a rival. The first step was to remove coastwise and intercoastal shipping from the regulation of the sympathetic U.S. Maritime Commission. To avoid "a great deal of confusion"[12] and "to achieve an integrated and balanced national transportation policy administered by a single agency, and free of any built-in preferences for particular modes,"[13] the Transportation Act of 1940 transferred jurisdiction to the Interstate Commerce Commission which for many decades had been a tool of the railroads.

The entry of the United States into World War II modified but did not change the railroads' goal of eliminating coastwise and intercoastal shipping. By early 1942 the War Shipping Administration had requisitioned almost the entire domestic fleet of the United States, a nearby and readily available shipping resource that proved to be invaluable during the first year of the war. All the cargo previously carried by water, as well as the new wartime traffic, now went to the railroads, whose net income rose 1,700 percent. Naturally, they did not want to lose this cargo once the war ended: "Without reflecting on the fine job performed by the rails, their position in this case seems merely to represent an effort to retain a wartime windfall based on the misfortunes of their competitors."[14]

The navy, impressed in two world wars by the military value and convenience of a domestic merchant fleet, strongly supported the War Shipping Administration's requests to operate in the coastwise and intercoastal trade after the war. The railroads bitterly contested this claim and argued before the Interstate Commerce Commission against granting certificates of operation. Since the War Shipping Administration operated under emergency powers subsequently ratified by Congress, the legislative mandates took precedence over regulatory proceedings, and a hostile Interstate Commerce Commission was forced to accept, at least temporarily, the following scenario:

> The proposed operation contemplates an orderly return to private operation. It does not contemplate indefinite government operation. At the outset, prewar private operators will act for the United States, but only operators holding certificates in their own names will be eligible for this service. This temporary arrangement is necessary for many reasons. Over half the vessels used before the war in these trades are no longer available. Many have been lost from war causes; other are still immobilized for military purposes. Legislation permitting the sale of government owned vessels as replacements probably will not be adopted for several months. Other physical facilities, such as terminals, have been taken over by the Army or Navy and must be restored. Vessels now owned by the government must be modified to meet the needs of the domestic trades. Traffic departments must be rees-

tablished and trade contracts restored. The labor relations problem must be clarified and stabilized. The freight rate structure must be renewed and revised, if necessary, to permit successful operation under the increased labor costs, increased capital charges and other increased expenditures that will govern future operations.

Since the government has disrupted these services and has a vital interest in their restoration, the government owes the industry every assistance in finding a solution to these difficulties. The domestic trade steamship industry suffered from several years of financial anaemia before the war. It was a very sick industry as fully set forth in the Maritime Commission survey of 1939.[15]

When the War Shipping Administration was dissolved on 1 September 1946, its domestic shipping services fell under the control of the U.S. Maritime Commission, whose authority to operate those vessels would expire on 28 February 1947. The Office of Defense Transportation was deeply concerned about any abrupt cessation of the domestic intercoastal trade, and, in conjunction with the shippers and the U.S. Maritime Commission, obtained authorization from Congress to continue government operations until 1948. The Truman administration, eager to get rid of the last remainders of wartime government operation, used this Congressional authorization to grant an extension, but only until July 1947. The U.S. Maritime Commission, now more concerned with supporting those lines reaping record high profits in the foreign trade, did not press the issue very hard; only the Office of Defense Transportation made the vigorous claim that "there should be no experimentation in the matter before next spring."[16] The Truman administration refused to make any further use of the Congressional authorization, so that government operation in the coastwise and intercoastal trade came to an end on July 1947. The private "lines were thrown on their own" to try to pick up the slack by either buying or chartering vessels from the U.S. Maritime Commission.[17]

The task facing those steamship lines, such as Pope and Talbot, Luckenbach, Coastwise, and American-Hawaiian, was enormous. Most of their ships had been sunk during wartime service, so that the government could return few vessels, most of which were too old anyway. Since the companies had no ships to use as collateral, banks were unwilling to extend them loans, and the insurance money from the lost ships did not cover the purchase price of surplus ships, even at their reduced price. Furthermore, most war surplus ships had been built for the deep-sea foreign trade, and so generally they were too big or otherwise not well suited to the coastwise and intercoastal service. Not surprisingly, many prewar operators simply took their insurance money and invested it in less risky businesses on land. Even Luckenbach Steamship, which chartered ships from the government, preferred to run them in the foreign trades that were lucrative until 1948, leaving few ships for the intercoastal service. In spite of these obstacles, "a few hardy souls battled tirelessly to reestablish deep water domestic common carrier service," and soon a modest flotilla was offering regular service on the coastwise and intercoastal routes of the United States.[18]

Thus in 1948 the weak and struggling domestic fleet was maneuvered into the position the railroads had carefully prepared for it since 1940. While a conspiracy on the part of the railroads cannot be ruled out, the fact that the Interstate Commerce Commission was staffed mainly by persons with railroad backgrounds and was faced daily with the problems of the railroads, its largest constituency, automatically stacked the verdicts against the domestic water carriers. Because of the enormous increase in cargo volume during the war, the railroads were able to retain the same low rates after the war for some years in spite of the postwar inflation. When finally forced to raise rates, the upward readjustments still lagged behind rising costs, keeping a competitive stranglehold on the gasping domestic steamship lines. The railroads then targeted special large bulk items for selective rate cutting as a way to convince the shipper to avoid the water carrier. Thus, when the railroad increases went into effect, the shipper found that he still enjoyed low rates for lumber and canned goods, the preferred items on the eastbound intercoastal service of the domestic lines. Interstate Commerce Commission approval was taken for granted; the agency either dismissed summarily the objections of the water carriers or, more likely, buried them in endless proceedings.[19]

High labor costs, particularly since World War II, have been a constant obstacle to the survival of the U.S. merchant marine, and just after the war two additional complications made the domestic fleet's labor situation even more critical. First, the wages of railroad employees rose more slowly that those of seafaring personnel. Second, an upward spiral in the foreign-trade operations drove the wages of seafaring personnel to record highs, but while lines in foreign operations could cover the pay demands and still reap huge profits, the domestic lines could not easily afford to pay such high wages because they were already struggling to compete with the low rates of the railroads. To complicate things further, 17 unions represented the seafaring personnel, each trying to outdo the next one in concessions for employees: "Each union leader makes it his business to see, if possible, that his union fares a little better in the way of concessions granted, than any other union" until the pay received "is so fantastically high, it is beyond comprehension."[20]

Not surprisingly, the share of domestic shipping within the merchant marine of the United States declined from almost 70 percent in 1939 to 30 percent in 1953. While water transportation had remained by a large margin the cheapest way to carry goods, the cargo-handling expenses at the dock traditionally had been so high that they swallowed up a large share of the savings associated with water transport. The inauguration of scheduled container service between the Gulf and the East Coast by Pan-Atlantic in April 1956 promised drastic cuts in cargo-handling expenses, but unfortunately the container revolution came too late to save the moribund coastwise and intercoastal shipping. By that date, only a handful of domestic coastwise lines remained, operating old ships whose replacement by modern container vessels presented a staggering capital investment none were in a position to make. The railroads, however, immediately realized the implications of containers and, to keep their shippers loyal and away from domestic shipping, proceeded to incorporate the containers into their rail services. And in 1957–60, the railroads launched a final furious campaign of selective rate cutting in order to liquidate the coastwise and intercoastal lines before they had time to adopt the new container technology.[21]

The U.S. Senate conducted hearings in 1960 to study the dramatic collapse of domestic shipping; among other events, the senators were able to witness first hand the bankruptcy of Coastwise Line, which suspended operation of its last vessel in late February 1960, thereby ending all common-carrier steamship service in the entire Pacific Coast region. The last two regular operators on the intercoastal service, Pope and Talbot and Luckenbach Steamship, suspended service in 1961; however, lines primarily engaged in foreign trade continued to provide intercoastal service, although with frequent interruptions, sometimes in only one direction, and never on the regularly scheduled routes that had previously existed. Common-carrier coastwise trade between the Gulf and the East Coast lasted the longest, with Seatrain not pulling out until 1963; Sea-Land, the successor of Pan-Atlantic, remained in the route thanks to its modern container ships, but finally the trucking competition, in addition to the railroads, forced Sea-Land to abandon the trade in January 1978.[22]

The United States government, by massively subsidizing the construction of modern expressways like the Interstate Highway System, in effect had artificially fostered a trucking industry whose operating costs were the highest in surface transportation. Perhaps inadvertently, the government also had contributed to the final destruction of the coastal and intercoastal shipping, which never even partially recovered from the official requisitions of World War II. More ironically, the trucking industry became the most formidable adversary of the railroads, whose efforts to destroy domestic shipping had left them depleted and weakened, prone to bankruptcy from the late 1960s on, and generally unprepared to face the onslaught of the trucking industry. If the Interstate Commerce Commission really had wished to favor the railroads, it should have kept them from engaging in the ruinous competition against the water carriers.

In the end, higher transportation costs because of trucking meant that the shipper had to pay higher rates that were ultimately passed on to the consumers; that "hidden" cost made U.S. goods even more overpriced in the highly competitive world market after World War II. To try to reduce their costs, some U.S. industries have continued to own or charter vessels for their own cargoes and to handle them in their own private docks, thereby reaping enormous savings not otherwise possible by other modes of transportation. Clearly, if the United States wishes to restore its position in the world economy, a second look will have to be taken at coastwise and intercoastal shipping as part of a more efficient and integrated transportation network.[23] Unlike coastwise and intercoastal shipping, however, one specialized segment of domestic shipping did escape extinction, although not without serious difficulties, as the next section explains.

□ The Decline of the U.S. Tanker Fleet

When the War Shipping Administration was dissolved on 1 September 1946 and its remaining functions assumed by the U.S. Maritime Commission, no change occurred in the tanker shortage, which remained just as critical as during the war. Because Congress had specifically ruled out chartering the government-owned tankers (unlike the freighters discussed in the previous section), the U.S. Maritime Commission was left with no choice but to continue operating the tankers in both foreign and domestic routes. On the assumption that the high rates would convince U.S. and foreign buyers to acquire tankers through the generous provisions of the 1946 Ship Sales Act, the government's authority to operate tankers ran only until 28 February 1947.

Private investors were overly cautious, however, and, while some did purchase tankers, the rush to buy did not materialize. By the time the authority was supposed to expire on 28 February 1947, the U.S.

Maritime Commission was still operating 240 tankers "at a considerable net profit to this government," and with no signs of a break because "current demands for tanker tonnage are at a peak and it is well nigh impossible to prophesy how long such demands will continue."[24] Reluctantly the Truman administration extended the authority to operate tankers until June 1947, and again one last time until the end of the year. Despite the fact that the U.S. Treasury was receiving $20 million a month from the tanker and shipping operations of the U.S. Maritime Commission, the political pressures to demobilize at any cost and the ideological arguments against any government enterprise were so strong that no further extensions were possible beyond 1947.

Ships are power, and because the U.S. Maritime Commission operated the largest tanker fleet in the world and owned the largest reserve fleet, it was in the quasimonopoly position of "price leader." The agency's share of the world market was so great that it could set high rates; foreign competitors, rather than attempting to undercut, preferred to see their rates rise upward to meet the government's. This was true to a lesser degree in the freighter market, where the possibility of chartering vessels tended to keep the rates from rising as rapidly, but in the tanker market the U.S. Maritime Commission reigned unchallenged.

Because of ideological reasons the United States refused to build a strong competitive position upon the overwhelming strength, profitability, and efficiency of the U.S. Maritime Commission's tanker operations. As a lone concession, the navy was allowed to operate 55 T-2 tankers, which subsequently became the nucleus fleet of the Military Sea Transportation Service when the latter was organized in 1949. From 1947 until the present, navy operation and inactivation of its tanker fleet has been an ongoing struggle between private profit for the few versus public service for national defense. Given that navy tankers were limited to the resupply of the naval fleet and military installations throughout the world, the task of defending the U.S. share of the world tanker market fell by default to a motley group of small operators, mainly newcomers, who were generally referred to as the "Independents."[25]

Many had started operations in 1947 with their first purchased ships while still under the protective rate umbrella of the U.S. Maritime Commission. Consequently some had formed an exaggerated opinion of their prowess and business strength. According to the Independents, they had proven a supposed obstacle to be insubstantial: "Notwithstanding the cultivated tradition that American seamen are unwilling to make long voyages, we were able to man our vessels in the States for voyages of a year or more."[26] Unfortunately for the Independents, by the time most of them raised the money to buy the ships, foreigners had bought the best tankers, either by purchasing directly from the U.S. government or, more disgracefully, through dummy American corporations. The fact that the U.S. oil companies replenished their prewar tanker fleets under the flags of convenience did not alarm the Independents, who, "in their avidity for lucrative tanker tonnage, were even led to buying those Liberty type tankers designed as a war emergency and never contemplated as commercial carriers."[27]

The withdrawal of the U.S. Maritime Commission from tanker operations by the end of 1947 left the Independents on their own, and by late 1948 the tanker market was in a sharp slump. Foreign operators, hesitant to take on the U.S. Maritime Commission, felt no hesitation about knocking off the new U.S. rivals one by one: "The amount of available tonnage has reached such proportions that competition has become quite sharp, resulting in foreign vessels with low operating costs cutting their rates to unheard of lows."[28] The main European countries were struggling to regain a share of the world's tanker market, but the headlines went to Aristotle Onassis and the Stavros Niarchos, colorful Greek entrepreneurs who quickly built up the largest tanker fleets in the world, initially with U.S. surplus tankers. The largest U.S. Independent was Daniel Ludwig, but not for long, because following the example of the Greeks, he proceeded by various subterfuges and maneuvers to acquire a tanker fleet flying flags of convenience, despite the strenuous opposition of the U.S. Maritime Commission. Indeed, Ludwig was only doing what the U.S. oil companies had previously done—acquiring only enough U.S.-flag tankers to supply the domestic trade, while operating all other tankers under foreign flags.

Some Independents had at last realized the futility of operating Liberties as tankers and had converted a number to a more suitable use as dry bulk carriers. Nevertheless, by June 1949 the situation had become critical, with 93 tankers left idle and the plunge in tanker rates showing no signs of ending. The Independents, who had pressured the Truman administration to end U.S. Maritime Commission operations in 1947, now came rushing back to seek government protection. They needed a simplistic formula to try to gain government support, and they decided to make the navy's 55 tankers the scapegoat for their predicament. Under intense political and ideological pressure, the Military Sea Transportation Service, in spite of its vigorous protests, was forced to inactivate 17 tankers, the last of which entered the reserve fleet on 4 July 1950, 10 days after the outbreak of the Korean War. That same month these tankers had to be reactivated. All these operations caused enormous expenses to the U.S. Treasury, and they were just one more example of subsidizing private profits with public funds.[29]

The 55 tankers of the Military Sea Transportation Service and the chartering of private tankers met the needs of the Korean War. For better coordination a voluntary tanker pool was organized in December 1950 and lasted until March 1953. The Korean War had saved the Independents, providing enough shipments to compensate for the loss of most cargoes on the foreign trades, yet even in 1952, before the war had ended, tanker rates resumed their downward trend. Except for military cargoes, the U.S. tankers had retreated basically into the coastwise and intercoastal trade, but nevertheless their situation was precarious: "They are concerned over (1) the approaching block obsolescence of their T-2 and Liberty tankers; and (2) the difficulty of obtaining financing for the construction of additional new vessels; and (3) the threat of competition by projected pipelines; and (4) their inability to compete with foreign flag vessels in foreign trade. They enjoy no benefits under the Merchant Marine Act such as those available to the subsidized lines."[30]

The slump in the tanker market became critical in 1954, and once more the Independents resumed their campaign against the navy's 55 tankers. Again under protest the Military Sea Transportation Service began the inactivation of 17 T-2 tankers in the autumn of 1954, a task completed by fall of 1955. The pressure upon the navy to inactivate ships eased off, and the reason became obvious when tanker rates began to spiral upward in November 1955: unusually large grain shipments had booked most of the U.S.-flag tankers. In the first half of 1956, rates continued to skyrocket 75 and 125 percent higher than the normal rates, and finally the Military Sea Transportation Service could not obtain any tankers, either U.S. or foreign; they simply were not available at any price. Once again, private operators had gone elsewhere to reap personal profits, forgetting about the public good of national defense, and the Navy was forced to withdraw from the reserve fleet the 17 tankers just recently inactivated at great expense because of the pressure from the Independents. Thanks to its tankers, the Military Sea Transportation Service could continue to supply U.S. forces deployed worldwide.[31]

When on 1 November 1956 Egypt sank blockships to close the Suez Canal in response to a British and French invasion, the world tanker market became a seller's paradise. Middle East oil that previously had flowed to Europe and the United States via the Suez Canal now had to take the longer route around the Cape of Good Hope, and the longer transit times required more tankers. Speculation reached a zenith, and it could have been stopped only if the United States government had dumped its reserve fleet into the market at least until the Suez Canal reopened. The Military Sea Transportation Service was allowed to withdraw only 12 tankers from the reserve fleet in December 1956 and January 1957, and all were promptly returned by November 1957. Huge windfall profits went into the hands of foreign private shipowners, although some crumbs went to those Independents active in the voyage charters of the "spot" market. Without the intervention of the U.S. government to stabilize the market, some U.S. private investors rushed to order tankers, speculating that the tanker boom would long outlast the reopening of the Suez Canal in early 1957. The get-rich-quick speculators had little knowledge of or interest in the volatile history of tanker movements; once again the market mechanism misfunctioned, in this case providing capital when it was not advisable, while in other shipping situations it failed to invest in indispensable ships and facilities.[32]

The tanker slump reappeared in 1958, and by late 1959 it had reached a critical point, especially for those who had ordered new tankers in the post-Suez rush: "Because of the high cost of construction and operation, and the existing low tanker rates, it is now impossible for American-flag tankers to continue in operation. Modern vessels which have been built within the past 18 months are unable to obtain employment. In cases where they have been able to obtain employment, this generally has been at loss rates. As a result, many of these vessels face foreclosure and layup unless a remedy for the existing situation is found promptly."[33]

The Independents did not give up their old struggle against the navy tankers with the usual charge of unfair government competition against private business, but now they concentrated their efforts on a different solution. Simple figures clearly showed that the share of oil imports carried by U.S.-flag tankers had declined from 81 percent in 1945 to 4 percent in 1961, and the Independents asked Congress to approve cargo-preference legislation to require a 50 percent share of oil imports for U.S.-flag tankers. As a bargaining tactic the 50 percent claim made sense, but it was clear that for the Independents, in dire straits and seeing their domestic routes gradually shrinking, any share of oil imports over 5 percent would allow comfortable survival, while anything over 10 percent would mean a return to boom time. However, Congress could not be convinced of the need of such stringent cargo requirements, and gradually the Independents, now joined by powerful labor unions, reluctantly concluded that cargo-preference legislation for oil imports had to await the arrival of another crisis.[34]

□   The Dollar Line Case

As the United States undermined or destroyed each of the supports sustaining the U.S. merchant marine in the postwar years, government ownership of American President Lines remained as one major pillar. Chapter 7 explained how the U.S. Maritime Commission, in order to stave off the bankruptcy of Dollar Steamship, had acquired the firm in 1938, henceforth known as American President Lines. The government poured funds into the company, held off the creditors, and established sound management, so that by the time World War II broke out, American President Lines was more than ready to make a major contribution to the nation's war effort. Thus, in 1938 American President Lines became another example of government-owned steamship firms—along with the Panama Line of the War Department and United States Lines—(1921–1929). During government operation the three companies produced an unbroken record of efficiency, profitability, and overall success, in stark contrast to the generally mediocre if not shoddy performance of most private operators. Indeed, when World War II ended, the biggest worry of European steamship companies was having to compete against a vastly enlarged government merchant fleet.

However, long-term considerations were not in the minds of the U.S. Maritime Commission in 1945: "I am convinced we should get rid of this property. So long as we continue to own it, rumors will persist in the industry that the Commission or Commissioners are attempting to foster government ownership and operation of the merchant marine. Such rumors do persist now in influential quarters in the industry. I believe the best interests of the government, the Commission, and the merchant marine will be served if we liquidate the property while its net worth is high."[35]

The U.S. Maritime Commission allowed itself to be stampeded into taking opening bids for the company on 27 June 1945. A first call for bids in 1940 had failed, because prospective investors still considered the bankrupt company a high-risk gamble. Now in 1945 there were four good bids, and the spread between the top three was less than a million dollars. The winner was businessman Charles U. Bay, a major stockholder of American Export Lines who wanted to combine the two companies' operations, but before he could take possession of American President Lines, an unforeseen development occurred. Stanley Dollar had not been able to scrape up enough money to make his own bid in 1945 to recover his pre-1938 control of the company, and he was in a precarious financial situation, so he decided to try to pull off one last coup against the government. After sending numerous letters to government officials demanding the return of Dollar's supposed 93 percent ownership of American President Lines, Dollar's lawyers filed a lawsuit on 6 November 1945 in the United States District Court in Washington, D.C.; they obtained a restraining order blocking the sale of American President Lines to Charles U. Bay until the litigation had been decided.[36]

Dollar argued that he only had pledged his 93 percent stockholdings in the Dollar Line as collateral until the company itself repaid the debt to the U.S. Maritime Commission and that therefore no sale had taken place to the government. Nevertheless, the 1938 agreement stated "transferred, sold, and assigned," Dollar in public statements as well as private letters claimed he had sold the stock, he did take an income tax deduction for losses in the sale, and, furthermore, the new American President Lines assumed not only his debts to the U.S. Maritime Commission but also his many other overdue obligations.[37] The pressure of the private creditors had been instrumental in pushing the government to take over the Dollar Line in order to recover the sums otherwise uncollectible under bankruptcy proceedings. The overwhelming evidence made Dollar's claim appear so outrageous that the government initially missed the true nature of the challenge. As part of the mounting postwar conservative reaction against government intervention, the Dollar Line case was a political struggle, of which only a part transpired within the courtroom. Thus, whenever judged on the merits of the case, the government always won, but on the round of appeals the issue was considerably clouded and was decided more through complex political maneuvering.

Failure to realize the political dimension made government lawyers concentrate initially on collecting evidence rather than challenging the moves by Stanley Dollar's lawyers to focus rather exclusively on isolated, narrow issues. The evidence was so overwhelming that in the various trials the district courts invariably ruled in favor of the government, but enough doubt had been inserted in the record to give the court of appeals a base to overturn the lower courts' decisions. Dollar, wise in the ways of Washington, D.C., began to search for allies, and although labeled a "reactionary Republican," he began to bankroll the campaigns of notable Democratic incumbents, notably Senator Pat McCarran, as well as many Democratic friends of Truman administration officials. To a country drifting into a conservative mindframe, the charges of socialism and unfair government competition against private business were guaranteed to evoke considerable public support, especially when the Truman administration was portrayed as a ruthless tyrant unwilling to return private property to its rightful owner.

The government appeared to have lost on 7 April 1947 after an unfavorable Supreme Court decision, but the case was soon back in district court, which for a second time ruled against the Dollar family on 2 December 1948. The Dollars confidently counted on reversals upon appeal; nevertheless, by the end of 1948 they had made a mistake that would eventually cost them ownership of the company. Even though the Dollars lost formal control in 1938, they remained fully informed about company affairs (with offices right next door on the same floor) and thus retained some influence. Most decisively, Stanley Dollar had repeatedly soft-pedaled any large-scale expansion attempts by the company during and after World War II. This reluctance to seek surplus ships had been noticed by Vice President Thomas E. Cuffe, who decided to fill the gap with his own steamship line, as the next chapter explains. But when George Killion became president on 12 August 1947, he wanted to rule without interference over a large and expanding corporation and not just over a modest family venture. Relations with the Dollar family remained outwardly friendly, but they were soon strained. The break came in 1948 when Killion decided to order three large vessels from domestic shipyards. The Dollars were scared about the debt and the expenses of running a vastly enlarged American President Lines, and in late 1948 they began for the first time to have second thoughts about the litigation. About Killion they had no doubt, and soon it was clear that if and when the Dollars regained control of the company, Killion would be out of a job.[38]

Lines of communication remained open, and Killion had been careful to break with the Dollars only after he was sure he had linked his fate to a new rising star, Ralph K. Davies, his former boss at the wartime Petroleum Administration. While still in government, Davies had judged correctly that the conservative reaction would eventually force the government to give up control of American President Lines, and as early as 1944 he had quietly begun to buy stock for the takeover struggle, until by 1952 he was the single largest minority stockholder in the company. Since the government owned 93 percent of the voting stock, such a takeover attempt would have been foolhardy if the company had been privately owned. But Davies had learned well that in a fight between private profit and public service, the private investors enjoyed unusual advantages that more than canceled the overwhelming presence of the government. Davies now had the standing to intervene in the lawsuits. His most significant intervention was a brief filed on 1 March 1951 praising "the outstanding achievement of the present management"; Killion thus had his future position guaranteed in writing.[39]

In January 1950, the financial situation of the Dollar family became sufficiently serious to consider a settlement, independent of the specific court verdicts; even if the Dollars won, the new debt obligations of American President Lines made the company too heavy a burden for the Dollar family, whose priority now became a cash settlement rather than actual return of ownership. In May 1950 when the Reorganization Plan abolished the U.S. Maritime Commission and replaced it with the Maritime Administration within the Department of Commerce, the government's goals also changed. Secretary of Commerce Charles Sawyer stated clearly the new position: "While the government operation had been successful, I have felt that it should not continue to compete with private industry any longer than was necessary."[40] However, both sides failed to perceive that the other's bargaining position had softened, so that when on 17 July 1950 the U.S. Court of Appeals again reversed the district court verdict and ruled in Dollar's favor, the latter made one last dash for an all-out victory.

Another inevitable round of appeals and reversals followed, until it seemed that the Dollars had gained the upper hand when they obtained contempt-of-court citations against Sawyer and Killion for failing to turn over the shares of American President Lines. Just a few days away from the first-ever jailing of a cabinet secretary, the government obtained a stay from Chief Justice Frederick M. Vinson. The government was off the hook, and now at last the Department of Justice rolled out its heavy artillery and promised to win not only in the district courts but in the appeals as well. The key lay in that the case would be retried now on behalf of the United States, rather than on behalf of the former head of the abolished U.S. Maritime Commission. At last the government had decided to handle the case as part of a larger political struggle rather than just a narrow legal issue based solely on merits. At the very least, the case would drag out: "We are still faced with years of litigation."[41] But realization of the political nature of the struggle also brought awareness that in the presidential election year of 1952, a Democratic ticket facing an electorate sharply veering toward conservatism could not afford charges of government ownership and socialism in the shipping industry; the government's seizure of the steel mills was already more than the Democratic party could handle.

Secretary of Commerce Sawyer had proposed a settlement by a friendly letter as early as 25 May 1951, but the Dollar lawyers decided to score some publicity points by an arrogant reply—which, however, did not completely rule out the possibility of a settlement. The financial situation of the Dollar family had taken a turn for the worst, and Stanley Dollar did not relish further litigation. Nevertheless, a deadlock had been reached, and although Sawyer still wanted a settlement, he could not risk another public rebuff. In January 1952 the president of the Bank of America, L. Mario Giannini, approached Killion to say that "as a citizen, taxpayer, and San Francisco businessman interested in shipping affairs"[42] he wanted something done fast to end the intolerable stalemate. Killion agreed, and correctly explained that Stanley Dollar was the obstacle to a compromise with the government. "I'll bring Stanley Dollar around," said the banker confidently, and most certainly he did: after a few words with the banker, Stanley Dollar was never the same again.[43]

The old fight totally vanished, and Stanley Dollar promptly put out feelers through Killion and Sen. McCarran. At a decisive meeting on 3 March 1952 in Washington, D.C., Stanley Dollar was apologetic toward Sawyer and meekly agreed to the compromise settlement. The formula, previously worked out with Killion, called on the government to open bids for the purchase of American President Lines; the proceeds from the highest bid would be divided in half between the government and the Dollar family. Stanley did ask Sawyer whether the government had any objection to his bidding on the company, partly to find an excuse not to bid and partly to gain assurances of a fair allocation of subsidies in the unlikely case his bid won. Sawyer replied that "while I had been very badly treated and unjustly criticized in connection with this matter, I would not let that interfere with my attitude as Secretary of Commerce and that the line would be treated under his management, if he should become the controlling owner, exactly as it would under the management of anyone else."[44]

Killion had kept Davies, a member of the board, fully informed of these negotiations, so that the latter was ready to put a package of investors together to make the highest bid. The Dollars' lack of interest was reflected in their low bid (4 million dollars below that of Davies), in spite of the fact that half of the money would be promptly returned to them. Matson Navigation Company had an interest in neutralizing this formidable competitor and made a bid only 2 million dollars lower than the winning offer of Davies. Announcement of the bids on 29 October 1952 was not the final chance for the Dollars to regain control but rather was the closing episode in their long involvement with the steamship line. Half of the proceeds from the sale was more than enough to restore the family fortune of the Dollars, who then could remain in lumber, trade, and sundry smaller businesses. The U.S. Treasury had recovered part of the investment made in the revival of the company. The Democratic party trusted that the end of the Dollar Line case, as well as the end of the government operation of the steel mills earlier in 1952, would safely put to rest charges of socialism in the November presidential election. Davies gained control of the company he had long coveted, and Killion retained his job as president.[45]

Satisfied as the interested parties were, the Dollar Line case had long-term negative consequences for the U.S. steamship companies. First, there would be no nucleus in any government-owned company for the survival of even a small merchant fleet able to carry a bare minimum of 10 percent of U.S. oceanborne commerce. Second, although the Dollars scored many points with the public through their attacks on government ownership, the countercharges of private mismanagement and milking of public funds for private profit had left the image, repeatedly reinforced by later events, that the steamship companies were privileged groups concerned only with their own personal profit at the taxpayers' expense. Third, the government had learned too well the lesson of taking over bankrupt steamship companies: no matter how many legal precautions the government took, the seller of a bankrupt steamship company could always wave the flag of socialism to capture the public's sympathy immediately. Henceforth, as U.S. steamship companies started to fold one after another, the government had no choice but to remain a passive witness.

10

Challengers Old and New

WHILE THE UNITED States was busy disman-
tling its maritime supremacy, how did the rest of the world react to this
unilateral withdrawal? Without exception, the industrialized nations,
whether Allied or former enemies, strove to rebuild their merchant
shipping services. As if they were not enough of a challenge, new competitors appeared in other parts of the world, particularly in South
America.

The revival of European shipping services began with France, a
country whose merchant marine had been reduced by the war to one-
third of the prewar level. By 1952, after great and sustained efforts,
France had regained its prewar position in merchant shipping. Private
and official steamship companies, in particular the state-owned Compagnie Générale Maritime, supported France's slow but sure economic
effort to return to the ranks of the world's richest nations by the 1960s.
For Italy, World War II had been disastrous, with 90 percent of its merchant fleet destroyed, yet a timely switch in sides had allowed the country to escape a lengthy occupation. Italy thus could begin the
reconstruction of its merchant fleet after 1945. It was an urgent task,
because shipping earnings formed a major part in that country's balance
of payments. Thanks to ship purchases from the United States (even
greater than France's), by 1954 Italy's tonnage exceeded its prewar fleet.
A shipbuilding program guaranteed the timely renovation of the fleet,
and shipping earnings served to cover the deficits in Italy's balance of

payments, thereby allowing the country's gradual rise into the ranks of the world's richest nations. By the 1990s Italy's national income rivaled Great Britain's.[1]

While the other European countries raced after 1945 to rebuild their prewar fleets, occupied Germany could not do the same. Allied vessels carried Germany's foreign trade, and already in 1947 United States Lines and other U.S. firms were squabbling with British steamship companies over their respective shares of occupation cargoes. Finally in April 1951 Allied controls were lifted over shipping and shipbuilding. Germany began to build as well as purchase some ships abroad, but it decided against a crash program, in part because only through excessive borrowing could shipowners acquire vessels. In 1954, German steamship companies closed the last link in their world network when they resumed service to Australia, yet their tonnage was still less than half that of their prewar fleet. Nevertheless, the upward trend in German shipping was unmistakable, and as the German economy released more capital to finish rebuilding the country's fleet, a formidable competitor arose almost imperceptibly, reaching an elevated position by the 1960s. In the 1980s German lines even broke into trades formerly considered privileged preserves for U.S. steamship companies, such as routes from the U.S. West Coast to South America.[2]

What about England? No less than the other European countries, the nation bought ships abroad and built new vessels, but the harder England strove, the more remote became its prewar status. Unlike the rest of the European countries with specific trade needs, England's goal was to resume its rank as the world's number one maritime nation. Charges that England "was played out" were premature, but the nation was simply unable to recover its former commanding position.[3] But whether English, French, Italian, or German, the European routes to Latin America, Africa, and Asia were tightly blanketed and ferociously defended by European steamship companies, which were well aware that their countries' livelihoods depended on profitable export trades. The U.S. lines, once the Allied occupation of Germany ended, retreated into the trades between the United States and Europe, where a decades-long holding action was possible. The prospects in the Pacific Ocean appeared to be much more favorable, at least in the initial postwar years.

□ The Pacific Ocean 1945–50

In 1945, the United States reigned supreme over the Pacific Ocean. The most dangerous rival before the war had been Japan, whose entire fleet had been sunk or destroyed with the exception of one vessel. Against this background, the United States now boasted the largest navy and the largest merchant fleet in the world; meanwhile, Japan under U.S. occupation was not allowed to rebuild its merchant fleet and what was left of its shipping routes were monopolized by U.S. steamship companies. The United States also expected to reap benefits from the wartime alliance with Nationalist China. In exchange for help in the gigantic task of constructing a fleet for China's inland and coastwise shipping, the United States expected to displace the Japanese and the British as the major carrier of China's oceanborne trade.[4] Should any of the above calculations have proved unfounded, government ownership of American President Lines remained as a final barrier to defend U.S. shipping in the Pacific Ocean.

Overconfident in its ability to repulse challenges, the United States gave up without protest a powerful weapon for reprisals against foreign line competition: the Philippine Islands. Tired of overseeing this possession, the United States gave the war-devastated Philippine Islands their independence on 4 July 1946. Unfortunately, the United States had never fully grasped the crucial role these islands had played in keeping foreign competition under control in the prewar period. By not extending the coastwise exclusion laws to these islands, the United States had in effect taken the foreign lines hostage. Fear of losing the profitable Philippines cargo made British lines reluctant to challenge U.S. steamship companies in the other Pacific routes. But in one swift gesture in 1946, the United States threw away the weapon that had been effective in keeping the transpacific foreign competition within limits.[5]

The loss of the Philippines privilege was later sorely missed, but the initial U.S. belief was that by hastening the pace of independence in Asia, doors would open elsewhere to U.S. steamship lines formerly excluded by imperial barriers. Nationalist revolts erupted in the Netherlands East Indies and in French Indochina; the Dutch finally accepted with great resentment the Republic of Indonesia in 1949, while the French managed to hang on until 1955. The greatest change had come about peacefully in August 1947 when England granted independence to India and Pakistan. Without the grip on the commerce of the Indian subcontinent, England's return to a position in the Pacific Ocean even remotely near its shipping supremacy in the prewar period was simply impossible. English steamship companies did return to the Pacific, and England retained control of Malaysia (including Singapore) until the late 1950s, but the once-dominant nation essentially left a shipping vacuum waiting to be filled by a rival bold and persistent enough to assume the lead England had lost.

At that time, American President Lines was ideally positioned to become the largest shipping company in the Pacific Ocean. Careful management had reaped profits every year, and the company had administered very successfully a large fleet for the War Shipping Administration. The transfer of government ships to American President Lines, also government-owned, appeared a logical consequence of this success, and just knowing the fact that the U.S. government stood behind this profitable and well-run company sent a clear warning to would-be rivals. But as the United States drifted into a more conservative mood after World War II, the primary policy concern for the company became not to antagonize private shipping firms. Government ownership of American President Lines, no matter how successful, was becoming a political liability. The steamship line had to wait until private firms, including foreign buyers, had first crack at the wartime surplus ships. Only when it was clear that not the slightest charge of socialism could be raised by some aggrieved private firm did American President Lines tentatively attempt a modest purchase program.[6]

The shackling of American President Lines was so obvious, that one of its executives, Thomas E. Cuffe, seized the opportunity in 1946 to create his own firm, Pacific Far East Line. To fill the gap in shipping services to the Pacific, he chartered eight refrigerated vessels from the U.S. Maritime Commission, and later in 1947 he bought five freighters. The company prospered, and in 1951 it purchased three more vessels from the government. Cuffe was a knowledgeable and hard-driving shipping executive, who to get enough staff to run the operation had no choice but to lure employees away from American President Lines. Predictably, this turn of events greatly pleased the opponents of government enterprise. Even happier were the foreign rivals who now faced a divided front rather than one united steamship company. Cuffe himself was forced after January 1953 to operate under subsidies from the Maritime Administration in order to survive the then-ferocious Japanese competition in the Pacific.[7]

Other U.S. steamship companies, such as States Steamship, resumed their transpacific services after the war, but none made a greater sensation than Isbrandtsen Company whose founder, Hans Isbrandtsen, was determined to repeat the tactics of his prewar career. He emerged from the war without any ships of his own, running only those vessels he could charter from the U.S. Maritime Commission. When he attempted to buy C-2 freighters, he was rebuffed and placed at the bottom of the waiting list with the government-owned American President Lines. The hostility to Isbrandtsen was understandable, because his opposition to conferences and subsidies, as well as the disruptive effect of his hit-and-run tactics, had made him obnoxious both to private shipping firms and government officials. The urgency to sell ships was so great, however, that the U.S. Maritime Commission after incessant pleas finally sold him a ship in December 1946, and others followed until he owned 10 vessels. With these ships he was able to resume service from New York via Suez to Japan and back (by the same route) in 1947.[8]

The 10 ships he had purchased at bargain prices were a nucleus but not the key to his success in the last stage of his business career. Part of the explanation lay in the 33 ships he chartered on average, the number fluctuating according to the demand for cargo space. Equally important and less well known were his supplementary activities as a merchant; he made money not only on shipping services but also on the commodities he carried from the Far East. Speculating in commodities became very profitable and provided a subsidized floor for his much more publicized steamship activities. The inauguration of around-the-world service in 1949 placed his ships near most of the world's ports, and if a sizable volume of cargo materialized in any, Isbrandtsen promptly had one of his passing ships change course to pick up the cargo—often buying it as well for his mercantile dealings. His behavior as a raider irritated the established lines who had been patiently trying to build up a particular trade—for example, tin from Thailand. He grabbed his cargoes by undercutting the conference rates, usually by 10 percent, and once he had skimmed the cream of the business, he disappeared to wherever the next lucrative cargo materialized.[9]

One of his characteristics was to carry cargo for anybody without asking too many questions. While he tried to avoid blatantly illegal situations, otherwise he considered it a sacred right to sail anywhere without any government interference, an attitude that soon provoked some famous international incidents. Blockade running became his specialty, and one of his ships, the *Martin Berhman*, was detained in 1947 by Dutch warships when it tried to deliver supplies and load rubber in an Indonesian region held by Republican insurgents. A Dutch police report claimed in 1948 that another of his ships, the *Flying Clipper*, had attempted to deliver explosives to Jewish forces in Palestine, but British vigilance had forced the shipment to be rerouted through North Korea. The cargo, now headed for Indochina rebels, caused tremors within the State Department: "I should like to stress my view that all possible precautions should be taken to prevent an incident arising in a North Korean port as a result of a call by an American flag vessel."[10]

That mishap was averted, but another came in 1949 when Communist forces had gained control of most of China. The Nationalist government in Taiwan declared a blockade, and its warships fired upon

Isbrandtsen's vessels in October and again in November 1949, severely damaging two as they ran the blockade. Communist China desperately wanted foreign trade, and Isbrandtsen in his own way sensed that the trade with China was crucial for the survival of U.S. steamship services in the Far East. Pacific Far East Line's profits were adversely affected by the loss of the China trade in 1950. American President Lines, under the pressure of the powerful China lobby determined to isolate the Communist regime from the rest of the world, likewise regretfully abandoned its routes to mainland China.[11]

Isbrandtsen was very suspicious of not trading with countries simply because of beliefs or ideologies, and one of his favorite sayings was, "I am a Presbyterian, yet I would soon find business slack if I were to deal only with other Presbyterians."[12] The China lobby mounted a smear campaign against Isbrandtsen because he continued to run the ineffective Nationalist blockade. Further international incidents were avoided when, in December 1950, in response to the Communist Chinese intervention in Korea, the United States declared a trade embargo on China. The loss of the China trade was cushioned for U.S. steamship companies by the temporary boost that the Korean War provided after its outbreak in June 1950. How American lines would continue to compete once normal peacetime conditions returned remained an open question.

□ Far East Rate War

Polemical as some of the Isbrandtsen services to the Far East had been, the most controversial of all was the Japan trade. Beginning in 1947, Isbrandtsen ships had sailed from the U.S. East Coast via Suez as far as Japan and then retraced their steps. In 1949, the company instituted around-the-world service, so that the ships kept going eastward after reaching Japan and returned to the East Coast of the United States via the Panama Canal. Isbrandtsen had instituted this change in order to tap into the outward cargo from Japan, which was then just beginning its phenomenal reconstruction from wartime ruins. The Japanese eastbound shipments became so valuable that the company's ships often refused to load bulk, low-paying cargo as they raced via Suez to the ports of Japan.

As long as the U.S. occupation of Japan lasted, there was nothing the Japanese could do to end their total dependence on foreign shipping to carry on their crucial overseas commerce. The Transpacific Freight Conference of Japan (eastbound from Japan to the U.S. Pacific Coast) and the Japan, Atlantic, and Gulf Freight Conference (eastbound from Japan to U.S. Gulf and Atlantic ports) were furious about what they saw as Isbrandtsen's blatant exploitation of the situation: "Isbrandtsen actually wants conferences to be strong enough to hold aloft the rate umbrella under which he can free ride, but weak enough so that they cannot take the steps necessary to meet his competition and keep their loyal shippers competitive with those who ship at his cut rates."[13] Isbrandtsen traditionally had quoted 10 percent under conference rates, but if the other steamship lines decided to lower their rates, they knew they still couldn't win: "We go through all the machinery and headaches and everything else to put out these tariffs. Isbrandtsen wants the conference system with its cumbersome democratic ways of making rates so that, while we are acting like a bunch of saps trying to establish rates, he in five minutes can cut the rates."[14] As an outsider, Isbrandtsen depended on two variables to guarantee his success: his own operating costs, which he always calculated very accurately, and the published conference rates, so that he could quote a lower price.

Undercutting the conferences by 10 percent did not mean that Isbrandtsen was more efficient than the other steamship lines; instead, it meant that by handling a larger volume and, in particular, by guaranteeing that his ships were filled before the others with the available cargo, Isbrandtsen maintained a higher profitability for individual voyages, which compensated for the lower rate. After 1950 the European conferences began to squeeze Isbrandtsen out of the Mediterranean, Middle East, and Indian Ocean trades by the deferred rebate (a discount refunded by the company usually six months or a year after the date of shipment), illegal in the U.S., and dual rates (lower prices for shippers who pledge to use only the conference lines). In retrospect, the conferences covering the eastbound traffic from Japan should have taken similar countermeasures, but since U.S. jurisdiction extended to the Japanese routes, the steamship lines were reluctant to start legal battles. In any case, as long as the U.S. occupation lasted, there really was enough cargo for all. The conference lines hauled 90 percent and Isbrandtsen about 10 percent of the eastbound cargo.

The U.S. occupation of Japan came to an end in 1951. As part of the withdrawal of Allied controls in August, four Japanese lines "were allowed to reinaugurate their merchant marine service to world ports,"[15] and they were joined by four more in 1952. Some ships had been purchased abroad, but as part of the strategy of sparking the economic reconstruction of the country, the Japanese government insisted on building most of the ships in Japan. The Japanese officials, unlike the U.S. government, immediately understood that for national commercial success, a merchant marine was indispensable. Government subsidies poured into steamship lines like Nippon Yusen Kaisha, which now rose phoenixlike from the ashes. The Japanese government charged the eight steamship companies with regaining the prewar position for shipping services at any cost, and, as a first step, Japanese ships were expected to carry at least 60 percent of the country's overseas cargo. To achieve these goals, the steamship companies took out heavy loans, whose repayment was possible only by having the ships haul cargo— even, if necessary, at low rates.[16]

Beginning in 1952 the Japanese lines burst upon the trade routes already overtonnaged by the conference lines and Isbrandtsen. The only way the Japanese could break in was by aggressive tactics: "Rebating, or such similar practice of under-the-table dealing, is quite common in Japanese business. It is another example of the Oriental philosophy that it is perfectly legal unless you are caught in the act. The method which has been used is the cash rebate, with a bill of lading carrying the correct conference tariff rate and ocean freight."[17]

The Japanese considered their main rival to be Isbrandtsen, whose share of the eastbound Japan cargoes had risen from 10 to 26 percent. Japanese lines had captured 49 percent of their nation's shipping volume by 1952, an impressive jump from zero in 1950 when the country was still under the U.S. occupation. The big losers, of course, were the non-Japanese conference lines; their market share collapsed from 90 percent to 25 percent. After much discussion and negotiation, the U.S. and European lines convinced both the Transpacific Freight Conference of Japan and the Japan, Atlantic, and Gulf Freight Conference to lower their rates by 10 percent in November 1952, whereupon Isbrandtsen promptly cut his rates by 10 percent below the new conference level. Isbrandtsen was now coming dangerously close to his operating costs, and the only way he could maintain these low rates was by increasing his sailings, even though he had already increased them from one to three a month. He now announced even more sailings for the future, and the conferences were now forced to announce dual rates, a powerful weapon against outsiders, although not as effective as the deferred rebate illegal in the U.S. trades. When the conferences filed the dual rate contract with the Federal Maritime Board in December 1952, Isbrandtsen quickly blocked approval with a delaying order from a U.S. Court of Appeals, a sure guarantee of months, if not years, of endless litigation.

With each month that passed, the U.S. and European lines were pushed out farther from the trade that increasingly became a preserve of Isbrandtsen and the Japanese lines. Yet the latter were far from comfortable with Isbrandtsen, whose hit-and-run tactics, maverick behavior, and fanatical hatred of conferences and government support clashed with cherished principles of Japanese society. Orderliness, stability, and consensus were the ideals the Japanese sought, and, while they were ready to use the most unethical tactics to preserve their market share, the constant instability symbolized by mavericks like Isbrandtsen profoundly disturbed the steamship executives as well as the shippers of Japan. They decided that Isbrandtsen had to be taught a lesson, and in a historic meeting in Tokyo on 18 March 1953, the two eastbound conferences agreed to lift the formal rates from most of the items carried by Isbrandtsen; each line would be free to quote privately whatever rates it wanted, thereby sidestepping the prohibitions and restrictions of U.S. legislation, which has traditionally encouraged indiscriminate and erratic rate cutting.[18]

The ensuing rate war turned very bitter, with rates dropping as low as 80 percent below the previous conference figures. Having to face the other lines on equal terms, Isbrandtsen no longer knew whether he was undercutting them or not, and his blind guesses were not always right. When some of his ships were carrying cargo for less than the cost of loading and unloading, Isbrandtsen knew he was beaten. In a desperate attempt to end the rate war, he flew to Tokyo to talk to the Japanese steamship executives who, under strong pressure from their shippers, were receptive to his pleadings. However, the European lines were adamant, and their commercial rivalry was accentuated by personal reasons: Isbrandtsen's cousin, A. P. Moller, was determined to crush his former partner at any cost. Isbrandtsen at last had met his match; he returned from Tokyo a defeated man, and while making a transfer of planes in Wake Island, he died of a heart attack on 13 May 1953.[19]

His son Jakob now had the opportunity to end the rate war, but he was initially hesitant to break with his father's tradition; he not only continued the unequal struggle but also pressed in the U.S. courts his father's case against the dual rates. The company lost $3 million in 1953 and $4 million in 1954, and finally in 1955 Jakob dropped the around-the-world service. Stopping the eastbound service from Japan did not effectively end the motive for the rate war, which nobody had expected to last this long, since Isbrandtsen remained running some nearby routes and could resume service at any moment. And at times his ships did return for spot cargoes, an action that did nothing to erase his father's reputation as a hit-and-run raider.[20]

The rate war continued even after the disappearance of the Isbrandtsen menace. The previous ferocity did vanish, and rates rose, but a 10 or 20 percent increase was still needed formally to end the rate war. The Japanese lines now wished to keep a mild rate war going for as long as possible, since their mission had now changed. For the Japanese shipper, the early phase of the rate war in 1953–54 had been a harrowing experience, because of the volatile rates and fluctuating sailings. Predictable rates and reliable services were essential for Japan's export strategy, and clearly the U.S. and European lines, with their predatory tactics, could not perform to Japanese standards. Instead the Japanese steamship lines were extremely sensitive to the needs of the shippers, besides being locked into the web of cultural, personal, and family relationships so typical of Japanese business. While the mission of Japan's steamship companies before the rate war had been to carry a majority of the country's overseas commerce, the new mission became to carry almost all of Japan's commerce, as well as sizable chunks of the world's ocean commerce as well. As a first step, in 1955 eight Japanese lines began to quote the same rates, a practice that continued even when their number temporarily increased to nine by 1957. These were not conference rates, and, according to the individual lines, they were determined independently after a careful study of the market; the coincidence in the rates merely reflected the accuracy of the techniques. The Japanese lines only confessed to having occasional luncheon meetings, but this was simply the revival of a prewar custom "to enrich our knowledge by mutual exchange" in a "purely social gathering."[21]

The U.S. lines wanted to retaliate in the same way by quoting similar rates, but antitrust injunctions against price fixing in the United States made them reluctant to risk prosecution. Instead they counted on the approval of the dual rates, once Isbrandtsen's lawsuit had been dismissed. Meanwhile, United States Lines decided to counter the Japanese challenge by being the first to order the government-designed Mariner-class vessels. First employed in early 1957 in the Japan trade, these ships carried more cargo at a faster speed and lower cost, effectively undercutting the Japanese companies. Panic seized the Japanese steamship executives, and although they rushed to order similar, if not faster, vessels from their own shipyards, they remained exposed to losing part of their market share because of the Mariners. In February 1957, the Japanese lines could not hide their eagerness to end the rate war and restore the conference system:

> These Japanese representatives will prove to be extremely smooth salesmen. They are all nice people and their intent will be joint action to promote a splendid selling job with the foreign lines so that they may gain their objectives. They will be the most

affable people the foreigners ever met. I cannot blame them for this as their livelihood is at stake.

These nine lines, I believe, will agree to everything if they can have the rates closed, and they will promise everything in the way of a complete stoppage of malpractices. At the time they make their statements they will mean every word they say, but when they return to Tokyo, ways and means will be found to violate agreements made. This, as you know, is an old Oriental custom which entails under the table dealing. As to malpractices, all the agreements in the world, plus bonds posted, plus conference memberships, will not prevent the Japanese lines from exercising the malpractice policy.[22]

United States Lines had originally wanted to wait for the Supreme Court decision on the Isbrandtsen lawsuit, but the Japanese representatives were so persuasive that, after further discussions in the Tokyo meeting of March 1958, all the steamship lines finally agreed to end the rate war the following month. Since malpractices (violations of conference agreements) continued to be denounced, the Japanese lines agreed to set up "neutral bodies" composed of persons who would decide what, if any, malpractices had been committed.[23]

Without any doubt, the real winners in the rate war were the Japanese lines, whose 52 percent share of Japanese cargoes in 1958 climbed rapidly afterward. The entry of Mitsui into the Europe–Far East trade had sparked a similar bitter rate war between June 1953 and February 1956, also resulting in another Japanese victory. Japanese ships not only rose to a near-monopoly position in the carrying of their country's overseas trade, but soon appeared through the world's seas competing in many runs previously considered U.S. preserves, such as trade between the Gulf of Mexico and Africa, and by the 1970s even in the North Atlantic trade. The only effective competition to the Japanese lines emerged in the 1970s with the entry of other Far East countries, such as Hong Kong and Taiwan, into the ocean trades.[24]

The rebirth of the Japanese steamship companies after World War II was truly remarkable, and a formidable competitor had appeared much more quickly than anyone in the United States had believed possible. To match the determination and drive of the Japanese lines required vast resources and, most of all, a clear sense of the crucial role of merchant shipping in world commerce. And whatever the exact response to the Japanese challenge, U.S. steamship companies would no longer be able to count on a near-monopoly over the South American routes.

□   South America

From the early twentieth century on, Brazil, Chile, and Peru had operated steamship companies in foreign trade. These companies had limited resources while Lloyd Brasileiro, the biggest, was deeply involved
in the coastwise trade. They posed no threat to U.S. steamship companies whose main competition came from English firms and increasingly from German and Japanese steamship companies. W. R. Grace
and Company had served the west coast of South America since the
nineteenth century, in 1919 the Delta Line began to sail between the
Gulf and the east coast of South America, and, from the late 1930s to
the 1980s, Moore-McCormack ran ships from the Pacific and Atlantic
coasts of the United States to the east coast of South America. Lykes
Brothers and United Fruit Company had regular sailings to the Caribbean side of South America, essentially Colombia and Venezuela.

South America suffered serious shipping shortages in World War
I and even more critical interruptions in World War II. The abrupt way
in which the United States pulled almost all its ships from the South
American routes and left that area starved for shipping services was the
last straw. Most South American governments decided never again to
be left in such a dangerously exposed situation because of the excessive
shipping dependence on Europe and the United States. The internment
of enemy or neutral ships in the ports of South America provided a
convenient nucleus to start a merchant fleet, as in the case of Argentina;
Chile agreed to turn over the seized ships to the United States in exchange for surplus vessels after the war. U.S. steamship companies,
reaping large profits from chartering all their vessels to the government
during World War II, did not sense the mounting movement in South
America, and, rather than promptly enlarging their prewar services,
pondered at leisure their gradual return to these routes. Thus, even
after the war was over, South America continued to pay excessively
high rates and all too often waited anxiously for promised sailings; the
high charges and delays convinced any remaining skeptics about the
need to have their own merchant fleets, whether government or
private.[25]

The most dramatic and significant increase occurred in Argentina,
whose fleet grew over four times in size between 1939 and 1952 and
temporarily eclipsed Brazil's fleet, which had always been the largest in
South America. Only Peru's fleet showed a similar comparable growth,
more than tripling its size during the same period, but among South
American fleets Peru's still remained in fifth place. In Argentina a state-
owned fleet and the steamship firm of the Dodero family, the latter

acquired by the state in 1949, were primarily responsible for the expansion. Brazil's merchant fleet doubled in size between 1939 and 1952 and soon after reclaimed its title as the largest in South America. Expansion was mostly concentrated in the state company of Lloyd Brasileiro. All the South American countries acquired or expanded their fleets by purchasing surplus ships from the United States or by placing orders mainly in European and Canadian shipyards. At least in the case of Latin America, the policy of selling U.S. surplus ships abroad to prevent the rise of foreign shipyards had been successful, but few new orders from Latin America came to U.S. shipyards.

The sharp postwar expansion of the South American merchant fleets appeared to promise bitter confrontations, but they did not materialize. Many South American ships remained tied down in river and coastwise navigation, and in the foreign trade the companies had to distribute ships among routes to Europe, the United States and Canada, and later Asia. The slow expansion of the U.S. lines left plenty of room for the South American fleets, so that although some diplomatic squabbles over privileges and discriminatory treatment erupted, the South American merchant fleets reached a position of regional supremacy by the 1960s without undue notice.[26] The only real attempt to stop the upward spiral of the South American fleets was made by W. R. Grace and Company against a new contender, Flota Mercante Grancolombiana.

This new merchant fleet began service in 1947 and was the creation of Venezuela, Colombia, and Ecuador, who had joined forces in 1946 to create Grancolombiana. Before that time these countries had lacked fleets, except for Venezuela, which had offered limited coastwise service. W. R. Grace and Company had realized the menace posed by Grancolombiana and had tried to block its entry into the conference and the trade route, but Grace had underestimated the resourcefulness of its manager, Alvaro Díaz. W. R. Grace and Company, through a network of agents, retained a stranglehold on the South American coffee cargoes, and shippers of southbound cargo did not want to experiment with the new line. Grancolombiana countered in early 1948 by accepting payment in pesos for southbound cargo, an action that was technically in violation of conference accords. Since the Colombian peso was a local currency worthless outside the country, shippers rushed to dump their pesos on Grancolombiana whose share of the southbound cargo became larger than all the other lines combined.

The Grace Line sought diplomatic and financial action against Colombia, but private ownership of Grancolombiana, unlike the public ownership of most of the other South American fleets, made government pressure meaningless. By threatening a rate war the Grace Line finally forced Grancolombiana to stop receiving pesos as payment for southbound cargoes, but only after considerable delaying tactics. In 1950, just when the Grace Line was about to claim victory, the wily Alvaro Díaz began to accept pesos as payment for the northbound cargo! In exchange for promises from Grancolombiana to stop receiving pesos, the Grace Line agreed to create a pool whereby the former would receive 35 percent of the northbound coffee cargoes. The promises to stop receiving pesos went unfulfilled, and since the 35 percent slice of the coffee cargoes had only whetted the appetite of Díaz, the Grace Line decided the time had come for a knockout blow.

Lobbying with a compliant dictator in Venezuela, the Grace Line obtained Venezuela's formal withdrawal from Grancolombiana. At one stroke Díaz saw his fleet reduced nearly by half, which was not only a physical loss but also a psychological one—one from which he never really recovered, since he had held very dearly the dream of a merchant fleet uniting the three countries of Colombia, Ecuador, and Venezuela. When a dictator likewise came to power in Colombia, all that was needed was a nudge from Grace Line to have Díaz removed from his post; but once again Grace Line underestimated its opponent, confidently trusting that the loss of the Venezuelan share had served as adequate warning. Evidently Díaz had not learned the lesson; indeed, his personal power had actually been increased with the departure of the Venezuelans. Grancolombiana replaced the ships lost and became the nemesis of Grace Line all along the Pacific Coast in the 1950s and 1960s. This affair strongly contributed to Grace's disenchantment with shipping services to Latin America.[27]

Grancolombiana was not as big as the new and enlarged lines in Argentina and Brazil, particularly Lloyd Brasileiro, yet the rise of the latter did not provoke bitter clashes with Delta and Moore-McCormack, in part because of the characteristics of that trade. From the Gulf of Mexico, Delta sailed south with cargoes mainly of lubricating oil and grease; from 1947 the line installed deep tanks to carry some of these petroleum products in bulk rather than packaged as before. The line went as far as Buenos Aires in Argentina, but the essential return cargo was coffee from southern Brazil. The return cargoes were basically the same for Moore-McCormack serving the Pacific and Atlantic coasts of the United States. Moore-McCormack shipped south a greater variety of products, in particular automobiles, heavy machinery, equipment, and coal. Traffic was booming immediately after World War II because Argentina and Brazil, unable to import during the war, had accumulated large dollar reserves and were eager to buy every conceivable type of

U.S. product. By the second half of 1947 the spending spree was over, and to preserve scarce dollars, those countries imposed import restrictions; with the drop in cargo volume, Delta and Moore-McCormack ships sailed south with half their space empty.

Thanks to the Korean War boom and the granting of a loan from the U.S. government's Export-Import Bank to Argentina, the traffic situation improved in the second half of 1950. Again having ample dollars, the South American countries resumed large-scale imports, and both Delta and Moore-McCormack shipped cargoes such as agricultural parts and implements to Argentina. But by 1953 the dollar shortages had returned, sharply curtailing the flow of southbound cargoes. Once again the U.S. ships sailed south half empty, making the coffee cargoes from southern Brazil crucial for the survival of the U.S. steamship companies. Since the share of northbound coffee carried by Delta and Moore-McCormack had been slowly but steadily diminishing from 1945 on, this development was not a very encouraging prospect for the 1960s.[28]

Prior to World War II, northbound cargoes from Argentina had been largely monopolized by European and Japanese lines. They were only partly displaced by the new Argentine steamship companies, so the U.S. lines, in spite of their efforts, remained largely excluded from Argentina's northbound cargoes. Lloyd Brasileiro, a steamship company dating back to the nineteenth century and having more accumulated experience than the U.S. steamship companies, had a ready solution to the dwindling share carried by U.S. ships. Before World War II and on several occasions afterward, Lloyd Brasileiro had proposed a 50/50 agreement: All cargo would be evenly divided in half between the U.S. and Brazilian steamship companies. If one country could not provide enough vessels, the other would be given right of first refusal on the remaining cargo before turning to other foreign lines or the tramps. Here was the life-saving formula that would rescue the U.S. steamship lines from extinction in the South American trade; the agreement could be made binding at either the company or the government level, and Brazil was convinced that once it was signed, Argentina would eventually join the agreement.[29]

Lloyd Brasileiro's formula was not the vicious rate cutting of the Japanese lines during the Far East Rate War. Unfortunately the U.S. government, which had ineffectively responded to the Japanese takeover of Pacific shipping, refused on ideological grounds to sanction or even consider the 50/50 sharing proposals. The results were not long in coming. While Lloyd Brasileiro and the Argentine lines held their market share of the cargoes, the U.S. position was gradually whittled away by the entry of Norwegian and other foreign competitors, including the appearance of Japanese service between South America and the United States. As the next best thing, Moore-McCormack in 1964 entered into pooling arrangements with Lloyd Brasileiro whereby each steamship line received a share of the coffee cargo. These pools, which were to share traffic revenue, cargoes, or both, were bitterly attacked in the Federal Maritime Commission by the European steamship executives who rightly saw in this a first real effective menace from the U.S. lines.

The U.S. government has never been comfortable with cargo-sharing plans because of possible antitrust complications. As a legal expedient, informal agreements between the Brazilian government and the Maritime Administration tried to provide a more secure foundation for such plans in the late 1970s. But by then this mechanism of 50/50 sharing—which, if boldly and decisively instituted in the late 1940s, would have worked well—came too late to save the U.S. steamship companies. Starting in the 1970s a host of other problems overwhelmed the U.S. lines, whose market shares dwindled to insignificance by the 1990s.[30]

11

Ineffective Responses

BY THE 1950s THE revival of strong foreign competition was undeniable. The United States continued to drop in rank among the world's merchant fleets, and only the most vigorous measures could hope to reverse, or at least slow, the steady fall. Would the United States use the opportunities of the 1950s wisely to preserve at least a minor share of the world's oceanborne trade, before time ran out?

☐ New Government Agencies

One last round of changes molded the government agencies in charge of official policies toward steamship companies during the second half of the twentieth century. It would be reassuring to report that the purpose of these administrative shifts was to bolster the rapidly tottering position of the U.S. merchant marine, but invariably this larger goal was displaced by secondary considerations.

The U.S. Maritime Commission, created as an independent regulatory agency in 1936, had satisfied no one, and proposals for its overhaul frequently surfaced in the late 1940s. President Harry S. Truman did not want to deal with this messy topic, but finally he was forced to act when the comptroller general charged the majority of the five-member commission with maladministration. In May 1950 Reorganization

Plan Number 21 abolished the U.S. Maritime Commission and created in its place, within the Department of Commerce, the Maritime Administration and the Federal Maritime Board; the latter awarded subsidy contracts and performed all regulatory functions. The three-member board served four-year terms and was appointed by the president with the consent of the Senate. No more than two members could be of the same political party. The chairman also headed the Maritime Administration, which was in charge of implementing the subsidy contracts and other aspects of government policy toward shipping.[1]

The first chairman was retired U.S. Navy Admiral E. L. Cochrane. Under him, the Maritime Administration mobilized the reserve fleet effectively to meet military shipping needs when the Korean War began in June 1950. Harmonious cooperation characterized the work of the Federal Maritime Board, and Cochrane reported: "It is noteworthy that in these two years the three members have been without exception to come to unanimous decisions."[2] When Cochrane resigned on 1 October 1952, President Truman promoted Albert W. Gatov, another board member, to the chairmanship. But Truman did not fill the vacated position, leaving the board with two members who coincidentally were both Democrats.

Cochrane's political affiliation of Independent had sufficed to prevent the worst abuses, but without his moderating presence, the remaining two board members—who both had strong links to the steamship companies—were left free to do as they pleased. The incoming Republican administration of Dwight D. Eisenhower had to clean up the mess, which was described in a confidential assessment: "The present board members have a seemingly strange concept of public duty, due probably to their former connections and their present and/ or anticipated future connections. When they are not busy "whitewashing" the corrupt or at least highly questionable transactions of the old Commission, they seem to be busy thinking up new deals that would make their predecessors look like 'pikers.' "[3]

The appointment of two Republicans, first to the vacant position and then to the chairmanship (as soon as the incumbent's term had expired on 30 June 1953), changed the behavior of the Federal Maritime Board; for a while it appeared that Eisenhower was delivering on his campaign promises to clean up the mess in Washington. The new chairman, Louis S. Rothschild, soon found that the Eisenhower administration was more concerned with slashing the federal budget, with no thought for how agencies would be able to perform their legally mandated tasks after the cuts: "The administrative staff of the Maritime Administration has been sharply curtailed in 1955 to the point that serious deficiencies exist in the performance of its regular recurring duties."[4] Clarence G. Morse, the next chairman of the Federal Maritime Board, was no more successful in restoring the budget cuts, yet he soon rationalized the problem away. Morse had seen the red tape as a real stumbling block and promised to reduce the excessive paperwork burdening the shipping industry. It would take time to streamline procedures; meanwhile, the Federal Maritime Board could not seriously pretend to police the hundreds of conference agreements between the steamship companies. A staff ten times bigger, if not more, was needed to keep track of the long and detailed rate agreements covering most of the trade routes in the world's oceans. Self-regulation by the steamship conferences tied in well with the Republican policy of limiting government intervention; just handling the grievances of steamship companies kept the Federal Maritime Board swamped with cases.[5]

There was only one problem with Morse's highly accurate prescription. The Federal Maritime Board, in the tradition of its first predecessor, the U.S. Shipping Board, had routinely approved "dual rates" for conferences, which essentially meant that steamship companies could charge lower rates to shippers who exclusively patronized conference carriers rather than nonconference firms. The 1916 Shipping Act had been enacted with a built-in contradiction: one clause outlawed dual rates, but at the same time it gave the U.S. Shipping Board the power to authorize any type of conference agreements. In accordance with prevailing international practice (the U.S. was the only country in the world to have a clause in its codes outlawing dual rates), the Federal Maritime Board had continued the tradition of approving those dual-rate conference agreements brought to its attention. This practice ended and consternation began when, on 19 May 1958, the U.S. Supreme Court ruled in *Federal Maritime Board v. Isbrandtsen Co.* that the 1916 Shipping Act had excluded dual rates from any government approval. Hence, all the conference agreements with dual rates were illegal, and the steamship companies were subject to prosecution under the antitrust laws.[6]

The spectacle of the U.S. government jailing all its shipping executives would have made the United States the laughingstock of the world and would have destroyed the U.S. merchant marine. Instead, a decades-long agony was in store for the steamship companies: Congress quickly tried to pick up the pieces by passing a blanket amnesty exempting from prosecution all past and present steamship operators, whether or not they had filed dual-rate agreements with the government. The Supreme Court decision undermined the already weak conference system, and *Federal Maritime Board v. Isbrandtsen Co.* also set

in motion the events leading to more bureaucratic changes. The antitrust subcommittee of the Senate, under the chairmanship of Emanuel
Celler, undertook a massive investigation into the conference system.
A large staff poured through company and government files, interro-
gated witnesses, and held extensive hearings. Sen. Celler triumphantly
paraded the many rebates, illegal practices, and additional violations of
the antitrust laws uncovered by his tireless committee staff. The blanket
amnesty protected the executives, yet the Celler Committee was a public relations and bureaucratic disaster for the steamship companies, rein-
forcing and confirming the previous fears about monopoly abuses
whenever regulation was not rigorously enforced.[7]

On 12 August 1961, Reorganization Plan Number 7 abolished the
Federal Maritime Board and created the new Federal Maritime Commission as an independent regulatory agency. The five members of the
new commission (no more than three of the same party) were appointed
by the president with the consent of the Senate for five-year terms, but
no longer was the chairman also the chief of the Maritime Administration, which remained within the Department of Commerce under a separate maritime administrator. The isolation between the two agencies
was virtually complete, and while the precise jurisdictions established
in the legislation had eliminated conflicts, the possibility of influencing
regulatory decisions to favor U.S. steamship companies disappeared. In
effect, the Maritime Administration lost one of its last remaining tools
to save the U.S. merchant marine.[8]

From the first years of its creation, the operations of the Federal
Maritime Commission had been "subject to delays, excessive paperwork, and lack of clear-cut program priorities." Congress had over the
years enlarged the agency's regulatory function, yet problems remained: "The Commission has not been granted the amount of staff
increase which it felt was necessary to discharge both new and old functions. Lacking clear-cut priorities, the Federal Maritime Commission
has allowed itself to get 'snowed under' by routine regulatory matters,
while non-routine issues of broad significance have been virtually
neglected."[9]

The Federal Maritime Commission became a lawyers' paradise, as
the ever more complex regulations required hiring larger legal staffs by
litigants and the commission itself. Increasingly foreign steamship companies found themselves obliged to contract the services of one of the
prestigious law firms able to decipher the regulatory maze at the
agency. For the U.S. steamship companies, the Federal Maritime Commission became still another barrier of red tape, countless delays, and
outright fear. So while the U.S. steamship companies declined during

the rest of the twentieth century, the Federal Maritime Commission saved the maritime lawyers whose livelihood was virtually guaranteed by the need to disentangle the complex and never-ending quasijudicial regulatory procedures.[10]

Curiously enough, the commission made its most effective contribution not to the U.S. steamship companies but rather to the international shipping community. The United Nations maritime organizations had become too politicized, and steamship companies were feeling the need for an organization to set some limits and at least save appearances in messy situations. To provide these services, the Federal Maritime Commission became a combination doorkeeper-umpire to a very exclusive club. To cite one example, excessive secrecy had previously characterized the conference agreements, but finally, thanks to the Federal Maritime Commission, certain types of information became equally available to all shippers and steamship companies. At first foreign governments had rejected this intrusion by an agency of the United States, but once the harmlessness of its intentions was confirmed, foreign steamship companies reconciled themselves to an expensive but not altogether useless Federal Maritime Commission.

What was left for the Maritime Administration? To this agency fell the depressing task of prolonging the agony of American steamship companies through the remainder of the twentieth century. Rather than providing swift and effective responses, it gradually sank into a quasijudicial mindset, with cumbersome judicial procedures surpassed in complexity only by those of the Federal Maritime Commission. The Maritime Administration did distribute a dwindling amount of subsidies for shipbuilding and operation, but the procedures to qualify and to remain qualified, as well as the reporting requirements, were so strict and intricate that they partially—if not totally—negated the benefits of the subsidy. To prevent a repetition of the abuses of the 1920s and the 1930s, Congress imposed on the Maritime Administration so many legal safeguards that the crippled agency lost its capacity to counter effectively the many crises befalling the U.S. steamship companies after the 1960s.[11]

The inability of the Maritime Administration to halt the decline of U.S. shipping was evident by the mid-1960s, but, rather than restore its powers and freedom of action, the government proposed to transfer the agency to the Department of Transportation, newly created in October 1966. Even before that department was created, skillful lobbying by labor leaders had blocked the transfer of the Maritime Administration. Nevertheless, organized labor failed to achieve its goal of an independent maritime administration, which would be essentially proindustry and prolabor; the scheme raised the specter of the giveaway policies of the old U.S. Shipping Board, and it floundered in the waning years of the Lyndon Baines Johnson presidency. In 1981, after the Ronald Reagan landslide, the Maritime Administration was transferred from the Department of Commerce to the Department of Transportation, but without any noticeable impact upon the rapidly dwindling U.S. steamship companies.[12]

◻ The Passenger Ship Myth

As World War II drew to a close, government officials and steamship executives found themselves divided over the future prospects for passenger service. One view claimed that keen airplane competition would eventually displace passenger sea traffic, but not before the useful life of existing ships had expired. Another line of thought, based on an analysis of the prewar travel figures, concluded that the surge in demand for passenger services would be greater than the capacity of airplanes to handle and that consequently new superliners had to be ordered. The proponents of the new passenger liners found their position conveniently reinforced by military advisers who argued strongly for the fast troopships required in any future conflict.

Irrespective of the merits of either school, both sides refused to come to grips with the fundamental change in the economics of superliners. The pre–World War I liners had depended on a combination of destitute immigrants and cargo to reap maximum profits; the luxury accommodations for first-class passengers generated little if any gain. The key to the ships' success had been cramming the lower decks with wretched immigrants, so that whatever revenue the cargo brought was pure profit. When the immigrant traffic dried up after 1920, the superliners entered into a period of permanent decline. First-class passengers did pay very high fares, but they expected only the finest service in return. The companies did not have to cater so carefully to second-class passengers and to the rapidly growing tourist class of passengers, who, however, if not treated minimally well, could easily switch to rival European liners. As explained in a previous chapter, the inexorable decline in the profits of passenger liners began in 1920 and continued unchecked.[13]

U.S. steamship companies running passenger service to Latin America and the Far East never quite made the transition to the full passenger liners of the North Atlantic. In South America Grace Line and Moore-McCormack employed combination vessels for carrying cargo as well as passengers, and so did the many lines serving Cuba. The same was the case for the Asiatic services, where the long sailing distances from the United States and the particular characteristics of Asian trade made almost obligatory the loading of cargo aboard the passenger liners in order to forestall competitors. Yet even in the Far East and Latin America, keen competition from airlines was making large inroads into the services of the combination vessels. With foreign lines aggressively seeking freight, passenger traffic became a useless if not financially harmful luxury.

The realization that passenger services had to be sharply curtailed and eventually abandoned was the true mark of entrepreneurial vision after World War II, and by that standard U.S. steamship companies failed miserably. An acute shortage of passenger services in the immediate post–World War II years was welcome ammunition for the proponents of new superliner construction. By a curious omission, the crash wartime shipbuilding program had left out passenger vessels, so that the government had to meet the tremendous need for troopships during the war by adapting ill-suited freighters such as the slow Liberties. At war's end, the troopships were reconverted to passenger ships with disastrous results, producing vessels that the Coast Guard labeled a "disgrace"; on one ship with 950 aboard, conditions were incredibly bad: [The passengers] are carried like cattle. These vessels are boarded by women going down in the ship wearing orchids. The toilet facilities and the like are just exactly what the troops had, if you can visualize that. There are just banks of toilets, no privacy at all. They sleep—I don't believe any of them sleeps less than ten in a room, and they go from forty to fifty. These people are being carried in the cargo holds."[14]

For Americans and foreigners, such as the war brides desperate to reach the United States, and for those needing to travel abroad as well as to the offshore possessions of Puerto Rico, Hawaii, and Alaska, these ships were the only transportation available in the immediate postwar years. The horrible facilities damaged the reputation of the U.S. lines enormously, and many persons lost their desire to travel again by sea.

To end this intolerable situation and to restore the tarnished reputation of U.S. passenger services, John M. Franklin, president of United States Lines, proposed nothing less than the construction of the most modern liner in the world. The company had previously bought as a war surplus vessel the *America*, which was reconstructed at government expense in October 1945, and since bookings far exceeded space in the immediate postwar years, Franklin concluded that the demand for passenger liners on the North Atlantic would remain strong at least during the 20-year life of another new passenger liner, to be called the *United States*. Yet the economics of the venture were not completely reassuring: first, because the investment was initially estimated at $50 million; and second, because nobody knew exactly what to do if the market suddenly changed, "if Europe went completely Communistic or something of the kind and we couldn't run this ship and the trouble with this big unit is she is not suited to run anywhere else."[15] In any case very substantial government backing was obviously needed, and to allay fears about his real intentions, Franklin stated that "we don't believe that a great deal of money can be made out of building and operating such a ship. We are anxious to do it from a patriotic point of view."

Franklin's pleas touched a responsive chord, and not only did the Truman administration agree to his request, but a sympathetic Congress passed legislation increasing the government's share of the construction costs. On 3 July 1952 the *United States* sailed on its maiden voyage from New York City, and its most serious rival, the British Cunard Line, watched the developments with great interest:

> Well, the great *United States* is off on her maiden voyage. I have seen her and she has good lines but rather ugly funnels. It seems to me that the first of Mr. Gibb's extravagant claims for her is already busted, that this much smaller ship can carry as many people as the much larger Queens. The United States Lines have been quick to say the lower number 1660 against the 2200 claim for her capacity is due to so many single occupants of double and three bed cabins. We now have to see what her sustained speed is and how her lighter alloy metals stand up to the North Atlantic on a winter rampage. I remember talking to Patterson about a sustained sea speed of 34 to 35 knots and his reply was that he would have to have another ship alongside to carry the extra machinery and fuel.[16]

The *United States* steamed across the North Atlantic setting a new (and still unbroken) speed record of 35 knots, making the ship the fastest superliner in the world. The technical and navigational success was unfortunately overshadowed in the public mind by a very embarrassing controversy. The newspapers trumpeted charges that the company had bought a $78 million ship for the bargain price of $28 million and, on top of that, had received the normal operating subsidy necessary to compete against the British and French superliners. In spite of company denials, the idea of giveaway legislation by the government to favor a very narrow interest group remained in the public mind. When the Eisenhower administration came into office eager to root out corruption in official circles, the government threatened to present "a strongly worded counterclaim, which reportedly contained a strong inference of fraud on the part of the company and the U.S. Maritime Commission."[17] To preclude further harmful disclosures, the company finally accepted an out-of-court settlement and agreed in May 1954 to pay the government an additional $4 million for the superliner.

The dispute over the price of the *United States*, which followed so closely upon the Dollar Line case, served to confirm in the public's mind that the only concern of the U.S. steamship companies was to make private profit using public funds, a conclusion certainly not disabused when the struggle to find a replacement for the aging *America* erupted in 1958. To avoid charges of favoring only a single company, both United States Lines and American President Lines each requested one superliner. United States Lines justified its request on the consideration that, while the subsidized *United States* earned $3 million profits annually, the older *America* earned considerably less. The company expected a new superliner to be as profitable as the *United States*.[18]

A bitter dispute had preceded American President Lines' decision to order its superliner, to be called the *President Washington*. Younger executives argued that, even in the Dollar Line days, passengers had never generated more than one-third of the company's revenues and that competition from the jet airlines would soon threaten the gigantic investment in a new superliner. Furthermore, signs of radical shifts were evident in the side of the freight business, which would soon demand all the attention and resources American President Lines could muster. Unfortunately for the young executives, passenger traffic on the Pacific route was sharply rising—from 40,000 in 1951, to 91,510 in 1955, to a record high of 110,768 in 1956—and it seemed to the chairman of the board, Ralph K. Davies, who also shared romantic visions of the floating palaces, that unless the company ordered a superliner of its own, American President Lines would miss substantial profit opportunities.[19]

Nevertheless, enough doubts remained about the solidity of the demand for passenger services that both companies felt it advisable to transfer as much of the risk as possible to the federal government. Rather than begin construction immediately under the shipbuilding subsidy measure of the Merchant Marine Act of 1936, which only required approval from a willing Maritime Administration, the companies decided to increase the subsidy payment by special legislation from Congress, just as in the previous case of the *United States*. But the companies went one step further and demanded federally guaranteed low-interest loans for their share of the investment. That last demand was too much for budget-conscious President Eisenhower, who felt the whole thing was a classic case of pork-barrel legislation. Congress dutifully rubber-stamped the proposal, but the president wanted to veto the bill.

The companies and organized labor were not about to give up. The United States was in a recession in 1958, and mounting political pressures called for massive federal spending projects, such as the two new superliners, to revive the national economy. Furthermore, the two vessels would be built in a New Jersey shipyard split among two congressional districts where Republican congressmen had barely managed to stay in office by narrow majorities, in one case by only 1,850 votes. If the superliner bill were vetoed, the shipyard would lay off more than ten thousand angry workers, who would certainly not vote Republican in the 1960 election. Eisenhower knew he was cornered, and reluctantly he allowed the bill to become law.[20]

The law authorized the expenditures, but the funds could be tapped only when they were included in the annual budget, a requirement Eisenhower used to extricate his administration from what he considered on ideological grounds undue government intervention in the economy. A labor leader later explained: "Unfortunately President Eisenhower was able to block the action called for by Congress through budgetary maneuvering which was shortsighted, misguided, and as phoney as a nine-dollar bill."[21] The 1958 drop in American President Lines' passenger traffic changed the company's mind about further expansion, and the company belatedly recognized that Eisenhower's delay had prevented a major investment blunder. United States Lines still continued to pressure for the construction of its superliner, and it was dissuaded only by the realization that the federal funds would never be forthcoming. Executives knew that once the *America* became overage, no replacement was possible. Again, the government's rejection turned out to be a blessing in disguise, because a second superliner would have stretched the company's financial position to the breaking point.[22] By the early 1960s the main concern of U.S. steamship companies became not how to replace but how to dispose of all their passenger ships with the least possible loss. The myth of the passenger liner had been exploded at last, but not before many steamship companies had suffered irreparable damage.

□ The Panama Line Episode

Since 1904 the Panama Steamship Company had run with military precision a cargo and passenger service from New York to the Canal Zone.

Over the years the line added a stop in Haiti, soon becoming the vital steamship service for that Caribbean republic. The ships belonged to the Panama Canal Company, which provided all services necessary for the operation of that waterway linking the Pacific and Atlantic oceans. The Panama Canal Company with its own shipping line belonged to the group of large U.S. corporations—such as Alcoa, Grace, and United Fruit—that shipped large amounts of their own cargo overseas, and so were forced to operate their own vessels to supply part or all of their shipping requirements. Unlike the other corporations, the Panama Canal Company was owned by the federal government, and even though it was hard to separate the activities of the steamship line from the parent company, in most—if not all—of its years of operation its ships had turned a profit.

Ever since the 1920s a number of individuals seeking private profit and obsessed with ideology had tried to take the ships away from the Panama Canal Company. Tired of waiting for the Panama Canal Line to sink into bureaucratic quicksand and heavy losses, in the 1920s private steamship companies launched a lobbying campaign against the government line; the charge was unfair public competition against private operators. The revelations of the Senate investigative committee under Hugo Black abruptly ended that campaign. The huge sums of money the U.S. Shipping Board had poured into private operators had resulted only in personal profit and the bankruptcy of many private steamship companies. Instead, the Panama Line earned profits year after year without additional government subsidy, and its commitment to long-term service stood in stark contrast to the get-rich-quick attitude of most private operators subsidized by the U.S. Shipping Board.[23]

The enemies of government ownership had to lay low for a couple of decades, until the probusiness Eisenhower administration came into office. The Panama Canal Company beat off attempts early in that administration to take away its ships (which miraculously had not been sunk during the war), but the antigovernment pressure was mounting. In a surprise move in 1956, the assistant secretary of the army offered all the cargo and passenger traffic of the Panama Canal Company to the Grace Line; the latter, however, declined the offer because its vessels were overflowing with cargo. By November 1958 the cargo glut had given way to partially empty ships because of the competition from Flota Mercante Grancolombiana. To compound the problem, the Grace Line had just received two new vessels ordered during the boom times, and unless they ran with full cargoes, the company would have to curtail existing services sharply, as well as cancel plans to order three new vessels.

The Grace Line decided that the solution lay not in more vigorous competition against foreign lines but rather in taking away the ships of the Panama Line, in effect sacrificing a public service for the sake of private profit. The Washington office launched a high-powered lobbying campaign in July 1959 under the leadership of the new Grace Line president, Admiral Wilfred J. McNeil, who as a former assistant secretary of defense was supposed to neutralize U.S. Army opposition within the Defense Department. Opposition in Congress was also a serious danger: since the legislation for the Canal Zone had been passed by Congress, all its members had the right to free passage on the Panama Line's ships in order to inspect the facilities of the Panama Canal. McNeil quickly dragged a reluctant United Fruit into the battle, so that both corporate names appeared in key petitions, but the real lobbying was done by the Washington office of the Grace Line.[24]

The same old charge of unfair government competition against private business was used by Grace lobbyists against the Panama Line. Although ideologically attractive to some in the Eisenhower administration, the argument could not withstand sharp scrutiny: the Grace Line was so heavily subsidized in the construction and operation of its ships that it hardly qualified as a purely private line. When in August 1960 the Grace Line offered to buy the last two remaining ships of the Panama Line, its bluff was quickly called by the Federal Maritime Board: because the ships after the sale would become eligible for subsidies, calculations showed that the government would actually save money by continuing to run its own ships. Over the years, as a result of its excellent service and competitive rates, the Panama Line had built up a 70 percent share of commercial cargo to Haiti and the Canal Zone (the rest was government cargo). If the government surrendered this business, what guarantee was there that Grancolombiana or some other foreign competitor would not take away that new cargo from the Grace Line?[25] Furthermore, the Panama Line claimed to provide a vastly more dependable service. The governor of the Canal Zone complained about the Grace Line, stating that "they couldn't even deliver the Ambassador on time—he was five days late."[26]

Secretary of the Army Wilber M. Brucker was now convinced that the Panama Line was essential to the operations of the Canal Zone; more welcome support for the Panama Line came from newspaper columnist Drew Pearson, for whom this was simply another issue of public service versus private gain. Labor leader George Meany, head of the AFL-CIO, sided with the Grace Line, partly because he was opposed to government enterprise and also because the revenues from union dues would be higher in the Grace Line ships than in those of the Panama Line. The need to fill cargo space became even more critical for the Grace Line after the failure of both the Great Lakes service and the container operation to Venezuela (chapter 12), yet the struggle had already assumed larger proportions. The Eisenhower administration was determined "to disclose the importance of this case to the enforcement in other fields of the government's policy on competition with business. This is an open and shut case of flagrant violation of clearly applicable policy. If we don't mean business here, we don't mean business anywhere. The business community, and labor unions, are watching this one."[27]

President Eisenhower decided on 21 December 1960, virtually on the eve of his departure from the White House, to place the two ships of the Panama Line in the reserve fleet, so that henceforth all cargo and passengers would have to use the Grace Line. The incoming John F. Kennedy administration granted a reprieve to review the decision, but the new president soon learned that this issue was no longer to be decided on the merits of the case but instead had become a litmus test to determine whether the new administration was pro- or antibusiness. The grip of big labor and big business was too strong, and the Eisenhower order was ratified, but as a consolation prize, the Panama Canal Company was allowed to keep one vessel to carry government cargoes. With only one ship (the *Cristóbal*), the Panama Line could not serve the New York–Haiti run adequately, so it shifted to the Canal Zone–New Orleans route. The lone vessel continued to provide an economical service long after the Grace Line had quit its Latin American runs. Only when the Panama Canal treaties came into force in the 1980s did the need for this service gradually cease.[28]

□   McLean's First Gamble: Containers

Waterman Steamship Corporation had emerged from World War II in a strong and very prosperous position. Taking advantage of the surplus ship sales, the company acquired the third-largest fleet of merchant vessels in the United States and reaped very high profits from the acute postwar shipping shortage. The Pan-Atlantic division operated mainly in the coastwise and Puerto Rican routes, while Waterman itself provided the foreign services. As an unsubsidized line, the company enjoyed flexibility to change routes and sailings in quick response to the shifting needs of the disrupted postwar trade patterns. Although it did provide regularly scheduled liner service, often its behavior resembled that of a tramp, coming and going wherever the highest rates for cargo appeared.[29]

Looking past boom periods such as the highly lucrative postwar years, founder John B. Waterman had carefully provided before his death in 1937 the resources for the steamship company to survive once the shipping market weakened. The corporation owned a modern office building in Mobile, Alabama, the Grand Hotel with surrounding lands at Point Clear across Mobile Bay, terminals and warehouse properties in Tampa, Florida, and Puerto Rico, 181 acres of land on which a shipyard and repair facilities were located, and, most importantly, the Ryan Stevedoring Corporation. With these assets, Waterman Steamship could survive the inevitable boom and bust shipping cycle: it could retreat back to land activities during the downturns and sail out in force to profit from the upturns. Yet the operating costs for U.S. vessels compared to foreign flags were still so high that the above strategy normally had to be combined with government subsidies—or, in their absence, some foreign-flag operations—if a U.S. steamship company wished to guarantee its survival.

The easy cash of the immediate postwar years went to the head of Waterman's successor, Chairman E. A. Roberts, who overextended himself in his personal investments, while also attempting to launch Waterman Airlines, a venture that foundered in 1947. Thus, when the shipping market began to decline in 1948, the task of carrying out Waterman's policy for survival during the downswing fell to the president, Captain Norman G. Nicolson. Ryan Stevedoring Company emerged as the real money-maker, keeping profits high until 1949. The collapse came in 1950, and if the outbreak of the Korean War in June had not sent shipping rates soaring, the company would have faced large losses, cutbacks, and layoffs. The company had not heeded the warning signs of 1948 to seek either subsidies or flags of convenience.[30]

Roberts's neglect of Waterman Steamship Corporation had been so great that not even the Korean War managed to rescue the company; essentially, the company had no liquidity to meet operating expenses. Thirteen ships were lying idle, and it seemed the company would fold, when a windfall charter from the Military Sea Transportation Service sent the vessels to carry tanks and other military equipment to French Indochina in 1951. The military cargo helped the firm avoid bankruptcy, and the parent company continued to limp along because of Ryan Stevedoring, whose cargo-handling profits kept the fleet sailing. As a further precaution, management shut down the shipyard on 1 January 1952, but the land was retained as a valuable asset. Yet the adoption of real remedies—subsidies or flags of convenience—was postponed indefinitely by another consideration.

Like stockholders of many other closely held companies in the Deep South, as the Waterman stockholders grew older, they increasingly feared the federal inheritance tax that their heirs would not be able to pay. Doubtlessly some arrangement could have been made, as the case of the highly successful Lykes family in the very same shipping field suggested, but Roberts, tired by then of the whole steamship business, had a different idea. He gradually swayed stockholder opinion to accept the idea of selling the company as the best way to sidestep the inheritance tax, while at the same time obtaining cash to pay whatever tax still accrued on the stockholders' remaining assets.[31]

The Waterman Steamship Corporation had been a crucial factor in Mobile's survival and growth during the previous 30 years; only the company's unceasing struggle against Lykes Brothers Steamship had kept New Orleans from overshadowing Mobile as a shipping center. Yet throughout Waterman Steamship's existence, only a handful of persons had appreciated its decisive role in Mobile's prosperity, so that the rest of the business community watched with indifference the impending sale of the company. However, the profits from Ryan Stevedoring were just too good to be overlooked, and a spin-off kept this subsidiary under local control. The significance of Ryan Stevedoring was missed by Malcom McLean, the best prospective buyer, who was initially interested only in the coastwise trade and wanted to buy the subsidiary Pan-Atlantic division. After he completed the purchase, the banks loaned him additional sums to acquire the rest of Waterman Steamship (minus Ryan Stevedoring), one month after the original purchase of the Pan-Atlantic division.[32]

McLean was a trucker from North Carolina whose firm had risen to become one of the 10 largest in the United States. From careful study of cargo movements, he realized many trucks traveled between port cities in the Gulf and the East Coast; if he could somehow load the trailers on ships and sail them around Florida to hook up to waiting tractors in the destination port, he could drastically undercut his competitors because of the immensely lower cost of water transportation. Implementing this sound idea had been difficult, and not the least of the problems was the prohibition upon carriers in the domestic trade from owning more than one type of service. Therefore, in January 1955 McLean sold his stock in the trucking firm, purchased Pan-Atlantic division with the proceeds, and with borrowed money bought Waterman Steamship as well. The fact that McLean was sailing alone, without the safety net of his trucking firm or Ryan Stevedoring Company to fall back on in case of trouble, did not bother him; risk taking right to the brink had always been a key characteristic of his management style.[33]

McLean knew that Seatrain shipped railroad cars from New York and New Orleans to Havana aboard specially fitted vessels that allowed the cars to be lifted from and lowered right on the tracks. McLean's original scheme called for ordering seven "trailerships": special tractors pushed the trailers on board and pulled them out for hookup to the waiting rigs. These trailerships were one of the variants of the "Roll on–Roll off" ships whose origins are unclear but which had appeared in various forms by the early 1950s. One problem remained, however: no one could find an economically feasible way to meet the Coast Guard safety requirements to drain the fuel from the vehicles and disconnect the batteries. Only in the 1960s did the installation of special ventilation systems more than adequately satisfy safety regulations at an acceptable cost. McLean, by having tractors push the vans aboard to their places on the decks, initially avoided the safety rules of the Coast Guard, but he soon realized that the amount of space wasted because of the chassis and wheels of the trailers made the whole operation uneconomical.

McLean was never one to admit failure, and rather than drop the issue, he instead returned to a World War II discovery. Under the wartime emergency, major savings in speed, efficiency, and cost had been made by sending mixed cargo inside palletized boxes (boxes stacked on top of flat trays). So impressed was the War Shipping Administration with the savings in time and labor that it conducted special trial runs using containers instead of palletized boxes and achieved phenomenal results. The end of the war abruptly halted the agency's plan to impose by government order the widespread use of containers, but before it was disbanded the War Shipping Administration shared its discovery in numerous published reports that strongly stressed the advantages containers would bring to ocean trade.[34]

Admittedly the steamship industry had sinned because of inordinate traditionalism, and in the case of waterfront activities, except for increased mechanization, the essential loading and unloading procedures had changed little from the days of the Phoenicians. After World War II, a number of steamship companies puttered around with containers and conducted studies; two firms, Alaska Steamship Company and Bull Steamship Company, actually began to use containers in their scheduled services, but they handled them like just oversize items of regular cargo. When McLean removed the wheels and chassis from the trailers and loaded by special cranes the resulting containers into a ship adapted to carry them, he simply duplicated the War Shipping Administration's discovery and previous operation. His claim to fame lay in being the first to introduce a permanent commercial container service, which opened the door for a whole series of gradually widening changes loosely defined as the "container revolution," whose end is still not in sight.

The seven new trailerships henceforth became "containerships," but McLean could not wait for their delivery from the yards. With money he raised by issuing shares in January 1956, he purchased three

World War II T-2 tankers, on which workers erected two-level wooden decks (spar decks) to stow the containers above the tanker's main deck. The converted ship could carry a total of 58 containers, but since this small number made the trip uneconomical, McLean had counted on shipping oil from the Gulf to the East Coast in the tanks below deck, a proposition that the Coast Guard rejected on safety grounds. Thus when the *Ideal X* sailed on its maiden voyage on 26 April 1956, the advantages and economies of handling containers were amply reconfirmed, but the trip itself and subsequent voyages all lost money. Later the company sold the T-2 tankers; to cover the accumulated losses, the sale of the Grand Hotel with the surrounding 367 acres of property was necessary. Over the next five years, McLean disposed of the main company assets so patiently accumulated by John B. Waterman and so carefully managed by Capt. Nicolson over the three previous decades.[35]

The problem of how to finance the containerships under construction was now compounded by Waterman's gradually weakening position, the result of mounting foreign competition in the shipping lanes. In a very ill-advised move, McLean attempted in 1957 to revive the shipyard; after a year the corporation realized that only further losses, rather than profits, could come from shipbuilding, and the venture was dropped. The decision put off by Roberts in the late 1940s now came back to haunt the company, which at last in 1957 created a foreign subsidiary as the first step toward placing most of the ships under flags of convenience. McLean quickly realized this last solution would generate profits only after the vessels were operational; to pay for the containerships (now reduced to six) under construction, he had to devise instead a separate scheme. In December 1957 Waterman and Pan-Atlantic sold five of the six containerships to another company; the latter promptly placed them with Pan-Atlantic in long-term charter lasting until 1968. The containers and the rolling equipment were almost all likewise leased, and when a new terminal was needed for Pan-Atlantic in Newark, New Jersey, it too was leased. Through all these steps McLean had continued to borrow to the maximum from eager bankers who ranked him among their best customers.[36]

The successful financing of the coastwise container operation still did not address the problems of Waterman. Ever since the purchase in 1955, McLean had left the day-to-day operations of Waterman to his brother James K. McLean, who became the new president. By 1957 James McLean had concluded that only subsidies could save the foreign service, and he began a long struggle to obtain them from the Maritime Administration. Meanwhile he tried to survive by relying on government cargoes and by using the flexibility that unregulated lines enjoyed to move ships from one unsubsidized route to another. Malcom McLean distanced himself even more from Waterman and instead concentrated on the container services of Pan-Atlantic division, which he renamed Sea-Land in 1960. Sea-Land became the jewel in the crown, and whatever profits Waterman generated were syphoned off to Sea-Land. Malcom himself moved to New Jersey in 1965, leaving James behind in Mobile to run what was left of Waterman.

The delays in approving the operating subsidy worsened the financial prospects of Waterman, which not only made cutbacks but continued to sell assets. The Tampa terminal and warehouse facilities were sold in 1960, and they were followed by the 181 acres of the shipyard facilities in 1961. The assets of Waterman Steamship Corporation, once the third-largest U.S. fleet, had been drained away to finance McLean's dream of container operations.[37] If the new containerships were the first step in the revival of the U.S. merchant marine, then the sacrifice of Waterman Steamship Corporation had been more than justified.

☐   The Tramps' Last Try

At the end of World War II, U.S. operators of tramp ships fell into two groups later represented by rival trade associations. The first group comprised the survivors of the post–World War I tramps, who by the 1930s had shifted their remaining vessels to foreign flags to take advantage of labor and maintenance costs that were much lower abroad. The War Shipping Administration had turned over many vessels to these operators during the period of hostilities, so that by 1945 the fleet under their control had vastly increased. Neither the regular steamship lines nor the existing tramp operators could absorb all the vast output from the crash building program in the shipyards, so the War Shipping Administration recruited for the task 30 steamship agents who had never owned or operated vessels before. These "war babies" formed the second group of tramp operators, who were looked down upon by the older and more established first group.

A year before World War II ended, the War Shipping Administration decided to give preference in assigning ships to those tramp operators with sufficient capital to carry on the business in peacetime. After Congress passed the Ship Sales Act of 1946, many operators rushed to buy surplus vessels at rock-bottom prices from the U.S. Maritime Commission, which was also authorized to offer on "bareboat charter" (without crews, officers, fuel, or supplies) hundreds of ships from the reserve fleet. The number of ships under the control of the U.S. tramps, whether purchased or chartered, rapidly mushroomed in 1946–48, essentially because of the acute shipping shortage in the immediate postwar years.[38]

The disappearance of the German, Italian, and Japanese merchant fleets and the temporary eclipse of the British and Norwegian fleets left a tremendous vacuum in shipping services. U.S. steamship lines tried to fill the gap, but the demand was so large that U.S. tramps enjoyed the greatest bonanza in their history. The disrupted trade patterns in the aftermath of World War II created one acute shipping bottleneck after another in the most unlikely places, sending the tramps scurrying all over the world. Rates shot up so high that in some cases a single trip paid for the purchase price of the vessel. The temptation to reap windfall profits was too great for the lines, who began pushing into the tramp trades, rather than merely sailing back and forth between two points. A showdown between the tramps and the lines seemed imminent, but it was avoided by the additional demand in 1947 to ship emergency-aid cargoes of grain and coal to a devastated and destitute Europe. In its appropriations, Congress stipulated that 50 percent of all foreign aid cargoes had to be shipped in U.S.-flag vessels, a measure that in later hard times kept many U.S. tramps alive.[39]

The 50 percent preference on aid cargoes could not by itself compensate for the irreparable damage done by the Ship Sales Act of 1946. Foreign tramps reappeared under the British, Greek, and Norwegian flags during the shipping downturn of 1948. A coal strike in the United States and the decline of aid cargoes to Europe triggered the shipping recession of 1948, which lasted until 1950. Once again U.S. tramps realized that, just as in the 1930s, they could not compete against foreign-flag shipping. Only the protection of the U.S. government saved the tramps from extinction in 1948–50. In addition to the 50 percent cargo preference on foreign-aid cargoes, the government also reserved for U.S.-flag vessels all military cargo, including the trade of occupied territories. However, these guaranteed cargoes were not enough, because U.S. steamship lines actively competed for them as well. Many tramp operators laid up their ships, other slashed their staffs by half, while the rest barely covered expenses. Hope of a future upswing kept them in the business, but as a precaution they began lobbying Congress for subsidies.[40]

Relief came in June 1950 with the outbreak of the Korean War, which caused a shipping shortage comparable to the one at the beginning of World War II. The government's need to transport military goods across the Pacific plus a surge in coal and grain exports to Europe drove rates sky-high. Tramp operators now returned the laid-up vessels

204 □ PART III

to service and like the steamship lines began bareboating from the reserve fleet, until altogether more than six hundred vessels had been chartered. Bareboating ships from the reserve fleet was a profitable and risk-free business, because when the war ended, the vessels were simply returned and the operator was left with a tidy profit. But when the ships were bought, even at below market prices, the owners had to recover the original investment as well as pay interest on the sums borrowed for the purchase. The end of the U.S. occupation of Japan and Germany in 1950 had deprived U.S. tramps of a major share of the guaranteed cargoes, and while this loss was adequately offset by Korean War demands, the presence of foreign tramps hovering just beyond the range of the U.S. government's protective shield should have counseled considerable caution.

Instead, the tramps rushed to buy ships on borrowed money, and to the nearly 70 Liberty vessels bought in 1946–48 they now added 90 more in a spree of panic buying from December 1950 to January 1951, when the Ship Sales Act expired. The only possible explanation for this impulse investment was either a belief in a Korean War of long duration or the assumption that it was merely the opening drama of a much larger war.[41] The tramps' gross miscalculation was evident already in November 1952, even while the Korean War was still in progress, when they sought to make the Military Sea Transportation Service their scapegoat:

> The current tribulations of the American-flag tramp operators are not attributable to the chartering procedures followed by the Military Sea Transportation Service, and the allegation that MSTS makes the market today for American-flag tramp vessels is without foundation in fact. These operators find themselves in a dilemma which has its roots in the basic law of supply and demand. They seek to alleviate this situation by suggesting that the government adopt an artificial and arbitrary basis of compensation for the hire of their ships. Overlooked entirely is the fact that in the recent past, when cargoes were plentiful and rates at a high level, all but a few of the tramp operators were reluctant to charter their ships to MSTS, even at the market rates then current. As a procurement agency, MSTS has no authority to pay for the tonnage it requires, more than the owners of such tonnage could obtain from other sources.[42]

The end of the Korean War in July 1953 further reduced the military cargoes, plunging the tramps deeper into the 1952–55 shipping recession. Quite expectedly, they now revived their pleas for help from Congress.

As a preface to a discussion of that legislative battle, a statement on the nature of U.S. tramping after 1948 needs to be made. The true tramp chased after cargo from port to port, charging the maximum that the shipper was willing to pay for one voyage. Without any regularly scheduled service and with no fixed home, the tramp was a true wanderer, to the point that many European tramp owners and their wives lived aboard with their household belongings. With a tendency to carry bulk cargoes (coal, grain, ores, etc.), the tramps ultimately were ready to stuff anything that would fit aboard, especially to avoid sailing with just ballast on return legs. After 1948, however, although some U.S. tramps wandered about, the majority sailed back and forth between two ports to deliver military and foreign-aid cargoes; the sailings were usually irregular, but otherwise the pattern was like the one of the steamship lines, which explains the latter's readiness to participate. When the U.S. tramps carried grain abroad, invariably they returned home empty, because foreign tramps could deliver cargoes to the United States at a rate that was always lower than the Americans could offer. Once in the United States, the foreign tramps again undercut rates until they found enough cargo to sail to anywhere else in the world, thereby limiting most U.S. tramps to the government–mandated cargoes. Thus, according to one's perspective, the U.S. tramps were either a curious hybrid between true tramps and steamship lines or simply another U.S. shipping distortion.

To escape from the 1952–55 recession in tramp shipping, the owners petitioned Congress and the Maritime Administration for two specific measures. The first was to extend the operating subsidies received by steamship companies to the tramps. In the 1930s England had operated a successful program to subsidize British tramps, but other examples were hard to find, and in the American context of regulation a subsidy program for tramps seemed unsuitable, though perhaps not entirely impossible. The second was to authorize U.S. tramps to establish steamship conferences under Federal Maritime Board supervision, like those in force for liner services. More valuable as another indication of the drift of U.S. tramps to quasiliner operations, the proposal was totally unworkable and noncompliance by foreign tramps could be taken for granted.[43]

Congress was reluctant to adopt any of these proposals, but because the tramps had "caused considerable difficulty in proceedings"[44] at the Maritime Administration, the steamship lines gradually moved to an accommodation with the tramps. Steamship companies normally chartered some vessels for their liner services, and after 1954 they made it a point to sign long-term charters for some of the tramp vessels. Most of the older group of pre–World War II tramp operators had by the

1950s either transferred their vessels to flags of convenience or altogether abandoned vessel operations; many of the World War II operators had likewise returned to the status of steamship agents. One of the largest tramp outfits, South Atlantic Steamship with four vessels, had sold out to United States Lines in 1955. Thus by the end of the 1950s, the remaining U.S. tramp vessels belonged mainly to the "Korean War babies," those who had bought during the impulse buying of 1950–51 and who continued to carry foreign-aid and Military Sea Transportation Service cargoes.

The business was not lucrative, but the profit levels were tolerable enough to entice the owners to remain in the tramp trades. The biggest difficulty was vessel replacement, since the "Korean War babies" had bought Liberty ships that would all reach their 20-year statutory life in the first half of the 1960s. The American Tramp Shipowners Association in 1960 shifted their lobbying campaign in Congress from operating to construction subsidies, so that the owners could replace their vessels, which numbered less than a hundred; however, Congress declined to act on the request, probably because of opposition by the steamship companies. As a partial substitute, some owners added new midsections to increase the capacity and economic life of their vessels.[45]

The American Tramp Shipowners Association and the American Maritime Association, the rival tramp groups, both also tried to convince the federal government to eliminate unfair practices under the 50 percent cargo preference in foreign-aid cargoes. U.S. tramps were being delayed needlessly at foreign ports while delivering aid cargoes, thereby incurring additional expenses. More importantly, the intent of the cargo preference, which was to leave 50 percent of the cargo to the recipient country, was not achieved, since many countries without their own steamship lines simply relied on European tramps to haul their 50 percent share of the cargoes. This practice was not generally the case in South America, but it was rather frequent in Africa and in some Asian countries.[46]

The lobbying strategy of 1960–65 yielded few results, and the tramps' associations (which had never merged into a single body) resumed in 1965 the plea for operating subsidies. This time the tramps enjoyed the support of the steamship lines because the latter felt that if the shipping industry, which was already in critical decline, was to survive at all, it must present a unified front when dealing with the government. Through a series of unfortunate coincidences, the reform of maritime policy foundered during the Johnson administration, and no permanent rescue was forthcoming for the tramps or the steamship companies. However, by 1964 the tramps had gained another lease on life: the Vietnam War. The overage tramps were operated past their service lives; vessels were withdrawn from lay up and from the reserve fleet, and some already under flags of convenience were brought back into U.S. registry.[47] But the lesson of the Korean War had been well learned, and rather than order new ships, the tramps used the Vietnam War as a very profitable way to depart permanently from shipping. As the Vietnam War drew to a close in the early 1970s, the number of U.S. tramps declined, until at some time in that decade they vanished altogether from the high seas.

12

In the Shadow of the Cuban Revolution

NEW YEAR'S EVE, 1958: In Havana high military and government officials came with their wives to welcome the New Year in the company of their president, Fulgencio Batista. Unlike previous grand celebrations, this time the dictator invited only those closely connected with his regime. The invitation promised a memorable party, perhaps even historic. Once the party was under way the dictator dropped the bombshell: His regime, in spite of numerical superiority in forces and weapons, had collapsed under the weight of staggering corruption and could no longer oppose the rebel guerrilla units of Fidel Castro. Batista himself fled at 3:00 a.m. on 1 January 1959. The ensuing stampede included high officials fleeing with caches of money and their wives with jewels. The old Cuba came to an end, and power was assumed by a new revolutionary leadership that, whatever its defects, could not be ruled by money.[1]

Shipping executives, always avid for news of revolutions, concluded from the press reports that there was no cause for alarm. Whatever the political system of Cuba might be, no one could imagine the island existing without a substantial volume of trade with the United States. This initial assessment soon was proved false, and when the loss of the Cuba trade became a reality, the U.S. government concentrated on bringing the Castro regime to its knees by means of an economic and shipping blockade that after three decades still has not succeeded. The U.S. government left steamship companies such as Lykes Brothers,

Seatrain, W. R. Grace, and United Fruit to overcome the loss of the crucial Cuban share of their total cargoes as best they could.

□ Lykes Brothers Steamship Company

The Cuban Revolution found Lykes Brothers just beginning the transition from a family-owned firm to a publicly held stock company. Chairman Solon B. Turman had made the decision to go public in 1958, because he wanted to raise funds in the stock market for the vessel replacement program. Since the 1950s Lykes Brothers had rivaled United States Lines, and the size of Lykes's fleet, which sailed to all the continents, made Turman hesitant about relying exclusively, as had past generations, on family and company savings to finance new vessels. Furthermore, with new technologies and growing ship size, the cost of replacement was escalating rapidly, and new vessels cost three and four times more than duplicates of the older versions.[2]

The task of grappling with financing and vessel replacement was complicated immensely by the Cuban Revolution. Lykes Brothers believed that continued trade with the new Castro government was entirely possible, and its first reports confirmed this view: "Political events in Cuba have had little, if any, effect on traffic."[3] As late as 20 October 1959 Lykes could report that "conditions in Cuba continue relatively normal," and the firm strove by all means to maintain friendly relations with the revolutionary government, but events were beyond the control of the steamship company.[4] By early 1960 the U.S. government had decided to overthrow the Castro government. In effect, this meant a quasiwar against Cuba, and just as in previous U.S. conflicts, the steamship companies would bear the brunt of the losses. The Cuban government, trying desperately to escape from the U.S. stranglehold, now began to strike against any available U.S. targets.

The Castro government, after having seized most private properties of Cuban nationals, now proceeded to expropriate all U.S. assets. However, this wave of nationalizations left the Lykes ships untouched, as well as those of other U.S. steamship companies. Vessels could freely sail in and out of Cuban ports, but already by March 1960 a "very serious deterioration of traffic conditions" was evident so that "overall conditions in the trade [were] most abnormal."[5] The end soon came:

> Through the spring and summer months, the traffic situation to Cuba deteriorated to the point where less and less cargo was available to Conference Lines' vessels, the Cuban government, to a large extent, utilizing its own tonnage. The death blow came

in late July, when the Cuban government took over most impor-
tations and decreed that henceforth all freight must be collected
and paid in pesos. Under these conditions, we were forced to
suspend service to Cuba, and have not had a sailing to that country since the early part of August 1960.[6]

With the rather sudden cessation of the Cuba service, what could
the company do with the excess vessels not easily shifted into other
already overtonnaged routes? Fortunately for Lykes, a number of its
vessels had been on long-term charter from the reserve fleet of the U.S.
government. The Maritime Administration quickly agreed to the re-
delivery of these vessels in September 1960, thereby removing part but
not all of the burden from the company. As was usual with U.S. steamship companies in times of crisis, they rediscovered Puerto Rico, that
U.S. island possession in the Caribbean, but since its cargo volumes
could never replace Cuba's, Lykes adopted a special strategy: "Since the
suspension of our Cuban service in August 1960, it has been our practice to schedule bi-weekly sailings to Puerto Rico, with alternate voyages extending to Venezuela/Colombia and the others serving Haiti and
the Dominican Republic."[7]

Lykes still had too many vessels, but this surplus proved a temporary bargaining chip: Japanese lines had been eating into the profitable cotton exports from the Gulf to the Far East, and Lykes, which had
just lost the Cuba trade, could not afford to continue looking the other
way. Lykes threatened to start a rate war with the Japanese, who knew
the U.S. company could back up the threat because the firm actually
would save money by running its otherwise idle ships in the competition for the cotton cargoes. The Japanese lines, surprised by this unexpected show of force, quickly capitulated; the ensuing "Cotton Pool"
(to distribute equitably the cotton cargoes) helped Lykes regain its share
and restored stability for years to the cotton trade from the Gulf.[8]

Another solution also came out of the Far East. The Kennedy
administration was carefully preparing the groundwork for the Vietnam
War: "The 'crash' military program to Saigon, on which earliest arrival
in Saigon was of paramount importance to the highest level of our government, required several additional Saigon sailings the first four
months."[9] The prospects were good for cargoes: "Of major importance
has been the great increase in Military Sea Transportation Service Shipments to Saigon, where the precarious situation shows no signs of eas-
ing."[10] In effect, Lykes had been the first U.S. steamship company to
discover in the Vietnam War a temporary substitute for the cargoes lost
because of the Cuban Revolution. Other steamship firms soon followed

suit, and in effect the Vietnam War became the temporary bailout for many of these troubled companies, since the vast sailing distances across the Pacific Ocean guaranteed more than ample cargoes. In the period of rapid buildup, the Maritime Administration even had to take more than a hundred World War II vessels out of the reserve fleet (including all the Victories, but none of the Liberties). After a few years most of these vessels were returned to the reserve fleet, and the resupply of military forces in Vietnam was continued by the companies' traditional shipping services.

If Lykes had been the first to realize the potential of the Vietnam War, it had also been among the first to understand that the war was a temporary phenomenon and could never replace the permanent cargoes characteristic of the Cuba trade. How could Lykes survive in a post–Vietnam War shipping world? The results of alternative strategies were not very encouraging. Great hopes were placed on the Soviet wheat purchases of 1963–64 as a means of generating profitable cargoes, but the plan did not work out: "In fact the eventual effect was to the contrary in that it enticed from layup considerable tonnage whose continued operation has depressed the market to the extent that in some segments it is lower than prior to the wheat purchases."[11] Into the routes from Puerto Rico to the Gulf came Seatrain in 1964 to offer "formidable and damaging competition."[12] In the Far East, as part of its quest for economic supremacy, Japan continued to build one of the most powerful merchant fleets the world had ever seen, which was "now being regrouped and realigned in such fashion as to create a greater competitive force in this trade"; this news evoked scant interest in a U.S. government obsessed with the Vietnam War. Also, Lykes's success in reducing crew size from 46 to 32 through mechanization soon was copied by foreign lines, thereby erasing any momentary advantage.[13]

Chairman Turman believed the real answer lay in diversification away from shipping, a policy he initiated in 1962. Yet, *diversification* was a term that did not quite reveal the complexity of Lykes Brothers. The early activities of Lykes discussed in previous chapters revealed that a web of relationships tied the steamship company to a larger family investment group. Starting about the same time as the Dollar family, the Lykes had grown into a clan of more than a hundred members by the 1960s, so that shifting alliances in the already complex panorama of family properties and wealth served as backdrop for diversification. Going public in 1958 had been advantageous for the company, but the strategy had failed in its main goal of raising capital, since investors proved reluctant to buy shipping stock. By diversifying into other fields, Lykes Brothers hoped to improve its image among prospective stock investors. Turman had established a subsidiary company to engage in nonshipping activities in 1962, and the next president, Frank A. Nemec, secured government approval for transferring the legal reserve funds into nonshipping areas.[14]

The company Nemec received in 1965 had plenty of cash and no debt (the last loan dated from 1933), was at the end of the vessel replacement program, and had started a very modest diversification. As a first step, he decided to convert Lykes from a shipping firm into a holding company, a maneuver that released $50 million in cash and allowed him to borrow $150 million more from the banks for his takeover goals. Nemec began with purchases of an insurance company and an electronics distributor; then he felt ready to make his big takeover move. After careful examination of what companies were up for grabs in the United States, Nemec concluded that natural resources was the best field. Oil companies with their steep entry prices were beyond reach, but with the $200 million he had raised he could pick up Youngstown Sheet and Tube, a steel company that owned its own iron ore and coal deposits. After a somewhat bitter takeover fight, Lykes prevailed, and in February 1969 the merger of both firms into a new Lykes-Youngstown Corporation was announced; Lykes Brothers now became the steamship subsidiary.[15]

The purchase of the eighth-largest U.S. steel producer was not the excuse to leave shipping; as a matter of fact, the diversification, by spreading the investment over a larger area, lowered the risks inherent in shipping. Lykes Brothers proceeded with the construction of a new type of vessel, the SEABEES. Lykes claimed that "more than a new vessel design, it is a complete new system of ocean transportation"; the three ships ordered in 1966 were supposedly "destined to revolutionize ocean freight transportation," and they did have many unique features.[16] Originally called a barge carrier, the large ship (27,183 deadweight tons) could load and unload barges through a special elevator (Syncrolift) at the rear of the ship. The novelty was that besides being a barge carrier (like the LASH ships discussed in the next chapter) the ship also allowed vehicles to drive on and off, since the elevator lowered a whole deck to whatever dock level was required. Furthermore, the ship could carry containers with the same ease.

Impressive as the technical aspects were, the commercial achievements were no less so. The three vessels were well suited for military cargoes, earning enthusiastic backing from the U.S. Navy and civilian agencies. Their role was not limited to the Vietnam War, and afterwards they found profitable employment in many shipping routes. The large dimensions of the ships and the elevators made them ideal for transporting oversize equipment formerly too big to load on board. When cargo was scarce, the ships could be filled with vehicles, containers, or just about anything else. Best of all, here was a technological innovation that foreign competitors were slow to copy, because Lykes had found and comfortably captured the demand slot for SEABEE services in the world market. Foreign lines instead turned to containerships, which handled containers much faster and cheaper than the SEABEES could. Even before the first SEABEE entered service early in 1972, Lykes Brothers itself had ordered, in 1970, nine ships (and subsequently four more) to be converted to containerships; the shipyard added a midbody section as well, thereby enlarging the capacity of the converted vessel.[17] Thus, as a diversified company, Lykes Brothers moved successfully into the container age of shipping, thereby overcoming the earlier loss of its long-standing trade with Cuba.

□   Seatrain

Not all the companies affected by the Cuban Revolution had been as successful as Lykes Brothers. Since 1900, the Peninsular and Occidental Steamship Company of Miami (no relation to Peninsular and Oriental Steamship of England) had been running passenger-cargo vessels between Cuba and Florida. Because of the Cuban Revolution, this service ended in the middle of 1960, and Peninsular and Occidental was left stuck with ships ill-suited for other routes. The company, owned by several railroads, made an effort to enter the cruise business by sailing to the Bahama Islands from Miami, but this attempt merely prolonged the agony, since U.S.-flagships from the early 1960s on had proved their inability to hold even the smallest share of the cruise business permanently. In December 1967 the stockholders finally liquidated Peninsular and Occidental.[18]

Another casualty was the Ward Line, which up to 1960 had provided service to New York, Havana, and Mexico. After the liquidation of the Atlantic, Gulf, and West Indies Company in 1955, Jakob Isbrandtsen eventually bought its main shipping subsidiary, the Ward Line. He quickly disposed of the Ward Line's six old vessels and replaced them with two chartered ships of larger size under Panamanian registry. Operations under these new arrangements remained profitable until the Cuban Revolution disrupted trade. Losses began to pile up early in 1960, but the Ward Line was reluctant to suspend sailings until the legal question of its lease from the University of Chicago of the dock and warehouse in Havana harbor had been cleared up. The run to Mexican ports had only served to fill up ("top off") the open spaces left after the main cargo had been loaded in Havana, so that once the Cuban trade ended in the fall of 1960, service to Mexico likewise ceased. Isbrandtsen was left with two ships under long-term charter that he was forced to dispose of at a heavy loss in order to qualify for operating subsidies for the remainder of his fleet. The whole Ward Line venture had turned out to be a failure; indeed, for the Isbrandtsen family, the origin of the family's ruin dates back to the suspension of the Cuba service in 1960.[19]

Another company slated for disappearance was Seatrain. Like Peninsular and Occidental and the Ward Line, it had relied heavily on trade with Cuba for a very profitable livelihood since 1929. Seatrain's six vessels had been specially designed to drive on board railroad wagons subsequently lowered into the holds by ingenious devices. Lumber, sugar, and general cargo were transported aboard these ships, linking the ports of New Orleans and West Palm Beach with Havana. The onset of the Cuban Revolution led the company to suspend the lucrative service in 1960, and with no other choice left, Seatrain strove to place its excess ships in additional runs within the coastwise trade of the United States. Late in 1960 the company opened service from New York to Texas City, with calls in major ports like New Orleans and Savannah. The company counted on carrying railroad wagons and truck vans at a cheaper rate than hauling by land. Soon the ships began to carry containers as well, but to no avail, because the railroad companies united to drive this competitor against the wall. To cut costs, Seatrain convinced the unions to reduce the crew sizes by five on each vessel, but as losses continued to pile up in 1963, the selective cuts in railroad rates finally forced the company to suspend its coastwise service.[20]

Seatrain had seen the end coming and wisely decided to redeploy its ships to Puerto Rico in May 1963. Puerto Rico, a U.S. island possession in the Caribbean with many similarities to Cuba, promised to become a suitable replacement. Seatrain purchased marine terminal facilities in Puerto Rico to acquire a permanent base for the trade with the U.S. mainland. Try as it might, the service to Puerto Rico could never replace the trade to the island of Cuba, which was 10 times bigger in size and which had a much larger economy. It did improve Seatrain's prospects to the point that in August 1963 U.S. Freight Company, a holding company of freight forwarders, made a purchase offer. Since both companies were in domestic transportation, the Interstate Commerce Commission had to approve the merger. The regulatory process dragged on for nearly two years, giving plenty of time for Transeastern Associates, a rival company not subject to the jurisdiction of the Interstate Commerce Commission, to snap up Seatrain in May 1965. A new phase in Seatrain's history, which would last more than 15 years, had begun.[21]

Transeastern was really Joseph Kahn and Howard Pack, two ex-furriers who hated the fur business and wanted something different. In 1950 they had bought surplus Liberty ships, and they soon branched out into buying tankers for chartering or operating on their own. By 1965 they owned the *Manhattan*, then the largest U.S.-flag tanker, and they were looking for an addition to their growing shipping empire. In 1966 they made Seatrain their headquarters, the older firm providing the corporate structure and the prestige needed to run a major shipping organization.

Wonderful as the tankers were for Seatrain, they still did not solve the problem of what to do with the ships that the Puerto Rico trade could not absorb. Precisely this problem had made Seatrain a risk as well as a cheap acquisition for Kahn and Pack, but they confidently counted on the Vietnam War to solve the excess ship problem. Military cargoes soon overflowed the capacities of Seatrain, and the company received ships from the government reserve fleet for wartime duty. With the Military Sea Transportation Service opening additional bids for carrying cargoes to Southeast Asia, Kahn and Pack had no difficulty securing loans to finance Seatrain's expansion.

Seatrain increased its tanker fleet and placed the new vessels either in long-term charters with the oil companies or in the "spot" market for voyage charters. Seatrain devised a technical innovation that allowed cleaning the tanks while sailing from one port to another. This method changed the tanker business, and confirmed Seatrain's tradition of innovation: tankers loaded with aid cargoes of U.S. wheat went to India, then on the return voyage cleaned their tanks prior to reloading Persian Gulf oil for Europe.

If Kahn and Pack had mastered the intricacies of the tanker trade, certainly the transition to containers would have posed no problem. Seatrain, with such a rich tradition in handling railroad cars and vans, had not the slightest doubt that containerization was the wave of the future. The immediate decision was how best to enter the container age: whether to scrap its modern freighters and build new containerships, or simply to convert the existing vessels to full container capacity. Seatrain poured its vast store of data into computer simulations until enlarging four of its vessels emerged as the best alternative. An additional midsection was added to each and the enlarged ships, besides each being 110 feet longer, also had more powerful engines. Afterward a new generation of containerships was ordered.[22]

With this lead in containers, Seatrain hoped to capture major portions of the container market; and once the Vietnam War was over, the firm hoped to have its future assured. Kahn and Pack had other ideas as well—they were always trying something new. The discovery of Alaska oil on the North Slope promised large volumes of cargo for U.S.-flag tankers carrying the crude to the East Coast. One possibility that had never been explored was sailing through the Northwest Passage past the Arctic Circle and into the North Slope fields. Over half the route through Canadian waters remained frozen except for a few weeks each year; icebreakers were not enough, so the tankers would have to be specially adapted for these path-breaking voyages. Computer models did not have enough data to provide a definitive answer to this exciting and challenging possibility. Kahn and Pack duly fitted the *Manhattan* for a trial run from Philadelphia in 1969; the vessel was chartered to an oil company for one voyage. Would the *Manhattan* make it through the ice? Seatrain executives waited anxiously, and with joy they received the news that the *Manhattan* had returned with only minor damage from the historic crossing. But when the voyage data was fed into the computers, the analysis confirmed that the route was uneconomical. The oil companies opted instead for building a pipeline from the North Slope to the port of Valdez in the south; from there the tankers would load the crude for transport mainly to the East Coast via the Panama Canal.[23]

The *Manhattan* setback, although minor, did counsel the need for caution before plunging into high-risk situations. This was especially true for Seatrain, whose rapid expansion had been financed by bank loans exceeding $100 million. Yet even while the *Manhattan* experiment was taking place, in January 1969, Kahn and Pack had made a crucial decision that would have the greatest impact on the company's future, as a later chapter explains. Nevertheless, as the 1960s came to a close, most observers agreed that Seatrain had managed to recover from its Cuban losses and was branching out to explore many new areas in a creative and productive manner.

□ W. R. Grace and Company

The Cuban Revolution caught W. R. Grace and Company by surprise, but it was not among the hardest-hit shipping companies. The Castro government did nationalize some of the firm's small properties on the island, but those losses were easily recovered through generous U.S. tax clauses. More serious was the loss of cargo for its ships, a setback Admiral Wilfred J. McNeil had to face when he took over the presidency of the Grace Line in October 1959. Fortunately for Grace, the bulk of its trade was with Peru, yet the Cuba share was still highly significant. While fully loaded ships sailed south from New York to the Pacific Coast of South America, northbound cargoes were generally insufficient, except during the harvest season when ships loaded sugar at Cuba for the last leg of the return voyage. The Cuba trade, by making the northbound voyages profitable, held a place all out of proportion to the limited volume of the sugar cargoes. Thus, when service to the island ended in 1960, Grace Line posted losses for the first time in many decades.[24]

The parent company, W. R. Grace, was impatient with this deficit. As a first urgent step, McNeil reduced the number of voyages between the New York and the Pacific Coast of South America, a solution that left him with idle ships. What could the Grace Line do with the excess ships? McNeil tried to enter the Puerto Rico trade, and he made a bid for Bull Steamship's route (but not its ships), hoping that the Grace Line could operate the excess ships on the New York–Puerto Rico run. However, before the deal could be closed, Manuel Kulukundis, a Greek shipper, bought all of Bull Steamship in 1961; even if the Grace bid for just the route had been successful, it still was not clear how the company could have obtained Maritime Administration approval when, by law, ships built and operated with subsidies were excluded from the Puerto Rico trade. With no quick end to the problem in sight, Peter Grace, the president of the parent company, stepped in and sold eight of the Grace Line's vessels at a loss in 1962; he was stopped from selling the entire line only by the lack of a buyer.[25]

The drastic surgery was effective, and the Grace Line began to show profits again in 1963, although its position in the market remained vulnerable. For Peter Grace, president of the parent company since 1945, the Cuban Revolution merely confirmed what he had long ago foreseen—that the company was sitting on top of too many powder kegs in Latin America. While the swiftness of the Cuban Revolution had caught him by surprise, he was far from unprepared. Soon after becoming president, he made his first major decision: The company must withdraw from Latin America and shift the bulk of its investment back into the United States. But in what sector would he invest? For years a task force of young professionals studied every nook of the U.S. economy and finally boiled down the choices to three: electronics, oil, and chemicals. After careful thinking Grace finally picked chemicals, prompting the president of DuPont to remark: "What is the chemical industry coming to when even steamship companies are getting into it?"[26]

Undaunted by outside carping or in-house skepticism, starting in 1952 Grace invested heavily in chemicals until by 1963 that division generated 60 percent of the income and 70 percent of the profits. Earnings from Latin America were used for chemical diversification, but a majority of the expansion was financed through loans from U.S. banks. The transition from a steamship company to a chemical giant did not go smoothly, numerous mistakes and setbacks occurred, but ultimately the transition was successful, raising again the question of the Grace Line's future within the new corporate structure. Shipping in the 1960s accounted for only a 10 percent share of both income and profits, yet Peter Grace toyed again with the possibility of retaining the steamship line as a support system for the company's remaining investments in Latin America, particularly in Peru. Within the limits of corporate policy, McNeil tried to steer the Grace Line through the remainder of the 1960s, always seeking ways to convince the parent company to remain in the steamship field.

One of the first experiments failed miserably, in spite of lengthy studies. The Grace Line was the first to adopt containers for international routes, but when two specially constructed ships went into service in 1960, longshoremen in Venezuela refused to unload the vessels because they feared their jobs would become superfluous. Only major diplomatic pressure could convince the Venezuelan government to force the dockworkers to handle the cargo, but in the wake of the Cuban Revolution, the State Department was extremely reluctant to antagonize foreign governments whose support was crucial to stop the spread of Castro-inspired revolutionary movements in Latin America. The successful introduction of container services would have given the Grace Line a temporary lead over its Latin American rivals, who inevitably would have been forced to counter with their own containerships. The Grace Line sold the two container vessels, and not only was the widespread use of containers in Latin America postponed until the late 1970s, but enthusiasm for rushing into container service in the North Atlantic was dampened considerably.[27]

Besides regular freighters, the Grace Line had traditionally operated combination cargo-passenger vessels from New York City to the Pacific coast of South America. From the late 1950s passenger traffic had been hit hard by increasing air travel, but a substitute appeared in the growing number of persons seeking cruises to the sunny Caribbean during the winter months. The Grace Line ships could not handle the seasonal volume, and the overflow of cruise passengers became a lucrative alternative for the operators of transatlantic service, in particular United States Lines and American Export, whose passenger liners were ideal because of scant demand during the winter months. Moore-McCormack soon wanted to withdraw its Mediterranean liners for passenger cruises, and this "blanketing of Grace's entire Caribbean service" produced an "oversaturation", until the Grace Line saw the winter cruise passengers driven from its older and smaller cargo-passenger vessels to the floating palaces of the Atlantic.[28] Clearly a decision was needed: either the Grace Line abandoned its passenger service altogether to concentrate on freight, or it built specially designed tourist vessels for Caribbean cruises. An indication of which way the company was leaning came in 1967, when W. R. Grace sold its 50 percent share in Panagra Airlines to Pan-American Airlines; Panagra would have been a crucial link to any tourist strategy by offering combination sea-air cruise packages.

Bethlehem Steel shipyards delivered the last of the three cargo-passenger vessels in 1963, a year behind schedule. The Grace Line had sued the shipbuilder for breach of contract and for designing insufficient refrigerated space for bananas on four freighters delivered during 1963 and 1964. Grace also had litigation pending against Sun Shipbuilding and Dry Dock Company for excessive delays in making unanticipated changes in vessel technology. The complex litigation was not finally settled until the 1970s, but for a parent company doubtful about the Grace Line (which was made a separate subsidiary in 1965), the shipyard complications were not very reassuring. Starting in the 1960s, foreign shipyards have tried to lure U.S. steamship companies away from domestic shipyards whenever possible. They have treated shipping executives like kings and have offered every conceivable service to guarantee the customer's satisfaction with the final product, at prices as low as 50, 100, and sometimes even 150 percent below those quoted by U.S. shipyards. In contrast, when U.S. steamship companies have dealt with domestic shipyards, both have acted more like strangers or intermediaries on the road to the U.S. Treasury. In effect, the domestic shipyards have built ships to receive their subsidized prices, and steamship companies, to qualify for their own subsidies, have had to use U.S. shipyards. The only sure winners have been the shipyard workers employed at uncompetitive wage rates on the world market. Not surprisingly the Grace Line was reluctant to repeat its past experiences with U.S. shipyards. But to build abroad also meant adopting foreign-flag operations as well as redefining the Grace Line's rationale.[29]

McNeil tried one last gamble to save the shipping line for W. R. Grace. Because of the U.S. Shipping Board's insistence on small firms in the 1920s, W. R. Grace had not been allowed to serve both coasts of South America and had remained limited to the Pacific side. A motley succession of U.S. companies, the latest of which was Moore-McCormack, had served Brazil and Argentina on the Atlantic side. Facing divided and generally small U.S. lines, the Latin American steamship companies had thrived since the late 1940s, until they had become formidable rivals. Grace had continued to feel the pressure, but McNeil believed he had finally found a way to outflank the Latin American rivals in one bold gamble.

His ideal solution was to fuse Moore-McCormack with the Grace Line. The plan began to unfold when, as a first step, in May 1966, he acquired one of Moore-McCormack's routes, around the Straits of Magellan between the U.S. Pacific Coast and Brazil/Argentina. By integrating this new route into the existing Grace Line services, a vastly enlarged itinerary with tremendous profit potential emerged because coffee from Brazil and meat from Argentina provided very valuable return cargoes. Massive opposition immediately materialized from the Latin American steamship executives who saw this move as a grave threat, since Grace Line could then undercut rates in any of the countries. Latin American steamship companies did not believe that they could stop this formidable competitor, but to try to prolong their resistance in the anticipated rate war, they formed a common front. McNeil was still convinced that his strategy was sound and wished to press forward, but he was overruled, and the Grace Line, without having made a second move, announced the cancellation of its proposed service around the Straits of Magellan in November 1966; McNeil retired shortly afterward in May 1967.[30]

Devaluations in Latin America reduced W. R. Grace profits in 1967, and Peter Grace by now had gone sour on Latin America and wanted to liquidate the firm's holdings. The Peruvian government seized the sugar lands in 1969, and other seizures and sales followed, until the investment in Latin America narrowed to chemical-related ventures. The Grace Line alone remained as a reminder of former times, and finally in October 1968 the parent company made the decision to find a buyer. After an intensive year of search and negotiations, Prudential Lines, owned by Spyros S. Skouras, purchased the Grace Line in December 1969; W. R. Grace's 50 percent share of Gulf and South American Steamship Company was bought by Lykes Brothers Steamship Company, the owners of the other 50 percent.[31] After more than a hundred years in shipping, W. R. Grace had come full circle: from its beginnings in ocean transportation, the company invested widely in South America, only to return to the United States and sell its steamship line as a last step. Whatever may have been the losses, both economic and sentimental, the hard fact remained that the diversification away from merchant shipping had saved W. R. Grace and Company and propelled it into the ranks of the leading U.S. industrial enterprises.

□ United Fruit Company

For many Latin American countries, the Great White Fleet was the most visible sign in their waters of the presence of the U.S. merchant marine. Since the end of the nineteenth century, the Great White Fleet had plied Latin American seas carrying mainly bananas and also sizable sugar cargoes; with more than 55 vessels in the late 1950s, no signs of decline were apparent. Yet unknown to all but a handful of high executives, United Fruit Company had been in deep trouble since the late 1940s. The profit margin had fallen from 33.4 percent in 1950 to 15.4 in 1957; the value of the company's stock had dropped almost by half, and in the summer of 1959, for the first time in the company's twentieth-century history, it skipped a quarterly stock dividend.

The parallel with W. R. Grace and Company was striking: both companies had reached the limit of their expansion in Latin America. Unless new areas could be found for investment, the downward turn would soon become impossible to reverse. It was a sad commentary on the prospects for development in Latin America when companies with ample capital concluded that no further expansion was possible in a continent whose populations lacked so many basic necessities of life. But corporate survival must be the first rule of company executives, and here the vision of Peter Grace stood out: he detected the problem in the late 1940s and after 1952 began to transform W. R. Grace and Company into a chemical company. The fact that he and his family were major stockholders gave added impetus and authority to the change. At United Fruit, management owned little stock, and ownership until the late 1950s was scattered among 95,000 stockholders, with no individual having more than 1 percent of the nine million shares. The Boston-based management was old and highly conservative in its business methods, and the executives' policy was simply to keep doing more of the same until an upswing automatically returned the company to high profit margins. An ace in the cards was mainly responsible for the management's lack of concern over the downward trend: the two profitable sugar mills in Cuba had bailed out United Fruit at critical moments, and they were expected to do so again. Initial indications seemed to back the old-timers' claims: since 1954 the two sugar mills had entered a period of high profits large in both amount and margin, a cyclical upswing expected to peak in the early 1960s.[32]

At this time executives had long forgotten their former employee Angel Castro, who had gone on to become a small landowner on his own. Local United Fruit officials remembered two of his children, Raúl and Fidel, just as two nice kids, so when Fidel Castro came to power with his brother in January 1959, United Fruit initially expected continuation of the good times under Fulgencio Batista. Gradually the Cuban government started nibbling away at the company, until in March 1960 it expropriated its Cuban lands (the firm's largest holding in any Latin American country). As usual with the nationalizations, the Cuban government had not seized the ships, but United Fruit Company had lost the vital sugar profits, and without the sugar cargoes the Great White fleet could not operate as a lucrative venture. United Fruit had dealt with problems like this before, most recently in Guatemala where it had helped the CIA overthrow a nationalistic regime in 1954. In a repeat performance, United Fruit lent to the CIA two of its freighters needed for the invasion force sailing to topple the Castro government in April 1961. Bad luck continued to plague United Fruit: not only was the invasion force defeated and captured, but Castro's air force, which had sunk other ships of the invasion flotilla, had unfortunately failed to sink those of the company. No compensation for the vessels was possible from the CIA, and the company was stuck again with the two freighters to add to its ships idled by the lack of sugar cargoes.[33]

Generous tax credits indemnified United Fruit and other U.S. companies for the loss of their Cuban properties, but this still did not replace the expected profits from the sugar mills, nor the lost cargoes for the ships. A decade after W. R. Grace and Company, and at about the same time as Lykes Brothers Steamship, United Fruit at last decided to diversify away from Latin America in a two-step process. To reduce its exposure to future expropriations, United Fruit attempted to sell all its lands. But after strenuous efforts, the firm could dispose of less than one-third of its properties; indeed, many countries did not want the company to leave, and occasionally it found itself buying additional lands. Even W. R. Grace and Company, which today still has investments sizable by local standards in some Latin American countries, had discovered that breaking away completely was impossible. For United Fruit, with few buyers willing to purchase the plantations, the task could never be finished. With the proceeds of the few land sales as well as the generous U.S. tax credits, United Fruit began to invest in other food industries. In 1961 freeze-dried shrimp and chicken as well as other instant foods led the way; the company acquired the A and W Root Beer drive-in chain in 1966 and Baskin-Robbins ice cream in 1967.[34]

When all was done, however, the company wasted too many years without having found either a substitute for the profits of the Cuban sugar mills or an alternative to Latin American trade. More than before, the company remained tied to bananas, its traditional main activity, but here too its main rival, Standard Fruit and Steamship Company, was rapidly closing in. To eradicate the Panama disease from its banana plantations, Standard Fruit abandoned the old vulnerable Gros Michel bananas and adopted instead a new resistant variety, the Valery banana, which however could not be shipped on stems but had to be boxed. United Fruit resisted this change until it was almost too late, but it finally shifted to the new Valery variety and boxes just in time. In fact, the company made a small comeback when, as part of a very successful public relations campaign, it introduced the Chiquita label on its bananas, raising the banana from commodity status to an identifiable product with personality. This success could not erase the growing shadow cast by Castle and Cooke's acquisition of Standard Fruit and Steamship Company. United Fruit had always looked down on its smaller banana competitor, but now it was threatened by a food conglomerate much larger and more powerful than United Fruit itself.[35]

The Great White Fleet had been an orphan of the company ever since the loss of the Cuban sugar cargoes had left its ships idle or running with partial loads. Even more significantly, Cuba had provided the bulk of the company's scarce southbound cargo. The Central American countries shipped bananas north but could afford few goods in return. Instead, Cuba's sizable import commerce had filled the company's vessels when steaming southward to load the sugar, and by ingenious routing the Cuban market was worked into the company's Caribbean sailing schedules to improve the profitability of the voyages. The inevitable attrition of vessels began in 1963, when at last the company started to find buyers for them. Since the vessels had been designed specifically for the Caribbean trade, they could not all be disposed of easily.

The sales of the ships continued, so that less empty cargo space was left in the remaining vessels, but the volume still did not suffice to prevent another policy change. Traditionally a mix of foreign-flag and U.S.-flag vessels had comprised the Great White Fleet. After World War II, the company did not ask for operating subsidies, yet it nevertheless continued to bring about 50 percent of banana imports on U.S.-flag vessels, whose operations were obviously subsidized by the greater profits and lower costs of the foreign-flag ships. With the policy of diversification away from Latin America in full force, the parent company refused to release funds for the renovation of the Great White Fleet. The old ships were run as long as possible, and the shrinking fleet was left to refinance its own vessel replacement program. When the possibility of receiving government subsidies while keeping its foreign-flag vessels was rejected in 1965 by the U.S. government, United Fruit proceeded to transfer its remaining U.S.-flag vessels to flags of convenience and the ships remained firmly under the control of the Boston headquarters. By the early 1970s, the use of the term "Great White Fleet" had gradually lapsed, although recent publicity campaigns may bring it back.[36]

The parent company's refusal to release funds for vessel replacement was justified only so long as the diversification campaign was vigorously carried out. But leaving large sums of money lying around, when they could have been invested in shipping operations that were now very profitable under flags of convenience, was a serious mistake. Lykes Brothers Steamship Company, with $50 million in cash, had borrowed $150 million more to acquire a steel company, yet United Fruit, after nearly a decade of frittering away sums in small acquisitions, still had $100 million left untouched in cash. United Fruit acted as if it had all the time in the world. Its tradition of making presidents and overthrowing governments in Latin America had given the executives a heady sense of their power, while the sobering experience of the Cuban Revolution had not quite sunk in. With no debt, $100 million dollars lying around, and a very low stock price, United Fruit had created the ideal conditions for a hostile takeover as part of the wave of acquisitions that swept through the U.S. economy in the late 1960s.

Company executives had ignored earlier warnings. In previous years modest chunks of stock had started to appear in the market, and, to keep the price from dropping further, United Fruit had started to rebuy some of its own shares. This was a rather novel practice. Management failed to pursue the stock repurchase aggressively, and the opportunity to acquire stock holdings large enough to ward off raiders was lost. After a bitter takeover fight that left deep resentment among executives, the former rabbi Eli M. Black gained control of United Fruit in February 1968. His other main businesses were manufacturing and meat packing, but bank loans had provided the funds for the takeover, and he had bought the shares mostly from institutional holders. Black hoped to be able to repay the loans and at the same time restore the fortunes of United Fruit, which henceforth became just a division of the larger holding company, United Brands.[37]

The new holding company posted losses in 1970 and 1971; the result of the takeover had been immediate, and in less than a year Black had transformed a cash-rich firm into one crushed by debt. In 1972 and 1973, United Brands appeared to rebound, but in reality the profits were the result of the sale of the Guatemalan properties to Del Monte Corporation. This sale had been agreed upon in 1958, as part of an antitrust agreement, to restore competition to the banana trade. United Fruit had accepted the spin-off of part of its business in order to create a medium-size firm equal in assets to United's only rival at the time, Standard Fruit and Steamship Company. The payment of debts swallowed up the Del Monte money, yet Black still needed a big upturn in 1974 so that he could quiet the banks, which were anxious about the repayment of other loans. The energy crisis in 1973 added to United Brand's problems, with the higher fuel costs of the ships driving the United Fruit division into the red. When the Central American countries appeared to organize a cartel to raise banana prices, United Fruit neutralized the danger with bribes to a Honduran cabinet minister, yet the banks became even more insistent. The pressures were simply too much for Black, who finally on 3 February 1975 jumped from his forty-fourth–story office in the Pan Am Building of New York to his death.[38]

United Fruit division and the parent United Brands never recovered from this blow. Waiting in the wings was Castle and Cooke (named Dole since 1991), which soon took first place as the nation's major supplier of bananas. Even Del Monte Corporation, which owned the spin-off from the United Fruit's previously larger holdings, was handling a larger volume of bananas than United Fruit division itself. This sharp change in market shares was reflected as well in the fleet sizes of the companies. The ships of United Fruit division, in deep trouble prior to the takeover in 1969, now faced worse problems. The vice president for shipping, who had worked ceaselessly to keep the fleet alive, suffered a coronary because of the pressure and finally retired in 1972. By 1975 the division was down to 37 refrigerated ships, and it continued to decline rapidly, soon to be overtaken by the fleets of its rivals. Castle and Cooke had originally ratified the policy of Standard Fruit and Steamship Company, which had sold its ships in the early 1960s and preferred to charter vessels or ship the bananas aboard the Latin American steamship firms. A number of difficulties with the service had finally taught Castle and Cooke an important principle for bulk operators of commodities like bananas and oil. It learned that, although a firm did not have to own all the vessels for its cargoes, it must own a nucleus fleet for smooth operations, generally under flags of convenience. In tonnage, Castle and Cooke soon had the largest banana fleet. Del Monte had its own fleet that rivaled the ships left in the United Fruit division, the latter having fallen from first to third in tonnage. United Fruit Company, for nearly a century a powerful force in Latin America, by the end of the twentieth century found it had fallen down to the level of a division within a second-rank U.S. corporation, and its remaining ships were only a pale reflection of the vanished Great White Fleet of an earlier era.[39]

13

Scramble to Survive

THOSE STEAMSHIP companies not seriously affected by the loss of the Cuban trade did not use the 1960s wisely to prepare for the inevitable onslaught of foreign competition. Takeovers, turf wars, and squabbles absorbed the deeply troubled U.S. steamship lines as they scrambled to reach positions most likely to ensure their survival. The struggle weakened the strong companies and left them all vulnerable to foreign rivals.

☐ United States Lines

The year 1960 found United States Lines to be the leader among U.S. steamship companies, as well as the holder of a significant and prestigious position in world shipping. Under the leadership of John M. Franklin, the fleet had grown to 53 cargo vessels, and since 1952 it had also included the *United States*, the fastest passenger liner ever built. In one last acquisition, Franklin had purchased the ships and routes of the South Atlantic Steamship Company in October 1955. More significantly, Franklin had navigated the treacherous transition from the old International Mercantile Marine strategy, based on bigness and foreign-flag ships, into the postwar system of competition and U.S.-flag subsidized ships. Yet the company's routes revealed that even greater and more dangerous obstacles awaited United States Lines in the 1960s.[1]

The North Atlantic carried until 1982 the largest volume of world commerce, and the route between the East Coast of the United States and Europe formed the heart of the company's operations. Thirty-seven of its fifty-three freighters provided the service, and prospects were good for a greater cargo volume; in 1962 the company had requested an increase of both its maximum sailings to Europe and the total number of subsidized sailings allowed under the government subsidy contract. Fears that the European Common Market would decrease commerce with the United States had proven groundless. Provided United States Lines met the increasingly strong competition from European steamship lines on time, the company could count on profitable service to ports in Germany, United Kingdom, Belgium, Netherlands, Atlantic France, and northern Spain for decades to come.[2]

Originally, World War II C-2 freighters had sufficed for the routes to Europe and Australia, the latter served by seven of those reliable ships. By 1962, however, economics and geography dictated a change in the Australian service: "Speed is especially desirable for the so-called "long trades," one of which is the Australian service encompassing some 25,000 miles on a round voyage. Speed in such trades is important since it usually attracts better paying cargo and as in this instance will permit the replacement of a greater number of ships with a lesser number."[3]

While faster ships were the solution to keep the Australian service profitable, much more than speed was needed in the Far East routes. The Pacific rate war of the 1950s awakened United States Lines to the serious danger posed by the Japanese lines, and to counter this menace, the company had placed its Mariners, then the fastest freighters in the world, into the route between the East Coast of the United States and the Far East. The ships sailed via the Panama Canal, called in Japan, Formosa, Hong Kong, Vietnam, Thailand, and the Philippines, then returned home after the traditional stop in Hawaii. Over these long routes, an additional problem was the constant and growing presence of "outsiders." The weakening of the conference system because of U.S. policy had allowed outsiders like Isbrandtsen to survive and expand. The presence of rate-cutting outsiders, almost indistinguishable from the tramps except that the former claimed to offer regular liner schedules, became a permanent and growing part of world shipping. The argument that these outsiders would also hurt the Japanese was not borne out: "Our most serious competition comes from Japanese flag lines who receive most of their support from Japanese firms. We know from experience, and this after many years in this trade, that unless strict routing instructions are furnished the supplier in Japan, most of the shipments will move via Japanese flag vessels with no benefit whatsoever to the buyer at this end."[4]

United States Lines faced a vessel replacement program critical to the company's survival. The World War II vessels had become overage by the 1960s, and with such a large fleet, the cost of ordering replacements was simply staggering. The company continued the emphasis on speed. The first group of 20-knot ships was contracted on 7 September 1960, and according to the original plan the last group would be ordered from the shipyards by 1 February 1967. To reduce borrowing by $20 million and save approximately $10 million in interest, soon after the company decided to stretch out the planned last groups of vessel orders, so that final contracts would not be awarded until mid-1969. Unlike the World War II fleet acquired at bargain prices from the U.S. government, these vessels forced United States Lines to dip deep into its pockets to put up its share of the bill, since the construction subsidy merely reduced the incentive to order at low-cost foreign yards. The International Mercantile Marine had no trouble financing its expansion, because it could draw upon the large profits of its foreign-flag vessels to cover the losses of its U.S.-flag ships. Now without any foreign-flag operations, United States Lines had to replace its entire fleet of U.S.-flag vessels. There simply was no room for mistakes, no margin for error; one false step and the whole company would be irretrievably lost [5]

With such a momentous decision facing Franklin and his beleaguered executives, they gradually found the passenger operations an increasingly heavy and distracting burden. As discussed in chapter 11, the passenger liner had become an endangered species by the 1950s, yet the fascination generations of Americans had felt for these floating palaces made a break with this past hard to face. Besides the *United States,* the company also owned the *America,* built in 1940. Generally ships over 20 years old are considered overage and ready for replacement, but since the *America* had been totally reconstructed at government expense in October 1945 and then sold to the company as a surplus vessel, there were solid grounds for claiming that overage would not begin until 1965. As far as seaworthiness and physical condition, the ship was impeccably maintained and even had a loyal following of regular passengers. But as new generations less in love with sea travel and with different tastes appeared, the success of the ship was less certain: "Passenger ships deteriorate not only by reason of physical deterioration but also by reason of obsolescence of design, styling, services, and comforts offered the passengers, and are at a considerable disadvantage versus modern ships."[6] The Maritime Administration allowed the *America* to qualify for subsidies past the 20-year limit in the hope that the 1958 law authorizing the new superliner construction would finally be translated into appropriations for funds. With mounting losses, the ship was finally withdrawn from service in 1964 and later sold to a Greek line for operation as a cruise ship.

United States Lines had tried from the 1950s to break into the cruise business by sailing the *America* and the *United States* on off-season voyages to the Caribbean during the winter months. Travel to the sunny Caribbean was in peak demand precisely when the volume of passenger traffic to Europe was lowest. On the cruise ships, constant attention to every whim of the passenger was necessary to compete against the many rivals, but since this translated into intensive labor demands, U.S.-flag ships with their higher wage scales were put at a greater disadvantage than was already the case with freighters. If the wages of 37 crewmen seemed high on U.S.-flag freighters, the bill for a cruise staff numbering in the hundreds seemed astronomical.

What about the *United States*? Its record as the world's fastest passenger liner and its more modern attractions produced a considerable following among the traveling public, yet the vessel also faced a hard uphill battle. To meet the heavier than expected demand for tourist-class accommodations, toilet and shower facilities were added to 47 rooms, reducing the capacity to two beds, rather than the previous three or four. This met the competition of the *France* in the Atlantic and made the *United States* more attractive to travelers on the off-season cruises; yet the hard fact was that the arrival of the jet plane merely hastened the end of profitable passenger service. Out of a very different conception that prevailed before World War I, the superliners had evolved over the decades into a very specialized form of travel soon left behind by a changing reality. At the same time that the *America* was sold, the *United States* should have been laid up, but the emotional attachment was too great for Franklin to make such a drastic move.[7]

One measure of entrepreneurial vision in the postwar shipping world was the realization that passenger liners were finished, but United States Lines, along with other U.S. as well as foreign lines, failed to accept this fact. Although this delay weakened the position of United States Lines in the 1960s, in meeting another radical new development, the company reacted more than adequately: "United States Lines has been developing various types of container operations over the past ten years and has participated in a number of experiments, both from the physical and commercial viewpoints, with the aim of trying to ascertain the most practical, efficient, and financially successful methods of handling cargo in containers."[8]

The Grace Line's fiasco with containers in Venezuela counseled caution before rushing into a full-scale shift to containers; as a compromise, transitional formula, United States Lines concluded that "the general concept is that of developing a ship which will be efficient both as a container carrier as well as a break-bulk cargo carrier."[9] In December 1964 the company ordered five ships, each with a 228-container capacity and with the fast freighter speed of 23 knots.

United States Lines' hopes for a gradual and orderly transition into the container age were dashed when Malcom McLean's Sea-Land established full containership service on the North Atlantic in April 1966. The next month United States Lines took evasive action and decided to change the last three ships on order into full containerships each carrying 638 containers. This redesign was sufficient to counter the challenge from McLean's old World War II vessels, but as Sea-Land continued to draw cargo away because of the novelty of its service, United States Lines prepared to deliver a knockout blow to McLean. The company again changed the design of the vessels under construction and created a new ship of the Lancer class, each of which would have a speed of over 22 knots and carry 1,178 containers. The economics of utilizing these ships were so great that as soon as they entered service, McLean's Sea-Land would be driven off the seas. Equally significant, the strong position of United States Lines against foreign competition was assured for many years.[10]

An increasing share of all these developments had become the responsibility of W. B. Rand, the president of United States Lines and also the son-in-law of the chairman of the board, John M. Franklin, who gradually was retiring from an exhausting life spent in the shipping world. To Rand, the two separate issues of vessel replacement and containerization had become one incredibly expensive problem to solve, and while he had made the right decision in waiting until May 1966 to order the large containerships, he felt increasingly uncomfortable about the future of a company beset not so much by Sea-Land's maneuvering as by the ever-tougher foreign competition. He had watched Lykes Brothers, W. R. Grace and Company, and even United Fruit Company diversify away from shipping, and, with the ever-escalating costs of replacing older ships with faster and larger vessels, Rand decided it was time to pull back. As a first step, United State Lines sold its profitable Australian service to Farrell Lines for $7 million in June 1965. The excuse was the need to raise capital to finance the new containerships under construction, but the real reasons were, first, to reduce the company's exposure in shipping (and avoid another costly vessel replacement program for that service), and, second, to add those proceeds to other funds Rand was gathering to finance the company's entry into nonshipping but less unpredictable fields. The company had never quite broken the earlier International Mercantile Marine mindset that J. P. Morgan was always there to finance and back the firm; for Rand, the sooner the company realized it was otherwise alone and without any fallback on land to offset risks in the highly volatile steamship business, the better the chances of success for a survival strategy in its remaining steamship routes.[11]

Before Rand could fully implement the survival strategy for what he considered a dangerously exposed company, an unforeseen event took place that might not have caused any problem in a more solidly placed company. In November 1966, the marriage of Rand to Sloane Franklin, daughter of the chairman of the board, ended in a messy separation, and Rand was eased out of the president's office. When a company is in a vulnerable position, any disruptive event can cause its downfall; in the case of United States Lines, the downward plunge began with the breakup of Rand's marriage in November 1966, and, once started, the chain of events unfolded at an impressive and unstoppable pace.[12]

Neither Rand nor John Franklin was at the helm, and, without leadership, the company drifted. McLean, who realized that his business was in mortal danger once United States Lines' containerships were delivered, saw the last chance to save himself. Posing as a friendly adviser, he spread the news that United States Lines was vulnerable to a takeover attempt. Because of his limited financial resources, McLean could not carry out the takeover himself, but at least he could earn goodwill with John J. McMullen, who was interested. McLean painted a rosy picture of United States Lines' prospects and urged quick action to seize the company while it remained leaderless. What was in this move for McLean? He had convinced McMullen that United States Lines simply lacked the capability to handle containerships, and that to save the company from bankruptcy, McLean, the popularizer of containers, would be more than glad to run the new ships for United States Lines on a long-term charter.

Soon McMullen had 5 percent of the company's 2,085,000 outstanding shares, more than twice the number held by all the members of the board of directors. Unfortunately for McMullen, acquisition news spread fast in New York City, especially during the takeover mania of the late 1960s. Thus his plan to gain control of the company with only a small percentage of the shares collapsed. The conglomerate of Walter Kidde and Company had grown by repeated acquisitions, but to continue growing it needed a big undervalued firm, and United States

Lines was one of the few left. In what has been described as a "lightning raid," Walter Kidde and Company launched its first hostile takeover and put out a bid for 45 percent of the stock in the middle of December 1967.[13] The board of directors did not resist; in fact, quite a few used the opportunity to leave the steamship business while they could do so at a profit. Stockholders rushed to sell their shares, and by the middle of January 1968, Walter Kidde and Company controlled more than a third of the company's shares.

The only hitch in the otherwise effortless hostile takeover came from an unexpected source: Matson Navigation Company, then locked in a bitter struggle against American President Lines, had placed a separate tender for the shares. Matson Company, which headed a consortium with U.S. Freight (45 percent) and Waterman Industries (5 percent), wanted control of United States Lines to scare off American President Lines from its invasion of the Hawaii trade. Matson's bid was a few weeks too late, and by the middle of January 1968 Walter Kidde and Company, allied with John McMullen, had gained control of United States Lines, which now entered the most exciting period of its existence.[14]

□ Isbrandtsen's Merger with American Export

The death of Hans Isbrandtsen on 13 May 1953 permanently changed the U.S. shipping scene. Previous chapters have recounted his highly aggressive if not destructive practices, which were more suitable to an earlier age. Control of Isbrandtsen Company now passed to his son Jakob, who had already tired of most of his father's antics and who in any case did not want to devote every moment of his life to the steamship business. Above all, Jakob wanted to show that he had arrived, and he now sought entry into the conferences, those very exclusive clubs his father had done so much to weaken. As a first step, and in a reversal of his father's lifelong opposition to government support, Isbrandtsen Company applied for operating subsidies from the Federal Maritime Board in 1955. Rather than grabbing this olive branch, the other steamship companies blocked the application. Trapped in a corner, Jakob Isbrandtsen had no choice but to proceed with his father's lawsuit against conference dual rates.

The lawsuit was less a genuine grievance than a bargaining lever to pry open a door for Jakob among the exclusive ranks of U.S. steamship owners, so when the Supreme Court handed down a favorable verdict, this immensely complicated the situation for Isbrandtsen Com-

pany. First, the rest of the steamship companies closed ranks in anger
against Jakob, who in the following years found his applications both
for subsidy and for entry into the conferences hopelessly bogged down.
Second, when the Supreme Court struck down dual rates, the conference system was irretrievably weakened. Over the long run its members would be left with gradually shrinking protection against ruthless
"outsiders" like Hans Isbrandtsen.[15]

Would Jakob always have to remain an outsider? He continued to
look for ways to escape his status as owner of the largest nonsubsidized
line until finally the right opportunity appeared. Ever since the death
in 1955 of Charles Ulrich Bay, the chief executive and main stockholder
of American Export, that steamship line had been drifting. Control of
American Export passed to Bay's widow, who later remarried, and she
and her new husband, Michael Paul (another employee of the company), soon decided that running a steamship line was not the best way
to enjoy the rest of their lives. When Jakob Isbrandtsen heard of this
situation, a bid from another buyer was already on the table, but he
had no trouble convincing Mr. and Mrs. Paul to accept his higher offer
of $8.5 million. The actual sale took place on 3 October 1960, where-
upon the Pauls resigned all their positions and Jakob Isbrandtsen acquired full control of American Export.[16]

The matter was far from over, however. Minority stockholders
claimed the Pauls had inflated stock prices to make bigger profits in the
sale to Isbrandtsen, and in a lawsuit they demanded damages for their
exclusion from this lucrative transaction. Yet the lawsuit was just one
more embarrassment compared to Isbrandtsen's deeper problem. He
simply did not have enough cash; he had borrowed the $8.5 million
from Irving Trust Company, but how would he repay the loan? He
arranged for American Export to purchase Isbrandtsen's fleet of 14 ships
for the same amount of money, thereby reimbursing the loan, but only
after having incurred substantial interest charges that burdened American Export's account. Jakob had been hesitant to move from a simple
purchase to a merger of two major companies, but he had no choice,
since Isbrandtsen Company had just taken a heavy beating with the loss
of the Cuban trade handled by its subsidiary, the Ward Line. The
shadow of the Cuban Revolution hung over Isbrandtsen, and to save
the company, he had to expose himself in a high-risk merger. He
cleared a major hurdle when the antitrust division of the Justice Department, surprisingly enough, voiced no objections to the proposed
merger.[17]

This transaction still required Federal Maritime Board approval,
because of the existing subsidy contracts of American Export as well as

the subsidy applications of Isbrandtsen. The Federal Maritime Board imposed two harsh conditions. First of all, Jakob had to abandon his father's cutthroat practices and make a formal promise to operate ever afterward within the conference system. After some hesitation, Jakob finally agreed:

> In the light of your letter we have reviewed our position and submit the following which we believe to be in accordance with your requirements.
>
> We hereby agree, if subsidized, to participate in conferences on the same basis as other subsidized operators in all the areas in which we will operate subsidized services. Naturally we will, on our part, comply with the rates, rules, and regulations of all conferences of which we are members. There is no reservation whatsoever as to our commitment on this matter.
>
> In any areas where conferences do not exist, we will use our best efforts to work toward stabilization of rates and conditions.
>
> We feel that the position which we present here is in harmony with the policies and practices of the other fourteen American-flag subsidized lines.[18]

This agreement was difficult for Jakob to accept, but more dangerous was the second condition imposed by the Federal Maritime Board: it demanded the divestiture of virtually all the foreign-flag vessels of Isbrandtsen Company. As many other steamship operators before him, Jakob had continued his father's practice of having a mixed fleet of U.S.- and foreign-flag vessels. Under normal circumstances the profits from the foreign-flag vessels (usually chartered) financed the U.S.-flag ships. This balancing act between foreign and U.S.-flag vessels had been at the base of Hans Isbrandtsen's shipping services. Now "at great sacrifice," his son Jakob divested himself in 1961 of his foreign-flag fleet, cutting himself off from the self-financing mechanism his father had so carefully nurtured.[19] Jakob had met the two conditions imposed, and the Federal Maritime Board now promised approval for the subsidies and the merger, provided no other steamship line raised objections.

At this moment, Spyros S. Skouras decided to make his debut in the shipping world. Skouras's father had put him in charge of Prudential Lines, a small outfit with five vessels, and the son felt that the merger would threaten Prudential's few sailings to the Mediterranean. Isbrandtsen, who had gone to extreme lengths to make peace with all the large steamship lines, was not about to let a young upstart spoil all his arrangements. Jakob decided it was time to draw on his father's arsenal of tactics. He threatened Skouras with "a fight that you will regret for the rest of your life; you had better accept my handshake and my promises if you want to survive."[20] When Skouras went on the witness stand to sustain his charges against the merger, he did not hold up under questioning in the hearing conducted at the Federal Maritime Board. He revealed himself to be ignorant not only of the most basic details about the proposed merger and the Isbrandtsen routes but even of the operations of his own company! With Skouras's credibility as a witness destroyed, government approval was assured, and Isbrandtsen's merger with American Export was formalized in June 1962.

Isbrandtsen left most of the management team in place, and he himself did not become president of the steamship line but rather of the new holding company American Export Industries, which he created in 1964. The holding company reflected his concern for diversification, a policy he had begun earlier, and already in 1961 he claimed that his nonshipping activities generated slightly more income than his steamship business. The subsidy program did provide some tax shelter protection, but actually there were not that many shipping assets to diversify away from. Neither Isbrandtsen Company nor American Export had enjoyed a century to accumulate capital and sundry investments in land, as was the case for W. R. Grace and Company and United Fruit Company, so there were no large stashes of capital waiting to be plowed into diversification. Prompt payment of interest on the merger loans earned Isbrandtsen's companies an excellent credit rating and effortlessly opened the door to more borrowing as the easiest way to finance the diversification policy.

Each additional acquisition increased the debt obligation, which at least in the immediate years could only be repaid out of the ships' proceeds. A stock swap in June 1967 with Dragor Shipping did bring the latter's five tankers under the control of American Export Industries, but no other interest-free deals were available.[21] Clearly the future of American Export depended on how effectively it could repay the many loans contracted for diversification until the new investments began to generate sufficient cash flows. Meanwhile, the main burden of repaying the company's obligations depended on the ships' earnings, and with a decision on vessel replacement pending, the late 1960s promised to be a crucial time for American Export Lines.

□ West Coast Rivalries: Hawaii

Matson Navigation Company had its near-monopoly over the Hawaiian trade seriously challenged in the 1960s. The expansion of the Hawaiian economy made its trade much more lucrative than in the pre–World War II period, and other U.S. steamship companies were eager to incorporate a greater share of the Hawaiian business into their Far Eastern services. American President Lines had called in Hawaii since the Dollar Company days, and it requested Federal Maritime Board approval to increase the number of calls. Matson wanted American President Lines limited to the 1936 volume, but the latter's claim of "a right to grow with the trade" convinced the government in 1960.[22] Since the mid-1950s, Pacific Far East Line had been requesting permission to enter the Hawaiian trade, but as a subsidized operator, the Federal Maritime Board had steadfastly refused. When the U.S. Court of Appeals upheld the right of the company to serve Hawaii in February 1960, Pacific Far East Line was already under the control of Ralph K. Davies, who temporarily postponed any additional challenge to Matson's position.[23]

From 1961 to 1965, Matson faced a permanent challenge from States Steamship. Pacific Transport Lines had called on Hawaii since 1950, and when the company was acquired in 1954 by States Steamship, the latter inherited the right to make 13 outbound calls on the islands during each calendar year. When Matson announced a 10 percent rate increase in 1961, the public outburst in Hawaii gave States Steamship the perfect opportunity to seek an increase in calls to 26 per year. Matson bitterly denounced these additional stops as "raids" but to no avail, since the Maritime Subsidy Board granted the permission. The president of Matson stated that the decision of the board "was an absolute mystery, I am shocked"; subsequent appeals failed to revoke the permission.[24] The most Matson could obtain was the requirement to review the decision after a three years' period. The importance of the struggle against States Steamship was not so much the volume of the business lost, because with less than a 3 percent market share States Steamship barely dented the Hawaiian cargo, but rather the warning sent to all prospective rivals about Matson's determination to conserve at any cost its near-monopoly position over the Hawaii–West Coast route.

The outburst of public opinion in the island against Matson led to antitrust proceedings, and the company had to act swiftly to cover this exposed flank. Worse, at the antitrust division of the Justice Department, the case had fallen into the hands of "a most intense young man with a very sincere mission to promote competition . . . in addition, he has apparently placed almost total credence on the stories reaching him from one particular viewpoint."[25] To avoid unforeseen and costly complications, the antitrust suit had to be quickly settled. Alexander and Baldwin, one of Matson's stockholders, decided to buy the shares of the other three main stockholders, C. Brewer and Company, American Factors, and Castle and Cooke, in 1964. The whole argument of the antitrust case had been that these four firms (part of the "Big Five" of the islands) had conspired to manipulate Matson's rates for the benefit of their own cargoes. Now that Alexander and Baldwin was the single parent company, all grounds for antitrust action vanished.[26]

The problem of the high freight rates provided a rallying cry against Matson, and the need to pacify the shippers was behind the decision to shift to containerships. Extensive computer programming as well as pilot experiments had convinced Matson beyond the slightest doubt that containers would reduce costs drastically. In July 1964, the company enhanced its goodwill even more by saving some of the older container vessels for service to the other islands in the archipelago, not just Oahu. The majority of the population now became convinced that Matson was really interested in the welfare of Hawaii. Matson's early and complete shift to containerships was an example that all U.S. steamship companies should have followed. The change, however, was bad news for Matson's older partner, Isthmian Lines. For nearly 30 years, Matson had run a joint freighter service to Hawaii from the East Coast and the Gulf of Mexico with Isthmian Lines, but finally on 1 May 1964, Matson canceled the arrangement. The cargo henceforth moved overland across the United States to West Coast ports for reloading into Matson's new containerships, while a scorned Isthmian was left with empty and increasingly obsolete freighters.[27]

Matson pushed ahead with its container expansion and confidently believed no more rivals would dare challenge its monopoly. Thus when American President Lines announced in February 1966 its entry into the Hawaiian trade, Matson was rudely awakened. Maritime Subsidy Board approval was of course necessary, but American President Lines counted on approval because of the chink in Matson's armor: the operation of a separate subsidized service to the Far East weakened considerably Matson's claim that it was a purely domestic, unsubsidized operator in the West Coast to Hawaii route. The president of American President Lines, Raymond W. Ickes, unveiled in April 1966 the next part of his strategy—essentially a merger with the Pacific Far East Line and American Mail Line. All three companies belonged to Ralph K. Davies, who up to then had run them as separate entities, but the advantages of consolidation had grown too great to be delayed any longer. From the combination of the three lines' services, American President Lines emerged with excess ships just right for the lucrative Hawaiian trade.

Matson, joined by States Steamship, promptly protested the merger, only to be confronted with another surprise. In August 1966 American President Lines announced the formation of a new steamship company, Hawaiian Lines, in which American President owned a 40 percent share, Isthmian Lines another 40 percent, and Castle and Cooke held the remaining 20 percent. By this clever move, Ickes had eliminated any grounds for monopoly accusations; the prospects for blocking the merger of Davies's three shipping lines were at best very slim.[28]

Continually caught off balance by the moves of an aggressive and determined rival, Matson desperately groped for solutions. As soon as American President Lines' containerships began their regular Hawaii to West Coast service (and not just the limited calls as before), a ruinous rate war would ensue. Hawaii was big enough for only one shipping company, but for American President Lines, with such strong West Coast connections, the nearby islands were too tempting an opportunity to forsake for too long. A fusion between Matson and American President Lines would have eliminated the needless and weakening competition arising from their respective geographic bases, and it certainly would have better prepared one single large firm to face the ruthless shipping behemoths of the Far East. But for Matson in the 1960s, its only option was to retain the near-monopoly on Hawaii.

In December 1966, Matson fired a warning shot over the bow when it announced the formation of a pool with Nippon Yusen Kaisha, the largest of the Japanese steamship lines. Details were vague, and although forming pools to share cargo was not necessarily a hostile act in world shipping, Matson hoped American President Lines would heed the warning to leave the Hawaiian trade alone. The attempt to repeat by bluff the shameful capitulation of Stanley Dollar in 1930 failed, and American President Lines opened for business the office of the Hawaiian Lines in San Francisco and Honolulu in February 1967. Matson promptly responded by signing a "basic agreement" with Nippon Yusen Kaisha in March 1967 to share land facilities and containers in the Far East. For the Japanese line, this rivalry between two U.S. companies was a precious opportunity to drive another wedge into the trade routes still served by U.S. steamship companies. As always, while the Japanese carefully presented a united and solid front in the ceaseless quest for world shipping, the U.S. steamship companies indulged in costly and unproductive rivalry only benefiting the foreign lines.[29]

The Japanese were not the only weapon Matson was using to repel the invasion by American President Lines. Matson skillfully applied pressure until Isthmian Lines decided to back off from the Hawaiian Lines operation in May 1967. This momentary gap was quickly filled in August by American President Lines, which assumed two-thirds of Hawaiian Lines stock, while Castle and Cooke increased its share to one-third. Davies soon regained the offensive when the Federal Maritime

Commission approved the merger of Pacific Far East Line and American Mail Line into American President Lines in December 1967.[30]

The antitrust division of the Justice Department might still challenge the merger but Matson could not afford to wait. In a calculated gamble, the firm made a last-minute bid for United States Lines, then in the middle of a takeover attempt by Walter Kidde and Company. Matson with a 50 percent share headed a consortium composed of United States Freight (45 percent) and Waterman Industries (5 percent). Matson's bid failed, and left without any other alternative, the company pressed forward with the Japanese. The Maritime Subsidy Board approved Matson's basic agreement with Nippon Yusen Kaisha in August 1968, although fully sharing the fears that it was "but the opening wedge to a more permanent, more embracing and ever closer affiliation by Matson with foreign-flag lines."[31] The helplessness of the Maritime Subsidy Board (bogged down by a myriad of legal precedents and restrictions) was more than reconfirmed when, in November 1968, it approved the creation of Hawaiian Lines. Such contraordinary moves revealed the inability of the federal government to respond to the divisive struggle raging between two U.S. steamship companies. This very dangerous situation could lead to a ruinous rate war at any moment, but the next move was up to American President Lines.

Before launching the final offensive, Davies surveyed his companies, and he soon realized that a problem had emerged with Pacific Far East Line. Justice Department action on his proposed merger could not be ruled out, and Pacific Far East Line had turned into a liability. In such an exposed situation, a confrontation with Nippon Yusen Kaisha over Matson would be very risky. In January 1969, when the U.S. Court of Appeals blocked the merger, the time for decision had come. American President Lines abandoned its proposed Hawaiian Lines venture and canceled plans for the merger. Just as in the days of the Dollar Company, American President Lines backed off, but this retreat was no rout; the line retained its traditional right to make calls in Hawaii. Later in 1969, Davies took advantage of the opportunity to dump Pacific Far East Line for a tidy profit. After some time had passed and through quiet lobbying, the merger of American Mail Line with American President Lines was finally achieved in October 1973.[32]

Matson had once again repulsed the challenge from the West Coast, but the price had been very high for the U.S. merchant marine. The constant fighting among the U.S. steamship lines had given the foreign lines like the Japanese even more opportunities to consolidate and advance their respective positions. In spite of all the sacrifices, Matson still did not feel secure, and to make a rock-solid case for the near-monopoly over the Hawaiian trade, the company sold its last subsidized Far East service. Henceforth Matson remained limited to the purely domestic operation of the Hawaii-California service. Barely had the danger from American President Lines receded in January 1969, when later that same year Seatrain delivered on its oft-repeated promise to enter the Hawaiian trade; since its vessels were unsubsidized, no legal obstacle was possible. After some heavy slugging and relentless competition, Seatrain finally called it quits in April 1974, selling its island properties and three ships in the Hawaiian service for $14.5 million. With this acquisition, Matson's share of the Hawaiian cargoes passed to 90 percent, and its triumph appeared complete, yet it could never quite rest knowing that over the horizon lurked American President Lines.[33]

□ Malcom McLean and Daniel Ludwig

American-Hawaiian Steamship Company tried after 1945 to return to the less hectic pattern of operations existing during the period between the two world wars. The War Shipping Administration had requisitioned its entire fleet in World War II, but with the return of peace and the purchase of surplus ships, the company soon was back in operation. The intercoastal service between the East and West coasts through the Panama Canal remained the company's main operation, supplemented by a revival of the prewar route to the Far East. By 1950 the shrinking of the intercoastal service, increasingly undercut by aggressive railroad rates, was evident to American-Hawaiian, but once again the Korean War provided a temporary shot in the arm to keep high profits rolling. The end of the U.S. occupation in Japan, however, suggested caution before embarking on any expansion of Far East Shipping. In spite of this and other warning signs, American-Hawaiian was stampeded, along with many of the tramp operators, into panic buying of six additional surplus ships in January 1951, before the authorization under the Ship Sales Act expired.

Along with many other U.S. steamship companies, American-Hawaiian had overestimated the cargo demands of the Korean War; as a result, even before that conflict was over, the company's prospects were bleak. As a first step to recovery, the money-losing intercoastal service was suspended in March 1953. Because American-Hawaiian had ample assets as well as pending war claims against the U.S. government, one group among the board of directors confidently expected the company to survive until the ships were all redeployed into the foreign routes. In the worst-case scenario, the ships could be placed under flags of convenience since, as an unsubsidized line, the company retained this option.[34]

Another group of executives was not so certain the company could survive, and to prevent a collapse, this faction preferred to hand over American-Hawaiian to an expert in foreign-flag operations, the American billionaire Daniel Ludwig. A very bitter takeover battle ensued in 1955 until Ludwig gained majority control, which, however, did not satisfy him. The following year Ludwig instructed American-Hawaiian to draw up a very pessimistic annual report, hoping that the rest of the stockholders would be panicked into selling at bargain prices. The Securities and Exchange Commission denounced this maneuver but to no avail; soon Ludwig had over 99 percent of the shares and proceeded to convert American-Hawaiian from a public corporation into a private company. Also in 1956, Ludwig sold off or otherwise disposed of the fleet of American-Hawaiian, the company henceforth surviving as a real estate venture but still retaining some of the tax advantages steamship companies enjoyed.[35]

The vessels sold had been built with government funds, so by law the total proceeds of $11 million could be spent only on new ships. Curiously, Ludwig had not forgotten the intercoastal service, and he planned to order ten new Roll on/Roll off ships (Ro/Ro). This new transportation technology appearing in the early 1950s was expected to compete successfully against the railroads; but upon closer analysis, Ludwig changed the order to 10 new containerships. Other issues in Ludwig's far-flung empire now commanded his attention, and he put off a final commitment on the intercoastal containerships. He easily could have ordered the ships with the $11 million from the American-Hawaiian deal and his own assets, but he had not become a billionaire by risking his own capital.

Ludwig duly requested the federal government to underwrite 87.5 percent of the mortgage insurance for the ships, and, not unexpectedly, the application languished at the Maritime Administration. When Pope and Talbot dropped out of the intercoastal service in 1960, followed by Luckenbach Steamship Company in February 1961, Ludwig felt the time was propitious to push his application, reduced by then to three containerships worth in total $68 million. Because of the competition from the railroads, the Maritime Administration refused to provide the mortgage guarantee to more than one intercoastal operator, and when Luckenbach made a last bid to revive its former service, Ludwig easily pushed aside this venerable 100-year-old company. With approval almost in his grasp, Ludwig was forestalled by the last-minute bid of

Malcom McLean for the mortgage guarantee. McLean was backed by the powerful conglomerate of Litton Industries, a large stockholder in his ventures; the Secretary of Commerce, Luther Hodges, a fellow North Carolinian, was also a close friend. To gain more time against Ludwig, McLean's domestic company, Sea-Land, began intercoastal service in June 1962, running ships of the Pacific service eastbound and claiming that by ingenious scheduling the ships would somehow make the return voyages. The service was tied by 1963 to Sea-Land's Puerto Rico routes from the East and West coasts.[36]

McLean after six years still had not secured the government subsidy for Waterman, his other steamship company, since Ludwig could apply enough pressure to block this application permanently. Sea-Land's intercoastal service was running losses, while Waterman Steamship, without subsidies, had continued to devour its remaining assets to the point that bankruptcy loomed on the horizon. McLean had to jettison Waterman, and he began negotiations in 1964 with Spyros Skouras of Prudential Lines, who was eager to buy, but only at giveaway prices. McLean was now desperately short of cash and no longer eager to continue in the intercoastal service. Ludwig, who wanted that intercoastal service, still had not obtained Maritime Administration approval, in spite of paring down his request for federal mortgage insurance from 87.5 percent to 50 percent for the three containerships. Both men had reached a deadlock, but for Ludwig this deal was only one of many ventures, while for McLean this was a life-or-death business matter. A mutual understanding was reached, whereby Sea-Land left the field open for American-Hawaiian and in exchange Ludwig bought 800,000 shares of McLean stock; the sorely needed cash infusion saved both Sea-Land and Waterman.

From this vastly strengthened position, McLean was now able to negotiate a fair sale of Waterman Steamship to the shipping group of the Walsh family in May 1965. Waterman Steamship Corporation's gyrations were far from over, but at least McLean could start to carry out the next step of his plans for Sea-Land. To complete the conversion to containerships, McLean repeated his earlier maneuver of selling six of his ships to Litton Industries and then taking them back on long-term charter once they had been transformed into full containerships in the Litton shipyards. Since he could no longer operate his ships in the intercoastal run, McLean had no choice but to inaugurate container service to Europe in April 1966 without government subsidies. McLean was determined to prove the principle that the new technology made operations feasible in foreign routes without subsidies. In July, Sea-

Land began container service to the Far East, and soon almost all the Far East vessels were profitably engaged in supplying the Vietnam War.[37]

In spite of all the publicity about operating containers on foreign routes without subsidies, Sea-Land was not making real profits and was mainly kept afloat by the Vietnam War; the proceeds were not enough to raise the capital needed to finance the next generation of container-ships. The impact on the European lines serving the Atlantic had been noticeable but not substantial; how long Sea-Land could stay ahead of foreign competitors who were planning their own containerships was not at all clear. Sea-Land had made a dent in United States Lines' Atlantic operations, but, as explained in the first section, that steamship company had just ordered a group of containerships, the Lancers, destined to drive out McLean's older converted vessels. Once again, McLean was up against the wall, waiting for United States Lines to deliver a knockout blow as soon as the shipyards delivered the new Lancer containerships.

Ludwig's 50 percent application for the three containerships had finally been approved by the Maritime Administration in 1964, but by then he had totally abandoned plans to enter the intercoastal service. Instead, Ludwig needed to wiggle out of the contract, in such a way that the Maritime Administration assumed the blame. He floated the trial balloon of making the proposed containerships nuclear-powered, and, with other delaying tactics, he finally obtained a cancellation from the government. Now with a straight face he could claim that for more than 10 years he had tried to reinvest the reserve construction funds of American-Hawaiian into new ships, but he had been permanently blocked by the bureaucracy.[38]

With the funds finally released by the Maritime Administration, Ludwig acquired more McLean shares in 1967. Sea-Land now could order a new generation of containerships, the SL-7s, from the ship-yards, although the final payments were not so certain. Nevertheless, with the latest cash infusion from Ludwig, McLean could show a solid balance for Sea-Land, certainly glossing over the essential unprofitabil-ity of U.S.-flag containerships in nonsubsidized routes and without U.S. government cargoes. If the image fooled most players in the ship-ping business, companies in other fields could not be expected to detect the weaknesses. Whether R. J. Reynolds Tobacco Company realized these weaknesses existed or not, they were seemingly irrelevant to this huge conglomerate, which was looking for both profitable diversifica-tions as well as losses for tax write-offs. When R. J. Reynolds bought

Sea-Land in May 1969, Ludwig received for his shares $60 million, almost five times the original cost of the investment. McLean himself became a major stockholder in R. J. Reynolds with a seat on its board of directors.[39] Yet the perpetual gambler instinct in McLean would not let him stay quiet and enjoy the fruits of his many close calls and risky maneuvers. Soon he was deeply involved in schemes to bag the biggest game in American shipping, United States Lines.

14

Energy: Crisis and Opportunity

THE ARAB OIL EMBARGO in October 1973 and the ensuing rise in fuel prices sent another shock wave through the already shaky U.S. steamship companies. The effect was immediate: ships ran out of fuel abroad, foreign governments saved the scarce fuel for their own merchant fleets, and until an international allocation system appeared, mayhem reigned throughout the world's shipping lanes. When the Arabs resumed pumping oil for export, the immediate shortage ended, but the long-term crisis did not disappear so easily.

As oil prices steadily rose in the years after 1973, fuel economy suddenly became the overriding priority for steamship operators. The previous rush for speed vanished, but what to do with the fuel guzzlers? Almost all the steamship companies were stuck with vessels ill-suited for the energy crisis and, as a stopgap measure, they ran the ships designed for fast sailing at lower speeds to save fuel. Older and smaller ships with lower fuel consumption received a new lease on life, and engineers hit the drawing boards to design fuel-efficient vessels, which among other changes, would use the slow-speed diesel engine, whose fuel consumption was the lowest.[1] For companies in the midst of the transition to containers, the added burden of rerouting ships, rethinking schedules, and reducing fuel expenses posed a staggering challenge. Not surprisingly, the pressures were too great for some companies, as the last two sections reveal. But crisis has often meant opportunity as well, and, for the first time since World War II, the downward trend in the U.S. merchant marine was arrested. After the mounting setbacks discussed in previous chapters, it is comforting to find in section 2 the story of the establishment of a highly successful steamship company, the first created in over two decades. In fact, the greatest opportunities came from the energy crisis itself. The first section addresses the question: Would the U.S. let the chance to revive its tanker fleet slip by?

□ The Revival of the U.S. Tanker Fleet

The post–World War II decline of the U.S. tanker fleet had continued without interruption into the early 1970s. The coastwise trade of the United States had employed the majority of U.S. tankers, yet this base suffered permanent erosion. Crude-oil production reached its limits in the United States, thus sharply reducing the opportunities to ship from domestic fields to refineries. The construction of the Colonial pipeline from Houston to New York City in the early 1960s (whose capacity was doubled in the early 1970s) virtually eliminated the refinery products as a source of cargoes. As a demand for tankers shifted to hauling the imported foreign oil, the U.S. tankers, built without construction subsidies and without access to operational subsidies, were simply overpriced. They could not compete in foreign markets except during brief periods of marked instability or acute shortage of vessels.

Two circumstances, however, kept the U.S. tankers afloat during the 1960s. Once again, the Vietnam War was a lifesaver. As long as the war lasted, the legal requirement to charter only U.S. tankers through the Military Sealift Command ensured their employment for hauling oil over the vast ocean distances to Southeast Asia. Less glamorous, but more permanent, was a second circumstance. Coupled with the ever-increasing size of tankers, a new technology at last allowed the vessels to carry return cargoes, in particular grains, but also ores and coal. Special fittings were necessary, and eventually ship designs were changed to build the Oil/Bulk/Ore (OBO) ships. Some construction continued for just tankers or carriers that specialized in the bulk trades, but the difference became blurred, and, in the case of vessels hauling either grain or oil, the difference virtually disappeared. The ship operator could now seek a solution to the otherwise inevitable problem of how to find a return cargo for the tanker that had delivered its oil and up to now always had to sail back empty. This cost advantage was particularly valuable in the trade with the Soviet Union: U.S. ships, which by law had to carry a share of the cargoes, sailed for Russia loaded with grain and returned with Soviet oil. The foreign tanker operators were quick to adopt the new technology, eventually reaping an even larger financial advantage than their U.S. counterparts.[2]

From the late 1960s on many U.S. tanker owners had foreseen a bleak future and had gradually reduced or sold their fleets. The 1971–72 tanker recession, provoked partly by the winding down of the Vietnam War, saw many operators abandon the business. Daniel Ludwig had long before replaced his U.S.-flag fleet with ships built, manned, and controlled abroad. The major oil companies, such as Exxon, Gulf, Mobil, and Texaco, simply increased the size of the large foreign fleets they had always owned through their overseas subsidiaries. Of the shrinking U.S. tanker fleet, the oil companies still owned about half, while the rest was distributed among the unsubsidized independent operators who owned most of the ships they ran. Clearly the Independents, the real competitors in the U.S. tanker operations, were gradually getting squeezed out by both the shrinking market size and the oil companies who had always preferred foreign ships.

The unsubsidized operators ranged from one-tanker outfits (the tramps of the trade) to larger firms such as Ogden Marine and Keystone Tankship Corporation. They all sought to place their ships in long-term charter with one of the oil companies, but failing that, the Independents engaged in the "spot" market, both domestic and more rarely foreign, to meet any unexpected demand for tankers. When Raphael Recanati fused several small companies into the Overseas Shipholding Group in 1969, he was responding to a subtle but significant change in the tanker market. Traditionally the oil companies owned most of their ships, but since the late 1960s they had begun shifting to long-term charters of 10 and even 20 years for many of their vessels, while always retaining, however, a substantial fleet of their own. Who would provide these new tankers? This was the task that Overseas Shipholding Group proposed to accomplish, by raising money on the stock market to finance tankers destined for long-term charters with the oil companies. Initially all these ships would be foreign-built and foreign manned, and indeed the bulk of Overseas Shipholding Group's fleet has retained that characteristic. Only in 1973 did the company, under the direction of Morton P. Hyman, take the crucial decision to order U.S.-flag tankers from domestic shipyards for operation in the Alaska crude-oil trade. But before these ships were ready for service in 1978, a ferocious struggle erupted over the U.S. tanker fleet.[3]

The Arab Oil Embargo in 1973 and the onset of the energy crisis awakened in most Americans a temporary awareness of the crucial importance of natural resources, particularly oil. Soon Congress was flooded with proposals to reduce the adverse effects of the oil shortage. Sensing a favorable climate, a coalition of organized labor, independent-tanker operators, and shipbuilders pushed through Congress the Energy Transportation Act of 1974, which mandated carrying 30 percent of U.S. oil imports on U.S.-flag vessels. Out of the welter of laws, bills, and proposals that had passed through Congress since World War II, the Energy Transportation Act was the single most important piece of legislation affecting U.S. shipping operations. Indeed, it was nothing less than recovering in a different way the "Philippines" privilege under whose shadow the U.S. merchant marine had enjoyed unusual protection from foreign competition. Ever since the independence of the Philippines in 1946, the U.S. had lacked a tool of immediate impact with which to challenge other shipping nations. Compared to the cumbersome regulatory proceedings of the Federal Maritime Commission that were always decisions after the fact, the 30 percent cargo preference provided a ready reprisal against trade discriminations. The key lay in the waiver requirements; since only a prohibitive crash program could have built the U.S. tankers needed to meet the 30 percent cargo preference, constant waivers to foreign-flag ships would become the rule. The fear of losing these waivers, when coupled with a modest shipbuilding program, would keep foreign competitors from becoming too aggressive.[4]

A failure to understand the dynamics of world shipping competition and a slavish adherence to ideology convinced President Gerald Ford to veto the Energy Transportation Act of 1974, thereby scuttling the last chance to reverse the downward trend in the U.S. merchant marine. Before concern for energy issues ran out, proponents of cargo legislation decided to make one more try in 1977 under the next president, Jimmy Carter. They pared down the cargo preference to only 9.5 percent of oil imports, but this time the united opposition of the oil companies (in 1974 Mobil and Gulf had bolted ranks and supported cargo preference) boded ill for the bill. The Carter administration thoroughly bungled the issue when leaked memorandums showed the White House was primarily concerned with repaying organized labor for its support during the 1976 election. The 1977 cargo preference legislation failed to pass even in the House, and thereafter the U.S. tanker fleet returned to a holding action to preserve its gains, most important of which was Alaska crude.[5]

The constant legislative battle had not been a total defeat, because the oil companies, kept on the defensive for so long, had not been able to pursue the preferred course of action—namely, to bring their tankers built with construction subsidies into the Alaska trade. Of course the oil companies would refund the subsidies to the government, but the strenuous opposition had convinced them to charter all available unsubsidized U.S. tankers before trying to introduce their own ships. A prime beneficiary was Overseas Shipholding Group whose tankers, built in U.S. yards without subsidies, were ready for chartering when Alaska oil started to flow. Once all the existing independent operators were chartered, the Maritime Administration received a large number of requests for waivers to allow ships built with construction subsidies into the Alaska trade. Some waiver requests were for a few voyages, others for the normally maximum six-month period, but the unusual cases were not lacking. If there were no unsubsidized tankers able to meet all the specific requirements of a shipper, then the Maritime Administration granted waivers; for example, it would grant a waiver to a refinery that needed a large tanker to carry the oil around Cape Horn rather than the smaller ones employed in the usual Panama Canal route. In order to allow the *Stuyvesant* to operate permanently in the Alaska trade, the government allowed Seatrain to refund its entire construction subsidy. These waivers had the effect of blurring somewhat the line between the domestic protected fleet of tankers and ships built in U.S. shipyards for the overseas trade.[6]

At least as long as Alaska oil flowed, the independent tanker operators would survive, and the oil companies would also have to maintain U.S.-flag ships for the domestic trade. Indeed, the wave of Alaska oil saved the U.S. tanker fleet from extinction. The importance of this achievement still could not disguise the loss of the priceless opportunity to revive the U.S. merchant marine on a permanent base over all the seas.

□ The Creation of Navieras de Puerto Rico

Puerto Rico, an island in the Caribbean acquired by the United States from Spain in 1898, had long remained the neglected child of U.S. maritime policy. An invariable pattern of operation had emerged: if other opportunities seemed more profitable, U.S. shipping companies all too easily reduced or even abandoned their services to the island, only to return to dump their excess ships from other routes in Puerto Rico. Price gouging was a recurrent threat to the Puerto Rican shippers, who were trapped in a cycle of feast and famine. The latter was quite literally true when, during World War II, many Puerto Ricans (unlike mainland

Americans) went hungry not because of danger from German U-boats but because the War Shipping Administration had diverted the ships serving the island to the supposedly vital theaters of World War II. The U.S. coastwise laws excluded foreign shipping, such as the ever-present British or Norwegian tramps, and required instead U.S.-built and U.S.-flag ships to serve the island.[7]

Bull Steamship Lines, present in Puerto Rico since 1910, had come closest to understanding the real needs of the island, but its career was cut short by the Cuban Revolution. U.S. tramps and companies trying to stuff their ships from the Cuba trade into Puerto Rico smothered Bull Lines to death in 1962. There was not enough room for all new arrivals, and by the late 1960s the field had narrowed down to Sea-Land, Seatrain, and Transamerican; the three companies controlled the island's entire ocean trade. In 1970 these three lines began to pile up heavy losses, and, as a solution, they requested whopping rate increases of as much as 24 percent from the Federal Maritime Commission in early 1971. Shippers in Puerto Rico were outraged by these outlandish demands, and to block the hike the Commonwealth of Puerto Rico took legal action. The commonwealth learned that, because its legal arguments were backed up only with words and not by ships, it would only delay the hike, so ultimately, in 1972, the three companies prevailed in the proceedings.[8]

The uproar among shippers who protested against this blatant exploitation of the Puerto Rican trade to bail out steamship companies generated tremendous political pressures on the island. An additional shock soon came in early 1973: the commonwealth government learned that Seatrain was about to shut down its operations, leaving its 25 percent of the market share unattended. Once again the island faced a shipping shortage, but this crisis was the last straw for the commonwealth, which finally responded decisively. Governor Rafael Hernández Colón immediately proposed to buy Seatrain's Puerto Rico service and to have the government run the ships. Upon closer examination, commonwealth officials concluded that the "purchase of Seatrain's assets alone would not be economically sound."[9] Further discussions revealed that the other two companies were likewise only too glad to sell. On December 1973, after lengthy negotiations, Sea-Land, Seatrain, and Transamerican agreed to sell their ships and other assets in the Puerto Rico trade to the commonwealth. This agreement was subsequently ratified by the legislature on 10 June 1974.

The creation of Navieras de Puerto Rico, which began operations in October 1974 under the dynamic director Esteban Dávila Díaz, was greeted by jeers in many quarters: "They are going to lose their shirts," claimed a Washington, D.C., official.[10] Fears of an overbloated bureaucracy were put to rest when the Company signed a management contract with a private firm to run and maintain the company's ships. A small staff under director Dávila Díaz concentrated on the big decisions and the larger trends, while profit-sharing incentives motivated the private management firm to run ships in the most economical manner. Indeed, the consolidation of the three previous companies into one offered many opportunities to improve the efficiency of the third-largest U.S. fleet. After a brief dockworkers' strike, all of the unions accepted the new government company, which combined the advantages of government ownership with those of private management. The shippers soon were pleased with the quality of the service to the U.S. mainland and the neighboring Caribbean islands. Navieras de Puerto Rico also became a powerful tool to attract new firms to the island, not only by the guarantee of regular service and low rates but also by the initial incentive of below-market rates for companies planning to establish business on the island.

There was one major problem that could not be overcome so easily. To some Puerto Ricans and many Americans, Navieras smacked of socialism, pure and simple. Would Gov. Hernández Colón turn into another Fidel Castro? The creation of Navieras and the purchase of the telephone system from ITT sounded to some like the beginning of a wave of nationalizations that soon would sink Puerto Rico into communism. Unless the charge of socialism could be put to rest, opposition from Washington would wreck Navieras. Public relations and legal campaigns were not enough; the steamship company needed insurance for protection. Originally the commonwealth had planned to use its own funds to establish the shipping company, but to quiet the charges of socialism once and for all, the commonwealth decided to borrow most of the funds using its triple-A rating on the bond markets. Dávila Díaz secured a number of loans, the most important of which was for $50 million from Manufacturers Hanover Trust Company. These loans had the disadvantage of raising expenses because of interest payments, but in the long run they were the single most important step in ensuring the survival of Navieras.[11]

By 1974 the shipping company was buffeted by the high oil prices of the energy crisis, and the 1974–75 recession in the U.S. economy had affected Puerto Rico adversely. Much as Navieras tried to cushion the energy blows for shippers, it was forced to raise rates in 1975 and 1977; profits continued through 1975, but starting in 1976 the company began to show losses. Furthermore, in 1975 Seatrain and Sea-Land returned to the Puerto Rican trade, and, when joined by other smaller firms, they provided sharp competition. Navieras counseled patience, explaining that the competitors were the typical "here today gone tomorrow" companies whose only goal was to place excess ships or fill surplus cargo space and then disappear as soon as better opportunities appeared. This argument was not fully accepted, and instant analysis by the media gained support for another solution.

Puerto Rico elected a new governor who, among other things, promised to sell Navieras to the private sector. He argued on both ideological and practical grounds that with the return of Seatrain and Sea-Land, the need to subsidize the money-losing Navieras had passed. Not all the shippers were convinced, and many continued to patronize the government company in spite of the often tempting rates offered by the new competitors. Undaunted, the new governor insisted on selling the company, and in 1977 five purchase offers were on the table, not only from Seatrain and Sea-Land, but even one from the private firm that managed Navieras. This steamship company that was supposed to lack any future certainly had aroused a tremendous acquisitive fever! Before the commonwealth could favor one of the bidders, one last hitch had to be overcome. The bankers, in particular Manufacturers Hanover Trust Company, had to approve the transfer of the mortgages. The conclusion of the bankers was inescapable: none of the five bids offered sufficient guarantees for the repayment of the outstanding loans. A stunned governor, who was also feeling a backlash of sentiment from the shippers, was forced to recant, and finally in early 1979 the commonwealth announced that Navieras de Puerto Rico was no longer for sale.[12]

By a very narrow margin Puerto Rico had saved its steamship line and thereby prevented a return to the unreliable conditions of the pre-1974 period. Other U.S. companies could come and go as they wished, temporarily tempting shippers with low rates, yet price gouging became a thing of the past, because henceforth no price hike could enter into the force without the concurrence of Navieras, whose majority market share imposed maximum rates on other steamship companies much more effectively than the cumbersome regulatory proceedings of the Federal Maritime Commission. And if the private companies left for whatever reason, Navieras would always be there: for instance, when Seatrain suddenly suspended service in 1981, leaving many shippers stranded with their goods on mainland U.S. docks, Navieras by extra efforts was able to transfer the cargo to its ships and quickly fill the gap left by departing Seatrain. At least for the foreseeable future, Puerto

Rico had solved its shipping problems, and the island's success stands out boldly in the otherwise bleak panorama of the U.S. merchant marine during the second half of the twentieth century.

□ Pitfalls of Vessel Replacement

Was the success of Navieras de Puerto Rico an isolated event, or did it mark the reversal of the downhill trend for U.S. steamship companies? There was no real obstacle to imitating the Puerto Rican model, but this alternative was not even considered or even mentioned. Steamship executives saw Navieras as a maverick, a strange tropical hybrid whose example could not be followed under any circumstances. Indeed, an underlying tone of fear characterized the reporting about this government-owned firm. For both the U.S. steamship companies and the federal government, no change in course was conceivable, and, undaunted by past failures, they pushed on to try to clear the hurdle of vessel replacement.

By the middle 1960s the ships of U.S. steamship companies were almost all obsolete. The Vietnam War gave a breathing spell that ended in 1973 with the onset of the energy crisis. By then three companies that had not used the time wisely were in deep trouble. American Export, for so long saddled with passenger liners, tried to catch up with new containerships, but without subsidies. The last two cases on Pacific Far East Line and States Steamship Company reveal that not even subsidies could compensate for a tardy shift to containerships.

□ **American Export Lines**   The winding down of the Vietnam War left this company dangerously exposed and ill-prepared to make two much-needed transitions. The abandonment of passenger services was a change long overdue, but American Export delayed the transition to full cargo services until it was too late. The true mark of entrepreneurial vision in the 1950s was the realization that passenger liners across the North Atlantic were a thing of the past, yet American Export, along with other U.S. companies, rejected this logic. Only in 1969 were the *Independence, Atlantic,* and *Constitution* finally laid up, after all attempts to sell them had failed. The transition to "intermodalism" (providing shippers with an integrated land-sea transportation for their cargoes) had started early. Containerships had been ordered on time, but with so many other problems besetting the firm, American Export made a number of mistakes as it pushed into intermodalism.

Buying a trucking company, as well as other facilities needed for inter-modal services, tied in with the larger policy of diversification launched in 1960.[13]

The company repeated W. R. Grace's discovery that investment in fields different from merchant shipping was the key to survival. Heavy borrowing from banks allowed American Export to diversify into areas such as iron ores and trucking-related activities. The easy cash that the bankers eagerly lent provided a false sense of prosperity, so that when the Maritime Subsidy Board refused to grant operational subsidies for the new containerships, company executives did not grasp the serious consequences of this decision. Eager to dispose of a rival, Sea-Land had convinced the Maritime Subsidy Board that American Export could run the new ships (to be built with construction subsidies) at adequate profit because of the new container technology. Sea-Land's argument was valid, provided that the heavy past of American Export could be mirac-ulously erased—which was impossible. At this moment Jakob Isbrandt-sen, the president and owner, should have curtailed—and possibly even abolished—shipping services, but he pressed on. The pressure of the bank loans, the desire to live up to his father's reputation, and the false hope of repeating his father's tradition of operating without subsidies were all too much for Jakob to overcome.[14]

The possibilities of survival under this strategy were remote, but they completely disappeared when a rate war began on the North At-lantic in early 1970. United States Lines, Sea-Land, Seatrain, and American Export (the major U.S. steamship companies) competed against each other and against two powerful foreign consortia. Needless to say, the U.S. lines were left badly mauled, and by the time an agree-ment ended the rate war in June 1971, American Export was doomed. Jakob Isbrandtsen simply could not break with the past; he had allowed the company to be sucked into this struggle among Titans, when the rate war was the perfect excuse to suspend operations at least tempo-rarily or probably permanently. Too late for second thoughts, the com-pany plunged into a downward spiral, posting losses of $42 million in 1970, $58 million in 1971, and $23 million in 1972.

As a first stopgap measure, American Export negotiated a credit agreement with the banks in 1970, yet this failed to halt the plunge, and more drastic measures soon followed. The banks imposed a new management team on June 1971, and Jakob Isbrandtsen, the majority stockholder, saw himself displaced from the presidency of the company. Control had shifted from the stockholders to the creditors, whose main concern was to safeguard their loans. In order to pay off the short-term loans that fell due on a rotating basis, the company began selling off assets in 1970. At last in 1971 American Export found a buyer for the passenger liner *Atlantic.* In 1972 the Overseas Shipholding Group purchased three of its tankers, and in early 1973 two more, so that when the 1973 energy crisis began, American Export, without tankers, had forfeited the opportunity to reap windfall profits in oil transportation.[15]

No sooner had a loan payment been met than another due date loomed on the horizon. The sale at a staggering loss to Hong Kong shipping magnate C. Y. Tung of the last two passenger liners *Constitution* and *Independence* barely netted $2 million for both, a sum which by law could be reinvested only in new ships. The big bailout appeared to come when the city of New York bought the Staten Island Marine terminal for $47 million. This long overdue infusion of working capital revitalized the company, and in 1976 the new containerships at last showed a profit. But it was too late; the profits were simply too small to satisfy the creditors. The loan repayments kept ticking away, no more assets could be sold, and the several attempts to merge with other lines were blocked by the ever-vigilant antitrust division of the Justice Department. To forestall creditors who were preparing to foreclose on the company, American Export had no choice but to file for bankruptcy on 15 July 1977, bringing the hectic career of this steamship firm to a close.[16]

□ **Pacific Far East Line**   Another legacy of the Vietnam War were the LASH (Lighter Aboard Ship) vessels. Their ability to raise and lower fully loaded barges made them ideal for service to many ports in Southeast Asia, in particular those near the mouth of major rivers, such as the Mekong in Vietnam. Lykes Brothers had wisely sidestepped the LASH trap by designing instead the SEABEE vessels, which were suitable for both war and peacetime commerce, but this had not been the case for the shipping group owned by Ralph K. Davies. In effect, the question of whether to build LASH vessels had cluttered up and delayed the crucial issue of the inevitable transition to container vessels. What was best for American President Lines, American Mail Line, and Pacific Far East Line—container or LASH vessels? Not sure of the right answer, Davies put off the decision as long as possible, and he finally hedged his bets: Only Pacific Far East Line would order LASH vessels. In 1969, too late to reverse the decision, the superiority of containers was evident to all, and Davies realized that he had made a serious mistake. To make matters worse, by the time Pacific Far East Line received its first LASH vessel in 1970, the Vietnam War was winding down, eliminating the only profitable employment. The need to cover possible losses (later proved unfounded) in his Indonesian oil explorations was the perfect pretext to sell. Before anyone could discover the blunder he had made ordering the LASH ships, Davies sold Pacific Far East Line in 1969.[17]

The buyer was Consolidated Freightways, a trucking firm headed by William G. White, who wished to repeat the legendary performance of another trucker, Malcom McLean. White went one further, and to his control of a shipping line and his trucking firm he added an airline, all of which he believed would allow him to offer shippers a package of air, land, and sea services in the best ideals of intermodalism. Matson Navigation Company decided to dispose of its last South Pacific service, essentially the Australia route comprising two freighters and two passenger lines, the *Mariposa* and the *Monterey*. White, not asking why so many shipping services were up for sale, was eager to add these routes to those served by Pacific Far East Line, and he quickly closed the deal. After 1 October 1970, Matson no longer sailed to foreign ports, instead limiting itself to the protected trade between Hawaii and the West Coast.[18]

Consolidated Freightways soon came to regret its departure from the domestic trucking market inside the United States. Losses began to pile up: $4 million in 1972, and $19 million in 1973. The arrival of the first LASH vessel in 1970 proved a mechanical nightmare, but, without attempting to find out what exactly was wrong with the company, Consolidated Freightways decided it had had enough and wanted out. The company took the loss directly, writing down the investment from $24 million to $3 million, and then sold the Pacific Far East Line at the bargain-basement price of $4,622,000 to John I. Alioto, son of San Francisco mayor Joseph Alioto, in July 1974. The Maritime Administration believed the company would not survive the year, but the drama of Pacific Far East Line was not yet over: an unexpected surge in demand for cargo space, coupled with John Alioto's dynamic driving style, turned around the losses of the initial months into a profit of over $1 million by the end of December 1974. These unexpected shifts have always made shipping a fascinating as well as a treacherous business: the firm on the verge of collapse finds its life prolonged, while another on the way to recovery has its career cut short rather abruptly.[19]

At least Alioto was riding the upward wave, and if he planned to continue for long in the shipping business, he had to begin immediately the conversion of the LASH vessels to containerships. The next year, 1975, witnessed strong competition in the transpacific trade, supposedly instigated by the entry of FESCO, the Soviet shipping line in the Far East. Alioto jumped to make graphic public attacks on the Soviet line, but he was also facing competition from Sea-Land, which was offering illegal rebates to its favorite customers. Later it was learned that Pacific Far East Line had countered with rebates, and it was never satisfactorily explained whether FESCO's lower rates were simply a response to the rebates offered by the U.S. companies in competing against each other. In any case, faced with losses, Alioto sold the South Pacific route with four ships (including two LASH) to Farrell Lines in May 1975.[20]

This sum buoyed up Pacific Far East Line, and, although much of the money went to cancel old debts and cover previous losses, enough was left to reinvest in ships. This was the last chance to convert the LASH vessels to containerships, but Alioto had another strategy in mind. Tempted by the huge demand for goods in the Persian Gulf countries booming with oil revenues from the worldwide rise in oil prices, he decided to buy Roll on/Roll off (Ro/Ro) vessels to ship cars and other wheeled vehicles. The decision was not wrong in itself, since the Ro/Ro vessels were profitable and a sound business opportunity. But since he had left the South Pacific trade to assume start-up expenses in another part of the world and since Pacific Far East Line could not operate the existing LASH vessels at a profit, postponing the conversion to containerships was a serious case of mistaken priorities.[21]

In effect, from that moment Pacific Far East Line became a hostage to its Ro/Ro vessels, because the profits from that service balanced the losses in the rest of the company's operations. Finally, in January 1977, Alioto decided to spend $20 million to convert all the LASH ships to containers, but by then it was too late. The company, which had posted a $9 million profit in 1976, witnessed a slump in the demand for Ro/Ro service to the Persian Gulf. The race to the finish line was on: Would the Ro/Ro vessels manage to bring in enough revenue until the conversion to containerships was completed at the end of 1977? With only a few more months needed, just when it looked like the company had cleared the last hurdles, disaster struck. The East Coast dockworkers went on strike, paralyzing the Ro/Ro vessels in port. Revenues stopped coming in, the tied-up vessels generated costs, and the money ran out to finish the conversion of the LASH vessels to containerships.[22]

Rumors began to spread during the fall of 1977, and in January the company fell in arrears on its payments. In the Persian Gulf and the Suez Canal, its barges and ships were being seized for failure to pay dues and tolls. After several bailout attempts, in February 1978 Pacific

Far East Line filed for bankruptcy under Chapter 11. A succession of presidents after Alioto tried to steer the company out of Chapter 11, but they only succeeded in driving it to Chapter 10, a prelude to the total liquidation of the company.[23] A lesson in LASH and containerships had been learned—at the high price of leaving another gap in the services of the U.S. steamship companies.

□ **States Steamship Company**   The Dant family had established this company in 1921 to haul lumber from the Pacific Northwest to the Far East. States Steamship was a child of the Shipping Board, certainly the only surviving child that fully espoused the characteristics the Shipping Board had tried to impose on the U.S. companies. The firm had remained small and under family ownership, unlike the few other survivors. States Steamship, coming on the scene after the Dollar interests had carved up the best routes in the Pacific Ocean, could not grow; indeed it was the only U.S. company whose every move was jealously watched by the Dollars in the 1930s so that they could take effective countermeasures. In its beginnings, the Dant family's career showed many similarities to the early career of the Dollar family 20 years before, and if antiquated business notions had wreaked havoc with the Dollar Steamship Lines in the late 1930s, how could States Steamship survive?[24]

Generously subsidized by the Shipping Board during the 1920s and 1930s and stumbling upon a permanent shipping relationship with the Philippine Islands as the core for its Far East service, States Steamship was a well-run outfit that enjoyed a remarkable streak of good luck. The government charter of its ships in World War II and cargoes for the American occupation in Japan carried the company through the 1940s. The Korean War and the renewal of subsidies from the Maritime Administration launched the company into the 1950s. Lumber was the company's preferred cargo, and, in a reverse twist, States Steamship pioneered the development of the lumber trade from the Philippines to the West Coast in the early 1960s. The company's 13 old and small vessels were overdue for replacement in 1965, but once again good fortune, in this case the Vietnam War, gave the Dant family time to ponder at leisure the replacement program for its vessels, as well as the whole future of the business.

The company had no staff; the Dant family members refused to hire outside consultants to analyze the company's situation and, like the Dollars, they refused to accept the transition to a new generation of professionally trained managers. One company executive claimed that "experience and intuition" sufficed in making the correct choice; essentially he was saying that what had worked before would be good enough again. Its freighters had already begun to load containers on the top deck, but rather than seeing this growing trend as the future of shipping, the company declined to order full containerships. The five ships contracted in May 1966 and scheduled for delivery in 1969 were merely bigger freighters with a faster steaming speed and a higher fuel bill. When later in 1966 Sea-Land and American President Lines announced the conversion of their vessels to full containerships, States still had time to alter the vessels under construction, but relying on "experience and intuition," States Steamship refused to change the vessel designs. Not surprisingly, from their first day of operation the new ships were obsolete.[25]

Sensing danger—for the company was already doomed—the executives belatedly ordered five full containerships in 1969, but a little later States Steamship countermanded the order and substituted the construction of four Roll on/Roll off (Ro/Ro) vessels. When the ships were finally delivered, States Steamship found itself in the same predicament as Pacific Far East Line: Ro/Ro vessels are necessary for the cargo that cannot be packed in containers, but they can never replace containerships. In the 1960s and 1970s shipping executives had to decide among four choices for their vessel replacements: larger freighters, LASH, Ro/Ro, and containerships (a fifth choice, passenger liners, at last had dropped out). LASH vessels were the real trap, and in retrospect they should have been avoided at all costs. A mix of the other three was the right choice, provided that containerships always formed the bulk of the company's fleet. States Steamship badly bungled the decision, and, without any containerships, it had to try to survive the high fuel prices of the 1973 energy crisis with fuel-guzzling ships.

Meticulous operation and careful attention to detail kept the company afloat, but as oil prices shot up higher and higher, only infusions of capital from the Dant family could keep the company alive. In June 1978 States Steamship withdrew from the Pacific Conference, so that the company could quote lower rates in a vain attempt to attract customers. Losses piled up, and when in October 1978 the company missed a $1 million mortgage payment, this "triggered a frantic search for a buyer."[26] Only Lykes Brothers showed any interest, but, after desperate last-minute negotiations failed to produce an agreement among the government, Lykes Brothers, and the Dant family, States Steamship had no choice but to file for bankruptcy in early 1979. The last direct link with the legacy of the Shipping Board had vanished.

□   End of the Line for Seatrain

Seatrain's successful strategy to survive the loss of the lucrative Cuba trade was threatened by the winding down of the Vietnam War. The rapid buildup in Southeast Asia was over, and, although the resupply of the remaining forces would still generate sizable cargo volumes for a number of years, 1969 was not too early to prepare for a post-Vietnam shipping world. In January of that year, Joseph Kahn and Howard Pack, the ex-furriers who had bought Seatrain in 1965, leased the Brooklyn Navy Yard in New York City at a nominal rent. Tempted by federal and city funds, Kahn and Pack believed they could profitably enter ship-building, perhaps the only other business as volatile and risky as shipping itself. Running a bankrupt steamship company apparently had not been excitement enough for the owners—so now they had added ship-building to their original company. [27]

The beginning of construction on the first two tankers in Brooklyn Yard did not keep Kahn and Pack from experimenting even more creatively with their shipping services. Unlike Pacific Far East Line that had bungled its container conversion, Seatrain promptly ordered con-tainerships, starting in the late 1960s. But the story does not stop there: when the company received the first four container vessels in February 1971, Seatrain went on to establish the pioneering "landbridge" system destined to revolutionize transportation in the United States. In the "landbridge" system, the company arranged with the railroads to run special trains carrying containers across the United States for delivery either at the company's terminal at Weehawken, New Jersey, or at one of the West Coast ports for transfer aboard the company's container vessels sailing to the Far East. The trip from New York to Tokyo, which by the all-water route of the Panama Canal took 30 days, could now be reduced by as many as 10 days. Since Seatrain assumed full responsi-bility for the container cargoes, the shipper was spared having to ne-gotiate with anyone else. Some problems remained to be worked out, but the system was soon imitated by other steamship companies, most notably American President Lines and the Japanese firms. There was no doubt that in the 1970s Seatrain had once again become a leader in transportation innovations, overcoming the lead Malcom McLean had taken temporarily with the introduction of containers during the 1960s. [28]

This success could not immediately reverse the dismal financial picture. The long-term debt of Seatrain stood at $168 million and was two and a half times equity. By June 1973 the long-term debt had risen to $244 million, and the company was making principal payments of $16 million to the banks each month, surely a crushing burden. To meet pressing loan obligations, the company agreed to sell the Puerto Rico service to newly created Navieras in December 1973. This was still not enough, so Seatrain decided to abandon its Hawaiian service as well. Matson Navigation paid $14.5 million for the three ships in April 1974, thereby raising its market share of the Hawaiian trade to 90 percent. The infusion of cash allowed Seatrain to improve its remaining container routes to the Far East and to Europe, yet the danger of bankruptcy remained.[29]

Kahn and Pack realized they needed help, and, to save the company from bankruptcy, in late 1974 they hired Steve Russell, a financial expert, as executive vice president. The 34-year-old Russell soon had in place a team of young executives with strong financial backgrounds but no shipping experience; the takeover by financial people generally means that a shipping company has entered its last stage. Russell had mapped out a strategy to put the company on a sound basis, but before he could put his plan into effect, he had to neutralize a gaping hole that threatened to engulf the entire company: the Brooklyn shipyard.

Seatrain had received federal and city funds to run the shipyard on the condition that the company hire and train minorities, particularly blacks and Puerto Ricans. The task of converting the hard-core poor into skilled workers was enormous, and not unexpectedly the company incurred a $20 million overrun in building the first two tankers. Fortunately, the Maritime Administration reimbursed the company for the $20 million, and the tankers were placed on long-term charter with the oil companies. Two more tankers were under construction in the shipyard: The *Stuyvesant* (80 percent completed) and the *Bay Ridge* (20 percent completed) when the company ran out of funds in late 1974. Banks refused to extend any more credit until buyers or charterers for the tankers could be found, an impossible task when the world tanker market was glutted. A ready solution was at hand: the imminent passage of the Energy Transportation Act would instantly create a huge demand for U.S.-flag tankers built with construction subsidies. But when President Gerald Ford vetoed the act in December 1974, Seatrain promptly began to lay off workers, and by February 1975 all the 2,800 shipyard employees were without work. Operations resumed in June 1975, because the powerful political influence of the unions had helped Russell convince the Ford administration to assign further federal funds to complete the tankers.[30]

Russell then was free to pursue his strategy of stabilizing the firm. His first move was to shift the company away from shipbuilding and into energy ventures, and to that effect Seatrain purchased an oil refinery in Texas as well as some coal fields. Shipping continued to be a strong point, and the company consolidated its position in the container trades of the Pacific and Atlantic. Tight attention to financial controls remained the rule: Russell discovered that the company had too many high-interest loans, and by shopping around he was able to replace many of them with lower-interest loans. He also decentralized decision-making responsibilities, thereby encouraging the managers of the subsidiaries to seek ways to generate profits. The new management strategy seemed to be working, and after a record five years of losses, at last in 1976 Seatrain posted a $14 million profit and paid the first dividend since 1959, the last year of the lucrative Cuba trade.

A possible complication was quickly eliminated by the ever-resourceful Russell. When the *Stuyvesant* was finally completed in 1977, nobody wanted to buy or charter it. After several tries, Russell convinced the Maritime Administration to accept a refund of the construction subsidies, thereby qualifying the tanker to ply the Alaska trade. Since Seatrain lacked funds, the government accepted a 20-year promissory note rather than cash for the refund. This coup earned Russell a formal promotion to president of the company, a position he in fact had held unofficially.[31]

Russell finally identified the Brooklyn shipyard as a source of the company's problems, and as soon as *Bay Ridge*, the last of the four tankers, was finished in May 1979, he shut down the shipyard, which was running losses of $40 million annually. But the involvement with the shipyard would not end so easily: a federal court had overturned the Maritime Administration's decision to accept the construction subsidy refund. Seatrain was stuck again not only with the *Stuyvesant* but with the *Bay Ridge* as well. After considerable difficulty and at a great loss, the company sold the two tankers to financial institutions, thereby at last freeing Seatrain from the legacy of the shipyard, but by then it was too late.[32]

The long-term debt of the company had climbed to $270 million, and if not reduced quickly, it threatened to swallow up the whole company. There was only one alternative left. The container services in the Pacific and the Atlantic, joined by the landbridge, were turning over a nice profit, but not enough to bail out the company, which was sinking in accumulated debt. Under relentless pressure from creditors, Russell tried a last desperate gambit: if he could attract more cargo in the North Atlantic, his containerships, which were not running full because of intense competition, could pile up the profits needed to reduce the crushing debt load. Only lowering rates could attract more cargo, but such an action would violate the rates set by the freight conference in the North Atlantic.

European steamship companies have been very reluctant to start rate wars, preferring the cozy conference arrangements to the uncertainties and dangers of cutthroat competition, but when Seatrain fired the opening shot by bolting from the conference on 1 February 1980, they were not about to pass up such a tempting opportunity. This Atlantic rate war, the first since 1970–71, pitted the U.S. companies against the now fully containerized European lines, which were endowed with large capital resources and were either state-owned or backed by governments who understood the true nature of world shipping competition. Sea-Land and United States Lines managed to hold their own, but for debt-burdened Seatrain, it was soon all over. In three months of the rate war the company lost perhaps as much as $30 million, and in August it had no choice but to sell its Atlantic ships to an Australian firm.[33]

This sale was still not enough to stave off the creditors. At the insistence of Chase Manhattan Bank, which demanded payment of overdue loans, Seatrain sold its Pacific vessels to the Hong Kong firm of C. Y. Tung in December 1980. Seeing the end rapidly approaching, the team of financial experts quit their jobs in the first week of February 1981, with Russell seeking refuge in the presidency of a Caribbean subsidiary that Seatrain had formerly spun off at a million-dollar loss. An accountant then became president, and, left with no other alternatives, he filed for bankruptcy under Chapter 11 on 12 February 1981. A slow agony awaited the company as it desperately latched onto a succession of proposals to restore operations without success until liquidation was inevitable in 1982. The race to escape from its past was over: Seatrain had tried and failed to flee from its Cuban origins. There had been so many experiments and so many innovations, but nothing, not even reaching out to the Arctic Circle, had ever replaced the lucrative voyages to the fertile tropical island of Cuba.[34]

15

The Shakeout

THE 1980s SAW THE end of many steamship companies that had been prominent during previous decades. In each of the cases discussed in this chapter, the final outcome was the result of the gradually accumulating momentum of earlier mistakes. So many government steamship companies had already collapsed in the 1970s that the new Ronald Reagan administration adopted two innovations in maritime policy: the "buyout" scheme, by which the steamship firms received in accelerated payments subsidies that otherwise would have been strung out over as long as 20 years; and individual permits to build U.S.-flag vessels abroad (which, however, would be ineligible for subsidies). These two innovations were eagerly grasped by some steamship companies and greeted with skepticism by others; in any case, they were both ideologically attractive to a Republican administration determined to slash federal budgets. The rapid military buildup begun by the Reagan administration fooled some executives into believing that merchant shipping's wartime role would lead to greater direct government support, but except for additional Military Sealift Command charters for some U.S.-flag ships, the Republican administration mainly concentrated on praising the free-market mechanisms.

☐ Moore-McCormack

In the 1950s this company was prospering, with no signs of impending dangers. In its routes from New York to the east coast of South America, Moore-McCormack had successfully met the challenge of the local steamship companies. The long-standing relations with Lloyd Brasileiro remained firm, and after skirmishing with the new state-owned firm of Argentina, ELMA, Moore-McCormack had established a modus vivendi agreeable to both parties, avoiding the bitter clashes that had marred relations between Grancolombiana and the Grace Line on the Pacific side. Moore-McCormack's fleet of 40 freighters and 1 tanker also linked (through its subsidiary the American Scantic Line) the ports of Scandinavia and the Baltic with those on the East Coast of the United States. In an expansion move, the company acquired the Robin Line in 1957, thereby adding to its services from the United States the African ports stretching from Walvis Bay to Mombasa.[1]

To maintain its leadership in these routes, Moore-McCormack began a vessel replacement program in 1956. Fourteen new ships comprised the first wave, completed in 1965. The freighters were essentially bigger and faster versions of existing ones, and the two new combination vessels delivered in 1958, the *Argentina* and the *Brazil,* carried cargo and also provided luxury accommodations for 550 passengers per ship. Moore-McCormack realized that more of the same would not be suitable for the second generation of ships, and from 1965 on it decided upon a different type of vessel for its replacement program. The dawn of the container age was starting to break upon a shipping world that still could not rid itself of the obsolete passenger liners.

Moore-McCormack soon regretted having ordered the new passenger liners *Argentina* and *Brazil,* and it belatedly tried to get out of the passenger business altogether. At least the company realized that containers were the wave of the future, though the realization was not easily acted upon because Moore-McCormack did not want to get burned with containers, as happened to the Grace Line in Venezuela in 1960. The majority of the company's business was in South America and Africa—areas that, because of their rudimentary transportation and port systems, placed containers at least 10 and probably 20 years into the future. Thus Moore-McCormack needed a highly versatile vessel that could readily adapt to general cargo, containers, and Roll on/Roll off vehicles (Ro/Ro), without forgetting special defense measures particularly important in the Vietnam War period. The unique design Moore-McCormack created provided for false decks and the closing or opening of special hatches so that the vessel could increase its capacity of either container or Roll on/Roll off vehicles. The ships were quite well suited to the African and South American trades, but when Moore-McCormack launched the first regular container route to Europe in February 1966 (two months before Malcom McLean's Sea-Land) the higher cargo-handling expenses in European ports ate away almost all the profits.[2]

The ports in Europe soon installed facilities to handle containers economically, and the European lines ordered full containerships, the smallest of which had twice the container capacity of Moore-McCormack's vessels. The U.S.-flag company was sensing danger and, to raise capital, it sold its Straits of Magellan service to the Grace Line in 1966. This was only a temporary fix, so Moore-McCormack sought more permanent help in merger talks with U.S. Freight (1966) and Farrell (1969), but both attempts failed. Thus, when the North Atlantic rate war erupted early in 1970, Moore-McCormack had nothing to fall back on. The combination freighter-container-Ro/Ro vessels were simply no match for the European lines, which, running bigger and faster full containerships with fat profit margins, could afford to ride out a long rate war. In a few months it was all over for Moore-McCormack: the company abandoned the North Atlantic service, and even after selling the four vessels to American Export, it still suffered a $17 million loss in 1970.[3]

The company was on the verge of collapse, but in 1972 the sale of its two passenger liners, *Argentina* and *Brazil* (laid up since 1969), for cruise purposes to Holland-America brought a much-needed cash infusion that allowed the company to revive. Since February 1971 the company had been under the leadership of a new president, James R. Barker, who had learned well the lesson of other steamship companies—namely, that corporate survival depended upon diversification away from the highly risky and volatile shipping business. Diversification had begun timidly in 1964, but Barker made it his primary goal. He sold 20 overage vessels from the fleet, and kept only the most modern and efficient ships running on the South American and African services. With those proceeds, the $20 million from the sale to Holland-America, and loans, he invested in the natural resources field. The biggest acquisition was Pickands, Mather, and Company in April 1973, a supplier of raw materials for the steel industry. Pickands, Mather, and Company owned and operated iron ore and coal mines, as well as all supporting facilities, including Interlake Steamship Company, a Great Lakes fleet of bulk cargo ships.

Partly to meet legal requirements to reinvest in ships, Barker ordered three tankers in July 1973 for operation in the domestic routes.

Thus when the energy crisis struck in October 1973, he had already positioned Moore-McCormack to take maximum advantage of the situation. However, he allowed himself to be swept away by the sudden enthusiasm, and soon Moore-McCormack was too deeply involved in a myriad of energy ventures. A special subsidiary was searching for oil and gas in Texas, Louisiana, and the Rocky Mountains, while the parent company (whose name was now changed to Moore-McCormack Resources) had bought a small independent oil company, picking up along the way a cement factory as well. Initially all these energy ventures were modestly profitable, mainly because of the temporary worldwide shortage of resources, but they offered few long-term prospects. Indeed, the glitz of the energy ventures had overshadowed the less glamorous South American shipping service with its slow but sure growth. The no less solid Africa route was ignored until the opportunity appeared to consolidate the service with the other U.S.-flag line sailing to Africa; in 1980, with the purchase of Farrell's two 15-year-old U.S.-flag freighters (previously on that route), Moore-McCormack became the sole U.S.-flag service from New York to South and East Africa.[4]

When the energy bubble exploded in late 1980, the collapse dragged down all those like Moore-McCormack who had built their survival strategy on the short-term opportunities. One after another of the company's energy ventures sagged and began to pile up losses, with the exception of the three tankers now chartered to carry Alaska oil. Belatedly Moore-McCormack had agreed to lengthen 4 of its fleet of 13 ships serving South America and Africa to handle a larger number of containers, but the company, remembering how badly it had been burned with containers in the 1970 North Atlantic rate war, was still skeptical, so as Latin America finally entered the container age, Moore-McCormack was a reluctant participant. The losses of the parent company began to pile up from 1981, and Barker desperately sought to sell off assets while buyers could still be found for the rapidly collapsing energy ventures. At this moment Malcom McLean appeared, now the proud owner of United States Lines, who was preparing to establish a worldwide transportation network. As the popularizer of container services, McLean was judged the ideal person to handle the transition to containers in the African and South American routes; after quick discussion, McLean purchased the fleet and routes of Moore-McCormack in December 1982. The steamship tradition of another company dating back to 1913 had come to an end, but the sale had not saved the parent company: Moore-McCormack Resources remained locked in a tailspin, plummeting downward into the bottom ranks of corporate America.[5] Yet what remained of Moore-McCormack's fleet had been saved, and great hopes again appeared that under Malcom McLean a revitalized U.S.-flag fleet would continue to sail to South America and Africa.

□   Prudential Lines

Another casualty of the 1980s shakeout was Prudential Lines, a company founded in 1933 by the Greek immigrant Stephan Stephanidis. Operating initially as a tramp business, the company grew from one freighter to three by 1939; during World War II it operated vessels for the War Shipping Administration. After the war Prudential acquired three Victory ships, only to find itself in 1954 on the verge of bankruptcy, but it was saved by a timely investment by Spyros P. Skouras, a Hollywood tycoon who owned Twentieth Century Fox. In 1960, after the original founder Stephanidis had died, full control of the shipping line passed to Skouras who, however, relegated the management of the firm to his son, Spyros S. Skouras.[6]

The business ability of the son was soon brought into question: in hearings on the merger of Isbrandtsen with America Export, Skouras could not answer the simplest questions about his own company, his understanding of basic ideas of shipping left much to be desired, and his reputation as a playboy was not regarded as an asset, as was the case for the Greek shipping magnate Aristotle Onassis. Initially Skouras proceeded correctly, with the company receiving two new freighters in 1966 to bolster its fleet. Skouras still had not made it into the major shipping leagues, but a lucky break catapulted him to the top: W. R. Grace and Company was becoming desperate to dispose of its shipping service worth at least $75 million. With no other buyers in sight, W. R. Grace and Company slashed the price to $44 million, within Skouras's reach. On 12 December 1969 Prudential became the owner of the Grace Line, making complete its transition from tramp operation to one of the top steamship companies in the United States.[7]

Would Spyros S. Skouras be able to live up to the reputation and goodwill carefully built up by the Grace Line during its hundred-year history? He had already made the crucial decision in 1965 to order LASH ships for his vessel replacements, and he had been among the first to realize the potential of this type of barge carrier, which had many opportunities to unload at seaside locations without adequate ports in the Mediterranean. The first LASH vessel was delivered in 1970, and all were in operation by 1972, but as a pioneer in LASH, Prudential incurred the learning costs inherent in a new type of transportation technology. Cash problems began to plague the company, and the transition into LASH vessels required harsh cost-cutting measures. Skouras laid off headquarters staff, shook up management, and laid up the *Santa Paula* and *Santa Rosa* (combination cargo ships, each having a 225-passenger capacity). In spite of the ships being booked almost solid and the cargo hatches being filled with quality high-revenue cargo, the crew pay scales imposed by organized labor were so high that not even the subsidy covered the losses. When the National Maritime Union finally offered to reduce the wages, it was too late. Prudential also planned to lay up four other vessels with a smaller 90-passenger capacity, but a better alternative was arranged, in which the former Grace Line vessels would operate a service around South America from the West Coast of the U.S. carrying general and refrigerated cargo as well as passengers.[8]

With the onset of the energy crisis, Prudential Lines found itself riding a boom: Ecuador and Venezuela, two countries in its routes, were major oil exporters, and with their newly found oil revenues were buying every kind of consumer goods from abroad. Particularly in Venezuela, congestion at its ports reached monumental proportions, with ships waiting three weeks and longer to be unloaded. A brisk demand for cargo space made Prudential charter extra vessels for service in these routes until 1977 when Venezuela's orgy of impulse buying gradually declined to more normal levels of international commerce.[9]

The South American routes remained profitable, but they could no longer continue to compensate for the mounting losses Prudential faced on its LASH service to the Mediterranean. Crew costs were very expensive on the LASH ships, and the weather was so bad that often days would pass before the ships could discharge the barges. These unexpected delays were a surprise to the executives back at headquarters who had expected the Mediterranean to be a calm sea. Skouras compounded the problem when he stated, "We're no longer going to try to be all things to all people with LASH," and promptly removed the last containers from the vessels. Skouras could not be shaken from his steadfast faith in the profitability of LASH, but mounting losses caused by the operation of those vessels forced the company to sell its Latin American service to the Delta Line in July 1977. The sale transferred four freighters and the four passenger-cargo vessels to Delta; Skouras let go of only one of the LASH vessels, and, as unrepentant as ever, he paid off old debts with the $75 million purchase money and continued to operate his remaining LASH vessels to the Middle East.[10]

The Delta money allowed Prudential to survive in a gradually narrowing environment. Persistent rumors of a bankruptcy in 1981 were dismissed by the ever-optimistic Skouras, and its fleet—now reduced to three vessels—continued to operate thanks to Maritime Administration subsidy. Prudential gradually came full circle, returning to tramp operations typical of its beginnings in the 1930s. In May 1986 the company's three ships were seized in New York and Italy by creditors, and in September Prudential entered Chapter 11 bankruptcy proceedings. In 1989 the Military Sealift Command chartered the three vessels, prolonging indefinitely the bankruptcy proceedings. In 1990, the three ships were still in charter to the Military Sealift Command, and Prudential's prolonged agony appeared to have no merciful end. [11]

□ Delta Line

Holiday Inns acquired the Delta Line in 1969. Delta had begun a modest vessel replacement program in the 1960s, but the majority of its ships were still overage; steamship executives eagerly expected an infusion of capital from Holiday Inns to place new orders with the shipyards. The cash-rich parent company was willing to invest up to a point, but unfortunately Delta executives badly bungled what turned out to be the line's last opportunity. In the early 1970s it was still a bit too early for full container service to Latin America, but the growing container volume showed that no steamship company would be able to continue ignoring this new transportation method for long. Delta thought otherwise, and, still remembering how badly W. R. Grace and Company had been burned with containers 10 years before, the company decided against ordering containerships standard in the North Atlantic routes by the early 1970s.

Delta repeated the mistake of selecting LASH vessels as the next cautious step in technology beyond the traditional freighters. The shipyard delivered the first of three LASH ships in 1973, and soon after the other two. There was no question of placing them in West Africa: there the old freighters continued successfully to ply the traditional African routes. For the Latin America service (the bulk of Delta's business) the LASH ships provided only a fleeting advantage, and by the late 1970s the lower costs of container vessels were clearly evident. What the Latin American trade needed were those containerships with cranes rapidly becoming obsolete in the North Atlantic routes; European and U.S. ports had invested heavily in full container-handling facilities, but the Latin American ports lagged considerably, and in particular they lacked the cranes. [12]

In 1977 the full impact of the container revolution was still not completely clear, and Delta executives were able to convince Holiday Inns to purchase the Latin American service of floundering Prudential Lines. Included in the sale were six freighters and one LASH vessel; more of the latter would have been included had not Spyros Skouras, the owner of Prudential, remained so firmly attached to his other LASH ships. Delta and its parent Holiday Inns believed that combining the complementary routes into a unified service would put the company on a solid profit-earning track. Most of 1978 was spent unifying the routes and offices of Delta with Prudential's Latin American services, so that now the east coast of South America was served from both the Atlantic and Pacific coasts of the United States as well as from the Gulf coast, while the former Grace Line service from the U.S. East Coast to the Pacific coast of South America continued in addition to the traditional Caribbean and Central American routes. Delta's West African service continued to operate as well.[13]

By the time the first operating results appeared in 1978, it was becoming clear that Delta's takeover of Prudential's Latin American service could not overcome the earlier blunder of ordering three LASH vessels—and, to make things worse, the company bought a fourth one! One of the LASH vessels was laid up most of the time, and the other three barely eked out enough revenue to continue on the Gulf route to South America; Delta, like other U.S. steamship companies, was stuck with LASH vessels. Holiday Inns was becoming impatient, and a shakeup in management brought Andrew E. Gibson, former head of the Maritime Administration in the Republican administration of Richard Nixon, to become president of Delta. Holiday Inns counted on Gibson, with his many contacts in official Washington, to swing some arrangement that at least would unburden the company of the LASH ships. Gibson was unable to budge the Democratic administration of Jimmy Carter, but, as a staunch Republican, he was expected to achieve great success with the incoming Republican administration of Ronald Reagan.

Meanwhile the cargo situation continued to deteriorate in the Latin American routes, and at last Delta executives proposed adding midsections to six freighters so as to enlarge their container-carrying capacity. This conversion, if adopted in the early 1970s instead of buying LASH vessels, would have put the company in a very solid long-term position, and even in the early 1980s it was still a good step forward. But by now Holiday Inns had tired of pouring money into the apparently bottomless pit of steamship operations, and rather than approve the request for the midsections, it decided instead to dispose of its nonhotel assets.

It was not easy to find a buyer, but finally Thomas B. Crowley, the nation's largest tug and barge operator, decided to purchase Delta in December 1982 for $96 million.[14]

At first it was hard to understand how such a careful and conservative businessman like Crowley could want to plunge into the highly risky steamship field. Since Delta's prospects were none too favorable, he had been sold on the misleading proposal dubbed "buyout." Gibson and other steamship executives realized that increases in subsidies had no chance during the early years of the Reagan administration; instead, any plan to discontinue subsidies had a tremendous ideological attraction for the Republican government. Delta had contracts lasting until 1997 for operating subsidies eventually totaling $2 billion, and in 1982 it proposed to swap them for $762 million paid in five annual payments (i.e., a government buyout). With those funds Delta could buy a new state-of-the-art fleet capable of competing in the world market without need of any further subsidy payments. In addition, the prohibition on building U.S.-flag ships in the cheaper foreign shipyards had been temporarily waived as a substitute for construction subsidies.

Delta collected a number of individual permits to build U.S.-flag vessels abroad, and so did other companies like United States Lines, before the federal government's authorization to grant them expired in 1982 (previous permits remained valid). The rest of the buyout proposal smacked too much of a scheme more appropriate to the old Shipping Board, and doubts soon surfaced. Even if Crowley performed everything he pledged, it was still not clear how Delta could operate over decades without operating subsidies. Historically only steamship companies with foreign-flag subsidiaries or Oriental crews had been able to sustain U.S.-flag operations for any length of time without subsidies from the government or a parent company—unless they carried mainly U.S.-government or legally mandated cargoes. Crowley's buyout proposal encountered snags, and he repeatedly lowered his asking price for the buyout of the government subsidy contracts: from $762 million in 1982 to $575 million in 1983, then a short drop to $525 million, until finally in early 1984 he was willing to take $325 million—and was still willing to listen to any offer.[15]

Meanwhile, Crowley tried desperately to cut back his losses on shipping operations. He now regretted having bought "old junk ships with large crews"[16] and proceeded to slash his original fleet of 24 ships. This action took on an added urgency with the collapse of the Latin American market in early 1983, caused by the foreign-debt crisis that choked the region's commerce and also made local shippers more conscious about reducing handling costs in the remaining foreign trade.

Delta sold ships for the reserve fleet and laid up others that were eventually sold for scrap. To carry the remaining cargo, Crowley orches-
trated a complex swap arrangement with the Maritime Administration
and American President Lines, whereby as payment for turning freighters over to the Maritime Administration's reserve fleet, Delta received
two of American President Lines' older containerships. At last the company adopted the policy of buying castoff container vessels suitable for
the Latin American trade, but rather than continuing with this modest
but careful strategy, Delta fell to the temptation of ordering three new
U.S.-flag containerships in Danish shipyards, using the construction
permits the federal government had earlier granted. An added attraction
of the Danish ships was their 18-man crew, less than half the size of
the 45-man crews on the older ships. Wages were also slashed, and
when dockworkers refused to work for lower wages, Crowley moved
his terminals to smaller U.S. ports with cheaper dock labor, thus gaining popularity with the U.S. business community.

In spite of all these economy measures, Delta remained a drain on
the parent company, with losses of over $20 million in 1983 and higher
ones expected for 1984. With no hope left for the government buyout,
Crowley decided to bail out while he could. By now it was getting hard
to find anyone who would buy a U.S.-flag steamship company, and
very quickly the search narrowed down to the ever-optimistic Malcom
McLean, who was very eager to integrate what was left of Delta's Latin
American service (the African route had been abandoned in 1983) into
his scheme for a worldwide transportation system. Unfortunately
McLean was short of cash, so a complex stock-exchange arrangement
was worked out. Crowley took his huge losses courageously, but he
considered himself lucky to have at least stopped the drain on his tug
and barge business. McLean received Delta's active fleet, now dwindled
to four ships. Besides the three containerships still under construction
in Denmark, those four ships were all that was left of Delta, whose 55-
year existence as an independent service had come to an end.[17] Another
U.S. steamship company had ceased to exist, but any sadness or regret
was hastily erased by the tremendous expectations now riding on Malcom McLean, who had already revitalized a previously shaky United
States Lines.

□ McLean's Last Gamble

The quick takeover of United States Lines by Walter Kidde and Company in January 1968 saved Malcom McLean. United States Lines' new

container fleet would soon be in a position to deliver a knockout blow to McLean's Sea-Land, whose aging ships were simply no match. Too many coincidences suggest that McLean goaded Walter Kidde and Company's chairman, Fred R. Sullivan, into the hostile takeover of United States Lines, and in any case the steamship firm was immediately afterward bombarded with McLean's offers of a long-term charter of the entire new fleet of containerships. However, Sullivan's first goal was to reap a financial windfall by selling off the undervalued assets of the supposedly cash-rich United States Lines, but he soon suffered a tremendous deception when he learned that there were almost none. He soon tired of the grinding task of running a steamship business, but, wishing to retain the status that ownership of the nation's largest fleet conferred, he had another shareholder, John McMullen, become the president of United States Lines in June 1968. An Annapolis graduate with a Ph.D. in mechanical engineering, McMullen also had a rough and blunt manner more typical of an old sea captain, and this rare combination was supposed to make him the right chief executive needed to bring United States Lines into the container age.

Immediately upon arrival, McMullen canceled the contracts of all the white-collar employees and sacked 125; as a result of his bitter confrontational manner, he soon had a fight with a white-collar workers' union on his hands. McMullen correctly concluded that the conversion to containerships had to proceed at all possible speed, and to raise additional funds he sold 5 freighters (engaged in modestly profitable runs) to Farrell Lines in February 1969. McMullen had no hesitation about taking the inevitable action of ending passenger service, and in November 1969 the *United States*, the fastest passenger liner in the world, was laid up. A new problem was entirely McMullen's doing: after he fired the supposedly superfluous white-collar workers, nobody was left in charge of filing the subsidy renewals in time, so that in late 1969 the operating subsidy on the remaining 14 freighters expired. McMullen tried to publicly cover his colossal gaffe by claiming that henceforth United States Lines would operate 14 freighters as tramps, with freedom to pick and change routes, unlike the rigid requirements of the subsidized service. More realistically, he worked quietly in the background and through his old navy friends; soon he had most of the freighters profitably chartered to the Military Sea Transportation Service for hauling cargoes during the last stages of the Vietnam War. The rest of the freighters were placed in different domestic runs for minimal profits.[18]

For both Sullivan and McMullen, the steamship business was turning out to be a lot more complex than it had appeared to be from the outside, and in October 1969 they finally agreed to McLean's constant requests to lease for 20 years United States Lines' 16-ship container fleet, including the new Lancers. They believed that McLean was a pro who would take the hassle out of the steamship business, enabling them just to sit back and count the profits from what would be the largest peacetime charter in maritime history. In a sense, they were paralleling what Overseas Shipholding Group was doing when the latter leased out its tankers on long-term charter to the oil companies. But meanwhile McLean had upped the ante: he had exchanged his ownership of Sea-Land for shares and a director's seat on R. J. Reynolds, one of the nation's largest tobacco conglomerates. Reynolds now owned Sea-Land, and as soon as it chartered United States Lines' container fleet (then considered the finest in the world), it would gain control of 88 percent of U.S.-flag container capacity.

The Federal Maritime Commission soon was swamped with protests from other steamship companies, guaranteeing a long hard fight to secure government approval for the charter. All the time the losses from United States Lines continued to mount, and Walter Kidde and Company's debt had risen from $93 million in 1968 to $238 million in 1969. Sullivan decided to dump the whole mess on an eager R. J. Reynolds, and on 9 November 1970 he sold United States Lines to the tobacco conglomerate. Both sides were aware of possible antitrust complications, and in case the antitrust division of the Justice Department vetoed the sale, Reynolds promised to find a new buyer, although Walter Kidde and Company continued to manage the steamship company until the sale was officially approved by the federal government.[19]

The sale caught McMullen by surprise, because he had hoped to have his own bid for the purchase of United States Lines accepted; he tried to block the sale, leaving Sullivan no choice but to fire him after a bitter clash in December 1970. United States Lines now was left in limbo, with neither R. J. Reynolds nor Walter Kidde and Company having any real stake in its operations. Another 100 employees were fired, and the steamship firm's debt continued to mount, in order to cover operational expenses. In spite of these difficulties, between 1972 and 1977 the company had earned profits during some years, in part because a number of vessels had been shifted to foreign flags. The Federal Maritime Commission and the Justice Department killed the proposed sale, but since R. J. Reynolds still had to find a substitute buyer, to obtain a release from this contractual obligation, it paid Walter Kidde and Company a lump settlement of $4.5 million in 1976.[20]

McLean now had United States Lines within his sights, and he could only watch with satisfaction as Walter Kidde and Company struggled to find anyone who would take the steamship company. The many suitors who answered the bid inevitably were smaller outfits without the necessary financial backing, resources, or even experience. Sullivan nevertheless decided to try a sale with one of the small outfits, only to be promptly shot down by the Maritime Administration. Why did McLean now emerge on top of the list? He had been restless as a director of R. J. Reynolds, preferring the excitement of running a one-man high-wire show to the highly profitable but dull life in the corporate stratosphere. He quietly sold most of his Reynold's stock at a handsome price and resigned from the board, and, using other personal assets as collateral, he revealed an uncanny ability to loosen money from otherwise skeptical and wary bankers. In September 1977 Walter Kidde and Company was left with no choice but to sell, and McLean was at last the proud owner of United States Lines; thanks to a series of carefully plotted moves and deals, he had made it to the very top of the steamship business.

McLean could not long savor his triumph, because the company was sinking in problems. McLean very characteristically had his own home-grown remedies. With gusto he plunged into the company and put his own management team into place, "the boys from Mobile." His first course of action was to get the government off his back, and he insisted on wiggling out of low-interest government mortgages on ships, even though United States Lines was not receiving operating subsidies, which formerly had been the principal source of government interference in the company's affairs. McLean held the deeply ingrained belief that government with its red tape and regulation was the source of the problem and that once he was free to make and change his routes, the company would become profitable.[21]

The immediate challenge came from Sea-Land, which as an R. J. Reynolds subsidiary had easily financed the construction of the next generation of container vessels, the SL-7s with 50 percent more carrying capacity and a top speed of 33 knots compared to the Lancers' 24 knots. Sea-Land had become the largest U.S.-flag container operator, while United States Lines was barely holding onto third place. McLean's goal was to recapture first place, but if he did not take some drastic action, his container share would soon shrink to insignificance. In early 1979, McLean announced his dramatic play: United States Lines would build the 12 biggest containerships in the world (with capacity for 3,400 containers). These ships would be highly automated, so that the size of the expensive U.S. crews would be cut in half; furthermore, the ships would be built abroad in Korea and would operate under the U.S. flag once enabling legislation had been passed by Congress. McLean knew he could easily line up adequate financing from banks ready to lend against his good credit rating and ample other properties. The profitability of the venture was ensured by the bold strategy of sending the ships around the world, thereby eliminating the recurrent return-cargo problem on the two-way routes; to any doubters, McLean confidently explained that the lower rates on his around-the-world route "would suck up cargo like a vacuum."[22]

Many investors shared McLean's enthusiasm, but others felt he was placing too much weight on his small freighters and foreign-flag vessels, the less glamorous but more reliable money earners. Short of cash to finance his 12 containerships, he first dropped plans to order an additional 2, and then he did an amazing reversal: after a lifetime spent condemning federal government intervention, he now applied for operating subsidies for most of his fleet of freighters. His application for 20-year contracts was approved in the closing months of the Carter administration, without requiring McLean to dispose of his foreign-flag operations. Receiving a subsidy disqualified United States Lines from placing orders in foreign shipyards, but McLean had that problem under control as well. Legislation was rushed through Congress allowing steamship companies to build U.S.-flag vessels abroad without disqualifying the rest of their fleet for subsidies, provided the applications were presented before the expiration date of September 1982, a deadline duly met by United States Lines. But there was more: sensing the mounting public wave against government intervention reflected in the Ronald Reagan landslide, McLean now denounced the subsidy he was receiving and decided to embrace the buyout formula, whereby in exchange for giving up the 20-year subsidy, the company would receive during five years a smaller total amount.[23] A Reagan administration eager to end the subsidies agreed, and now McLean had the rest of the funds needed to finance the ship construction in South Korea.

The orders for the 12 containerships were placed in 1983, and McLean cut another shrewd deal with the shipyard and the government in South Korea, both of which were desperate to land this major contract. Too much time had elapsed since he had announced his plans in 1979, and modifications to the original ship design seemed advisable. McLean counted on oil prices remaining high and he dismissed the drop in fuel prices after 1981 as just a temporary phenomenon, so he insisted on maximum fuel efficiency and had slow-speed diesel engines installed. For the around-the-world service, the ships had to fit through the Panama Canal, so rather than making them longer and wider, he retained the square hull, blunt prow, and sharp angles that made the ships look more like floating shoeboxes. Rather than slicing through the water, the 16-knot speed was a throwback almost to the pre–World War II vessels. The tempo of activity seemed to the quickening in the 1980s, shippers wanted things faster than before, but when management tried to explain this faster pace to McLean, he revealed his own formula for success: "The secret is price, the customer says he wants speed, in reality the customer wants lower price."[24]

McLean did agree to extend United States Lines' services to Latin America by acquiring Moore-McCormack in January 1983 and Delta Line in December 1984, thereby covering both coasts of South America, which could be tapped as feeder lines for his main around-the-world service. Yet it was not clear how the Latin American cargo, which mainly moved on a north-south axis, would mesh with his eastbound around-the-world service; more significantly, the Latin American steamship companies did not feel threatened. To finish these acquisitions, McLean raised more funds by issuing shares for the first time in the stock market in August 1983. The issue was subscribed in a few hours thanks to a rosy prospectus, but no more capital could be raised in the stock market, and by 1984 McLean had exhausted both his assets and his lines of credit.[25]

The gamble appeared to work, and in July 1984 the *American New York*, the first of 12 new containerships, sailed on its maiden voyage and earned substantial profits. This was the high point of McLean's career. As the shipyard delivered over the next months the remaining vessels (each named after a state), the revival of the U.S. merchant marine appeared to have become a reality—and, best of all for McLean, under private control.

Foreign steamship companies had had at least a four years' warning about McLean's plans, and they had gradually accumulated reserves for a bitter rate war as soon as McLean's containerships finally hit the overtonnaged trades. The Europeans, the Japanese, and the Taiwanese dug in for a long fight and calculated that they could outlast McLean's lower costs by offering customers faster speed and absorbing their losses until their own new containerships were delivered. A new player from Taiwan, Evergreen Group, had matched United States Lines' expansion in volume, but Evergreen's containerships were smaller and thereby could easily enter a larger number of ports than could McLean's "floating elephants" or "moving bathtubs." The permanent undermining of the conference system by the Federal Maritime Commission and the U.S. antitrust policy left no authority to fall back on or to try to prevent the rate war.

To keep the cargo from going to McLean's ships, competitors reduced rates to retain customers in 1984, forcing McLean to counter with cuts that eventually fell to 40 percent below the pre–rate war level. United States Lines was now operating below cost, a situation the competitors because of their reserves could sustain for a long time while still offering faster delivery time. In the around-the-world service, Middle East cargo failed to materialize, and in other areas many ports were too small or lacked the facilities to handle the mammoth containerships; furthermore, the drop in fuel prices wiped out McLean's expected advantage of having economical slow-speed diesel engines. McLean struggled through 1985, keeping United States Lines afloat by balancing the subsidy payments on the remaining U.S.-flag ships and the solid profits from the foreign-flag freighters, but the pressures continued to mount during the next year. Losses piled up incredibly fast, reaching $236 million in the first nine months of 1986; at that pace another three months would have been fatal. Creditors began to hound the once rock-solid United States Lines for overdue payments, and to avoid foreclosures, on 24 November 1986 United States Lines filed for protection under Chapter 11 bankruptcy proceedings. "We just guessed wrong," McLean explained lamely.[26]

The moving bathtubs were docked at various world ports, in the vain hope that under Chapter 11 proceedings the small freighters could somehow earn enough to erase the monstrous losses incurred by the containerships. The 2,800 employees were promptly reduced to 600, but it was too late—United States Lines, a product of 65 years of corporate existence and the direct descendant of J. P. Morgan's once-powerful International Mercantile Marine, was beyond saving. The handful of surviving U.S. steamship companies backed attempts to revive United States Lines out of a concern that if the containerships fell into the hands of the strong foreign firms, they would become "killer ships" and easily dominate the world's ocean commerce. The fate of the killer ships remained unsolved, but United States Lines never revived, bringing to an end the turbulent and memorable career of what had long been the largest fleet of U.S. merchant vessels.[27]

CONCLUSION

THIS BOOK HAS COME FULL circle: The narrative ends with the collapse of United States Lines in 1986, the last direct descendant of the International Mercantile Marine, whose creation in 1901–1902 ushered in the twentieth century for U.S. merchant shipping. The direction of the momentum was clearly different: The foundation of I.M.M. formed part of a wave of U.S. firms expanding into the foreign trade routes, while the collapse of United States Lines reflected on the contrary the desperate struggle of the dwindling number of U.S. companies to survive. The downward plunges continues to the 1990s; the Gulf War provided but a momentary boost, and the end of the Cold War has been steadily reducing military cargoes, the main sources of business for the remaining U.S.-flag services. After almost a century of pouring incredible sums of money into the U.S. merchant marine, the question inevitably arises: why did the U.S. fail to create U.S. steamship companies able to resist competition in the world's sea lanes? Those seeking individuals, government agencies, or private companies to blame will easily find many in this book which has few heroes. Chance and the random events that make history unpredictable but so fascinating frequently manifested themselves, but a number of patterns or larger trends were also present. Of the latter, five stand out to this author as the most significant.

The pre-World War I history of United Fruit, Dollar Line, W.R. Grace, Pacific Mail and others revealed the surprise of how widespread was the prevalence of the British flag for the ships of U.S. companies. Other flags were also used, sometimes the Belgian, in one case the Cuban. With the flags came the opportunity to use foreign ships, crews, and officers, although generally the companies retained a small percentage of their ships flying the U.S. flag. That so many companies chose foreign flag operations powerfully suggested no mere coincidence, but rather the only business way to operate the merchant fleet without subsidies, government cargoes, or coastwise privileges. Nevertheless,

281

from World War I the rejection of foreign flag operations has become a generalized principle in U.S. policy. The flags of convenience (Panama, Liberia, and others) were a partial substitute to the end of the British Empire, whose collapse deprived British flag registry of most of its former benefits. Whenever the U.S. has accepted foreign flag ships for U.S. companies, the merchant fleet has grown, with even some U.S.-flag ships as a secondary subproduct. The opposite has likewise been true: the rejection of foreign flag ships at the cost of large government subsidies has pushed U.S.-flag companies into a precarious position conducive to decline and eventual disappearance.

Besides the repudiation of foreign flags, the rejection of large near-monopoly companies emerges as another reason in the decline of U.S. merchant shipping. The author does not believe blindly the dictum that "bigger is better," and the striking proliferation of tramps (whose demise was often predicted) confirms the presence of a very dynamic and significant sector of small shipowners; nevertheless, the twentieth century (particularly pre-1914 and post-1945) has been a period of consolidation for steamship companies, above all in the liner and tanker trades. The bigger a steamship firm became, the more it increased its chances of survival, on the assumption of course that management did not make irreparable blunders. I.M.M. was able to meet the fierce foreign competition on the North Atlantic only because the company combined bigness with foreign flags. I.M.M. at least could survive, yet its Achilles' heel remained public relations in the United States. To most Americans, I.M.M. was nothing but a huge British monopoly, a veritable Trojan Horse that undermined the U.S. merchant marine by keeping out smaller companies. I.M.M. was the most serious of many casualties of the obsession against bigness, an anti-monopoly campaign that intensified from the 1950s as the Justice Department targeted the shrinking U.S. merchant shipping industry for antitrust action.

The rejection or fear of bigness and of supposed monopolies among steamship firms often mixed with a blind faith in the miracles of competition. The heyday of competition was after World War I, when the Shipping Board spawned over two hundred new steamship firms. The pressures toward consolidations in world shipping were no less than before World War I or after World War II, but the Shipping Board's rash actions created the false impression that massive competition was making a comeback. In 1919-1920 reckless competition was the rule, as rival U.S.-flag subsidized lines competed against one another in the same routes, and each port sought to have its own line. The Shipping Board itself soon realized how senseless the competition had become, and began to consolidate the lines, a task it was never able to finish. Yet even when the Shipping Board was abolished, "the more the merrier" remained rampant as a principle for U.S. shipping. After World War II, a timely and prompt consolidation of U.S. steamship companies into the half dozen with the best managerial talent was essential to prepare for the coming onslaught of foreign competition once Europe and Japan rebuilt their fleets; instead the government continued to squander resources in costly rivalry between subsidized U.S.-flag ships. An excess of foreign competition has been the rule, yet an emotional attachment to an idyllic form of free market has kept the U.S. from marshalling its resources in order to reap the commercial benefits that having a merchant fleet brings in the foreign trades.

No matter how far the percentage of cargo carried by U.S. steamship companies dropped, the blind faith in competition as well as the rejection of bigness and foreign flags remained rock-solid beliefs. However, the sense that something was needed, or better yet, was wanting, to reverse the downward trend in the U.S. merchant marine, could not be avoided. New and supposedly superior technology became the cure-all and the new idol. There was no denying that a whole host of technological innovations revolutionized almost every aspect of the shipping business, but none gave U.S. steamship companies anything but a brief lead. U.S. firms pioneered the introduction of computers into their ship and cargo operations, only to see the computer methods rapidly adopted by foreign competitors. Speed became another technological edge, with faster U.S. ships supposedly outrunning their foreign rivals to the cargoes. But speed was a tricky thing, and fast ships were not always the answer to all routes and all decades, with the result that in vastly changed circumstances, Malcolm McClean sunk United States Lines when he mistakenly saddled the burdened company with literally slow boats to China.

Yet the worst technological disaster for U.S. companies were the containers. From the late 1960s the blind faith in technology as the solution for the companies' mounting problems triggered a movement towards Ro/Ro, LASH, and above all container vessels. While U.S. firms made the costly experiments, the Europeans and Asians waited until the last moment to make the most effective and appropriate conversion of their fleets to containers. U.S. companies countered with bigger containerships as the way to retain cargo, but the more U.S. companies plunged into containerships, the deeper most dug their own graves. Among other problems, the container technology created a contradiction: as the container ships increased in size, foreign companies could merge and become supergiants, but the U.S. firms could not because of the government rejection of bigness. The American blind faith in technology had actually backfired, at best merely prolonging the decline of some U.S. firms, at worst accelerating the companies' bankruptcies.

Many countries in the world have turned to state-owned merchant fleets in order to achieve their foreign trade goals. In the United States, however, any proposals for government ownership and operation of ships has met not only an indignant rejection, but provoked as well a paranoid fear. The two contradictory charges of inefficiency and unfair government competition have reappeared from the first decade of the twentieth century until the present. This spasmodic reaction has been all the more remarkable because the four historical cases of the twentieth century do not confirm, and on the contrary refute the fears about a government merchant fleet. The Panama Line (1904–79), the Military Sealift Command (1898 to the present), and the United States Lines during its period of government control (1921–29) were highly efficient organizations run with a near-military discipline. American President Lines (1939–52) and United States Lines (1921–29) were two bankrupt companies at the moment of government takeover; once they became profitable again, the government caved in to charges of socialism and sold the firms to private owners. The bottom line was no less telling: it has been cheaper for the government to operate its own ships than to use the 1936 act to subsidize private owners. The operating costs among government vessels using civil service crews compare favorably with some—but far from all—those for foreign lines. Government ships, because they do not have to sustain the huge "overhead" costs of rewarding management and owners, nor much less support and enrich a bloated labor leadership, can compete in a limited way in some of the foreign trade routes, an intriguing possibility violently rejected by most Americans.

To the five reasons listed above, many experts add a sixth: mistaken subsidy policies. This book takes a different approach, and considers subsidy policy not as an independent reason or factor, but simply a consequence or a response to the previous five. From the first congressional hearings on the merchant marine in the first decade of the twentieth century, legislators recognized subsidies as a feasible alternative to the politically unacceptable previous five reasons. When experts debate over subsidies, the focus should not be (as it has been) over whether they were too large (during the Shipping Board era) or too meager (under the 1936 act) but rather that they have been a compensation given to owners and never a solid foundation for long-term survival and expansion. Generalizing over many encounters between the government and the private sector, officials frequently offered the subsidies as a way to entice the owners to remain under the U.S. flag, and although completely legal, at times the impression could not be avoided that the government was trying to bribe the companies with the subsidies. The owners sometimes turned the tables around, and literally blackmailed the government, by saying that if subsidies were not provided, their ships would leave the U.S. flag. Whether in specific cases the threat was carried out or the bluff called the point remains that subsidies have been inevitably a result of a much larger struggle. For the above and other reasons, subsidies, the focus of the overwhelming majority of merchant marine studies, have been more a symptom than a cause or independent variable, and consequently subsidy policy by itself cannot explain the evolution of U.S. merchant shipping in the twentieth century.

What can be done to revive U.S. merchant shipping? To provide an answer, a veritable cottage industry has thrived, as over the last four decades many experts elaborated a varying list of proposals. This author is not afraid of providing for free what others have charged well to supply; my main concern remains that historical studies like the one completed in this book, should have preceded any attempt to offer recommendations. For those readers who became overly depressed by this tale of repeated failure and gloom, and who insist on some answers or gleam of hope, the five conclusions stated above are a logical starting point. The reader may combine these conclusions to begin sketching possible alternatives, but should not be scared by the apparent incongruity of some combinations; as a last hint, more than one proposal can be right.

In any case, a more basic goal of this book has been to draw the reader's attention toward U.S. merchant shipping. As the twentieth century comes to an end, the world increasingly splits into powerful trading blocks, while the end of the Cold War released ethnic and national struggles. As the growing population of the crowded planet clashes over markets and resources, the commercial need for a U.S. merchant shipping industry becomes greater. Without its own steamship companies, the trading position of the United States in the highly competitive world economy must necessarily continue to deteriorate. But to look to steamship companies to restore the U.S. trade balance is a wishful dream: as far as the twentieth century is concerned, the drama of the U.S. merchant shipping industry appears to have played itself out; perhaps the next century will bring a turnaround.

Notes and References

CHAPTER 1

1. Vivian Vale, *The American Peril: Challenge to Britain on the North Atlantic, 1901–1904* (Manchester: University Press, 1984), 33–39, 63–70; Thomas R. Navin and Marian V. Sears, "A Study in Merger: Formation of the International Mercantile Marine Company," *Business History Review* 28 (1954): 293–98.

2. Vale, *American Peril*, 38–39, 54–55, 76; Navin and Sears, "Formation of I.M.M.," 296–99; Francis E. Hyde, *Cunard and the North Atlantic, 1840–1973* (Atlantic Highlands, N.J.: Humanities Press, 1975), 137.

3. For this and the previous paragraph, *see* Vincent P. Carosso, *The Morgans: Private International Bankers, 1854–1913* (Cambridge: Harvard University Press, 1987), 481, 482; Navin and Sears, "Formation of I.M.M.," 300–302; Herbert L. Satterlee, *J. Pierpont Morgan: An Intimate Portrait* (New York: Macmillan, 1940), 372–73.

4. *The Daily Post* (Liverpool), 30 April 1901.

5. Lord Inverclyde to Sir William B. Forwood, 1 May 1901, Cunard Records, the University Archives, the University of Liverpool (manuscript collection hereafter cited as Cunard); Vale, *American Peril*, 56–57; Navin and Sears, "Formation of I.M.M.," 303–7.

6. E.H. Cunard to Lord Inverclyde, 6 May 1901, Edward J. Berwind to Vernon H. Brown, 29 May 1901, and Vernon H. Brown to David Jardine, 21 October 1901, Cunard; Vale, *American Peril*, 74–79; Hyde, *Cunard and the North Atlantic*, 138–40; Carosso, *The Morgans*, 482–83; Lamar Cecil, *Albert Ballin: Business and Politics in Imperial Germany, 1888–1918* (Princeton: Princeton University Press, 1967), 48–53.

7. Hyde, *Cunard and the North Atlantic*, 140–48; Vale, *American Peril*, 150–81; Vernon H. Brown to Lord Inverclyde, 21 January 1902, Cunard; Satterlee, *Morgan*, 1–145, 320–55.

8. Carosso, *The Morgans*, 483–85; Vale, *American Peril*, 90–91, 113, 208–9, 214; William H. Becker, *The Dynamics of Business-Govern-*

286

ment Relations: Industry and Exports, 1893–1921 (Chicago: University of Chicago Press, 1982), 187.

9. Navin and Sears, "Formation of I.M.M.," 320–22; Vale, *American Peril*, 208–9.

10. Navin and Sears, "Formation of I.M.M.," 320; U.S. Department of Agriculture, *Ocean Freight Rates and the Conditions Affecting Them* (Washington, D.C.: Government Printing Office, 1907), 5–11; Vale, *American Peril*, 208–9.

11. Hyde, *Cunard and the North Atlantic*, 114, and 110–16; for the outbreak and origins of the rate war, see Reports of the French consul at Hamburg, 1903–1904, F 12/6145, Archives Nationales, Paris, France.

12. James Bisset, *Tramps and Ladies: My Early Years in Steamers* (New York: Criterion Books, 1959), 269–307; Milton H. Watson, *Disasters at Sea: Every Ocean-Going Passenger Ship Catastrophe since 1900* (Northamptonshire, England: Patrick Stephens, 1987), 48–52.

13. Vale, *American Peril*, 212–14; Carosso, *The Morgans*, 492–93.

14. Hyde, *Cunard and the North Atlantic*, 117–18 Navin and Sears, "Formation of I.M.M.," 326; Vale, *American Peril*, 213–14; Cecil, *Ballin*, 61–62.

15. Navin and Sears, "Formation of I.M.M.," 326–27; Carosso, *The Morgans*, 490–94; Vale, *American Peril*, 214, 220.

16. John Niven, *American President Lines and Its Forebears, 1848–1984* (Newark: University of Delaware Press, 1987), 17, 37–40; E. Mowbray Tate, *Transpacific Steam* (New York: Cornwall Books, 1986), 35–37, 253–54; John H. Kemble, "A Hundred Years of the Pacific Mail," *American Neptune* 10 (1950): 125, 131–32.

17. U.S. Congress, House Committee on Merchant Marine and Fisheries, *Investigation of Shipping Combinations*, 4 vols. (Washington, D.C.: Government Printing Office, 1913), 2: 894–96; Kemble, "Pacific Mail," 136–38; Robert J. Schwendinger, *Ocean of Bitter Dreams: Maritime Relations between China and the United States, 1850–1915* (Tucson: Westernlore Press, 1988), 169–79.

18. House Committee on Merchant Marine and Fisheries, *Investigation of Shipping Combinations*, 2:897.

19. House Committee on Merchant Marine and Fisheries, *Investigation of Shipping Combinations*, 2:923; for previous paragraph, see also Niven, *American President Lines*, 40–41.

20. Kemble, "Pacific Mail," 139; Niven, *American President Lines*, 41; Schwendinger, *Ocean of Bitter Dreams*, 181–93.

21. Lawrence A. Clayton, *W. R. Grace & Co.: The Formative Years, 1850–1930* (Ottawa, Ill.: Jameson Books, 1985), 269, 335; Kemble, "Pacific Mail," 139–43; Tate, *Transpacific Steam*, 38–41. In 1925 Grace surrendered the name, house flag, trade emblems, and goodwill of the Pacific Mail, all of which were acquired in 1926 by the Dollar family and continued to be used in miscellaneous ventures at least until 1949; see

"Pacific Mail Steamship Company," box 10, Dollar Collection, Bancroft Library, Berkeley, California.

22.   Frederick E. Emmons, *American Passenger Ships: The Ocean Lines and Liners, 1873–1983* (Newark: University of Delaware Press, 1985), 54; William L. Worden, *Cargoes: Matson's First Century in the Pacific* (Honolulu: University of Hawaii Press, 1981), 4–5, 12.

23.   Fred A. Stindt, *Matson's Century of Ships* (Modesto, Calif.: n.p., 1982), 21; Tate, *Transpacific Steam,* 52–55; Worden, *Cargoes,* 19, 23.

24.   W. Kaye Lamb, "The Transpacific Ventures of James J. Hill," *American Neptune* 3 (1943): 185–95; for this and the previous paragraph, *see also* Emmons, *American Passenger Ships,* 55–56; Tate, *Transpacific Steam,* 120; Don L. Hofsommer, "The Maritime Enterprises of James J. Hill, "*American Neptune* 47 (1987): 197–202.

25.   Lamb, "The Transpacific Ventures of James J. Hill," 196–204; Watson, *Disasters at Sea,* 29–30. Requisitioned shortly afterward by the government, the *Minnesota,* according to seamen, at last was a happy ship, having found her true calling in the North Atlantic to carry the endless mountains of supplies to the American Expeditionary Force in France. The *Minnesota's* deep holds were filled to the top for the first time in her life, her decks were stuffed full, the top deck was piled high with freight, and cargo was even hung from her rigging. After her obsolete machinery was replaced, she was slightly faster than most freighters and was thus a godsend to the Shipping Board as she made voyage after voyage across the North Atlantic in the most productive and final stage of her career.

26.   Robert Dollar, *One Hundred Thirty Years of Steam Navigation* (San Francisco: Schwabacher & Frey, 1931), 131–34; Niven, *American President Lines,* 46–47; Robert Dollar, *Memoirs,* 4 vols. (San Francisco: Schwabacher & Frey, 1927), 1:78–79, 3:16–17, 27.

27.   Gregory C. O'Brien, "The Life of Robert Dollar, 1844–1932" (Ph.D. diss., Claremont Graduate School, 1968), 56, 58–61, 74–78; Niven, *American President Lines,* 47–50.

28.   O'Brien, "Robert Dollar," 109–111, 179–81; Niven, *American President Lines,* 50–54.

29.   Dollar, *Memoirs,* 2:13–17, 23, 44, 60, 104; 3:16–17, 70–73; "Robert Dollar Financial Investigation," 21 November 1921, box 842, Record Group 32, National Archives, Washington, D.C.

CHAPTER 2

1.   Lincoln Concord, "History of the American-Hawaiian Steamship Co.," unpublished manuscript, 3, 19–21, 23–26, 38, 40, 53; *Pacific Marine Review,* November 1926, 493–94.

2.   Concord, "History," 23–24, 120–24; Raymond A. Rydell, *Cape Horn to the Pacific: The Rise and Decline of an Ocean Highway* (Berkeley: University of California Press, 1952), 147.

3.   Thomas C. Cochran and Ray Ginger, "The American-Ha-

waiian Steamship Company, 1899–1919," *Business History Review* 28 (1954): 345–46; Concord, "History," 3–5, 96–108.

4. Cochran and Ginger, "American-Hawaiian," 348–49; Concord, "History," 77–87; Rydell, *Cape Horn to the Pacific*, 152–53.

5. *Marine Journal*, 9 April 1904; *see also* Cochran and Ginger, "American-Hawaiian," 349–50.

6. Concord, "History," 30–31, 125–35; Cochran and Ginger, "American-Hawaiian," 350, 352–53.

7. Concord, "History," 137–39. In 1906 American-Hawaiian had carried 200,000 tons of cargo through the Straits of Magellan. The amount had increased to 315,987 in 1907, the first year of the Tehuantepec route, and by the route's last year, 1913, it had jumped to 753,113.

8. Cochran and Ginger, "American-Hawaiian," 354–55.

9. Concord, "History," 156–59, 172, 180–89, 192–94; Cochran and Ginger, "American-Hawaiian," 357–60.

10. Stindt, *Matson's Century*, 29, 34; Worden, *Cargoes*, 47, 53; Cochran and Ginger, "American-Hawaiian," 360–62; Concord, "History," 203–210.

11. Cochran and Ginger, "American-Hawaiian," 362.

12. Worden, *Cargoes*, 1, 12, 23–24.

13. Stindt, *Matson's Century*, 19–20; for this and the previous paragraph, *see also* Worden, *Cargoes*, 25–28; Emmons, *American Passenger Ships*, 57.

14. Worden, *Cargoes*, 33.

15. Stindt, *Matson's Century*, 21–22.

16. Cochran and Ginger, "American-Hawaiian," 356; Concord, "History," 162–63.

17. Kemble, "Pacific Mail," 139–40.

18. Concord, "History," 206–210; Stindt, *Matson's Century*, 29–30; Cochran and Ginger, "American-Hawaiian," 361–62.

19. Stindt, *Matson's Century*, 29–30; Worden, *Cargoes*, 47, 51, 53.

20. Emmons, *American Passenger Ships*, 110–11, 116, 128–29, 133.

21. House Committee on Merchant Marine and Fisheries, *Investigation of Shipping Combinations*, 1:651–63; Emmons, *American Passenger Ships*, 83; John B. Waterman to N. O. Pedrick, 9 November 1926, Records of Waterman Steamship Corporation, Mobile Public Library, Mobile, Alabama.

22. House Committee on Merchant Marine and Fisheries, *Investigation of Shipping Combinations*, 3:285–88; Emmons, *American Passenger Ships*, 116–17; James P. Baughman, *The Mallorys of Mystic* (Middletown, Conn.: Wesleyan University Press, 1972), 214–16, 223–26.

23. Emmons, *American Passenger Ships*, 142–43.

24. *Mast Magazine*, November 1949, 6–7; House Committee on

Merchant Marine and Fisheries, *Investigation of Shipping Combinations*, 1:392–93, 2:1208–1210.

25. *Ships and the Sea*, July 1952, 55–56; House Committee on Merchant Marine and Fisheries, *Investigation of Shipping Combinations*, 1:393–402, 2:1212–20; *Mast Magazine*, November 1949, 7.

26. Baughman, *The Mallorys*, 202–213; Becker, *Dynamics of Business-Government Relations*, 187–88.

27. *Fortune*, September 1937, 176; Baughman, *The Mallorys*, 214–16, 223–26.

28. John H. Melville, *The Great White Fleet* (New York: Vantage Press, 1976), 8–13; Charles D. Kepner, Jr., and Jay H. Soothill, *The Banana Empire: A Case Study of Economic Imperialism* (New York: Russell & Russell, 1935), 50–54, 179–80.

29. Frederick U. Adams, *Conquest of the Tropics: The Story of the Creative Enterprises Conducted by the United Fruit Company* (New York: Doubleday, Page & Co., 1914), 81–85; Melville, *Great White Fleet*, 15; Carlos Funtanellas et al., *United Fruit Company: Un caso del dominio imperialista en Cuba* (Havana: Editorial de Ciencias Sociales, 1976), 43–79, 131–41.

30. House Committee on Merchant Marine and Fisheries, *Investigation of Shipping Combinations*, 1:712–14; Melville, *Great White Fleet*, 29–30, 32, 47; Kepner, Jr., and Soothill, *Banana Empire*, 178–80.

31. Adams, *Conquest of the Tropics*, 124–26; for passenger service, *see also* Melville, *Great White Fleet*, 18–21.

32. Kepner, Jr., and Soothill, *Banana Empire*, 180–83; Melville, *Great White Fleet*, 25–27, 106–7; Adams, *Conquest of the Tropics*, 106–8.

33. Thomas P. McCann, *An American Company: The Tragedy of United Fruit* (New York: Crown Publishers, 1976), 34; for this paragraph, *see also* House Committee on Merchant Marine and Fisheries, *Investigation of Shipping Combinations*, 1:712–13, 730–31.

34. Lawrence A. Clayton, *W. R. Grace & Co.: The Formative Years, 1850–1930* (Ottowa, Ill.: Jameson Books, 1985), 30–33, 50–51, 65, 72, 177, 180, 190–95; William Kooiman, "W.R. Grace's Ships and Lines, 1869–1969," unpublished manuscript; correspondence, particularly 9 June 1903, box 74, and June 1906, box 75, W. R. Grace & Co. Records, Rare Book and Manuscript Library, Columbia University (henceforth CU).

35. Letter, 26 June 1906, Box 75, CU; Clayton, *W. R. Grace*, ch. 11.

36. Ed Eyre to J. F. Fowler, 8 November 1895, box 82, CU.

37. Kooiman, "W. R. Grace's Ships and Lines"; Clayton, *W. R. Grace*, 261–62.

38. Vice-President to John Eyre, 12 June 1903, box 74. For the Chilean subsidy episode, which is reported differently in Clayton, *W. R. Grace*, 202, 257–58, 260, *see also* telegram of 5 December 1901, and letters of 14 January 1902, and 21 October 1902, box 74, CU.

39.   Letters, 4 May 1908, 19 April 1909, 3 September 1910, box 76, CU; House Committee on Merchant Marine and Fisheries, *Investigation of Shipping Combinations*, 1: 464; Mark T. Gilderhus, *Pan American Visions: Woodrow Wilson in the Western Hemisphere 1913–1921* (Tucson: University of Arizona Press, 1986), 123.

40.   Clayton, *W. R. Grace*, pp. 266–70; House Committee on Merchant Marine and Fisheries, *Investigation of Shipping Combinations*, 1: 465–67; Kooiman, "W. R. Grace's Ships and Line"; Gilderhus, *Pan American Visions*, 24, 42–43.

CHAPTER 3

1.   Baughman, *The Mallorys*, 232–34; Jeffrey J. Safford, *Wilsonian Maritime Diplomacy, 1913–21* (New Brunswick, N.J.: Rutgers University Press, 1978), 35–39; Burton I. Kaufman, *Efficiency and Expansion: Foreign Trade Organization in the Wilson Administration, 1913–21* (Westport, Conn.: Greenwood Press, 1974), 91–96.

2.   Safford, *Wilsonian Maritime Diplomacy*, 39–43; Kaufman, *Efficiency and Expansion*, 98–99.

3.   Safford, *Wilsonian Maritime Diplomacy*, 48; for rest of paragraph, *see also* Becker, *Dynamics of Business-Government Relations*, 145–46.

4.   Kaufman, *Efficiency and Expansion*, 98–100, 124; Safford, *Wilsonian Maritime Diplomacy*, 49–65.

5.   Baughman, *The Mallorys*, 235–38; U.S. Congress, House, *Foreign Vessels Admitted to American Registry*, House Document (H. Doc.) 1664 (Washington, D.C.: Government Printing Office, 1915), 1–17; Becker, *Industry and Exports*, 146–48.

6.   Report, 8 January 1915, and telegram, 24 January 1915, Public Record Office, London (PRO), Foreign Office (FO) 115/1993; U.S. House, *Foreign Vessels Admitted to American Registry*, 1–17.

7.   Tate, *Transpacific Steam*, 38–41; Safford, *Wilsonian Maritime Diplomacy*, 111–13, 195–96; Schwendinger, *Ocean of Bitter Dreams*, 181–93.

8.   Safford, *Wilsonian Maritime Diplomacy*, 91; for this and the previous paragraph, *see also* Safford, 67–69, 71–77, 84–85; and Becker, *Industry and Exports*, 144–45.

9.   Safford, *Wilsonian Maritime Diplomacy*, 86; for the rest of the paragraph, *see also* Safford, 71–77, 84–85.

10.   Kaufman, *Efficiency and Expansion*, 124–28; Safford, *Wilsonian Maritime Diplomacy*, 85–92; Becker, *Industry and Exports*, 145–48.

11.   Carl E. McDowell and Helen M. Gibbs, *Ocean Transportation* (New York: McGraw-Hill, 1954), 412–13; Becker, *Industry and Exports*, 131–33; Arthur S. Link, ed., *The Papers of Woodrow Wilson* (Princeton: Princeton University Press, 1966), 42:285–87.

12. Kaufman, *Efficiency and Expansion*, 129; Becker, *Industry and Exports*, 148–50; Link, *Papers of Wilson*, 43:50–51, 204–6, 233–34, 260–61, 285–86.

13. Edward N. Hurley, *The Bridge to France* (Philadelphia: J.B. Lippincott, 1927), 27–29; Safford, *Wilsonian Maritime Diplomacy*, 95–103.

14. Kaufman, *Efficiency and Expansion*, 120–22; Baughman, *The Mallorys*, 250.

15. Hurley, *Bridge to France*, 120–25, 129–32; Safford, *Wilsonian Maritime Diplomacy*, 176–77, 180.

16. Report, 8 April 1917, and "Data on German vessels seized by the United States," Secret and Confidential Correspondence of the Office of the Chief of Naval Operations and the Office of the Secretary of the Navy, Record Group 80, National Archives.

17. Hurley, *Bridge to France*, 31–38, 42–44.

18. Baughman, *The Mallorys*, 251–55; Hurley, *Bridge to France*, 94–100; Link, *Papers of Wilson*, 45:42–44.

19. Baughman, *The Mallorys*, 255–58; Hurley, *Bridge to France*, 101–5.

20. U.S. Shipping Board, *First Annual Report* (Washington, D.C.: Government Printing Office, 1917), 15–16; Hurley, *Bridge to France*, 209–214.

21. Robert B. Albion, *Seaports South of Sahara: The Achievements of an American Steamship Service* (New York: Appleton-Century-Crofts, 1959), 71–79; Kaufman, *Efficiency and Expansion*, 188–90.

CHAPTER 4

1. For this and the next quotation, *see* Albion, *Seaports South of Sahara*, 78–79; Hurley, *Bridge to France*, 132–34, 271.

2. Safford, *Wilsonian Maritime Diplomacy*, 174–75, 181–83; Baughman, *The Mallorys*, 263–64; U.S. Shipping Board, *Third Annual Report* (Washington, D.C.: Government Printing Office, 1919), 10, 56, 122–23; U.S. Shipping Board, *Fourth Annual Report* (Washington, D.C.: Government Printing Office, 1920), 54–57.

3. U.S. Shipping Board, *Fifth Annual Report* (Washington, D.C.: Government Printing Office, 1921), 194; comments on 1919–20 files based on examination of Record Group (henceforth RG) 32 in the National Archives (henceforth NA).

4. Safford, *Wilsonian Maritime Diplomacy*, 215; *see* Safford, 199–219 for the *Imperator*–Standard Oil tankers controversy.

5. Kaufman, *Efficiency and Expansion*, 241–42, 247–48; Safford, *Wilsonian Maritime Diplomacy*, 232, for quotation, and *see* 224–30, 237–38; Mary Klachko, *Admiral William S. Benson, First Chief of Naval Operations* (Annapolis, Md.: Naval Institute Press, 1987), 182, 184–87.

6. U.S. Shipping Board, *Fifth Annual Report* (Washington, D.C.: Government Printing Office, 1921), 194; U.S. Shipping Board, *Sixth Annual Report* (Washington, D.C.: Government Printing Office, 1922), 99, 105, 189–91; U.S. Shipping Board, *Ninth Annual Report* (Washington, D.C.: Government Printing Office, 1925), 6; Baughman, *The Mallorys,* 284–86, 293–94.

7. For this and the next two quotations, Josephus Daniels to President Woodrow Wilson, 18 November 1918, box 855, RG 32, NA; for the previous paragraph, *see* P. A. S. Franklin letters, 19 January, 7 June, 12 July 1918, box 855, RG 32, NA.

8. 25 November 1918, box 856, RG 32, NA.

9. H. Walter to William McAdoo, 15 November 1918, box 855, RG 32, NA.

10. President Wilson to Edward N. Hurley, 24 January 1919, box 855, RG 32, NA.

11. "I.M.M. Sale," 12 June 1919, box 855, RG 32, and John Nicolson to Franklin D. Roosevelt, 26 March 1933, box 856, RG 32, NA; minutes, 25 May 1927, item 33, Royal Mail Steam Packet, Manuscripts Room, University College, London.

12. P. A. S. Franklin to John A. Donald, 7 July 1919, box 855, RG 32, NA.

13. P. A. S. Franklin to Shipping Board, 19 July 1919, box 855, RG 32, NA. This discrimination was in favor of W. Averell Harriman, who established a joint deal with the Hamburg-America Line. This short-lived scheme later proved to be excessively favorable to the Germans (some claimed the 29-year-old Harriman had been bamboozled), consumed valuable time and resources, and distracted the U.S. Shipping Board from other issues of a more lasting impact on U.S. steamship companies. *See* Safford, *Wilsonian Maritime Diplomacy,* 239–43, and Klachko, *Admiral Benson,* 186–87.

14. W. S. Tower memorandum, 27 March 1919, box 855, RG 32, NA.

15. Note, 1 May 1920, box 855, RG 32, NA. *See also* British Embassy report, 6 October 1927, PRO, FO 115/3224.

16. Report of British Consul, 14 February 1921, PRO, FO 115/2681.

17. Sir Ashley Sparks to Sir Thomas Royden, 5 December 1922, Cunard.

18. *Journal of Commerce* (New York City), 2 November 1924.

19. Sir Ashley Sparks to Sir Percy Bates, 13 August 1930, Cunard. For the negotiations and sale, *see* minutes, 25 May 1927, item 33, Royal Mail Steam Packet, Manuscripts Room, University College, London.

20. Sir Thomas Royden to Sir Ashley Sparks, 6 January 1927, Cunard.

21. British Embassy report, 6 October 1927, FO 115/3224, PRO.

22.   *Fairplay*, 21 April 1930, 294; for the merger *see* letter to Sir Thomas Royden, 30 January 1930, Cunard.

23.   This and the next quotation from "United States Lines Operation," September 1921, box 125, Kermit Roosevelt Papers, Library of Congress, Washington, D.C. (henceforth LofC). For the previous paragraph *see also* W. S. Tower memorandum, 27 March 1919, box 855, RG 32, NA.

24.   British Embassy report, 16 July 1926, PRO, FO 115/3128; for this paragraph, *see also* British Embassy report, 28 December 1923, PRO, FO 115/2859, and U.S. Shipping Board, *Twelfth Annual Report* (Washington, D.C.: Government Printing Office, 1928), 81–82.

25.   This and the next quotation from British Embassy report, 16 July 1926, PRO, FO 115/3128.

26.   *U.S. Daily*, 9 November 1926; Lawrence R. Wilder to William Baldwin Shearer, 19 June 1935, box 1, OF 99, Franklin D. Roosevelt Presidential Library (FDR), Hyde Park, New York.

27.   Paul W. Chapman prospectus, June 1929, Cunard. For the bids, *see* Lawrence R. Wilder to William Baldwin Shearer, 19 June 1935, box 1, OF 99, FDR.

28.   John B. Waterman to Congressman John McDuffie, 17 June 1929, Waterman Steamship Corporation Records, Mobile Public Library, Mobile, Alabama.

29.   Paul W. Chapman prospectus, June 1929, and to Sir Percy Bates, 12 June 1929, Cunard; for this paragraph *see also* Report to the President, 3 December 1930, box 7, Records of the President's Advisory Committee on the Merchant Marine, Harry S. Truman Presidential Library (henceforth HST), Independence, Missouri, and *Journal of Commerce*, 26 May 1930.

30.   Report, 28 August 1929, PRO, FO 115/3887.

31.   U.S. Congress, Senate Special Committee on Investigation of Air Mail and Ocean mail Contracts, *Hearings*, 9 vols. (Washington, D.C.: Government Printing Office, 1933–34), 6:2470.

32.   Report to the President, 2 May 1933, OF 40, FDR; British Embassy report, 2 July 1931, FO 371/15132, PRO; memorandum, 27 July 1931, and "Chronology," 13 July to 21 August 1931, box 125, Kermit Roosevelt Papers, LofC.

33.   Memorandum, 2 September 1931, 5 October 1931 letter, and memorandum of discussion, 8 October 1931, box 125, Kermit Roosevelt Papers, LofC.

34.   Report to the President, 2 May 1933, OF 40, FDR; *San Francisco Examiner*, 10 June 1931; Senate Special Committee on Air Mail and Ocean Mail Contracts, *Hearings*, 3:1170–90; Niven, *American President Lines*, 99; *Journal of Commerce*, 21 June 1934.

35.   *Fortune*, March 1931, 127–28; *Business Week*, 25 May 1946, 32.

36. Memorandum and correspondence, March 1920 to October 1921, PRO, FO 371/14281; Stanley Dollar to Robert Dollar, 15 January 1932, box 8, Dollar Collection, Bancroft Library.

37. Baughman, *The Mallorys*, 289; for previous paragraph, *see also* 284–88.

38. Baughman, *The Mallorys*, 289–92.

39. Henry Herbermann letters, 27 October and 28 November 1925, box 844, RG 32, NA; memorandum, 18 December 1931, box 846, RG 32, NA; *Fortune*, September 1937, 148.

40. *Fortune*, March 1931, 122, 124; American Export to Shipping Board, 17 June 1931, box 845, RG 32, NA.

41. *Fortune*, March 1931, 86–87, September 1937, 146–47; Henry Herbermann to Shipping Board, 20 August 1927, box 845, RG 32, NA; report of 21 December 1932, PRO, FO 371/16601.

42. *Seamen's Journal*, 1 April 1934; *Fortune*, September 1937, 148; memorandum for files, 9 January 1935, box 845, RG 32, NA; *Journal of Commerce*, 6 May 1935.

43. Memorandum for President Franklin D. Roosevelt, 4 September 1935, box 846, RG 32, NA; *Fortune*, September 1937, 148–49, 152; *Business Week*, 25 May 1946, 38, 41.

44. Marylin Bender and Selig Altschul, *The Chosen Instrument: Pan Am, Juan Trippe* (New York: Simon & Schuster, 1982), 320–29; *Business Week*, 25 May 1946, 31, 41–42, 44.

CHAPTER 5

1. Kaufman, *Efficiency and Expansion*, 94–95, 236–37.

2. Senate Special Committee on Investigation of Air Mail and Ocean Mail Contracts, 3:1198, 1208; *Fortune*, September 1937, 176; John B. Waterman (henceforth JBW in chapter 5 notes) to W. E. Campbell, 25 April 1928, Records of the Waterman Steamship Corporation, Mobile Public Library, Mobile, Ala. (henceforth WSC).

3. Petitions and correspondence, 22 April to 10 June 1921, box 864, RG 32, NA.

4. Clayton, *W. R. Grace & Co.*, 336; William Kooiman, "W. R. Grace's Ships and Lines."

5. Memorandums and letters, 21 March to 30 December 1924, box 862, RG 32, NA; *Fortune*, September 1937, 176.

6. Gilbert M. Mellin, "The Mississippi Shipping Company" (Ph.D. diss., University of Pittsburgh, 1955), 223; JBW to Thomas M. Stevens, 11 June 1932, WSC.

7. Memorandums, 18, 19 April 1932, box 862, RG 32, NA; Thomas M. Stevens to Congressman John McDuffie, 12 June 1932, WSC; *Times Picayune*, 8 December 1932.

8. J. C. Peacock to Secretary of Commerce, 30 August 1934, box 863, RG 32, NA; for beginning of paragraph, *see also* memorandum to J. C. Peacock, 3 July 1934, box 863, RG 32, NA.

9. J. C. Peacock to Secretary of Commerce, 30 August 1934, box 863, RG 32, NA; *Washington Herald*, 6 December 1936.

10. Thomas M. Woodward memorandum, 23 May 1935, box 863, RG 32, NA.

11. Waterman Steamship Corporation, *Waterman Building*, March 2–4, *1950*, 1; U.S. Shipping Board, *Fourth Annual Report* (Washington, D.C.: Government Printing Office, 1920), 258; JBW to Shipping Board, 16 May 1919, WSC.

12. "List of Steamers handled by the Waterman Steamship Corporation," 9 November 1920, WSC; Jeffrey J. Safford, "World War I Maritime Policy and the National Security: 1914–19," in *America's Maritime Legacy*, ed. Robert A. Kilmarx (Boulder, Colo.: Westview Press, 1979), 141–43; U.S. Shipping Board, *Sixth Annual Report* (Washington, D.C.: Government Printing Office, 1922), 99–100; U.S. Shipping Board, *Seventh Annual Report* (Washington, D.C.: Government Printing Office, 1923), 4–5.

13. JBW to Norman O. Pedrick, 4 October 1924, WSC; rest of paragraph also based on JBW to C. W. Hempstead, 27 July 1926, WSC.

14. JBW to H. B. Arledge, 21 July 1926, WSC.

15. JBW to W. E. Campbell, 5 March 1927, WSC; this paragraph also relies on JBW to H. B. Arledge, 24 July 1926.

16. JBW to Mark Lyons, 28 May 1928, WSC; Samuel E. Eastman and Daniel Marx, *Ships and Sugar: An Evaluation of Puerto Rican Offshore Shipping* (San Juan: University of Puerto Rico Press, 1953), 45.

17. Norman A. Nicolson, interview with author, Mobile, Ala., 9 March 1989; Captain Oscar I. Geiger, interview with author, Mobile, Ala., 28 July 1988; JBW to C. W. Hempstead and Thomas M. Stevens, 8 June 1928, WSC.

18. U.S. Shipping Board, *Fourteenth Annual Report* (Washington, D.C.: Government Printing Office, 1930), 80; J. H. Burton to C. W. Hempstead, New York City, April 1930, JBW to C. W. Hempstead and Thomas M. Stevens, 27 July 1929, WSC.

19. JBW to C. W. Hempstead and Thomas M. Stevens, 27 July 1929, WSC.

20. JBW to M. Warriner, 8 October 1929, WSC.

21. *New York Times*, 10 September 1931; U.S. Shipping Board, *Fifteenth Annual Report* (Washington, D.C.: Government Printing Office, 1931), 85.

22. JBW to C. W. Hempstead, 23 November 1927, WSC.

23. Thomas M. Stevens to JBW, 24 July 1934, WSC; *New York Times*, 4 December 1933.

24. Capt. Geiger, interview with author; E. A. Roberts to JBW, 29 July 1930, JBW to E. A. Roberts, 11 August 1936, WSC. The company was riding an upward wave when it was surprised in 1937 by the suicide of John B. Waterman, a tragic loss for U.S. shipping. Personal and health reasons, rather than his remarkable business career, appear to have been the cause of his unexpected action.

25. Mellin, "The Mississippi Shipping Co.," 25–30; Thomas J. Conroy, *Delta Line: A Historical Sketch* (New Orleans: Mississippi Shipping Co., 1947), 2–3; Kaufman, *Efficiency and Expansion*, 236–37, 251.

26. Mellin, "The Mississippi Shipping Co.," 70, 79, 82, 86–88; Conroy, *Delta Line*, 3–5.

27. Mellin, "The Mississippi Shipping Co.," 87–88; H. B. Arledge to Norman O. Pedrick, 18 November 1924, 9 December 1924, WSC.

28. H. B. Arledge to JBW, 27 March 1929, WSC; for this and the previous paragraph, *see also* Mellin, "The Mississippi Shipping Co.," 91–95; memorandum, 16 March 1929, WSC.

29. Mellin, "The Mississippi Shipping Co.," 109; for this and the previous paragraph *see also* Mellin, "The Mississippi Shipping Co.," 108, 115, 191–92; memorandum for Senator Burton, 23 August 1929, and to President Herbert Hoover, 11 September 1929, WSC; *United States Daily*, 28 June 1930.

30. Norman O. Pedrick to JBW, 10 August 1928, WSC; Mellin, "The Mississippi Shipping Co.," 202, 209–10, 223; Conroy, *Delta Line*, 3.

31. Mellin, "The Mississippi Shipping Co.," 115–17, 178, 182, 184, 186, 196–99, 202–3.

CHAPTER 6

1. Report from French consul in Hong Kong, 1 March 1918, F 12/7748, Archives Nationales, Paris, France.

2. U.S. Department of Commerce, *Transpacific Shipping* (Washington, D.C.: Government Printing Office, 1916), 11–13, 22–23; Walter A. Radius, *United States Shipping in Transpacific Trade, 1922–38* (Stanford: University Press, 1944), 160–61.

3. Report of Robert Dollar Company, 6 August 1918, box 842, RG 32, NA.

4. U.S. Congress, House Committee on Merchant Marine and Fisheries, *Steamship Conference Study*, 3 vols. (Washington, D.C.: Government Printing Office, 1959), 2:375; *see* 2:373–74 for rest of paragraph.

5. O'Brien, "Robert Dollar," chapters 18, 20, 21, and 32.

6. Niven, *American President Lines*, 59–63, 74–75, 77–84; O'Brien, "Robert Dollar," 230–33, 237–39.

7. Niven, *American President Lines*, 63–75; O'Brien, "Robert Dollar," 280–84, 296–97, 308, 310–12.

8. Niven, *American President Lines*, 90–95, 97–105; O'Brien, "Robert Dollar," 314–22, 329–31, 371–76.

9. James Dugan, *American Viking: The Saga of Hans Isbrandtsen and His Shipping Empire* (New York: Harper & Row, 1963), 65–66; *see also* 62–64.

10. "Joint Meeting, Pacific Westbound Conference–Far East Conference, 16 June 1930," box 27, Transpacific Westbound Rate Agreement, San Francisco Maritime Museum; House Committee on Merchant Marine and Fisheries, *Steamship Conference Study*, 2: 376–78, 396–98; O'Brien, "Robert Dollar," 375–80.

11. Minutes of 24 February 1936, box 67, Dollar Collection, Bancroft Library.

12. "Position of the Japanese Shipping Industry to April 1937," PRO, FO 371/21043.

13. "Japanese Shipping Competition," 15 February 1937, PRO, FO 371/21032.

14. Cunard letter to John R. Ellerman, 20 June 1927, box 124, Kermit Roosevelt Papers, LofC; for this paragraph, *see also* letter to J. E. Sheedy, 14 October 1926, box 44, Kermit Roosevelt Papers, LofC; T. S. Catto letter, 27 March 1924, Cunard.

15. Letter to J. E. Sheedy, 14 October 1926, box 44, Kermit Roosevelt Papers, LofC.

16. T. Ashley Sparks letter, 21 June 1928, PRO, FO 115/3319.

17. Kermit Roosevelt to Admiral L. C. Palmer, 15 January 1925, F. G. Frieser memorandum, 21 January 1926, Roosevelt Steamship to Elmer E. Crowley, 3 March 1926, box 894, RG 32, NA.

18. Minutes, 2 May 1927, box 124, Kermit Roosevelt Papers, LofC.

19. Minutes, 15 June 1927, box 124, Kermit Roosevelt Papers, LofC.

20. "Report Concerning Meetings in England with the Ellerman and Cunard Interests," June 1927, box 124, Kermit Roosevelt Papers, LofC.

21. Fred Graham to Sir Thomas Rodney, 5 December 1923, Cunard.

22. British Embassy report, 17 August 1928, PRO FO 115/3319; for this paragraph, *see also* related correspondence in PRO, FO 115/3319, and *U.S. Daily*, 2 November 1928.

23. "Rate Agreements," 10 October 1928, box 124, Kermit Roosevelt Papers, LofC; *San Francisco Examiner*, 9 December 1930; Roosevelt Steamship Company to Merchant Fleet Corp., 24 April 1931, box 895, RG 32, NA.

24. John M. Franklin to Merchant Fleet Corp., 6 December 1932, box 895, RG 32, NA.

25. Cunard letters, 24 December 1932, 17 March 1933, Cunard.

26. F. G. Frieser memorandum, 25 May 1936, box 896, RG 32, NA.

27. Worden, *Cargoes*, 58, 71; Stindt, *Matson's Century*, 37–40, 75–82; *San Francisco Chronicle*, 31 October 1930.

28. Worden, *Cargoes*, 58–59, 61; *Fortune*, September 1937, 102, 104, 174.

29. *San Francisco Examiner*, 9 December 1930; *Fortune*, September 1937, 103, 170, 172; Worden, *Cargoes*, 71–72.

30. J. E. Saugstad to Charles S. Haight, 31 March 1936, box 5, Shipping Policy Files, RG 59, NA; for the stevedores' boycott, *see* telegram, 22 December 1931, PRO, FO 371/15142.

31. *New York Times*, 3 December 1933. For the previous paragraph, *see San Francisco Chronicle*, 6 May 1932; telegram from Prime Minister of Australia, 21 September 1933, PRO, FO 371/16601; "Matson Line Competition," May 1935, PRO, FO 371/18748; H. M. Cleminston to Charles S. Haight, 14 May 1936, box 5, Shipping Policy Files, RG 59, NA.

32. Memorandum, 24 October 1933, PRO, FO 371/16601. In the minutes of 29 September the Board of Trade decided that it "would like the whole question to be put to sleep once more" and again in 30 April 1934 "the Board of Trade view was that the game of retaliation was not worth the candle" (PRO FO 371/17573).

33. "Attitude of New Zealand and Australian Ministers," 4 July 1935, PRO, FO 371/18749.

34. Memorandum, 10 September 1935, PRO, FO 371/18749.

35. British Embassy report, 24 November 1936, PRO, FO 371/19832; minutes, 31 December 1936, PRO, FO 371/20654, and "Extract from Cabinet Discussion," 22 December 1937, PRO, FO 371/20655; note, 1946, box 8, Shipping Policy Files, RG 59, NA; *Fortune*, September 1937, 172.

CHAPTER 7

1. U.S. Congress, Senate, *Investigation of Air Mail and Ocean Mail Contracts,* Senate Report (S. Rept.) 898 (Washington, D.C.: Government Printing Office, 1935), 17; Samuel A. Lawrence, *United States Merchant Shipping Policies and Politics* (Washington, D.C.: Brookings Institute, 1966), 42–44; Paul M. Zeis, *American Shipping Policy* (Princeton, N.J.: Princeton University Press, 1938), 142–65; Hyde, *Cunard and the North Atlantic,* 246.

2. U.S. Senate, *Investigation of Air Mail and Ocean Mail Contracts,* 2; for rest of paragraph, *see also* Lawrence, *Shipping Policies,* 44–45; *U.S. Daily,* 2 April 1932.

3. *Journal of Commerce,* 8 August 1933; Lawrence, *Shipping Policies,* 44–46.

4. Albert U. Romasco, *The Politics of Recovery: Roosevelt's New*

Deal (New York: Oxford University Press, 1983), 186–214; "Re Shipping Board Bureau and Merchant Marine Policies," 15 May 1934, OF 40, FDR. The British Foreign Office was cluttered with all the Shipping Code drafts—for example *see* report, 28 December 1933, PRO, FO 371/17571.

5. U.S. Senate, *Investigation of Air Mail and Ocean Mail Contracts,* 22, 36, 39–40.

6. U.S. Senate, *Investigation of Air Mail and Ocean Mail Contracts,* 40–46; as early as November 1933, the Black Committee had suggested the government's return to ship operations—*Washington Post,* 1 November 1933.

7. Telegram to Foreign Office, 15 February 1934, PRO, FO 371/17571; "Re Shipping Board Bureau and Merchant Marine Policies," 15 May 1934, OF 40, FDR; Lawrence, *Shipping Policies,* 46–47. Cases of private profiteering were rampant in the 1940s, but the controlling legislation in those programs consisted of separate acts of Congress—*see* chapter 9 of this volume.

8. Zeis, *American Shipping Policy,* 186–205; *Journal of Commerce,* 11 February 1935.

9. U.S. Maritime Commission, *Economic Survey of the American Merchant Marine* (Washington, D.C.: Government Printing Office, 1937), 53–57; President's Advisory Committee on the Merchant Marine, *Report* (Washington, D.C.: Government Printing Office, 1947), 24–27.

10. Lawrence, *Shipping Policies,* 158–61, 212–14, 286–88, 296–97.

11. Niven, *American President Lines,* 99–100; U.S. Maritime Commission, *Financial Readjustments in Dollar Steamship Line, Inc., Ltd.* (Washington, D.C.: Government Printing Office, 1938), 2. In 1938, American President Lines quietly ignored the Dollar Line's agreement with Matson, and the latter filed no protest.

12. U.S. Maritime Commission, *Reorganization of American President Lines, Ltd.* (Washington, D.C.: Government Printing Office, 1939), 16.

13. U.S. Maritime Commission, *American President Lines,* 23–24; for the beginning of this paragraph, *see also* the same volume, 17, and Niven, *American President Lines,* 104–5.

14. U.S. Maritime Commission, *American President Lines,* 27–36; Niven, *American President Lines,* 111–13.

15. U.S. Maritime Commission, *American President Lines,* 36; Niven, *American President Lines,* 114–16.

16. Stanley Dollar to W. T. Mitchell, 23 January 1939, box 36, Dollar Collection, Bancroft Library; U.S. Maritime Commission, *American President Lines,* 3–7; Niven, *American President Lines,* 118–22.

17. U.S. Maritime Commission, *American President Lines,* 41;

for rest of paragraph, *see* Robert Dollar Co., *Highlights of the Dollar Line Case* (San Francisco: n.p., 1951), 22–26.

18.   Niven, *American President Lines*, 122–23, 126–56.

19.   Shipping Board, *Seventh Annual Report*, 64–66; Baughman, *The Mallorys*, 306–8; U.S. Maritime Commission, "Economic Survey of Coastwise and Intercoastal Shipping," 15 March 1939, 16; George S. Gibb and Evelyn H. Knowlton, *History of Standard Oil Company (New Jersey) 1911–27: The Resurgent Years* (New York: Harper & Brothers, 1956), 472–81.

20.   Baughman, *The Mallorys*, 296, 306–7, 317–18, 325–26; Shipping Board, *Seventh Annual Report*, 150; Henrietta M. Larson, Evelyn H. Knowlton, and Charles S. Popple, *History of Standard Oil Company (New Jersey) 1927–50: New Horizons* (New York: Harper & Row, 1971), 212–14; U.S. Maritime Commission, *Economic Survey of the American Merchant Marine*, 26.

21.   Larson et al., *New Horizons*, 220–21; U.S. Maritime Commission, *Economic Survey of the American Merchant Marine*, 37–38; Baughman, *The Mallorys*, 329–33.

22.   U.S. Maritime Commission, *Report on Tramp Shipping Service* (Washington, D.C.: Government Printing Office, 1938), 4–5; Baughman, *The Mallorys*, 263–80; U.S. Congress, Senate, *Tramp Tonnage*, Senate Document (S. Doc.) 297 (Washington, D.C.: Government Printing Office, 1923), 1–2.

23.   Memorandum of Edward Macauley, 14 January 1946, box 19, RG 178, NA.

24.   U.S. Maritime Commission, *Economic Survey of the American Merchant Marine*, 17–19; for this and the previous paragraph, *see also* U.S. Maritime Commission, *Tramp Shipping*, 7–11; Baughman, *The Mallorys*, 323–24.

25.   U.S. Maritime Commission, "Economic Survey of Coastwise and Intercoastal Shipping," 25. The government's prediction of the disappearance of the tramp was effectively refuted in Radius, *United States Shipping in Transpacific Trade*, 180–82.

26.   Giles T. Brown, *Ships That Sail No More: Marine Transportation from San Diego to Puget Sound, 1910–40* (Lexington: University of Kentucky Press, 1966), 17–38, 181–216; U.S. Maritime Commission, "Economic Survey of Coastwise and Intercoastal Shipping," 28–29, 38–40, 72.

27.   Ronald A. Shadburne, "Coastwise and Intercoastal Shipping," *Annals of the American Academy of Political and Social Science* 23 (1943): 29–36; U.S. Maritime Commission, *Economic Survey of the American Merchant Marine*, 32, 42; U.S. Maritime Commission, "Economic Survey of Coastwise and Intercoastal Shipping," 41–47, 51, 70–71, 73.

28. P. A. S. Franklin to Hugo Black, 29 December 1933, box 119, Kermit Roosevelt Papers, LofC. For the first two paragraphs, *see also* P. A. S. Franklin memorandum, 14 February 1934, box 119, Kermit Roosevelt Papers, LofC; British Embassy report, 19 March 1934, PRO, FO 371/17572; Hyde, *Cunard and the North Atlantic*, 208–14.

29. U.S. Maritime Commission memorandum, 13 January 1937, OF 1705, FDR; *Wall Street Journal*, 13 April 1934; on the *Leviathan* itself, *see* the six-volume history published between 1972 and 1978 by Frank O. Braynard, *The World's Greatest Ship: The Story of the Leviathan* (Sea Cliff, N.Y.: F.O. Braynard, 1972–78).

30. *New York Evening Post*, 12–14 February 1934.

31. *New York Evening Post*, 12 February 1934.

32. *New York Evening Post*, 15 February 1934.

33. Memorandum of 27 February 1937, box 119, Kermit Roosevelt Papers, LofC, for this and the previous paragraph; *see also Journal of Commerce*, 21 May 1935, and *New York Times*, 8 June 1937.

34. Memorandum of 27 February 1937, box 119, Kermit Roosevelt Papers, LofC.

35. Ibid.

36. "Proposed Plan for the Future Development of United States Lines," 28 April 1937, box 111, Kermit Roosevelt Papers, LofC; U.S. Maritime Commission memorandum, 13 January 1937, OF 1705, FDR.

37. Report to the Board of Directors of I.M.M., 1 December 1937, box 119, Kermit Roosevelt Papers, LofC; *New York Times*, 14 May, 7 June 1938.

38. *Moody's Industrials 1939*, 2360, 2362.

39. *New York Times*, 19 June 1942; *Moody's Industrials 1940*, 2351; *Moody's Industrials 1943*, 2018.

CHAPTER 8

1. Cordell Hull, *Memoirs*, 2 vols. (New York: Macmillan, 1948), 2:688–700; Rodney P. Carlisle, *Sovereignty for Sale: The Origins and Evolution of the Panamanian and Liberian Flags of Convenience* (Annapolis, Md.: Naval Institute Press, 1981), 71–72, 80.

2. *Time*, 20 November 1939, 12. For this paragraph, *see also* Carlisle, *Sovereignty for Sale*, 78–80, 82–84; Emory S. Land to President Franklin Roosevelt, box 188, PSF, FDR; Adolf A. Berle, Jr., diary, 17 January 1940, FDR.

3. Carlisle, *Sovereignty for Sale*, 72–73, 83, 90; *Moody's Industrials 1941*, 2390–91.

4. For this and the previous paragraph, *see* Hull, *Memoirs*, 2:1046–51; Carlisle, *Sovereignty for Sale*, 194–98; Stetson Conn and Byron Fairchild, *The Framework of Hemisphere Defense* (Washington, D.C.: Office of the Chief of Military History, 1960), 61–62, 101–2.

5. Carlisle, *Sovereignty for Sale*, 85–86, 90–96.

6. Carlisle, *Sovereignty for Sale*, 101, 104–6, 111–13.

7. *Time*, 29 January 1940, 65–66; *Moody's Industrials 1941*, 2390–91; Frederick C. Lane, *Ships for Victory: A History of Shipbuilding under the United States Maritime Commission in World War II* (Baltimore: Johns Hopkins Press, 1951), 21, 23; U.S. Maritime Commission, *Economic Survey of the American Merchant Marine*, 36–39; Felix Riesenberg, Jr., *Sea War: The Story of the U.S. Merchant Marine in World War II* (New York: Rinehart & Co., 1956), 26.

8. *Newsweek*, 23 March 1941, 39; *Moody's Industrials 1941*, 2390–91; Lane, *Ships for Victory*, 24–28.

9. C. B. A. Behrens, *Merchant Shipping and the Demands of War* (London: Her Majesty's Stationary Office, 1978), 35; for rest of this paragraph, *see* 108–11, 202–6, 225–27, and John Gorley Bunker, *Liberty Ships: The Ugly Ducklings of World War II* (Annapolis, Md.: Naval Institute Press, 1972), 8–9. Cargo-carrying capacity can vary drastically even with the same fully loaded ship. When the ship is steaming back and forth between two nearby ports the capacity is greater than when the ship is steaming between two distant ports during the same time period.

10. Lane, *Ships for Victory*, 44; for this paragraph *see also* Bunker, *Liberty Ships*, 6–7, 10–11.

11. *Newsweek*, 13 January 1941, 39; Lane, *Ships for Victory*, 44–45, 80–81; Bunker, *Liberty Ships*, 9–13.

12. *Newsweek*, 24 March 1941, 39; 12 May 1941, 15–16; 16 June 1941, 38. *Business Week*, 10 May 1941, 61; 24 May 1941, 60–61.

13. Emory S. Land to president of Isthmian Line, 24 July 1943, box 1, Emory S. Land Papers, LofC.

14. *Business Week*, 24 May 1941, 60–61; 1 November 1941, 60–63. For wartime profiteering, *see* the series of articles called "Operation Plunder: The Secret Scandal of World War II," *New Republic*, May–June 1946, and Niven, *American President Lines*, 146–49.

15. *Time*, 15 December 1941, 88, 90; Riesenberg, *Sea War*, 28, 37; Niven, *American President Lines*, 148–49; Robert Carse, *The Long Haul: The United States Merchant Service in World War II* (New York: Norton & Co., 1965), 38–42.

16. Lane, *Ships for Victory*, 14, and 10–21 for the previous paragraph; *see also Time*, 2 February 1942, 67.

17. Lane, *Ships for Victory*, 161–65, 750–72; Behrens, *Merchant Shipping*, 286–87.

18. For the best accounts in print on the War Shipping Administration, the reader must turn to the official history of *British* shipping and to the official histories of the U.S. *Army*.

19. Memorandum, 28 May 1942, box 1, Papers of William Radner, Harry S. Truman Presidential Library (HST).

20. Memorandum, 28 May 1942, box 1, Papers of William Radner, HST; Behrens, *Merchant Shipping*, 330.

21. Carse, *Long Haul*, 77–80, 157–65; Riesenberg, *Sea War*, 93, 154–62; Bunker, *Liberty Ships*, 19–23.

22. Emory S. Land to President Franklin Roosevelt, 24 April 1942, box 3, OF 1705, FDR; Telfair Knight to Senator J. W. Bailey, 5 July 1943, box 8, Emory S. Land Papers, LofC; Carse, *Long Haul*, 84–87; Riesenberg, *Sea War*, 94–103, 300–1.

23. Lane, *Ships for Victory*, 605; for previous paragraph, *see also* 574–607, and Bunker, *Liberty Ships*, 11–17.

24. Robert W. Coakley and Richard M. Leighton, *Global Logistics and Strategy, 1943–45* (Washington, D.C.: Office of the Chief of Military History, 1968), 559–60; Bunker, *Liberty Ships*, 18–19; Lane, *Ships for Victory*, 4–6.

CHAPTER 9

1. Memorandum, 22 June 1943, box 8, Emory S. Land Papers, LofC; Cordell Hull to President Franklin Roosevelt, 25 September 1944, box 4, OF 99, FDR.

2. Mr. Schell's comments on memo of 14 September 1944, box 6, Shipping Policy Files, RG 59, NA; *Business Week*, 7 October 1944.

3. Note of talk, 5 April 1945, Cunard.

4. Emory S. Land to President Harry Truman, 6 September 1945, OF 99, HST; for rest of paragraph, see *Time*, 11 March 1946, 78–79; McDowell and Gibbs, *Ocean Transportation*, 258–59.

5. "Significant Developments in the United States Maritime Commission," 10 October 1946, OF 126, HST.

6. G. H. Helmbold memorandum, 13 January 1947, OF 126, HST; for this paragraph, *see also* Jerry Shields, *Daniel Ludwig: The Invisible Billionaire* (Boston: Houghton Mifflin, 1986), 136–39, 147–51; Carlisle, *Sovereignty for Sale*, 110–11.

7. "Ship Sales," 10 September 1946, box 4, Papers of W. L. Clayton, HST; for the "global do-gooders," *see Business Week*, 23 February 1946, 19–20.

8. *U.S. News*, 21 February 1947, 40–43; *Business Week*, 20 March 1948, 55–57, 7 August 1948, 82, 84–85; "Transfer of Ships to Foreign Countries under the Marshall Plan," 26 November 1947, box 23, Files of Charles S. Murphy, HST; President's Advisory Committee on the Merchant Marine, *Report*, 29; *Newsweek*, 10 January 1949, 66–67.

9. Shields, *Daniel Ludwig*, 141, 145–47; McDowell and Gibbs, *Ocean Transportation*, 116; *Business Week*, 10 October 1953, 196, 198; President's Advisory Committee on the Merchant Marine, *Report*, 25; Carlisle, *Sovereignty for Sale*, 111–12, 146.

10.   U.S. Bureau of the Census, *Statistical Abstract of the United States 1962* (Washington, D.C.: Government Printing Office, 1962), 591.

11.   McDowell and Gibbs, *Ocean Transportation*, 102; Brown, *Ships That Sail No More*, 238–41.

12.   McDowell and Gibbs, *Ocean Transportation*, 403.

13.   Lawrence, *Shipping Policies*, 85.

14.   Emory Land to Interstate Commerce Commission, 4 September 1945, box 15, RG 178, NA; *see also* William Radner to Interstate Commerce Commission, 4 September 1945, box 15, RG 178, NA.

15.   Emory Land to Interstate Commerce Commission, 4 September 1945, box 15, RG 178, NA.

16.   Office of Defense Transportation to John R. Steelman, 10 July 1947, OF 173–A, HST.

17.   Dearborn Clark, "The Rise and Fall of Intercoastal Shipping," 9 September 1952, William Kooiman Files.

18.   U.S. Congress, Senate Committee on Interstate and Foreign Commerce, *Decline of Coastwise and Intercoastal Shipping* (Washington, D.C.: Government Printing Office, 1960), 135; testimony of J. Sinclair, president of Luckenbach Steamship, President's Advisory Committee on the Merchant Marine, box 10, HST.

19.   Senate Committee on Interstate and Foreign Commerce, *Decline of Coastwise and Intercoastal Shipping*, 74–77, 193, 223–26, and passim; McDowell and Gibbs, *Ocean Transportation*, 99–101, 404–6.

20.   Dearborn Clark, "The Rise and Fall of Intercoastal Shipping," 9 September 1952, William Kooiman Files.

21.   Senate Committee on Interstate and Foreign Commerce, *Decline of Coastwise and Intercoastal Shipping*, 93–94; Clinton H. Whitehurst, Jr., *The U.S. Merchant Marine: In Search of an Enduring Maritime Policy* (Annapolis: Naval Institute Press, 1983), 61–62.

22.   *New York Times*, 26 October 1961; Senate Committee on Interstate and Foreign Commerce, *Decline of Coastwise and Intercoastal Shipping*, 7, 73, 79, 715–16, 727–55; *Wall Street Journal*, 12 December 1977.

23.   Senate Committee on Interstate and Foreign Commerce, *Decline of Coastwise and Intercoastal Shipping*, 165–66; Whitehurst, *U.S. Merchant Marine*, 62–67.

24.   W. W. Smith to John R. Steelman, 5 February 1947, OF 126, HST; for the rest of this paragraph and the first paragraph, *see* U.S. Tariff Commission, *Petroleum* (Washington, D.C.: Government Printing Office, 1946), 13–14, 69; "Information on the Shipping Situation for the Secretary," 1 April 1947, OF 173-A, HST.

25.   "Memorandum re Tanker Rates and Oil Prices," 28 April 1947, OF 173-A, HST; "Information on the Shipping Situation for the Secretary," 1 April 1947, OF 173-A, HST; Leonard G. Fay and Francis

Goss, eds., *Tanker Directory of the World* (London: Terminus Publications, 1962), 41.

26. North American Shipping and Trading Co. to U.S. Maritime Commission, 15 June 1949, OF 99, HST.

27. Economic Cooperation Administration to John R. Steelman, 13 July 1949, OF 99, HST; for this paragraph, *see also Business Week*, 8 November 1947, 22; Shields, *Daniel Ludwig*, 138–47; Carlisle, *Sovereignty for Sale*, 110–11.

28. Economic Cooperation Administration to John R. Steelman, 13 July 1949, OF 99, HST; for rest of paragraph, *see* Carlisle, *Sovereignty for Sale*, 145–47; Shields, *Daniel Ludwig*, 141–47.

29. U.S. Congress, Senate Committee on Interstate and Foreign Commerce, *Tanker and Cargo Tankship Charter and Construction* (Washington, D.C.: Government Printing Office, 1956), 12–13; North American Shipping and Trading to the U.S. Maritime Commission, 15 June 1949, OF 99, HST; U.S. Maritime Commission to the Assistant Chief of Naval Operations, 20 July 1949, OF 173-A, HST.

30. Leslie C. Krusen letter, box 1, Papers of Robert L. Dennison, HST.

31. Senate Committee on Interstate and Foreign Commerce, *Tanker and Cargo Tankship*, 12–15, 17–18, 33, 38.

32. L. J. Davis, *Onassis: Aristotle and Christina* (New York: St. Martin's Press, 1986), 72–73; Fay and Goss, *Tanker Directory of the World*, 45; *Business Week*, 2 March 1957.

33. Committee on American Tanker Owners to the President, 21 January 1960, OF box 652, Dwight D. Eisenhower Presidential Library (henceforth DDE), Abilene, Kansas.

34. U.S. Bureau of the Census, *Statistical Abstract of the United States 1962*, 591; Committee of American Tanker Owners to the President, 21 January 1960, OF box 652, DDE.

35. John M. Carmody to U.S. Maritime Commission, 10 March 1945, box 7, RG 178, NA.

36. Clinton M. Hester to President Harry Truman, OF 810, HST; *Business Week*, 15 September 1945, 2; Robert Dollar Co., *Highlights of the Dollar Line Case*, 25–29.

37. *New Republic*, 18 September 1950, 17; Niven, *American President Lines*, 121–22.

38. *New Republic*, 25 September 1950, 23, 18 December 1950, 18; *Business Week*, 7 October 1950, 42; Senator Pat McCarran to John R. Steelman, 10 May 1947, OF 810, HST; Robert Dollar Co., *Highlights of the Dollar Line Case*, 92–93; Niven, *American President Lines*, 166–67; minutes, 20 April 1948, 6 December 1948, box 26, Papers of Robert Dollar Co., San Francisco Maritime Museum.

39. Leland M. Kaiser report, 2 March 1951, box 25, Papers of Rob-

ert Dollar Co., San Francisco Maritime Museum; Niven, *American President Lines,* 169–74.

40.   Charles Sawyer memorandum, 9 June 1952, box 105, Papers of Charles Sawyer, HST; minutes, 13 January 1950, 3 February 1950, box 26, Papers of Robert Dollar Co., San Francisco Maritime Museum.

41.   Charles Sawyer to President Harry Truman, 15 May 1952, OF 810, HST; for this paragraph, *see* Robert Dollar Co., *Highlights of Dollar Line Case,* 77–80; *New Republic,* 18 December 1950, 18; *Business Week,* 24 March 1951, 25.

42.   *Business Week,* 10 October 1953, 187–88; for this paragraph, *see also* Charles Sawyer memorandum, 3 March 1952, box 105, Papers of Charles Sawyer, HST; Robert Dollar Co., *Highlights of Dollar Line Case,* 82–83.

43.   Niven, *American President Lines,* 178.

44.   Charles Sawyer memorandum, 3 March 1952, box 105, Papers of Charles Sawyer, HST.

45.   Niven, *American President Lines,* 178–81; *Business Week,* 10 October 1953, 186–90; *Newsweek,* 23 June 1952, 70, 10 November 1952, 86; *Time,* 10 November 1952, 109.

CHAPTER 10

1.   Board of Trade, *France* (London: Her Majesty's Stationery Office, 1953), 108–12; *Newsweek,* 29 December 1947, 54–55; Board of Trade, *Italy* (London: His Majesty's Stationery Office, 1951), 83–86; Board of Trade, *Italy* (London: Her Majesty's Stationery Office, 1955), 69.

2.   "Allocation of Bizonal Cargo to Germany," 25 November 1947, box 2, Shipping Policy Files, RG 59, NA; Board of Trade, *Federal Republic of Germany* (London: Her Majesty's Stationery Office, 1955), 250–56.

3.   Harold Macmillan, *At the End of the Day* (New York: Harper & Row, 1973), 339–40; letter to Sir Percy Bates, 31 December 1945, Cunard; *Business Week,* 28 April 1945, 113–14.

4.   "Participation U.S. Flag Vessels Japan Trade," 4 August 1948, and memorandum for Dr. Steelman, 15 April 1949, OF 99, HST; Tate, *Transpacific Steam,* 9.

5.   Robert Shaplen, *A Turning Wheel: Three Decades of the Asian Revolution* (New York: Random House, 1975), 2, 203–5; *see also* chapter 6 of this volume.

6.   Niven, *American President Lines,* 148–54; "A Report on American President Lines," 1 May 1946, box 5, RG 178, NA.

7.   Pacific Far East Line, *Annual Report 1955;* Pacific Far East Line, *Prospectus,* July 1955; Niven, *American President Lines,* 196–97.

8.   Dugan, *American Viking,* 147–48; *Fortune,* October 1961, 115.

9.   Memorandum of 26 March 1947, box 2, Shipping Policy Files, RG 59, NA; House Committee on Merchant Marine and Fisheries, *Steamship Conference Study*, 1:592–96; *Business Week*, 17 October 1953, 117.

10.   Memorandum, 3 March 1948, box 2, Shipping Policy Files, RG 59, NA; Dugan, *American Viking*, 149–53; U.S. Department of State, *Foreign Relations 1947: The Far East* (Washington, D.C.: Government Printing Office, 1972), 901, 905–13.

11.   Dugan, *American Viking*, 176–92; American President Lines, *Prospectus*, 7 October 1952; Pacific Far East Line, *Prospectus*, July 1955; U.S. Department of State, *Foreign Relations 1949: China* (Washington, D.C.: Government Printing Office, 1974), 1131–59, 1164–88.

12.   *Business Week*, 17 October 1953, 119; for rest of paragraph, see *Fortune*, October 1961, 221, 223; Dugan, *American Viking*, 193–97.

13.   House Committee on Merchant Marine and Fisheries, *Steamship Conference Study*, 1:264; for beginning of section, see also House Committee on Merchant Marine and Fisheries, *Steamship Conference Study*, 1:244–45; *Business Week*, 17 October 1953, 117.

14.   Committee on Merchant Marine and Fisheries, *Steamship Conference Study*, 1:410–11; to undercut the conference system numerous mechanisms have existed, not all of which require quoting lower rates.

15.   U.S. Congress, Senate Judiciary Committee, *Monopoly Problems in Regulated Industries: Ocean Freight Industry*, 7 vols. (Washington, D.C.: Government Printing Office, 1960), 6:161; for rest of paragraph, see Dugan, *American Viking*, 287–88.

16.   Senate Judiciary Committee, *Ocean Freight Industry*, 6:202–5; Board of Trade, *Japan* (London: Her Majesty's Stationery Office, 1953), 91–94.

17.   Senate Judiciary Committee, *Ocean Freight Industry*, 6:203.

18.   For this and the previous paragraph, see House Committee on Merchant Marine and Fisheries, *Steamship Conference Study*, 2:622–25; *Fortune*, October 1961, 223, 225; Dugan, *American Viking*, 281–82.

19.   *Fortune*, October 1961, 225; Dugan, *American Viking*, 289–90.

20.   *Business Week*, 17 October 1953, 114, 117, 119; *Fortune*, October 1961, 224, 226.

21.   Senate Judiciary Committee, *Ocean Freight Industry*, 2:1209; for previous paragraph, see also Senate Judiciary Committee, *Ocean Freight Industry*, 2:1119–21, 6:33–34, and House Committee on Merchant Marine and Fisheries, *Steamship Conference Study*, 2:623–31.

22.   Senate Judiciary Committee, *Ocean Freight Industry*, 2:1214–15.

23.   Senate Judiciary Committee, *Ocean Freight Industry*, 6:30–35, 185, 310–15; minutes of owners' meeting, 12–15 March 1948, folder 248, Transpacific Westbound Rate Agreement, San Francisco Maritime Museum.

24. Senate Judiciary Committee, *Ocean Freight Industry*, 6:268, 293, 615–16, 631–35.

25. "Survey of Latin American Surface Transportation," 21 July 1953, OSS/State Department Intelligence and Research Reports, part 14, reel 3, University Publications of America.

26. George Wythe, *Brazil: An Expanding Economy* (New York: Twentieth Century Fund, 1949), 208–12; "Survey of Latin American Surface Transportation," 21 July 1953, OSS/State Department Intelligence and Research Reports, part 14, reel 3.

27. U.S. Department of State, *Foreign Relations 1948: The Western Hemisphere* (Washington, D.C.: Government Printing Office, 1972), 444–46; U.S. Department of State, *Foreign Relations 1950: The United Nations: The Western Hemisphere* (Washington, D.C.: Government Printing Office, 1976), 811–14, 816, 831–34; *Business Week*, 19 January 1952, 170, and 1 August 1953, 78; U.S. Department of Commerce, *Investment in Colombia* (Washington, D.C.: Government Printing Office, 1953), 116.

28. Mellin, "The Mississippi Shipping Co.," 270–75, 304, 315–21; Robert C. Lee, *Mr. Moore, Mr. McCormack—and the Seven Seas* (New York: Newcomen Society, 1957), 22, 26–28; "Trade Route No. 1," 19 June 1945, box 9, Shipping Policy Files, RG 59, NA.

29. Jesse A. Saugstad memorandum, 8 December 1947, OF 11, HST.

30. Federal Maritime Commission report, 17 December 1968, box 123, Confidential File, and 31 August 1964, box 17, White House Central Files, Co 37, Lyndon Baines Johnson Library (henceforth LBJ), Austin, Texas; *American Shipper*, April 1990, 34.

CHAPTER 11

1. President's Advisory Committee on the Merchant Marine, *Report*, 7–9, 67–69; "Reorganization of the Maritime Commission," 20 January 1948, Confidential File, HST; memorandum on Maritime Administration, February 1953, box 35, Confidential File, DDE; Lawrence, *Shipping Policies*, 256–57.

2. E. L. Cochrane to President Harry Truman, 13 September 1952, OF, HST.

3. Memorandum on Maritime Administration, February 1953, box 35, Confidential File, DDE.

4. Louis S. Rothschild to Major General Wilton B. Persons, 16 July 1954, OF box 651, DDE.

5. Senate Judiciary Committee, *Ocean Freight Industry*, 1:10, 24, 27, 97, 110, 113, 117–19; Lawrence, *Shipping Policies*, 257–58.

6. House Committee on Merchant Marine and Fisheries, *Steamship Conference Study*, 1:2–90, 159–67.

7. Senate Judiciary Committee, *Ocean Freight Industry*, 1:2, 73, 2:1629, 5:5322, and passim.

8. Senate Judiciary Committee, *Ocean Freight Industry*, 1:11, 142; U.S. Maritime Administration, *Decisions* (Washington, D.C.: Government Printing Office, 1965), iii; Lawrence, *Shipping Policies*, 258–61.

9. Report on U.S. Maritime Commission, 16 October 1963, White House Central Files (henceforth WHCF), FG 236, LBJ.

10. "Federal Maritime Commission," Administrative Histories, LBJ; U.S. Federal Maritime Commission, *Decisions*, passim; Lawrence, *Shipping Policies*, 202, 269, 347.

11. U.S. Maritime Administration, *Decisions* (1965), passim; Lawrence, *Shipping Policies*, 265–66, 279.

12. Correspondence, 1966, box 21, Office File of Mike Manatos, LBJ; Lawrence, *Shipping Policies*, 305–6; *New York Times*, 23 June 1981.

13. "U.S. Post-War Vessel Requirements," box 6, Shipping Policy Files, RG 59, NA; President's Advisory Committee on Merchant Marine, *Report*, vi–vii, 9–12.

14. Testimony of Coast Guard, box 10, Records of President's Advisory Committee on the Merchant Marine, HST; same reference for rest of paragraph.

15. This and next quotation from testimony of John M. Franklin, box 9, Records of President's Advisory Committee on the Merchant Marine, HST.

16. T. Ashley Sparks to F. A. Bates, 4 July 1952, Cunard.

17. "Settlement of the United States Lines Case," 8 June 1954, box 1, Papers of Robert L. Dennison, HST; for this paragraph, *see also* United States Lines, *Annual Report 1952*.

18. "Bureau of the Budget to Governor Adams," 8 June 1956, OF box 651, DDE; U.S. Congress, Senate Committee on Interstate and Foreign Commerce, *Superliner Passenger Vessels* (Washington, D.C.: Government Printing Office, 1958), 15–25.

19. Niven, *American President Lines*, 199, 201; Senate Committee on Interstate and Foreign Commerce, *Superliner Passenger Vessels*, 27–39.

20. Memoranda, 1958–59, OF box 652, DDE; *Washington Post*, 12 July 1958; U.S. President, *Public Papers of the Presidents 1958* (Washington, D.C.: Government Printing Office, 1959), 548.

21. Joseph Curran to President Lyndon Johnson, 1 September 1964, WHCF, TN 7, LBJ.

22. Reports, 13 April 1962 and 4 June 1964, QM 245, Maritime Administration (henceforth Marad); Niven, *American President Lines*, 202–3.

23. Senate Special Committee on Investigation of Air Mail and Ocean Mail Contracts, *Hearings*, 2:660–63; *New York Times*, 11 April 1961; David McCullough, *The Path between the Seas: The Creation of the Panama Canal, 1870–1914* (New York: Simon & Schuster, 1977), 471.

24. Assistant Secretary of the Army to the New England Industries, Inc., 2 February 1955, box 592, General File, DDE; Grace Line to Assistant Secretary of the Army, 26 November 1958, box 593, General File, DDE; U.S. Congress, Senate Committee on Interstate and Foreign Commerce, *Free or Reduced Rates on Water Carriers* (Washington, D.C.: Government Printing Office, 1958), 21–22; William Kooiman, interview with author, San Francisco, 11 January 1990.

25. "Federal Maritime Board Appraisal: September 1960," box 14, Phillip E. Areeda Papers, DDE.

26. *Panama American*, 21 September 1960.

27. "Panama Line," 8 November 1960, box 14, Phillip E. Areeda Papers, DDE; for previous paragraph, *see also Washington Post*, 30 October 1960.

28. Memorandum for the Secretary of the Army, 21 December 1960, box 14, Phillip E. Areeda Papers, DDE; *New York Times*, 25 December 1960, 11 April 1961; William Kooiman, interview with author, San Francisco, 11 January 1990.

29. Waterman Steamship Corporation, *Waterman Building*, 2–4 March 1950; Norman A. Nicolson, interview with author, Mobile, Ala., 9 March 1989; Captain Oscar Geiger, interview with author, Mobile, Ala., 28 July 1988.

30. *Moody's Transportation Manual 1955*, 1396; Norman A. Nicolson, interview with author, Mobile, Ala., 9 March 1989; *Mobile Register*, 1 January 1948.

31. Norman A. Nicolson, interview with author, Mobile, Ala., 9 March 1989; *Mobile Press*, 27 November 1951; *Mobile Register*, 27 December 1952.

32. *Port of Mobile News*, February 1955; *Mobile Register*, 2 April 1955; *The Story of McLean Industries, Inc.: Facts for Stockholders*.

33. *Business Week*, 9 April 1955, 26; Lane C. Kendall, *The Business of Shipping*, 5th ed. (Centreville, Md.: Cornell Maritime Press, 1986), 192–93; Malcom McLean affidavit, 7 February 1962, QM 251, Marad.

34. *Mobile Register*, 13 November 1955; *Business Week*, 12 August 1944, 76, 78; Niven, *American President Lines*, 212; Kendall, *Business of Shipping*, 194–97.

35. McLean Industries, Inc., *First Annual Report 1955; Mobile Register*, 5 November 1956; Kendall, *Business of Shipping*, 192, 196–98.

36. *Moody's Transportation Manual 1956*, 1492–93, *Moody's Transportation Manual 1957*, 1453, *Moody's Transportation Manual 1958*, 1445–46; McLean Industries, Inc., *Annual Report 1960*.

37. Captain Frank Murdock, interview with author, Mobile, Ala., 27 July 1988; Memorandum of Lawrence Jones, 20 June 1962, QM 251, Marad; James McLean settled permanently in Mobile, Mrs. Norman A. Nicolson, interview with author, Mobile, Ala., 9 March 1989.

38. American Tramp Shipowners Institute to War Shipping Administration, 30 July 1946, RG 178, NA; American Tramp Shipowners Association, *Tramp Shipping and the American Merchant Marine* (New York: American Tramp Shipowners Association, 1954), 8–9.

39. "Plan for Purchase of War-Built Vessels," 21 April 1947, box 2, President's Advisory Committee on Merchant Marine, HST; testimony of Ship Operators' Association, box 11, President's Advisory Committee on Merchant Marine, HST; Wytze Gorter, *United States Shipping Policy* (New York: Council on Foreign Relations, 1956), 110–12.

40. *Business Week,* 11 June 1949, 20, 19 January 1952, 132; Gorter, *Shipping Policy,* 112, 115.

41. Tramp Shipowners, *Tramp Shipping,* 13–14; *Business Week,* 19 January 1952, 132, 134.

42. Military Sea Transportation Service letter, 5 December 1952, box 1, Papers of Robert L. Dennison, HST.

43. Tramp Shipowners, *Tramp Shipping,* 13, 18, 26–32; F. Riker Clark letter, box 1, Papers of Robert L. Dennison, HST.

44. Senate Judiciary Committee, *Ocean Freight Industry,* 1:247, and for rest of paragraph, 1:159–60, 759, 2:1082–84; January–February 1954 correspondence, OF box 651, DDE; Lawrence, *Shipping Policies,* 168–69.

45. *New York Times,* 7 January 1960, 23 February 1962; Lawrence, *Shipping Policies,* 220, 222.

46. *New York Times,* 25 May 1962, 16 August 1962.

47. Report, 22 July 1965, box 8, WHCF, TN 7, LBJ; *New York Times,* 30 March 1965, 25 December 1965, 28 March 1968, 22 July 1968. In the wartime rush, the 1961 prohibition against the use of U.S.-built ships previously registered under foreign flags was overlooked; *see* Lawrence, *Shipping Policies,* 162.

CHAPTER 12

1. Hugh Thomas, *The Cuban Revolution* (New York: Harper & Row, 1977), 238–45; Ramon L. Bonachea and Marta San Martin, *The Cuban Insurrection, 1952–59* (New Brunswick, N.J.: Transaction Books, 1974), 311–13.

2. House Committee on Merchant Marine and Fisheries, *Steamship Conference Study,* 2:648–51; *Time,* 8 May 1964, 86.

3. "Traffic Report," 24 April 1959, QM 118/L25-3, Marad.

4. "Traffic Report," 20 October 1959, QM 118/L25-3, Marad.

5. Lykes Brothers to Federal Maritime Board, 15 March 1960, QM 118/L25-3, Marad.

6. Lykes Brothers to Federal Maritime Board, 28 September 1960, QM 118/L25-3, Marad.

7. Lykes Brothers to Marad, 2 February 1962, QM 118/L25-3, Marad.

8. "Informal Memorandum on Certain Matters as of January 1960," QM 118, Marad; *New York Times,* 29 November 1960.

9. Memorandum, 28 March 1962, QM 118, Marad.

10. "Review of Current Traffic Situation of Each Lykes Trade Route," 30 March 1962, QM 118, Marad. Rest of paragraph draws on Bunker, *Liberty Ships,* 197; Whitehurst, *U.S. Merchant Marine,* 114–15.

11. Memorandum, 2 June 1964, QM 118/L25-3, Marad.

12. This and next quotation from 1964 reports in QM 118/L25-3, Marad.

13. *Time,* 8 May 1964, 86; *Business Week,* 25 January 1964; *Wall Street Journal,* 27 December 1967.

14. Reports, 12 March to 23 July 1964, QM 118/L25-3, Marad; Lykes Brothers Steamship Co., *Annual Report 1962.*

15. *Forbes,* 1 April 1969, 30–31; *Florida Journal of Commerce,* October 1969, 14–15; *Wall Street Journal,* 4 November 1968, 6 April 1970.

16. S. B. Turman letter, 3 December 1964, WHCF, TN 7, LBJ.

17. *Florida Journal of Commerce,* November 1966, 10–13, May 1970, 21, April 1972, 18.

18. *Moody's Transportation Manual 1954,* 1401; *Florida Journal of Commerce,* February 1968, 15.

19. *Moody's Transportation Manual 1954,* 1402; memorandum, 26 May 1961, and Myron L. Black letter, 4 January 1961, QM 109, Marad.

20. Kendall, *Business of Shipping,* 199–200; *Moody's Transportation Manual 1952,* 57; *New York Times,* 25 March, 28 October 1961; *Wall Street Journal,* 21 May 1965.

21. *New York Times,* 20 July 1962, 2 May 1963; *Wall Street Journal,* 28 May 1965.

22. *Forbes,* 15 June 1969, 71–72; *Business Week,* 8 February 1969, 106–10.

23. *Business Week,* 8 February 1969, 100–104; *New York Times* reporting on Northwest Passage; *Forbes,* 15 June 1969, 71–72, 1 February 1971, 26.

24. Clayton, *W. R. Grace & Co.,* ch. 11; *Wall Street Journal,* 21 December 1960.

25. *New York Times,* 30 April 1961, 19 July 1962; *Time,* 23 March 1962, 84; Kooiman, "W. R. Grace's Ships and Lines,".

26. *Dun's Review,* July 1967, 23; this and the next paragraph also draw on *Fortune,* August 1963, 108–13, and *Time,* 21 May 1965, 98–99.

27. Henry S. Marcus, *Planning Ship Replacement in the Containerization Era* (Lexington, Mass.: Lexington Books, 1974), 7; Kendall, *Business of Shipping,* 294–97.

28. Grace Line to Federal Maritime Board, 31 July 1961, and other documents, QM 245/L25-3, Marad; *Forbes,* 15 June 1968, 36.

29. Maritime Subsidy Board, *Decisions* (Washington, D.C.: Government Printing Office, 1980), 4:376–96, 427–41, 505–21.

30.   René De La Pedraja, "Rise of the Latin American Merchant Marine," book manuscript.

31.   Kooiman, "W. R. Grace's Ships and Lines,"; *Wall Street Journal*, 31 October 1968, 7 February 1969.

32.   *Fortune*, March 1959, 97–100; McCann, *An American Company*, 14–16, 38; Funtanellas et al., *United Fruit Company*, 161–94 and graphs 13–16.

33.   *Time*, 16 May 1960, 34; McCann, *An American Company*, 41, 57–60, 93–94; *Wall Street Journal*, 6 April 1960; Melville, *Great White Fleet*, 113.

34.   *Business Week*, 25 February 1961, 8 July 1967; *Wall Street Journal*, 23 February 1962; *Time*, 20 April 1962, 92–93.

35.   Thomas L. Karnes, *Tropical Enterprise: The Standard Fruit and Steamship Company in Latin America* (Baton Rouge: Louisiana State University Press, 1978), 282–92; McCann, *An American Company*, 71–72; *Time*, 19 May 1967, 116, 118.

36.   United Fruit Co. to Nicholas Johnson, 18 May 1965, roll 58, microfilmed records of the Department of Commerce, LBJ; *Wall Street Journal*, 27 January 1967; *Business Week*, 8 July 1967, 92.

37.   *Wall Street Journal*, 29 August 1966, 6 October 1966; *Fortune*, April 1969, 132–34; McCann, *An American Company*, 101–4.

38.   *Wall Street Journal*, 21 January 1971, 2 November 1972, 18 December 1972, 14 February 1975, 7 May 1975; *New York Times*, 14 February 1975; McCann, *An American Company*, 1–5, 214–31; Karnes, *Tropical Enterprise*, 293.

39.   *New York Times*, 24 April 1972; McCann, *An American Company*, 192–93; U.S. Maritime Administration, *Foreign Flag Merchant Ships Owned by U.S. Parent Companies*, October 1975 and July 1989; Karnes, *Tropical Enterprise*, 273–74, 294.

CHAPTER 13

1.   United States Lines to Federal Maritime Board, 2 May 1960, QM 245, Marad; United States Lines, *Annual Report 1960*.

2.   "Narrative Summary of Traffic Conditions," 31 March 1959, and United States Lines to Maritime Subsidy Board, 7 August 1962, QM 245/L25-3, Marad.

3.   Memorandum, 17 January 1962, QM 245/L25-24, Marad.

4.   United States Lines to World Wide Enterprises, 15 August 1961, QM 245/L25-24, Marad.

5.   Correspondence and reports, 1959–62, QM 245/L25-24, Marad.

6.   Memorandum, 13 April 1962, QM 245/L25-23, Marad; for this paragraph, *see also* United States Lines, *Annual Report 1960*.

7.   Memorandum, 28 October 1964, Matson Navigation Co. to Federal Maritime Board, 27 July 1961, and Grace Line to Maritime Subsidy Board, 20 August 1963, QM 245/L25-3, Marad.

8.   United States Lines to Marad, 26 March 1963, QM 245/L25-23, Marad.

9.   Conference memorandum for file, 21 August 1963, QM 245, Marad.

10.   Marcus, *Planning Ship Replacement*, 58–61; *Wall Street Journal*, 8 October 1965.

11.   *New York Times*, 6 February 1965, 8 June 1966; *Wall Street Journal*, 1 June 1965, 17 November 1965.

12.   *New York Times*, 16 November 1966; *Moody's Transportation Manual 1967*, 1301.

13.   *Forbes*, 1 November 1969, 30–31; *Wall Street Journal*, 27–28 December 1967; *Business Week*, 24 February 1968, 158–59.

14.   *Wall Street Journal*, 4 January 1968; *New York Times*, 4 January 1968, 20 January 1968; *Forbes*, 1 November 1969, 30–31.

15.   *Business Week*, 17 October 1953, 117, 119; Dugan, *American Viking*, 290–93; *Fortune*, October 1961, 224, 228.

16.   *Newsweek*, 28 March 1960, 76–77, 80; *Wall Street Journal*, 4 October 1960.

17.   Jakob Isbrandtsen to Admiral Ralph E. Wilson, 19 September 1960, QM 109, Marad; *Wall Street Journal*, 16 December 1960.

18.   Jakob Isbrandtsen to Admiral Ralph E. Wilson, 30 December 1960, QM 109, Marad.

19.   Letter to Marad, 24 August 1961, and other correspondence, QM 109, Marad.

20.   *New York Times*, 1 February 1961; for rest of paragraph, *see New York Times*, 22 April 1961, and *Wall Street Journal*, 26 December 1961, 2 May 1962.

21.   *Moody's Transportation Manual 1964*, 1328–29, *Moody's Transportation Manual 1967*, 1308; memorandum, 23 July 1964, QM 118/L25-23, Marad; *Wall Street Journal*, 6 June 1967.

22.   Federal Maritime Board, *Decisions* (Washington, D.C.: Government Printing Office, 1964), 6:10.

23.   Pacific Far East Line to Gerald D. Morgan, 18 February 1960, GF box 338, DDE; Niven, *American President Lines*, 197; *New York Times*, 3 March 1960.

24.   *New York Times*, 1 November 1963. For this paragraph, *see* also *New York Times*, 1 April 1961, 20 April 1962, 8 July 1965; Maritime Subsidy Board, *Decisions* (Washington, D.C.: Government Printing Office, 1965), 1:60–81, 2:1–39.

25.   Letter of governor of Hawaii, 2 July 1964, WHCF, ST 11, LBJ.

26.   *Wall Street Journal*, 21 January, 15 July 1964.

27. *New York Times*, 15 March 1964, 7 May 1964, 24 July 1964; Marcus, *Planning Ship Replacement*, 77–80.

28. *New York Times*, 15 February 1966, 17 July 1966, 2 August 1966; *Wall Street Journal*, 16 September 1966; *Time*, 13 May 1966, 96.

29. *New York Times*, 16 December 1966, 20 February 1967; Maritime Subsidy Board, *Decisions* (1965–73), 2:307.

30. Maritime Subsidy Board, *Decisions* (1965–73), 2:231–32; *New York Times*, 27 May 1967, 27 August 1967; *Newsweek*, 8 January 1968, 56–57.

31. Maritime Subsidy Board, *Decisions* (1965–73), 2:320; for this paragraph, *see also* Maritime Subsidy Board, *Decisions*, 2:214–24; *New York Times*, 15 January 1968.

32. *Wall Street Journal*, 20 January 1969, 20 August 1973; *New York Times*, 20–21 January 1969; Niven, *American President Lines*, 232.

33. Maritime Subsidy Board, *Decisions*, 2:226–29, 3:721–32; *New York Times*, 16 April 1974, 13 September 1974; *Wall Street Journal*, 10 April 1974.

34. "American-Hawaiian," 1949, and "Notice to Shippers," 2 March 1953, William Kooiman Files; *Moody's Transportation Manual 1952*, 47–48; *Pacific Marine Review*, February 1947, 37–38.

35. Shields, *Daniel Ludwig*, 204–5, 219–20; *Pacific Shipper*, 25 April 1955, 9 and 30 May 1955; *Newsweek*, 6 February 1956, 74.

36. *Pacific Shipper*, 29 August 1955, 18 January 1956; *Moody's Transportation Manual 1957*, 1455; Shields, *Daniel Ludwig*, 204, 206–7; *Business Week*, 15 April 1961, 115–16; McLean Industries, *Annual Report 1963*.

37. Correspondence, December 1964, and memorandum, 15 April 1964, QM 251, Marad; *Moody's Transportation Manual 1965*, 918; Shields, *Daniel Ludwig*, 220–22; *Wall Street Journal*, 31 March 1965, 12 May 1965; Marcus, *Planning Ship Replacement*, 67–68.

38. Shields, *Daniel Ludwig*, 222–23; Maritime Subsidy Board, *Decisions* 1:263–79; *New York Times*, 21 December 1964.

39. Shields, *Daniel Ludwig*, 224; *Moody's Transportation Manual 1969*, 1555–56; Marcus, *Planning Ship Replacement*, 68–71.

CHAPTER 14

1. Maritime Subsidy Board, *Decisions* 4:981–1003; *Business Week*, 15 December 1973, 24.

2. "Current Condition of the Independent American Tanker Industry," 28 February 1975, box 1, Michael Raoul-Duval Papers, Gerald R. Ford Presidential Library (henceforth GFL), Ann Arbor, Michigan.

3. "The Tanker Industry Problem," 6 March 1975, box 48, Presidential Handwriting File, GFL; Kendall, *Business of Shipping*, 435–38; *Forbes*, 1 November 1970, 24–25; *Wall Street Journal*, 1 April 1972, 12 March 1974.

4. "Meeting on Cargo Preference Legislation," 18 December 1974, WHCF, TN box 6, GFL; *Florida Journal of Commerce*, May 1974, 42–44; Whitehurst, *U.S. Merchant Marine*, 44–48.

5. Paul Hall letter, 28 March 1977, WHCF, TN 5, Jimmy Carter Library (henceforth JCL); Whitehurst, *U.S. Merchant Marine*, 49–51; *Florida Journal of Commerce*, March 1975, 8; *New York Times*, 29 July 1977.

6. *Forbes*, 1 February 1977, 34–35; Maritime Subsidy Board, *Decisions*, 5:258–60, 266–68, 506–13, 669–91; *American Shipper*, July 1978, 44–45.

7. René De La Pedraja, "Rise of the Latin American Merchant Marine."

8. "Maritime Transportation Section Input," October 1978, box 82, Domestic Policy Staff, JCL; *Business Week*, 1 April 1972, 31; *Wall Street Journal*, 3 April 1972.

9. "Maritime Transportation Section Input," October 1978, JCL.

10. *Business Week*, 1 June 1974, 32.

11. *New York Times*, 18 June 1974, 25 March 1975; *Florida Journal of Commerce*, July 1974, 10–11, August 1975, 16; *Wall Street Journal*, 26 December 1975.

12. *American Shipper*, September 1976, 22–23, September 1977, 39, December 1977, 33, March 1979, 49; "Maritime Transportation Section Input," October 1978, JCL.

13. *Business Week*, 29 April 1972, 52; *Moody's Transportation Manual 1969*, 1541–42; *Wall Street Journal*, 27 December 1968.

14. Memorandum, 23 September 1965, WHCF, TN 7, LBJ; *American Shipper*, July 1976, 18–19.

15. *Wall Street Journal*, 5 May 1971, 18 June 1971, 2 May 1973, 25 June 1973; *New York Times*, 18 June 1971, 29 February 1972.

16. *Wall Street Journal*, 11 October 1973, 5 February 1974, 1 December 1977; *Moody's Transportation Manual 1974*, 1541, and *Moody's Transportation Manual 1977*, 1451.

17. U.S. Congress, House Committee on Merchant Marine and Fisheries, *Pacific Far East Line Oversight* (Washington, D.C.: Government Printing Office, 1978), 18, 149–50; Niven, *American President Lines*, 223–25, 230, 235.

18. House Committee on Merchant Marine and Fisheries, *Pacific Far East Line*, 19; *Wall Street Journal*, 23 April 1969, 14 August 1970; *Business Week*, 26 April 1969, 52, 3 October 1970, 44–45, 48; Worden, *Cargoes*, 153.

19. *Florida Journal of Commerce*, April 1975, 3; *Wall Street Journal*, 28 September 1973; House Committee on Merchant Marine and Fisheries, *Pacific Far East Line*, 32.

20. Reports on Soviet shipping menace, 1975–76, WHCF, TN 7, GFL; *Business Week*, 30 June 1975, 111–12; *American Shipper*, May 1977, 5; *Wall Street Journal*, 7 July 1975, 12 February 1979. The supposed Soviet

shipping menace in the Pacific disappeared just as mysteriously as it had appeared in the 1970s; the 1981 exclusion from U.S. ports in reprisal for crackdowns in Poland (as well as the 1979 Afghanistan invasion) merely hastened FESCO's retrenchment.

21. *American Shipper*, July 1976, 4, May 1978, 28–29; *New York Times*, 7 August 1978.

22. *American Shipper*, February 1977, 30–32, March 1978, 22, May 1978, 28–29; House Committee on Merchant Marine and Fisheries, *Pacific Far East Line*, 35–36, 87–90.

23. *Wall Street Journal*, 12 July 1978, 3 August 1978; House Committee on Merchant Marine and Fisheries, *Pacific Far East Line*, 9, 12, 16, 165–66; *New York Times*, 7 August 1978; *American Shipper*, January 1978, 28–29, September 1978, 14.

24. Minutes of weekly conferences, 20 August, 24 September 1934, box 67, Dollar Collection, Bancroft Library; *Business Week*, 20 November 1978, 46; *Moody's Transportation Manual 1960*, 1439.

25. "Jack R. Dant," 25 June 1958, box 9, Dollar Collection, Bancroft Library; 21 December 1961 letter, QM 245/L25-23, pt. 11, and M. N. Frochen letter, 17 March 1964, QM 227/L25-23, pt. 15, Marad; Marcus, *Planning Ship Replacement*, 47–50.

26. *Business Week*, 20 November 1978, 45. The last paragraph also draws on *American Shipper*, May 1978, 34; *Wall Street Journal*, 5 November 1976, 23 March 1977.

27. Dick Sharood to Paul N. McCloskey, 14 February 1975, box 6, WHCF, TN, GFL; *Business Week*, 8 February 1969; *Forbes*, 15 June 1969.

28. Kendall, *Business of Shipping*, 235–37; Whitehurst, *U.S. Merchant Marine*, 205; *Business Week*, 4 August 1973.

29. Worden, *Cargoes*, 155; *Wall Street Journal*, 21 November 1973, 10 April 1974; *New York Times*, 16 April 1974; *Moody's Transportation Manual 1974*, 1549.

30. Dick Sharood to Paul N. McCloskey, 14 February 1975, GFL; "Seatrain Shipyard," 8 April 1975, box 104, L. William Seidman Files, GFL.

31. *Forbes*, 15 October 1977, 116–17; *Business Week*, 5 February 1979, 34; *New York Times*, 9 April 1978.

32. *Forbes*, 5 March 1979, 10; *Wall Street Journal*, 9 May 1979; *Business Week*, 21 May 1979, 36.

33. *American Shipper*, March 1980, 8–9, November 1980, 6; *Wall Street Journal*, 8 September 1980; *New York Times*, 6 September 1980.

34. *Wall Street Journal*, 8 December 1980, 26 December 1980; *New York Times*, 10 February 1981; *American Shipper*, February 1981, 4.

CHAPTER 15

1. Lee, *Mr. Moore, Mr. McCormack—and the Seven Seas*, 28–29; Senate Judiciary Committee, *Ocean Freight Industry*, 4:3771.

2. Marcus, *Planning Ship Replacement*, 54–55; *Wall Street Journal*, 10 April 1969.

3. *New York Times*, 28 April 1966, 30 June 1966, 17 August 1966; Marcus, *Planning Ship Replacement*, 55–56; *Wall Street Journal*, 11 February 1966, 14 April 1966, 2 June 1966, 21 November 1969, 26 February 1970.

4. Report, 23 July 1964, QM 118/L25-23, pt. 41, Marad; *Wall Street Journal*, 15 April 1971, 24 June 1980; *American Shipper*, August 1980, 20; *Moody's Transportation Manual 1973*, 1545, *Moody's Transportation Manual 1975*, 1551; *New York Times*, 2 September 1973, 19 August 1975; *Florida Journal of Commerce*, February 1976, 9.

5. *Fortune*, 5 December 1986, 140; *American Shipper*, 36.

6. *Compass*, June 1967; Kooiman, "W. R. Grace's Ships and Lines"; House Committee on Merchant Marine and Fisheries, *Steamship Conference Study*, 1:1601–3.

7. *Compass*, June 1967; *New York Times*, 20 January 1970; *Moody's Transportation Manual 1970*, 1559.

8. Kooiman, "W. R. Grace's Ships and Lines"; *Business Week*, 7 August 1971, 74–75, 7 April 1973, 24; *Wall Street Journal*, 11 January 1971.

9. *American Shipper*, September 1976, 24; Kooiman, "W. R. Grace's Ships and Lines"; René De La Pedraja, *FEDEMETAL y la industrialización de Colombia* (Bogotá: Op Gráficas, 1986), 91–92.

10. *American Shipper*, May 1977, 6; for this paragraph, *see also New York Times*, 26 July 1977, and *American Shipper*, June 1978, 23, and William Kooiman, interview with author, San Francisco, 11 January 1990.

11. *American Shipper*, November 1981, 16, July 1986, 66, November 1986, 79, February 1987, 63; William Kooiman, interview with author, San Francisco, 11 January 1990.

12. Kooiman, "W. R. Grace's Ships and Lines"; U.S. Maritime Administration, *Decisions*, 4:1012–20; *Moody's Transportation Manual 1972*, 1552–53.

13. Kooiman, "W. R. Grace's Ships and Lines"; *American Shipper*, June 1978, 23, July 1978, 35.

14. *Moody's Transportation Manual 1979*, 1453; *American Shipper*, May 1979, 2, June 1982, 20, January 1984, 3, 6; William Kooiman, interview with author, San Francisco, 11 January 1990.

15. *Business Week*, 27 September 1982, 28–29; *American Shipper*, October 1982, 20, 22, May 1983, 36, 38; Kooiman, "W. R. Grace's Ships and Lines."

16. *American Shipper*, January 1984, 4, and for this paragraph *see*

also American Shipper, August 1984, 18, 20, 22; *Business Week,* 20 August 1984, 114, 188; William Kooiman, interview with author, San Francisco, 11 January 1990.

17. *Journal of Commerce,* 2 November 1984; *American Shipper,* December 1984, 42; *Business Week,* 3 December 1984, 75, 78.

18. *New York Times,* 11 January 1970; *Wall Street Journal,* 12 January 1970, 11 August 1971; Frank O. Braynard, *The Big Ship: The Story of the S.S. "United States"* (Newport News, Va.: Mariner's Museum, 1981), 266–70.

19. *New York Times,* 8 March 1970; *Wall Street Journal,* 11 February 1970; *Business Week,* 21 November 1970, 29–30; *Moody's Transportation Manual 1973,* 1561.

20. *Forbes,* 1 December 1971, 27–28; *Business Week,* 20 July 1974, 72–73; *New York Times,* 14 September 1976.

21. *Forbes,* 1 February 1977, 64–65, 15 October 1977, 156; *Wall Street Journal,* 28 September 1977; *American Shipper,* November 1977, 23, May 1978, 21, June 1978, 47.

22. *Business Week,* 16 April 1979, 82, and for this paragraph *see also* 80–81, 83.

23. *American Shipper,* January 1981, 10–11, July 1982, 40; *Business Week,* 19 April 1982. The other U.S.-flag ships of the company continued to receive operating subsidies, but since the 12 mammoth containerships still did not qualify for subsidies, the advantage of placing them under the U.S. flag is inexplicable. Did McLean plan at a later date to orchestrate some way to pry subsidies out of the Reagan administration?

24. Captain Frank Murdock, interview with author, Mobile, Ala. 27 July 1988; *American Shipper,* July 1982, 44, June 1983, 32.

25. *Wall Street Journal,* 22 August 1983; *Forbes,* 24 October 1983, 40–41; *American Shipper,* August 1983, 9, 11.

26. *Forbes,* 23 March 1987, 33; *American Shipper,* September 1984, 25–26; *New York Times,* 25 November 1986; *Business Week,* 8 December 1986, 40, 42, 30 March 1987, 20–21.

27. *New York Times,* 17 January 1987; *Forbes,* 23 March 1987, 82–83.

SELECTED
BIBLIOGRAPHY

Books and Articles

The following titles are intended only as suggestions for further reading; for book-length bibliographies, consult the entries below for Albion, Labaree, and Schultz.

Albion, Robert G. *Seaports South of Sahara: The Achievements of an American Steamship Service*. New York: Appleton-Century-Crofts, 1959. Much broader than its title suggests, this case study of the Farrell Lines illustrates U.S. shipping policy; Albion was for decades the dean of maritime historians in the U.S.

————. *Naval & Maritime History: An Annotated Bibliography*. Fourth Edition. Mystic, Conn.: Marine Historical Association, 1972. The standard annotated bibliography of publications and dissertations in English. Labaree has issued a supplement. For articles, see Schultz.

Baughman, James P. *The Mallorys of Mystic: Six Generations in American Maritime Enterprise*. Middletown, Conn.: Wesleyan University Press, 1972. Exhaustive use of Mallory family papers make this the most revealing account about a shipowner family; also contains information on a variety of related steamship enterprises.

Braynard, Frank O. *The Big Ship: The Story of the S.S. United States*. Newport News, Va.: The Mariner's Museum, 1981. This detailed chronicle of one ship's career contains much useful information on its owner, the United States Lines.

Brown, Giles T. *Ships That Sail No More: Marine Transportation from San Diego to Puget Sound, 1910–1940*. Lexington: University of Kentucky Press, 1966. A scholarly and detailed account of coastwise shipping in the Pacific Coast; nothing similar exists for the Atlantic and Gulf coasts.

Carlisle, Rodney P. *Sovereignty for Sale: The Origins and Evolution of the Panamanian and Liberian Flags of Convenience.* Annapolis, Md.: Naval Institute Press, 1981. This valuable but critical study explores the nature of flags of convenience, and should be contrasted with the more sympathetic account in this book.

Carosso, Vincent P. *The Morgans: Private International Bankers, 1854–1913.* Cambridge: Harvard University Press, 1987. Devotes considerable space to the International Mercantile Marine.

Carse, Robert. *The Long Haul: The United States Merchant Service in World War II.* New York: W. W. Norton, 1965. One of several accounts of the wartime exploits of seamen; mentions the companies incidentally.

Clayton, Lawrence A. *Grace: W. R. Grace & Co. The Formative Years 1850–1930.* Ottawa, Ill.: Jameson Books, 1985. The steamship side is well covered in this history of the parent company; a post-1930 sequel would be highly desirable.

Dollar, Robert. *Memoirs.* 4 vols. San Francisco: Schwabacher & Frey, 1927. Although rather disorganized, this is a rare first-person account by a shipowner.

Dugan, James. *American Viking: The Saga of Hans Isbrandtsen.* New York: Harper & Row, 1963. An official and very friendly account that contains useful information but generally skims over the commercial side of shipping.

Emmons, Frederick E. *American Passenger Ships: The Ocean Lines and Liners, 1873–1983.* Newark, Del.: University of Delaware Press, 1985. A very convenient reference work that, however, has minor inaccuracies.

Hofsommer, Don L. "The Maritime Enterprises of James J. Hill." *American Neptune* 47 (1987): 193–205. The most recent account; supplements the Lamb article.

Hurley, Edward N. *The Bridge to France.* Philadelphia: J. B. Lippincott Co., 1927. This memoir brims with facts and recaptures the mood of the U.S. Shipping Board during World War I.

Karnes, Thomas L. *Tropical Enterprise: The Standard Fruit and Steamship Company in Latin America.* Baton Rouge: Louisiana State University Press, 1978. A scholarly account of the main rival of United Fruit Co.

Kemble, John H. "A Hundred Years of the Pacific Mail." *American Neptune* 10 (1950): 123–43. This carefully crafted article remains the standard source for the Pacific Mail Steamship Co.

Kendall, Lane C. *The Business of Shipping.* 5th ed. Centreville, Md.: Cornell Maritime Press, 1986. For the mechanics of ocean transportation, this is the classic exposition which, however, avoids mentioning most individual companies. The somewhat romanticized chapters on Malcolm McLean and the origins of containers contrast with the less glamorous account in this book.

Labaree, Benjamin W. *A Supplement (1971–1986) to Robert G. Albion's Naval & Maritime History: An Annotated Bibliography.* Mystic, Conn.: Mystic Seaport Museum, 1988. A temporary updating; the annotated entries, along with titles published since 1987, will eventually be incorporated into a new combined edition of Albion's bibliography.

Lamb, W. Kaye. "The Transpacific Ventures of James J. Hill." *American Neptune* 3 (1943): 185–204. This standard article spares the reader from having to plow through the many Hill biographies; a more recent account is by Hofsommer.

Lane, Frederick C. *Ships for Victory: A History of Shipbuilding under the United States Maritime Commission in World War II.* Baltimore: The Johns Hopkins University Press, 1951. A massive study that happily digresses into the shipping activities of the U.S. Maritime Commission and the War Shipping Administration.

Lawrence, Samuel A. *United States Merchant Shipping Policies and Politics.* Washington, D.C.: The Brookings Institution, 1966. The single most revealing book ever written on the government's role in shipping, but as a government-commissioned study, the author was not free to discuss individual companies.

Marcus, Henry S. *Planning Ship Replacement in the Containerization Era.* Lexington, Mass.: Lexington Books, 1974. The classic for company decisions of the 1960s, this book is a model of what a keen analytical study should be.

McCann, Thomas P. *An American Company: The Tragedy of United Fruit.* New York: Crown Publishers, 1976. An insider's account of one of the most hated U.S. companies in Latin America.

Mellin, Gilbert M. "The Mississippi Shipping Company." Ph.D. Dissertation, the University of Pittsburgh, 1955. This account of a firm generally known as the Delta Line is one of the rare company-specific studies.

Melville, John H. *The Great White Fleet.* New York: Vantage Press, 1976. A history of the ships of United Fruit Co. Corporate events must be reconstructed from other sources, such as McCann.

Navin, Thomas R., and Marian V. Sears. "A Study in Merger: Formation of the International Mercantile Marine Company." *Business History Review* 28 (1954): 291–328. The best brief account of I.M.M.

Niven, John. *The American President Lines and its Forebears, 1848–1984.* Newark, Del.: University of Delaware Press, 1986. A scholarly account of one of the most important U.S. steamship companies; an indispensable book.

O'Brien, Gregory C. "The Life of Robert Dollar, 1844–1932." Ph.D. Dissertation, Claremont Graduate School, 1968. The author makes effective use of the unpublished Dollar diary.

President's Advisory Committee on the Merchant Marine. *Report*. Washington, D.C.: Government Printing Office, 1947. Good for overall trends, but in accordance with the "gag" rule on revealing "proprietary" information, does not discuss individual companies.

Radius, Walter A. *United States Shipping in Transpacific Trade, 1922–1939*. Stanford, Cal. Stanford University Press, 1944. Useful for statistical trends, but the author worked under the U.S. Maritime Commission restriction of not discussing individual companies, thereby sharply reducing the book's value for business history.

Riesenberg, Felix, Jr. *Sea War: The Story of the U.S. Merchant Marine in World War II*. New York: Rinehart & Co., 1956. Another account of the wartime exploits of seamen.

Safford, Jeffrey J. *Wilsonian Maritime Diplomacy, 1913–1921*. New Brunswick, N. J.: Rutgers University Press, 1978. A basic scholarly account that focuses on government actions and policies.

Schultz, Charles R. *Bibliography of Maritime and Naval History, Periodical Articles*. College Station: Texas A & M Press, 1974–. This very useful reference tool is published every two years and contains abstracts of articles in academic journals. For books, see Labaree.

Shields, Jerry. *The Invisible Billionaire: Daniel Ludwig*. Boston: Houghton Mifflin, 1986. A pioneering work that sheds light on the Surplus Ship Sales and American-Hawaiian Steamship Company.

Stindt, Fred A. *Matson's Century of Ships*. Modesto, Ca.: n.p., 1982. This good study of the company's ships complements the Worden history of the firm.

Tate, E. Mowbray. *Transpacific Steam: The Story of Steam Navigation from the Pacific Coast of North America to the Far East and the Antipodes, 1867–1941*. New York: Cornwall Books, 1986. An encyclopedic work that covers the freighters as well as passenger liners of the individual companies.

U.S. Congress. House. Committee on Merchant Marine and Fisheries. *Investigation of Shipping Combinations*. 4 vols. Washington, D.C.: Government Printing Office, 1913. A mine of information for the business historian.

———. Committee on Merchant Marine and Fisheries. *Pacific Far East Line Oversight*. Washington D.C.: Government Printing Office, 1978. Congress decided to take a rare peek into the activities of one steamship company, but apparently saw enough, and decided not to investigate other firms such as the much larger United States Lines when the latter went bankrupt in 1986.

———. Committee on Merchant Marine and Fisheries. *Steamship Conference Study*. 3 vols. Washington, D.C.: Government Printing Office, 1959. Contains valuable information on international rivalries over ocean transportation.

U.S. Congress. Senate. Committee on Interstate and Foreign Commerce. *Decline of Coastwise and Intercoastal Shipping.* Washington, D.C.: Government Printing Office, 1960. The starting point for any serious study on this topic. In a departure from the usual silence in government publications, contains information on the desperate plight of some of the coastwise companies.

———. Committee on Judiciary. *Monopoly Problems in Regulated Industries: Ocean Freight Industry.* 7 vols. Washington, D.C.: Government Printing Office, 1960. The decades of government silence on the activities of individual steamship companies were overshadowed by the virtual hemorrhage of company-specific information in these massive volumes whose contents resemble more a "portable archive". In quantity and quality, this is the single most important publication of the twentieth century on U.S. merchant shipping.

———. Special Committee on Investigation of Air Mail and Ocean Mail Contracts. *Hearings.* 9 vols. Washington, D.C.: Government Printing Office, 1933–1934. Reveals how the steamship companies milked the Shipping Board out of public funds; a rich lode of information.

U.S. Maritime Commission. *Economic Survey of the American Merchant Marine.* Washington, D.C.: Government Printing Office, 1937. Same characteristics as the *Report* by the President's Advisory Committee on the Merchant Marine.

———. *Financial Readjustments in Dollar Steamship Line, Inc., Ltd.* Washington, D.C.: Government Printing Office, 1938. The investment of public monies forced the government to temporarily lift the "gag" rule of not discussing the affairs of individual companies and to come out with this fascinating exposé of the Dollar Line bankruptcy. Continued by the next entry.

———. *Reorganization of American President Lines Ltd.* Washington, D.C.: Government Printing Office, 1939. Continues the previous entry and shows how the government rescued the bankrupt Dollar Line.

Vale, Vivian. *The American Peril: Challenge to Britain on the North Atlantic, 1901–1904.* Manchester: Manchester University Press, 1984. The fullest scholarly account from the British viewpoint on the creation of the International Mercantile Marine.

Whitehurst, Clinton H., Jr. *The U.S. Merchant Marine: In Search of an Enduring Maritime Policy.* Annapolis: Naval Institute Press, 1983. This is the latest discussion of the general problems of the U.S. merchant marine.

Worden, William L. *Cargoes: Matson's First Century in the Pacific.* Honolulu: University of Hawaii Press, 1981. This good study of the company nicely complements the Stindt book on the firm's ships.

Zeis, Paul M. *American Shipping Policy*. Princeton: Princeton University Press, 1938. Well-written study, but the author, in accordance with the then prevailing canons of scholarship, did not go beyond government publications and secondary sources.

Periodicals

By returning to the *Reader's Guide to Periodical Literature* and newspaper indexes, the reader can locate a large number of articles on steamship companies. Some periodicals of particular value should be mentioned.

American Shipper. Since 1975 this monthly has reported extensively on U.S. steamship companies and their foreign counterparts. A professional staff of journalists runs this independent magazine that is sympathetic to the problems of shipping, but does not hesitate to report critically disturbing events.

Business Week. This has been the only weekly magazine to provide continuous coverage of U.S. merchant shipping since the 1930s.

Journal of Commerce. This newspaper, whose publication began in the nineteenth century, is the most comprehensive and detailed periodical on merchant shipping; its contents appear virtually inexhaustible. Originally a New York City publication, its coverage is now worldwide. The lack of an index, however, limits tremendously the immense research potential of this source.

New York Times. Detailed reporting from the 1930s to the 1970s and an excellent annual index make this newspaper a pleasure to use.

Wall Street Journal. Given the difficulties in accessing the *Journal of Commerce*, a partial substitute is the *Wall Street Journal* whose widely available indexes allow the reader to glean easily additional news on steamship companies for the years since 1960.

Archives and Manuscript Collections

The previous items in this bibliography might mislead the reader into believing that the history of U.S. steamship companies is all easily available in published sources. Nothing could be farther from the truth, and the present volume could be completed only after extensive research in unpublished sources. The footnotes detail the unpublished sources which fall into three main categories.

1. Business records. The tragic loss of the overwhelming majority of steamship records leaves largely irreparable gaps in our historical knowledge. A few collections may yet appear, but so far little more than scraps have reached the following institutions: Manuscript Division of the Library of Congress, Butler Library at Columbia University, National Maritime Museum in San Francisco, Mobile Public Library, and the Bancroft Library of the University of California at Berkeley.

2. Government archives. In contrast to the scarcity of business records, the sheer bulk of government archives hinders research. Even more seriously, officials were reluctant to gather information on individual companies, so that the government files are less useful for business history than one might believe. In addition, the archives of the Shipping Board, the United States Maritime Commission and the Maritime Administration are scattered in different places in the metropolitan Washington D.C. area, and some are subject to restrictions, making access complex and cumbersome at best.

3. Foreign records. Many foreign companies and governments followed U.S. shipping developments, and their reports helped to fill gaps in the deficient U.S. documentation. The most informative collections of documents are found in England, particularly at the University of Liverpool and in the Public Record Office at London.

INDEX

THE AUTHOR

RENÉ DE LA PEDRAJA WAS BORN in Havana, Cuba in 1951. His parents sent him to the U.S. during the Cuban Revolution and subsequently he became a U.S. citizen. He received his B.A. from the University of Houston in 1973, and his Ph.D. in History from the University of Chicago in 1977. De La Pedraja spent over ten years teaching in universities at Bogotá, Colombia, and his deep interest in that country's history produced many publications, including three books, the latest of which was *Energy Politics in Colombia* (1989).

De La Pedraja was researching a book on Latin American merchant shipping when he accepted an offer in 1986 to come back to the U.S. to teach at Kansas State University. As mentioned in the Preface, the conversation that led to the present book took place in Kansas. In 1989 he was offered a position at Canisius College in Buffalo, New York, where he is now an Associate Professor. He has been married for 17 years and has one son. Currently De La Pedraja is writing a historical dictionary of the U.S. merchant marine, and in the coming years he hopes to finish his original project on Latin American steamship companies.